Evaluating Classroom Instruction:

A SOURCEBOOK OF INSTRUMENTS

Evaluating Classroom Instruction:

A SOURCEBOOK OF INSTRUMENTS

Gary D. Borich
The University of Texas at Austin

and

Susan K. Madden
The Research and Development Center for Teacher Education

ADDISON-WESLEY PUBLISHING COMPANY
Reading, Massachusetts · Menlo Park, California
London · Amsterdam · Don Mills, Ontario · Sydney

This work has been supported by the National Institute of Education Contract NIE–C–74–0088, The Evaluation of Teaching Project. The opinions expressed herein do not necessarily reflect the position or policies of the National Institute of Education and no official endorsement by that office should be inferred.

ISBN 0-201-00842-4
ABCDEFGHIJ-MA-7987

Contents

Introduction

It should be apparent to every educator that a large number of researchers have examined the effectiveness of a variety of teaching practices and techniques. In less than a decade, thousands of studies have been conducted on such topics as the instructional styles, interaction patterns, and personality characteristics of teachers, the organizational structure of schools, the technology of instruction, and the affective and cognitive growth of pupils, to name only a few. In the course of these investigations, researchers have developed hundreds of psychological and educational instruments to study teacher and pupil behavior in the classroom. This book is designed to bring before the educational community the instruments used in these studies, so that readers may extend and elaborate upon them.

Though intended as a straightforward presentation of available instruments for evaluating classroom instruction, this sourcebook was prompted by several considerations, discussed below.

In reviewing empirical studies of teacher effectiveness for the Evaluation of Teaching Project at the Research and Development Center for Teacher Education, the authors found the research generally characterized by four problems:

1. a narrow range of measurements frequently employed in individual studies of teacher behavior;
2. inconsistent use of specific instruments across studies measuring the same or similar hypotheses;
3. lack of a generic framework or guide from which to select behaviors to be measured in the classroom; and
4. use of instruments with inadequate psychometric characteristics to measure these classroom behaviors.

Problem 1: Range of Measurement

This first problem came to the authors' attention from an examination of literally hundreds of empirical studies investigating relationships between teacher behaviors and pupil outcomes (Borich, 1977; Kash, Borich, and Fenton, in press).

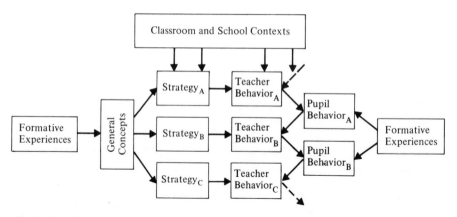

Fig. 1. A multivariate model of classroom behavior (after Biddle, Good, Hall, and Bank, 1975).

During this review, the authors noted the inordinate number of research studies which measured only a single criterion behavior. While it was apparent that a single criterion provided investigators with a parsimonious research design and a "clean" interpretation of results, the large number of nonsignificant findings produced by studies of this kind suggested that such simplistic methodology represented too narrow and theoretically vacuous an approach to measuring classroom behavior. A number of studies defined teacher behavior, treatments, or instructional programs so broadly that the reader was led to expect wide-ranging effects upon pupils. Yet in many of these studies only one treatment or teacher effect was actually measured. Even when multiple criteria were used, they were often applied to only one area of behavior (e.g., classroom interaction variables) or to closely related areas (e.g., self-, pupil, and supervisor evaluations of the teacher). Rarely did researchers employ instruments that captured a range of both pupil and teacher affective and cognitive behaviors. Surprisingly, concurrent measurement of teacher process and pupil product variables was infrequently incorporated into research designs, and few investigators focused on causal sequences of behavior which might have accounted for the effects of classroom instruction. This limited scope might have been avoided had researchers utilized a multivariate approach to the study of classroom behavior, perhaps similar to that illustrated in Fig. 1. Most of the research encountered in our review dealt with only a single "slice" of the classroom behavior shown in this model: Relatively few studies investigated the *sequence* of classroom behaviors, taking into account the interactive effects of context, classroom, school, pupil, and teacher variables.

Problem 2: Inconsistent Instrument Use

A second problem which emerged from the literature was the inconsistent use of any one instrument across studies purported to be conceptually similar. In a number of areas, there were as many instruments as there were studies, since no two investigations employed instruments which possessed the same reliability or validity and measured variables operationally defined in the same way, regardless of the supposed similarity between the constructs assessed. It was apparent that researchers preferred to develop their own instruments, rather than to use or adapt those already constructed for the same or similar purposes. This emphasis on new instrument development seems to have reduced the opportunity for researchers to improve upon existing measures, to replicate an instrument's reliability and validity, and to use the same operations to measure the same constructs.

Replication of research findings is more likely to occur under some conditions than others. For example, valid replicated results are most likely to be obtained when the same instrumentation is used across studies which test the same hypotheses. Less congruence between findings is expected when different instruments purporting to measure the same variables are used within the same study; and even less agreement is anticipated when such instruments are used in different studies. Although findings replicated across studies using different instruments are encouraging, the most systematic approach to replication involves use of the same instrument (and, therefore, the same operationally defined constructs) in different studies. Given that "no significant differences" are generally the norm in classroom research, we can place most confidence in those "no difference" findings which are replicated across studies using the same instrument, somewhat less confidence in those obtained with different instruments in the same study, and least confidence in those produced by different studies using different instruments.

Problem 3: Lack of a Measurement Framework

A third problem apparent from the literature was the absence of an overall framework or model to guide researchers in selecting teacher and pupil behaviors to be measured. Few researchers provided rationale· for the kinds of teacher behavior they assessed, and even fewer showed interest in (or knowledge of) the causal sequences of behavior possibly prerequisite to the single variable they did measure. Although promising process/product relationships (Rosenshine, 1971) sometimes encouraged researchers to collect both teacher and pupil data within the same study, other variables (e.g., context, ethnographic, presage, and affective) were frequently ignored. Researchers seemed averse to studying those behaviors which were prerequisite to teacher process variables or which were likely to confound the measurement of student achievement data. Figure 2 sketches the general type of eclectic framework from which investigators must work in order to assure that classroom, school, context, teacher, and pupil variables, *as well as the relationships among these variables*, are included in the research design.

Problem 4: Psychometric Standards

Our review of the literature also revealed the gross psychometric inadequacy of most tests and measures used in these research studies. The literally hundreds of instruments employed in the field of teacher effectiveness research had been subjected to little critical assessment, and in the rare cases when such assessment had

STAGE	DOMAIN	HIGH INFERENCE	LOW INFERENCE
Preoperational Measures	Affective	Personality, attitude	Attitudes related to teaching and learning
	Cognitive	Achievement, experience, and aptitude	Knowledge of teaching methods and content
Immediate Process Measures	Affective	Observations of general affective characteristics, e.g., teacher's warmth	Observations of specific affective characteristics, e.g., times teacher praises student
	Cognitive	Observations of general content-related characteristics, e.g., teacher's business-like or systematic behavior	Observations of specific content-related characteristics, e.g., teacher's lecture-to-discussion ratio
Intermediate Process Measures	Affective	Ratings of attitudes toward teaching and learning	Ratings of attitudes toward classroom tasks and lessons
	Cognitive	Ratings of teacher's knowledge of unit or grade level content	Ratings of knowledge of classroom tasks and lessons
Product Measures	Affective	Pupil attitudes toward learning, the school, and teachers	Pupil attitudes toward lesson content
	Cognitive	Pupil achievement of unit or grade level content	Pupil achievement of lesson content

Fig. 2. A measurement framework for evaluating classroom instruction (from Borich, G., *The appraisal of teaching: Concepts and process.* Reading, Mass.: Addison-Wesley, 1977).

been conducted and reported in a journal article or test manual, researchers seemed to be unaware of or indifferent to it. In addition, when psychometric evaluations were available, the instruments were generally judged according to absolute, rather than relative, standards. Few sources currently exist whereby one can judge the reliability and validity of an instrument in relation to the reliability and validity of other instruments with similar objectives. It was not uncommon, therefore, for researchers to choose an instrument with relatively low validity and reliability, apparently unaware that a more reliable and valid instrument was available and suitable for measuring the same construct. Revision and further development of an existing instrument would in many cases have been more appropriate and productive than construction of still another instrument of equal, or more questionable, reliability and validity. The inadequate psychometric properties characterizing many of the instruments in the studies reviewed, and the apparent availability of other more appropriate measures, suggests that, generally, no systematic approach was used in selecting these instruments.

It is important to note that researchers, for whatever reasons, rarely reported adequate psychometric data concerning the structural integrity of their instruments. They provided little information about replicability, constancy, uniformity, and stability of the measures they used, even when an instrument had not previously appeared in the research literature. Replicability refers to the extent to which a pattern or configuration of the behavior being measured recurs in essentially the same form in random samples on different occasions. Constancy is the degree to which a pattern or configuration appears in essentially the same form at different score ranges (e.g., Do pupils scoring low on an anxiety instrument demonstrate the same configuration of items as pupils scoring high on the instrument?). Uniformity refers to invariance in or similarity of the pattern across selected groups with varying characteristics (e.g., configurational similarity across race, sex, SES, age, etc.). And stability involves consistency of the pattern across two or more administrations of the instrument to the same subjects. The structural integrity of an instrument is determined by all four of the above characteristics, and the extent to which an instrument has structural integrity in turn determines the meaningfulness of the construct created to explain observed regularities.

An even greater number of studies failed to provide information about the validity, particularly the convergent and discriminant validity, of the instruments used. Convergent validity is a confirmation of traits (or variables or categories) by independent measuring methods that requires significant correlation between two methods measuring the same trait. Discriminant validity is a requirement that the correlation between different measures measuring the same trait exceed (a) the correlations obtained between that trait and any other trait not having method in common and (b) the correlations between different traits which happen to employ the same method. By determining intercorrelations among constructs in a multitrait/multimethod matrix, one can identify categories which pass specified tests of convergent and discriminant validity. (See, for example, the model by Borich and Malitz, 1975.)

Sourcebook Objectives

The four problems just discussed have had considerable influence upon the design and development of this sourcebook. Given these four problems, the objectives of this sourcebook are:

1. to provide a comprehensive review of currently available instruments selected across *different* areas of inquiry in order to encourage multivariate models of classroom research;
2. to provide a descriptive framework and organization that will encourage educators to return to the same pool of instruments, thereby promoting more consistent use of instruments across studies and investigators;
3. to report areas of inquiry and variables commonly researched, as well as those rarely studied (perhaps due to a lack of instrumentation); and
4. to provide data concerning the structural integrity of instruments and to evaluate these instruments according to relative standards by grouping them into conceptual categories which allow users to determine their comparative as well as their absolute psychometric value.

Generic Framework for the Instrument Search

In order to develop a framework to guide the selection of instruments for the sourcebook, the authors reviewed all relevant teacher behavior research and evaluations published during the period from which instruments would be chosen, i.e., roughly 1954 through 1975. Using Ryans' 1950s study of teacher characteristics (Ryans, 1960) and the publication of the *Second Handbook of Research on Teaching* (Travers, 1973) as approximate bounding points, the authors consulted significant journal articles, books, and monographs in order to define parameters for the sourcebook. From this review of the literature, two general dimensions were selected for the purpose of categorizing classroom behavior and the instruments used to measure it. These dimensions were: (1) type of behavior on a process/product continuum; and (2) level of inference required in measuring behavior.

Process/product stages

The inclusion of instruments covering a variety of process/product information stemmed from (1) the authors' conviction that researchers should explicitly state in advance the specific behaviors they are attempting to predict or observe; and (2) the fact that research produced over the past two decades has repeatedly revealed greater variance between than within process/product stages for both teacher and pupil behaviors.

The process/product continuum used in selecting instruments for the sourcebook contained four stages: (1) a preoperational stage characterized by the collection of antecedent, covariable, and predictor information such as personality, attitude, cognitive style, achievement, experience, and aptitude data on pupils and teachers; (2) an immediate process stage during which the ongoing, interactive behaviors of both the teacher and the learner are assessed, usually through systematic observation coding schemes and classroom climate inventories using either a rating or counting metric; (3) an intermediate process stage involving self-, peer, supervisor, and pupil ratings of the teacher; and (4) a product stage characterized by assessment of affective and cognitive pupil behaviors across content, subject, and grade level.

Level of inference

The second dimension used to guide the search for instruments—level of inference—has received increasing attention as a result of evidence which has shown that relationships between teacher behaviors and pupil outcomes differ depending upon whether teacher behavior is measured in a high- or low-inference fashion. High-inference behaviors are general characteristics of the teacher's performance, such as "enthusiasm," "organization," or "clarity," which are measured by overall ratings or observations. Low-inference behaviors, on the other hand, are discrete and easily observable units of activity, such as "teacher asks question," "student gives correct answer" or "teacher reinforces student." These behaviors are measured in terms of their presence or absence and are so clearly defined prior to coding that little inference is required of the observer in deciding whether or not a particular behavior occurred.

Contrary to initial expectation, high-inference measures of teacher behavior have often led to the strongest and most significant findings in the research literature. Such findings and related conclusions have recently stimulated interest in and examination of high-inference measures, while at the same time encouraging construction of low-inference techniques which offer the advantage of greater definition and specification of the teacher's performance vis-a-vis specific pupil outcomes.

Classification Scheme

Instruments in the sourcebook were organized according to who supplies information about whom. This informational approach, diagramed in Fig. 3, was designed to accommodate the instrument's intent as well as its place within a broader framework of classroom research.

The nine classifications represented on the grid are by no means mutually exclusive. Many measures, for example, can be used to obtain information about either the teacher or the pupil, and many can be completed by a teacher or an observer. Generally, instruments were placed in a particular category on the basis of previous or most likely use. Observation coding systems providing information about *both* the teacher and the pupil were classified under area III-C. The number of instruments varies from category to category, reflecting the state of instrument development which exists in the literature. There are, for example, many measures designed to yield data about the pupil, while comparatively few are available for assessing classroom climate, an area of relatively recent interest.

This classification scheme represents an attempt to place instruments in a broader research context, thereby encouraging educators to review the measures

About Whom / From Whom	Information		
	I	II	III
	About the Teacher	About the Pupil	About the Classroom
A. From the Teacher			
B. From the Pupil			
C. From an Observer			

Fig. 3. Sourcebook Classification Scheme.

in each column *and* each row before making selections. It is hoped that in this manner the sourcebook will promote replication of studies and more consistent use of multivariate designs for classroom research. The instrument classification pictured above avoids any single philosophical orientation toward the study of teaching in favor of a multivariate approach.

Criteria for the Selection of Measures

The following five criteria were used in selecting instruments for inclusion in the sourcebook:

1. Initially, instruments were reviewed without reference to the field of classroom behavior in order to cover all measures of possible use to researchers. Later screening focused more sharply on those instruments capable of providing a specific and/or unique contribution to the study of classroom behavior. The first criterion for selection, therefore, was that each instrument (a) relate to a major area of inquiry posited by the teacher research literature and (b) identify *specific* teacher or pupil variables for studying classroom instruction.

2. The second criterion for inclusion required that instruments apply to the classroom setting as opposed to the laboratory. Measures involving complex apparatus and contrived experimental devices were purposely excluded from the sourcebook. Recent writings (e.g., Rosenshine and Furst, 1973) have amply documented a need to establish general relationships between teacher behaviors and pupil outcomes in field classrooms before initiating intervention strategies to determine whether or not these relationships are causal. Therefore, instrumentation which can be applied in ongoing classrooms should be of most value at this point. The sourcebook focuses on those instruments which are appropriate for use in the classroom and compatible with time and administrative constraints associated with field settings.

3. The third selection criterion involved the instrument's availability to the research community. All instruments in the sourcebook are available from commercial publishers or public sources, such as journals, books, reports, monographs, dissertations, and reviews of research. The books and journals from which instruments were drawn were obtained from libraries or publishers. Reports and monographs were obtained either from their authors (who are identified in the sourcebook) or from the ERIC Document Reproduction Service, P.O. Box 190, Arlington, Virginia 22210. Dissertations were available either on a loan basis from the library at the degree-granting institution or from University Microfilms, University of Michigan, Ann Arbor, Michigan. Reviews of research were available as monographs, as chapters within commercially available texts, such as the *First* and *Second Handbook of Research on Teaching* (Gage, 1963; Travers, 1973), or as supplements to major educational and psychological journals.

When an instrument could not be obtained in full, either from the author or from one of the sources listed above, that instrument was not included in the sourcebook. Therefore, the reader can anticipate that each measure reviewed is available from the source cited at the beginning of each evaluation.

4. Each instrument included in the sourcebook was also required to have been employed in one or more studies wherein its psychometric characteristics were evaluated. Instruments which have generally remained unused were not included in this volume. Use, however, did not ensure inclusion. In some cases, measures used in pilot studies or exploratory designs were excluded because sample sizes were too small or research contexts too ambiguous to allow evaluation of the psychometric characteristics of the instrument. Many observation coding systems, already reviewed by Simon and Boyer (1970), were not evaluated in this volume since few research studies were available from which to judge their adequacy. Only the most widely used of the instruments appearing in Simon and Boyer were included. The bibliography which accompanies each review in the sourcebook reflects to some extent the instrument's past use and cites sources of further information about is psychometric properties.

5. The final selection criterion pertained to the test author's definition of the construct or constructs being measured. A statement of operationally defined constructs, referring to specific teacher, pupil, or classroom variables, or an attempt (past or in progress) to determine factorial validity, was required of each instrument included in the sourcebook.

Other Instrument Reviews

Before this sourcebook was compiled, four major instrument reviews were consulted in an effort to profit from the organizational insights of other authors and to avoid the pitfalls which seem to have diminished the usefulness of their work. The four sourcebooks most closely scrutinized were: *CSE-RBS Test Evaluations: Tests of Higher-Order Cognitive, Affective, and Interpersonal Skills* (Center for the Study of Evaluation, 1972) and its companion volumes; Johnson and Bommarito's *Tests and Measurements in Child Development: A Handbook* (1971); Shaw and

Wright's *Scales for the Measurement of Attitudes* (1967); and the Simon and Boyer volumes, *Mirrors for Behavior* (1970). Secondary works consulted for both style and content included Buros' *Mental Measurements Yearbooks* (1953; 1959; 1965; 1972), *Measuring Human Behavior* (Lake, Miles, and Earle, 1973), *Socioemotional Measures for Preschool and Kindergarten Children* (Walker, 1973), *Measures of Social Psychological Attitudes* (Robinson and Shaver, 1969), the ETS test file at the Carl Campbell Brigham Library at Princeton, New Jersey, and the Cornell University Test List (Cornell University, 1960).

After reviewing the above volumes, the authors determined that the present sourcebook should include the following information:

1. Name of instrument
2. Author of instrument
3. Type of measure: rating scale, self-report questionnaire, projective test, performance test, checklist, observational coding system, sociometric questionnaire, cognitive ability test
4. Availability of instrument
5. Description of instrument
    a) Purpose
    b) Population for whom it is appropriate
    c) Variables measured, with reference to other studies wherever possible
    d) Subscales or factors
    e) Context in which the instrument was developed
6. Illustration of sample items and response formats similar to those appearing on the instrument
7. Psychometric characteristics
    a) Reliability
        i. Internal consistency
        ii. Equivalence of forms
        iii. Stability
        iv. Intercoder agreement when appropriate
    b) Validity
        i. Content (source of items, adequacy of sample, item and factor analyses)
        ii. Predictive (criterion, number and type of cases, result)
        iii. Concurrent (criterion, number and type of cases, result)
        iv. Construct (type of evidence, result)
8. Norms
    a) Type and adequacy of norms
    b) Derived scores
    c) Suggestions for use
9. Administration and scoring
    a) Clarity
    b) Existence of manual or written directions

c) Administration time

d) Training requirements for administrators and observers

e) Type of scores obtained

f) Scoring procedures

10. Comments (evaluative remarks about the instrument's usability and psychometric adequacy)

11. Major references

These categories represent the organizational format of the reviews appearing in the sourcebook. The Description, Reliability, Validity, and Comment sections constitute the major part of each review. The descriptive and psychometric categories provide objective data from which the reader may draw his own conclusions about the adequacy of the measure, while a final, evaluative section presents the authors' perception of the instrument's strengths and weaknesses.

The authors of instruments are understandably reluctant to have parts of those instruments presented under other than actual measurement conditions. Therefore, the sample items included in these reviews, while true to the nature of their respective instruments, were originated by the authors of this sourcebook except where noted otherwise.

Sources of Instruments

Four kinds of sources were used in identifying instruments appearing in this sourcebook: (1) journal articles; (2) books; (3) reports; and (4) reviews of research. Though these sources were consulted for the years 1954 to 1975, the instruments in the sourcebook cover a broader period since the literature contained references to instruments currently in use but constructed prior to 1954. The starting point of the review intentionally corresponds to Ryans' classic study of teacher characteristics which began in the 1950s and culminated in 1960 with the publication of *Characteristics of Teachers* (Ryans, 1960). The authors feel that this research represents a milestone in the study of teacher behavior. Ryans' work, quite apart from the instruments it yielded, provided impetus for a decade of productive classroom research that followed. As the instruments in this sourcebook clearly reveal, interest in classroom research and evaluation has been increasing rapidly since the Ryans study and is now a significant field of inquiry.

Journals consulted for purposes of instrument selection included all those in which empirical studies related to classroom instruction might appear. Among these were education journals and several psychological journals noted for publishing teacher-behavior research. The periodicals of the American Educational Research Association (the *American Educational Research Journal* and the *Review of Educational Research*) were consulted along with the American Psychological Association's *Journal of Educational Psychology*. Other journals searched in the field of general education were the *Journal of Educational Research, Journal of Experimental Education, Journal of Sociology in Education, Journal of Teacher*

Education, Phi Delta Kappan, Curriculum Theory Network, Theory into Practice, Educational Researcher, the *Harvard Educational Review*, and the *Classroom Interaction Newsletter*. Several journals related to specific content areas were reviewed as well. These included the *Journal for Research in Mathematics Education, Journal of Research in Science Teaching, Science Education, Social Studies*, and the *Reading Research Quarterly*. Articles in these journals often served as leads directing the authors to still other journals which provided descriptions of additional instruments.

Professional texts and books provided a second source of instruments. Both major textbooks and less widely distributed monographs were reviewed. Typical of these were: Biddle and Ellena's *Contemporary Research on Teacher Effectiveness* (1964); Bolton's *Selection and Evaluation of Teachers* (1973); Dunkin and Biddle's *The Study of Teaching* (1974); Gage's *Teacher Effectiveness and Teacher Education* (1972); and Westbury and Bellack's *Research in the Classroom Processes* (1971). Other books, such as Rosenshine's *Teacher Behavior and Student Achievement* (1971) and Brophy and Good's *Teacher–Pupil Relationships* (1974), provided valuable leads to journal articles from which new instruments were eventually identified.

A third source of instruments included reports, monographs and unpublished dissertations. These works, though commonly circulated among educational researchers, were often otherwise unknown. Within this group were relatively obscure professional papers delivered to the American Educational Research Association and the American Psychological Association, the latter appearing in the proceedings of Division 15 (Educational Psychology).

Major reviews of research, such as those appearing in the *First* and *Second Handbook of Research on Teaching* (Gage, 1963; Travers, 1973) and in Smith's *Research on Teacher Education* (1971), served as a fourth source of instruments.

While no search can uncover all of the instruments of possible use to educators, the authors believe that the literature review described above was reasonably successful in identifying a significant subset of instruments for evaluating classroom instruction. The sourcebook contains a variety of strategic information needed by evaluators, researchers, and students of teacher behavior. Its mix of technical, research, and administrative information is designed to make this volume useful to the greatest number of educators.

References

Biddle, B. J., and W. J. Ellena (eds.), *Contemporary research on teacher effectiveness*. New York: Holt, Rinehart & Winston, 1964.

Biddle, B. J., T. L. Good, P. H. Hall, & B. J. Bank, *Institute for Research on Teaching: A proposal in response to RFP:NIE-R-76-0001*, Teaching Division, National Institute of Education, Washington, D.C., 1975.

Borich, G. D. *The appraisal of teaching: Concepts and process*. Reading, Mass.: Addison-Wesley, 1977.

Borich, G. D., and D. Malitz, "Convergent and discriminant validation of three classroom observation systems: A proposed model." *Journal of Educational Psychology*, 1975, **67**(3), 426–431.

Brophy, J., and T. L. Good, *Teacher–pupil relationships: Causes and consequences.* New York: Holt, Rinehart & Winston, 1974.

Buros, O. K., *The fourth mental measurements yearbook.* Highland Park, New Jersey: Gryphon Press, 1953.

Buros, O. K., *The fifth mental measurements yearbook.* Highland Park, New Jersey: Gryphon Press, 1959.

Buros, O. K., *The sixth mental measurements yearbook.* Highland Park, New Jersey: Gryphon Press, 1965.

Buros, O. K., *The seventh mental measurements yearbook.* Highland Park, New Jersey: Gryphon Press, 1972.

Center for the Study of Evaluation. *CSE-RBS test evaluations: Tests of higher-order cognitive, affective, and interpersonal skills.* Los Angeles: Center for the Study of Evaluation, Graduate School of Education, University of California, 1972.

Cornell University. *Cornell University test list.* Cornell University, Ithaca, New York, 1960.

Dunkin, M. J., and B. J. Biddle, *The study of teaching.* New York: Holt, Rinehart & Winston, 1974.

Gage, N. L. (ed.) *Handbook of research on teaching.* Chicago: Rand McNally, 1963.

Gage, N. L., *Teacher effectiveness and teacher education: The search for a scientific basis.* Palo Alto, Calif.: Pacific Books, 1972.

Johnson, O. G., and J. W. Bommarito, *Tests and measurements in child development.* San Francisco: Jossey-Bass, 1971.

Kash, M., G. Borich, and K. Fenton, *Teacher behavior and pupil self-concept.* Reading, Mass.: Addison-Wesley, in press.

Lake, D. G., M. B. Miles, and R. B. Earle, Jr. (eds.), *Measuring human behavior.* New York: Columbia University, Teachers College Press, 1973.

Robinson, J. P., and P. R. Shaver, *Measures of social psychological attitudes.* Ann Arbor, Michigan: Institute for Social Research, University of Michigan, 1969.

Rosenshine, B. *Teacher behaviours and student achievement.* Windsor, Berks, England: National Foundation for Educational Research in England and Wales, 1971.

Rosenshine, B., and N. Furst, "The use of direct observation to study teaching," in R. M. W. Travers (ed.), *Second handbook of research on teaching.* Chicago: Rand McNally, 1973.

Ryans, D. G., *Characteristics of teachers.* Washington, D.C.: American Council on Education, 1960.

Shaw, M. E., and J. M. Wright, *Scales for the measurement of attitudes.* New York: McGraw-Hill, 1967.

Simon, A., and E. G. Boyer (eds.), *Mirrors for behavior: An anthology of observation instruments.* Philadelphia: Research for Better Schools, 1970.

Smith, B. O. (ed.), *Research in teacher eduction: A symposium.* Englewood Cliffs, New Jersey: Prentice-Hall, 1971.

Travers, R. M. W. (ed.), *Second handbook of research on teaching.* Chicago: Rand McNally, 1973.

Walker, D. K., *Socioemotional measures for preschool and kindergarten children.* San Francisco: Jossey-Bass, 1973.

Westbury, I., and A. A. Bellack (eds.), *Research in the classroom processes: Recent developments and next steps.* New York: Columbia University, Teachers College Press, 1971.

Section I

IA

About the teacher from the teacher

Name: ACCEPTANCE OF SELF AND OTHERS

Author: Emmanuel M. Berger

Type of Measure: Rating scale

Availability: A copy of this instrument appears in: Shaw, M. E., and J. M. Wright, *Scales for the measurement of attitudes.* New York: McGraw-Hill, 1967.

Description: This instrument is directed toward the adult population. Although administered as a single test, it contains 2 distinct scales, 1 measuring attitude toward self, and 1 measuring attitude toward others. From an initial format of 47 statements on self-acceptance and 40 statements on acceptance of others, the 2 scales were reduced by item analysis to 36 and 28 items, respectively. The discriminating power of each item was determined by comparing mean scores of upper and lower criterion groups. The standard error of difference of the quartile means did not exceed .30 for any item. Selected items, except 3, had critical ratios of 3.0 or more; the remaining 3 had critical ratios close to 2.0.

Sample Items: The subject responds to each item on a 1-to-5 Likert scale. He or she may enter 1 for "not at all true of myself," 2 for "slightly true of myself," 3 for "about half-way true of myself," 4 for "mostly true of myself," or 5 for "true of myself." Items of the following type appear on the two scales:

Scale	*Item*
Self-Acceptance	I feel self-conscious and am shy in social situations.
Self-Acceptance	I think I might be neurotic or something.
Self-Acceptance	I do not condemn myself or worry if others judge me.
Self-Acceptance	If problems arise in the future, I feel confident that I can handle them.
Acceptance of Others . .	I am at ease with all types of people.
Acceptance of Others . .	I would not hesitate to encourage others to live by the same high standards I have myself.
Acceptance of Others . .	I really feel superior (or inferior) to most people I know.
Acceptance of Others . .	When others do things I feel are wrong, I can still be friendly with them.

Reliability: Split-half reliabilities, corrected by the Spearman-Brown formula, were obtained for five groups ranging in size from 18 to 183 (Berger, 1952). For the self-acceptance scale, these reliabilities were .894 or better for all but one group, which was .746. For the acceptance-of-others scale, reliabilities ranged from .776 to .884.

Validity: Several kinds of data were used in establishing validity (Berger, 1952). First, one group of subjects ($N = 20$) wrote about their self-concepts, while a second group ($N = 20$) wrote about their attitudes toward others. These paragraphs were evaluated by 4 judges and the mean ratings correlated with the corresponding scale scores. The Pearson product-moment correlations were .897 for self-acceptance and .727 for acceptance of others.

Second, a group of stutterers ($N = 38$) was compared with a group of nonstutterers on the self-acceptance scale. When matched for age and sex, the stutterers showed lower mean scores ($p < .06$) than the nonstutterers. Similarly, a group of prisoners was compared with a group of college students on the acceptance-of-others scale. Matched for age, sex, and race, the prisoners scored significantly lower ($p < .03$) than the students. In addition, the prisoners had lower scores on the self-acceptance scale ($p < .01$).

Third, clinical assistants rated members of a speech rehabilitation group for self-acceptance. These ratings correlated .59 with self-acceptance scale scores. This finding was not considered significant.

Norms: The initial form was administered to 200 students in first-year courses in either sociology or psychology. These subjects, ranging in age from 17 to 45, represented a variety of socioeconomic backgrounds and vocational interests. In determining reliability and validity, samples were drawn from college students, prisoners, stutterers, speech rehabilitation groups, and adults in YMCA classes.

Administration and Scoring: This instrument is self-administering; directions are printed on each form. There are 64 statements, the score for each of which ranges from 1 to 5. For negatively worded items, the direction of the scoring is reversed. A self-acceptance score and an acceptance-of-others score are computed by summing the appropriate item scores. A high score reflects a favorable attitude toward oneself or toward others.

Comments: This instrument has been carefully developed and has good reliability and validity. The nonsignificant correlation of .59 between clinical ratings and self-acceptance scores of a speech rehabilitation group is inconsistent with other validity data. However, this inconsistency may be attributable to the small number of subjects used and the unreliability of the clinical assistants' ratings. Generally, there appears to be sufficient evidence for validity.

References: Berger, E. M., "The relation between expressed acceptance of self and expressed acceptance of others." *Journal of Abnormal and Social Psychology*, 1952, **47**, 778–782.

Shaw, M. E., and J. M. Wright, *Scales for the measurement of attitudes*. New York: McGraw-Hill, 1967.

Name: ACTIVITIES INDEX

Author: George G. Stern

Type of Measure: Checklist

Availability: A copy of this instrument may be found in: Stern, G. G., *People in context*. New York: John Wiley & Sons, 1970.

Description: Adopted with some modifications from Murray's work (1938), the Activities Index (AI) may be used to measure 30 psychogenic needs in person/environment interaction. There are 300 items on the Index, each of which is, apparently, a manifestation of a particular functional need. It is assumed that functional needs are revealed in modes of behavior. Needs measured are Abasement, Achievement, Adaptiveness, Affiliation, Aggression, Change, Emotionality, Energy, Nurturance, Scientism, and Succorance.

 The prototype of the AI, the Interest Index, was developed after an inventory by Sheviakov and Friedberg (1939) suggested the format for a needs measure. The Interest Index differed from other activity/interest inventories because its design included variables which systematically represented an explicit personality theory. From an initial pool of over 1,000 statements, 400 items were selected by unanimous agreement among 8 psychologists. These items related commonplace activities and feelings which represented unambiguous manifestations of need processes. Modified to 300 items and renamed the Activities Index, this inventory has become a valuable research, and possibly diagnostic, tool for assessing specific elements in the need taxonomy. It may be administered to populations aged 13 and over.

Sample Items: The 300 statements produce 30 independent scale scores. Each scale consists of 10 items which are distributed randomly throughout the Index. The subject indicates whether an item describes an event or activity he or she would like or dislike, enjoy or reject, or find pleasant or unpleasant. He or she responds with either an "L" (like) or a "D" (dislike). Items of the following type appear on the Index:

___ Admitting failure.
___ Doing some crazy thing just for fun.
___ Listening to music that reminds me of sad things.
___ Suffering for a good reason or for a person I love.
___ Having others laugh whenever I make mistakes.

Reliability: Reliability has been assessed in several investigations by Stern (1970). Scale and cluster reliabilities were obtained for 122 school teachers, retested over a 7-month interval. Coefficients for the 10-item scales ranged from .47 to .93, with a mean of .69. Another sample group of social workers ($N = 11$) was retested over a 2-week period. Product-moment coefficients for the scale scores ranged from .67 to .94, with a mean of .88.

 Item analysis indices were computed for each statement. An index consisted of the upper and lower 27 percent of scores on each scale. Given 10 uncorrelated items of equal difficulty, the criterion coefficient was .32. The coefficients for the 30 scales ranged from .27 to .81, with a mean of .57.

Internal consistency reliabilities were computed by means of the Kuder-Richardson formulas 20 and 21. KR_{20} reliabilities, drawn from a group of 1,076 subjects, ranged from .40 to .88, with a mean falling in the low .70s. Computed reliabilities for 14 need scales fell below .70, while 5 scales had reported reliabilities of .80 or above. From another group of 4,021 subjects drawn from 34 institutions, KR_{21} coefficients ranged from .25 to .85, with a mean in the upper .60s. Reliability coefficients for 19 scales fell below .70 and for 4 scales reached .80 or above.

Validity: Stern (1970) conceptualizes 2 approaches to validity—Equivalent Validity and Consequent Validity. Equivalent validity is seen as the agreement of a given appraisal with other appraisals, either objective or judgmental. The AI profiles of 76 medical students were classified by vector summaries into 10 subgroups. These summaries were correlated with student ratings of personality traits of classmates assigned to each group. Differences between subgroup ratings were significant beyond the .001 level, and significant positive correlations were obtained between student ratings and vector angle (Scanlon, 1958).

Consequent validity refers to any behavioral event, unknown at the time of assessment, which seems to verify, or is consistent with, the personality traits suggested by the AI scores. One procedure used for consequent validation involves the instrument's ability to discriminate between predetermined groups. Stern (1970) cites a considerable number of studies which, using the AI, have found significant personality differences among various occupational, student, and sex groups.

No statistics are given for predictive validity. However, some applications of the AI have shown significant results. One such application yielded a multiple *r* of .63 crossvalidated between a 23-item subscale of the AI and a first-year general education examination average. Also, significant differences were found on AI subscales between extreme scorers on an index measuring positivity/negativity on TAT protocols.

A limited amount of information is provided for construct validity. Several studies tested predictions that groups having certain AI profiles would behave in certain ways. Other investigations showed that students in a given institution produced AI profiles consistent with known characteristics of that institution. Finally, factor scores for institutions based on a joint analysis of the AI and CCI (College Characteristics Index) showed patterns which might be predicted from general knowledge of the institutions. For instance, schools such as Bryn Mawr and Bennington were high on an Intellectual Culture factor.

Norms: The norms for the 30 scales were based on a group of 1,076 college students (men and women) from 23 institutions. The scales were combined into

12 first-order and 4 second-order factor composites. Item and scale character-istics were established by this sampling, and institutional norms for the factor scores were developed.

Administration and Scoring: The AI is self-administering. Instructions are given on a reusable Question Booklet, and answers are recorded on a single sheet using an electrographic pencil. The test takes 30 to 90 minutes to complete. There is no time limit.

The test may be hand scored with a single stencil or machine scored. Methods for computation of scores are listed in the Key and on a Diagnostic Summary Form. Scores are plotted as arcs forming a circular profile diagram.

Comments: The AI may be susceptible to response distortion. One group study ($N = 250$) showed a correlation of .75 between mean scale scores and mean social desirability scores (Stern, 1970). This high relationship may be due to individuals viewing their personal characteristics as desirable. The AI appears to be less susceptible to faking. A group sampling showed students unable to falsify or distort profiles on 2 administrations of the test, each taken with respondents role-playing different occupational groups.

The Activities Index is a carefully constructed instrument. However, little statistical information on reliability and validity is available. Evidence for re-liability is moderate, and evidence of substantial validity is scarce. Until psychometric properties have been better established, use of the AI should be confined to research.

References: Lake, D. G., M. B. Miles, and R. B. Earle, Jr. (eds.), *Measuring human behavior*. New York: Columbia University, Teachers College Press, 1973.

Murray, H. A., *Explorations in personality*. New York: Oxford University Press, 1938.

Scanlon, J., *The Activities Index: An inquiry into validity*. Unpublished doctoral dissertation, Syracuse University, 1958.

Sheviakov, G. V., and J. Friedberg, *Evaluation of personal and social adjustment. Progressive Education Association: Evaluation in the eight-year study*. Chicago: University of Chicago Press, 1939.

Stern, G. G., *People in context*. New York: John Wiley & Sons, 1970.

Name: ADJECTIVE CHECK LIST

Authors: Harrison G. Gough and Alfred B. Heilbrun, Jr.

Type of Measure: Checklist

Availability: Gough, H. G., and A. B. Heilbrun, Jr., *Manual for the Adjective Check List.* Palo Alto, California: Consulting Psychologists Press, 1965. A copy of the instrument may also be found in: Robinson, J. R., and P. R. Shaver, *Measures of social psychological attitudes.* Ann Arbor, Michigan: Institute for Social Research, University of Michigan, 1969.

Description: The Adjective Check List (ACL) is composed of 300 words describing personality traits. From the factor analytic studies of personality structure by Cattell (1943), a list of 171 adjectives was compiled and then supplemented with traits derived from the theoretical work of Freud, Jung, Mead, Murray, and others to produce an initial total of 279 words. Over a 2-year experimental period, this list was extended to 300 adjectives, which make up the current form.

 The ACL may be administered to high school, college, or adult populations as a measure of self-concept, ideal self, or perception of another.

Sample Items: This instrument yields 25 scale scores: 3 trait counts (number of total, favorable, and unfavorable adjectives checked), as well as scores for 15 of Murray's needs, and for personal adjustment, counseling readiness, self-confidence, self-control, lability, and defensiveness. The various scales are interpreted by indicative and contra-indicative adjectives marked by the subject. The self-confidence scale, for example, contains items of the following type:

Indicative Adjectives:	___ astute	Contra-indicative Adjectives:	___ uneasy
	___ candid		___ restrained
	___ forward		___ susceptible
	___ strong-minded		___ careful
	___ predominant		
	___ zealous		

Reliability: Determination of reliability has been approached through various investigations (Gough and Heilbrun, 1965). A group of 100 adult males was administered the Check List twice over a 6-month period. For each subject, a 4-fold point surface was computed—counting adjectives checked both times, neither time, first time but not second, and second time but not first. Test/retest phi coefficients ranged from .01 to .86 with a mean of .54 and a standard deviation of .19. From this same group, 5 subjects (the twentieth, fortieth, sixtieth, eightieth, and hundredth) were assessed on the ACL by 2 groups of raters (5 judges in each group) to investigate interjudge agreement. Totals from the rating groups were correlated to determine agreement between each rating group. The 5 inter-group reliability coefficients for each selected subject, corrected by the Spearman-Brown formula, were: .70, .63, .61, .75 and .61.

Test/retest reliabilities for a group of college males ($N = 56$) over a 10-week period ranged from .54 (Succorance Scale) to .85 (Nurturance Scale) with a median of .76. A group of college females ($N = 23$), tested over a 10-week period, yielded test/retest coefficients of .45 (Succorance) to .90 (Aggression), with a median of .76.

Validity: A variety of investigations have been performed to establish validity (Gough and Heilbrun, 1965). The ACL need scales were correlated with the college dropout rate among females, and it was found that 6 of the 15 scales were significantly related to dropping out of college. Further, an index combining these 6 scales enhanced the prediction of scholastic ability.

Heilburn (1958) correlated the ACL need scales with their counterparts on the Edwards Personal Preference Schedule (Edwards, 1954). Ten of the 15 needs were significantly correlated at the .01 level; the median correlation coefficient for all 15 needs was .31. The rank order of needs correlated .60. Between-scale correlations were low, ranging from .01 (Achievement) to .48 (Aggression).

Validity analyses have also been performed correlating self-ratings with ratings by observers. One hundred adult males were administered the ACL and then evaluated on it by observers. The obtained correlation between self- and observer ratings was .50. Similarly, a study of 66 student engineers yielded a correlation of .25 between self- and observer ratings. Also, a study using a group of 26 males, first tested as applicants to medical school and then again as graduating seniors, showed correlations ranging from .28 (Judgability) to .71 (Self-Insight) between self- and observer ratings.

Norms: Norms are based on sample groups of college students—1,364 males and 642 females. Interpretation of scores is complex since different norm tables are required depending on the number of adjectives checked. The manual provides the necessary tables for computation and translation of the 25 scale scores.

Administration and Scoring: This instrument is self-administering. It can be completed in about 15 minutes, either individually or in a group. It is available as a hand-scoreable, 4-page folder, or as a machine-scoreable single sheet. The ACL is scored first by counting the number of words checked. Then, among these words, the contra-indicative adjectives are subtracted from the indicative adjectives for each of the 25 scales. Each scale score is converted to a standard score according to sex and the total numer of checked items. Due to the extensive time involved in hand scoring, and the possibility of error, computer scoring is preferred.

Comments: Reliability and validity data for the ACL are not reassuring. Test/retest reliabilities are not consistently high, and validity coefficients are fairly low. The low median correlation between the need scales of the ACL and those of the Edwards Personal Preference Schedule make the appropriateness of the ACL as a diagnostic measurement of independent variables unclear. However, viewed as an instrument in research status, the ACL has potential for economical assessment of personality attributes. Accordingly, it may be of value in supplementing other personality indicators.

References: Cattell, R. B., "The description of personality: 2. Basic traits resolved into clusters." *Journal of Abnormal and Social Psychology*, 1943, **38**, 476–507.

Edwards, A. L., *Manual. Edwards Personal Preference Schedule*. New York: The Psychological Corporation, 1954.

Gough, H. G., and A. B. Heilbrun, Jr., *Manual for the Adjective Check List*. Palo Alto, California: Consulting Psychologists Press, 1965.

Heilbrun, A. B., "Relationships between the Adjective Check List, Personal Preference Schedule and desirability factors under varying defensiveness conditions." *Journal of Clinical Psychology*, 1958, **14**, 237–238.

Lake, D. G., M. B. Miles, and R. B. Earle, Jr. (eds.), *Measuring human behavior*. New York: Columbia University, Teachers College Press, 1973.

Robinson, J. R., and P. R. Shaver, *Measures of social psychological attitudes*. Ann Arbor: Michigan: Institute for Social Research, University of Michigan, 1969.

Name: ADJECTIVE SELF-DESCRIPTION

Authors: Donald J. Veldman and George V. C. Parker

Type of Measure: Rating scale

Availability: Veldman, D. J. and G. V. C. Parker, "Adjective rating scales for self-description." *Multivariate Behavioral Research*, 1970, **5**, 295–302. This in-instrument is also available in: Veldman, D. J. *Adjective self-description, RMM-11R*. Research Methodology Monograph 11 (revised). Austin, Texas: Research and Development Center for Teacher Education, The University of Texas, 1971.

Description: The Adjective Self-Description (ASD) grew out of Veldman and Parker's (1970) factor analysis of the Adjective Check List (ACL), which had been developed by Gough and Heilbrun (1965) to facilitate self-description across a wide variety of personality traits. Factor analysis of the 300-item Check List revealed 8 high-loading items for 7 factors of self-description (Attitude, Behavior, Efficiency, Orientation, Anxiety, Ideology, and Attractiveness). Identification and analyses of these 7 factors prompted the development of the Adjective Self-Description, which was designed to overcome the following short-comings of the ACL: (1) administration of the 300-item ACL was uneconomical if data on only the 7 empirical factors were desired: (2) the precision of measure-ment with a dichotomous-choice response format was questionable; and (3) the reliability and validity of the empirical factor structure obtained for the ACL had yet to be established.

The ASD may be administered to high school, college, or adult populations.

Sample Items: The ASD is a 54-item instrument which produces 7 scale scores. The 8 high-loading adjectives for each of the 7 factor variables are alphabetized and mixed randomly throughout the ASD. Each adjective is followed by a 1–5 response format: "No" over the column of ones and "Yes" over the column of fives. The Attitude Scale, for example, contains items of the following type:

	No				*Yes*
happy	1	2	3	4	5
good-hearted	1	2	3	4	5
agreeable	1	2	3	4	5
affectionate	1	2	3	4	5
compassionate	1	2	3	4	5

Reliability: Determination of reliability was approached through various investi-gations. Veldman and Parker (1970) computed test/retest reliabilities on a group of college students ($N = 61$) tested twice over a 2-week interval. Obtained coefficients for the factor scales ranged from .80 (Attractiveness) to .92 (Orientation).

Veldman and Parker (1970) obtained alpha coefficients of internal consistency for the items of each ASD scale. Based on a group of female college students ($N = 713$), these ranged from .64 (Ideology) to .88 (Orientation). Further investigation of the Ideology Scale revealed a similar degree of relationship for all 8 adjectives.

Analyses were also undertaken to determine structural invariance of the instrument (Parker and Veldman, 1969). A theoretical factor structure was constructed consisting of ones and zeroes, which represented assignment of the 56 adjectives to the 7 scales. Scores from each of 4 subject samples, who differed in one or more ways from the normative group, were separately item-factored. The resulting varimix structures were compared to the theoretical structure, with invariance coefficients ranging from .66 (Behavior: Adult Engineers) to 1.00 (Orientation and Anxiety: Adult Teachers). These data were offered as evidence of the invariance of the item structure across diverse populations (Veldman, 1971).

Validity: Validity has been investigated by assessing differences among predefined groups (Veldman, 1971). One-way analysis of variance was used to compare engineering students, engineering professors, and industrial engineers. There were major differences between student and adult groups. The means of student groups ranged from 17.1 (Behavior) to 31.3 (Attitude); adult means ranged from 14.4 (Behavior) to 30.7 (Attitude). For the 2 groups, differences on 3 of the 7 scales were significant ($p < .0001$).

Two-way analyses of variance were computed, comparing black and white, male and female students on each ASD scale. Group means ranged from 16.1 to 32.3 (white females); 16.0 to 33.5 (black females); 16.1 to 31.6 (white males); and 14.7 to 33.4 (black males). The results indicated 2 significant race effects and 3 significant sex differences (p levels ranging from <.0001 to .004); there were no significant interactions.

Two-way analyses of variance were computed with ASD scale scores, comparing 3 sample groups of education students (female elementary, female secondary, and male secondary) tested at 2 universities. The 3 groups showed significant differences on each variable (p levels ranging from < .0001 to .03). Groups from the 2 schools showed significant differences on 5 of the 7 scales (p levels from <.0001 to .04).

The ASD has been correlated with other instruments. Veldman and Parker (1970) computed cross-correlations between the ASD and 8 scales on the Self-Report Inventory (SRI). A sample group of female students ($N = 706$) showed cross-correlations ranging from −.39 (ASD Behavior vs. SRI Work Scale) to .44 (ASD Attitude vs. SRI Others). Although the SRI is concerned with "external" foci and the ASD with "internal" foci, cross-similarities exist for all scales and are further explained in the manual.

Eight variables on another instrument, the One-Word Sentence Completion, were cross-correlated with the 7 ASD variables (Veldman,

Menaker, and Peck, 1969). Correlations ranged from .24 (Efficiency vs. Depression Scale) to .25 (Anxiety vs. Anxiety Scale).

Norms: In the original factor analysis of the 300-item ACL, a group of college freshmen ($N = 5,017$) provided the empirical basis for the ASD. Since that time, a wide range of populations have annually provided systematic normative data for the ASD. These populations are composed of college undergraduates majoring in education, business and engineering, graduate students, black teachers, and white teachers.

Administration and Scoring: The ASD is self-administering. A 54-item list is presented on a single sheet, and the subject marks his response on a 1–5 basis. There is no time limit. All items are hand scored in a common direction, with the exception of the 3 items in Scale 4 (Orientation), which are reversed. A Likert (simple-sum) scaling approach is used. The scale scores are prorated for missing item data (the mean of valid item responses is substituted), provided at least one-half of the items in a scale are completed. Missing or double-marked items are left blank. Four or more items left blank result in a scale score of zero.

Comments: The ASD appears to be a carefully constructed instrument. Investigations of the 7 factors and inclusion of a 5-point response format have increased its sensitivity of measurement. Reliability appears to be good. However, validity, which is not high, warrants further investigation. Normative data are derived from large and varied populations. As an instrument in continued research status, the ASD shows potential for economic assessment of personality attributes.

References: Austad, C. A., and E. T. Emmer, *Personality correlates of teacher performance in a micro-teaching laboratory*. Report Series No. 51. Austin, Texas: Research and Development Center for Teacher Education, The University of Texas, 1970.

Gough, H., and A. B. Heilbrun, *Adjective Check List manual*. Palo Alto, California: Consulting Psychologists Press, 1965.

Parker, G. V. C., and D. J. Veldman, "Item factor structure of the Adjective Check List." *Educational and Psychological Measurement*, 1969, **29**, 605–613.

Veldman, D. J., *Adjective self-description, RMM-11R*. Research Methodology Monograph 11 (revised). Austin, Texas: Research and Development Center for Teacher Education, The University of Texas, 1971.

Veldman, D. J., S. L. Menaker, and R. F. Peck, "Computer scoring of sentence completion data. *Behavioral Science*, 1969, **14**, 501–507.

Veldman, D. J., and G. V. C. Parker, "Adjective rating scales for self-description." *Multivariate Behavioral Research*, 1970, **5**, 295–302.

Name: APTITUDE TEST FOR ELEMENTARY SCHOOL TEACHERS-IN-TRAINING

Author: Henry Bowers

Type of Measure: Projective test

Availability: Bowers, H., *Aptitude test for elementary school teachers-in-training.* Toronto: J. M. Dent & Sons, 1950.

Description: The Aptitude Test for Elementary School Teachers-in-Training (ATEST) was designed to predict the performance of individuals in a practice teaching program. Accordingly, it may be administered to adult populations.

This instrument consists of 7 parts: I (Opinions); II (Books); III (Occupations); IV (Interests); V (An Aspect of Judgment); VI (Performance); and VII (High School Percentile). Parts I–V are pencil-and-paper tasks. Apparently, Parts I–IV may be administered to both sexes. Part V, however, has not given satisfactory results for males. Part VI is essentially a concealed interview. The final section, Part VII, is a condensation of the subject's secondary school record.

Sample Items: The various parts of the ATEST require different tasks and modes of response. In Part I, the subject expresses his opinion of various personal experiences on a response scale from 1 (enthusiastic approval) to 5 (extremely opposed). In Part II, the subject indicates his willingness to read various books with fictitious titles, using the same mode of response as in Part I. In Part III, the subject lists his preference for 16 given occupations from 1 (greatest) to 16 (least). Part IV lists a number of activities in elementary school teaching. The subject responds to these on a scale from 1 (favor) to 5 (do not favor). From a list of assertions in Part V, the subject estimates the degree of truth in each statement. The response scale ranges from 1 (certainly true) to 7 (certainly untrue) to X (insufficient information). In Part VI, the individual selects a number of brief topics which he then discusses before an audience of fellow students and a rater. The subject is observed and evaluated by the rater. Part VII is a condensation of the subject's secondary school record, expressed as a percentile. It involves the areas of individual intelligence, group achievement, empathic ability, and vocational interests. Items of the following type appear on Parts I–V:

Part I: 1. Accepting a role in a play .... ( )
          2. Giving a recitation in public .... ( )
Part II: 1. Solitary Reflections .... ( )
          2. Eminent Music Composers .... ( )
Part III: 1. Secretary .... ( )
          2. Public Librarian .... ( )
Part IV: 1. Supervising library activities .... ( )
          2. Directing music period .... ( )

Part V: 1. Highly intelligent teachers will eventually become bored
         with routine subject lessons . . . . ( )
      2. A teacher who feels he is wasting his time in teaching, is also
         wasting the time of his students . . . . ( )

Reliability: Reliability of the 7 subtests has been investigated by Bowers (1950b). Split-half reliabilities were computed and corrected by the Spearman-Brown formula for the pencil-and-paper tasks. A split-half reliability coefficient of .67 ± .04 was obtained on Parts I–V for females ($N = 87$). A group of men ($N = 78$) yielded a split-half coefficient of .67 ± .04 on Parts I–IV.

On Part VI percentiles from a randomly selected pair of raters were correlated with those from another pair. Corrected by the Spearman-Brown formula, the obtained coefficient was .83 ± .02.

A rough analysis of the internal consistency of Part VII was made. Measures obtained from some of the components of this subtest were correlated with those obtained from the remainder. The resulting coefficient was .73. Application of the Spearman-Brown formula yielded a coefficient of .84 ± .02.

Validity: Validity has been investigated in several studies by Bowers (1950b). First, subtest scores and practice-teaching marks were correlated. On Parts I–III, females ($N = 87$) yielded a coefficient of .43 ± .06; for men ($N = 34$) the obtained coefficient was .57 ± .08. On Part IV a coefficient of .13 ± .07 for women students ($N = 87$) emerged; for men ($N = 34$) the coefficient was .39 ± .10. Correlations between Part V scores and teaching marks for women were .24 ± .07 ($N = 85$) and .13 ± .07 ($N = 87$). Between Part VI percentiles and teaching marks, correlations were .57 ± .05 ($N = 85$) and .73 ± .03 ($N = 90$) for women and .73 ± .05 for men ($N = 38$). In correlating Part VII percentiles with teaching marks, no distinction between the sexes was made. Obtained coefficients ranged from .17 to .47 for 9 groups of subjects. The quadratic mean was .29.

Another validation study compared leadership and sociability traits with ATEST predictions of performance in practice teaching (Bowers, 1950c). Near the end of the academic year, each of 76 female students nominated 3 fellow students for positions of leadership. These nominations were then compared with ATEST performance predictions. The ATEST predictions of success in teaching showed 19 students at the 74th percentile; these students also received the highest number of votes for leadership. The 34 students who received no votes fell at the 39th percentile. This same procedure was followed in comparing sociability and ATEST results. The 21 students who received the highest number of sociability votes ranked at the 61st percentile mark. The 12 who received no votes ranked at the 23rd percentile mark. A comparison between the average percentiles for ATEST predictions and the combined votes for leadership and sociability was also computed. The 16 students who received the highest combined votes ranked at the 75th percentile on the ATEST; the 15 who received the lowest combined votes ranked at the 21st percentile.

Norms: Normative data were based upon group studies in 3 Canadian schools. Approximately 258 teachers-in-training (209 females and 49 males) were tested.

Administration and Scoring: This instrument is self-administering. Instructions are printed on Parts I through V. There is no time limit. On Part VI the subject is required to deliver 3 to 5 speeches of from 3 to $3\frac{1}{2}$ minutes duration. The subject selects the topics about which he or she wishes to speak. Apparently Part VII, a percentile summary of the secondary education record, does not apply to those who have received secondary education outside of Ontario. For scoring, the manual provides keys for each subtest. Subtest scores are combined into a total percentile score for Parts I–V (women) and Parts I–IV (men). On Part VI (Performance) the subject is evaluated by a minimum of 5 raters. These evaluations involve Favorable Descriptions (amiable, self-assured, and pleasant) and Unfavorable Descriptions (shy, unclear, and uncertain). The manual gives directions for converting raters' impressions into a total percentile mark. To arrive at the final score, the percentile from Parts I–V (women) or Parts I–IV (men) is added to the Part VII percentile and twice the Part VI percentile. This total is then converted to a single percentile. When the test is used outside of Ontario, the percentile from Parts I–V or I–IV is added to twice the percentile from Part VI. A total score above the 50th percentile is recognized as a prediction of teaching success.

Comments: The Aptitude Test for Elementary School Teachers-in-Training is a carefully constructed intrument. It provides reliability and validity data of moderate significance. As a predictive inventory, however, several factors limit its usefulness. First, it was developed on a population exclusively Canadian. Second, a complex scoring procedure, particularly in Part VI, allows for a questionable amount of error. Third, the high validity coefficients obtained on Part VI may have been due to the raters' experience in validation studies, rather than to any particular characteristic of the instrument itself. Finally, this instrument assumes that effective performance can be predicted from measurement and observation. The ATEST does not consider given teaching situations; nor does it define or predict desirable changes in pupils. It does, however, effectively measure the interests and opinions of teachers-in-training.

References: Bowers, H., *Aptitude test for elementary school teachers-in-training.* Toronto: J. M. Dent & Sons, 1950. (a)

Bowers, H., *Manual descriptive of the Aptitude Test for Elementary School Teachers-in-Training.* Toronto: J. M. Dent & Sons, 1950. (b)

Bowers, H., "New data on the validity of the 'Aptitude Test for Elementary School Teachers-in-Training'." *Canadian Journal of Psychology*, 1950, **4**(1), 11–17. (c)

Name: ATTITUDE TOWARD EDUCATION

Author: Claude Mitchell

Type of Measure: Checklist

Availability: Mitchell, C., "Do scales for measuring attitudes have any significance?" *Journal of Educational Research,* 1941, **34**, 444–452. A copy of Scale A may be found in: Shaw, M. E., and J. M. Wright, *Scales for the measurement of attitudes.* New York: McGraw-Hill, 1967.

Description: The Attitude Toward Education Scale may be used to measure an individual's attitude toward education, school, and school practices. It is appropriate for high school or adult populations.

 The Attitude Scale consists of two parts, A and B, which contain 34 statements each. Scale A includes two kinds of items—some suggesting more serious and rigid school practices, others suggesting more lenient behavior toward the pupil. It is assumed that subjects checking items reflective of serious discipline tend to view school as preparation for life, while those checking items reflective of a more lenient arrangement are in school for reasons other than personal application and work. Scale B consists of the same items as Scale A, but arranged in a different order.

Sample Items: From either Scale A or Scale B, the subject marks those items with which he or she agrees. Each scale contains items of the following type:

 1. ____ Students should have more freedom to do what they wish.
 2. ____ Students should be compelled to study more.
 3. ____ School lessons need to be clearer and easier.
 4. ____ Teachers should explain difficult lessons more than they do.
 5. ____ Homework should not be assigned to students.
 6. ____ Students should be assigned about 2 hours of homework each day.
 7. ____ People usually manage to function adequately in life, regardless of whether or not they had any practice in high school.
 8. ____ Good study habits are learned only when intensive study is required.

Reliability: Reliability was computed by comparing Scale A scores with Scale B scores. The 2 scales were administered 12 weeks apart to a high school sample ($N = 382$). Test/retest reliability was .71 (Mitchell, 1941).

Validity: Validation was approached by correlating the scale scores with class grades. Mitchell (1941) assumed that students favoring strict discipline and rigorous school requirements would apply themselves more diligently to their studies and earn higher classroom grades than those students preferring a looser arrangement. The .73 correlation obtained between scale scores and class grades would seem to support this assumption.

Norms: The normative data are based on a group of 382 high school students.

Administration and Scoring: This instrument is self-administering. Instructions are printed on each form, and there is no time limit. The score is the difference between the number of checked items indicative of rigorous attitudes and those indicative of less rigorous attitudes. A positive score is interpreted as a favorable attitude toward strict school practices. A negative score presumably indicates a predisposition toward less strict school practices.

Comments: Although favorable, reliability and validity data on the Attitude Toward Education Scale are not extensive. Furthermore, no attempt has been made to determine the discriminating power of test items. The available evidence on the Attitude Scale, however, is basically positive and warrants continued research.

References: Mitchell, C., "Do scales for measuring attitudes have any significance?" *Journal of Educational Research*, 1941, **34**, 444–452.

Shaw, M. E., and J. M. Wright, *Scales for the measurement of attitudes.* New York: McGraw-Hill, 1967.

Name: ATTITUDE TOWARD THE FREEDOM OF CHILDREN SCALE

Authors: Helen L. Koch, Mame Dentler, Bonnie Dysart, and Helen Streit

Type of Measure: Checklist

Availability: Koch, H. L., M. Dentler, B. Dysart, and H. Streit, "A scale for measuring attitude toward the question of children's freedom." *Child Development*, 1934, **5**, 253–266. A copy of the instrument may also be found in: Shaw, M. E., and J. M. Wright, *Scales for the measurement of attitudes*. New York: McGraw-Hill, 1967.

Description: The Attitude Toward the Freedom of Children Scale measures opinions about the degree of freedom, independence, and self-management children should be allowed. Accordingly, it may be helpful in evaluating the effectiveness of adult or parental education programs, and in describing attitudes of various racial or socioeconomic groups.

From methodological characteristics listed by Thurstone and Wang, an initial pool of 123 statements was selected. These were then sorted by 200 judges, mostly college-trained. The final selection of statements was based on scatter, relatively low Q value, brevity, and similarity of item rating between the 2 groups of 100 judges. Two forms of the Scale (Scale I and Scale II) were developed; each contains 33 items.

Sample Items: Each statement on the 66-item format is assigned a scale value. Subjects respond to a statement by placing either a check mark (agree) or a cross mark (disagree) beside the item. Items of the following type appear on Scale I and Scale II:

Scale Values   *Scale I*

7.09   1. A young child has to be disciplined in order to learn not to handle things in his or her environment which he or she may damage or destroy.

2.56   2. Whenever there is conflict between the wants of a child and an adult, more consideration should be given to the child.

6.00   3. Parents should feel it necessary to give reasons for restricting a young child only when the child is capable of understanding.

Scale II

2.59   1. A child should be given an adequate reason to obey, except in dangerous situations.

7.72   2. Children should be taught to respect their elders.

5.25   3. Whenever imposing restrictions on a child, parents should consider the reasons and willingly explain them.

Reliability: Several studies were performed in order to establish reliability (Koch, Dentler, Dysart, and Streit, 1934). The reliability of scale values was determined by comparing sorted scale values from 2 groups, each consisting of 100 judges. A coefficient of .97 was obtained between the 2 sets of scale values.

Furthermore, the 2 forms of the Scale were correlated. The obtained coefficient between Scale I and Scale II was .68, based on the scores of 233 adults.

Validity: Various group criteria were used in order to establish validity (Koch, Dentler, Dysart, and Streit, 1934).

To determine the ability of the instrument to reveal group differences, Scale I was administered to 359 adults and Scale II to 233 adults in widely scattered parts of the country. The obtained scores for Scale I ranged from 3.50 to 8.50, the possible scores ranging from .55 to 10.43. The mean score was 5.62, and the distribution was bimodal. Scores obtained for Scale II ranged from 3.25 to 7.25, the mean score being 5.38. The mode was slightly in the liberal direction, a fact which may be explained by the composition of the Scale II sample. While students and professionals were heavily represented in both groups, they constituted proportionally more of the group given Scale II than that given Scale I.

Another group comparison involved educational differences. Results showed that the more formal education a respondent has the lower his score will be, and the more liberal his opinion. For a group of married females, obtained means ranged from 5.92 (for those with a high school education) to 4.75 (for those with graduate study). Married males yielded mean scores that ranged from 6.05 (high school) to 5.50 (graduate study). Obtained mean scores for a group of single females ranged from 6.09 (high school) to 4.72 (graduate study); for the single males, means ranged from 6.13 (high school) to 5.88 (graduate study).

When treated as a whole, or when grouped by age, education, marital status, and occupation, test data revealed sex differences. Females scored lower than males: those with a high school education had a mean score of 5.98, as compared to 6.09 for their male counterparts. Corresponding scores for respondents with a college education were 5.38 (female) and 5.60 (male), and for those with graduate study, 5.11 (female) and 5.54 (male).

The effect of an adult's contact with children was also investigated. A group of males produced mean scores that ranged from 5.74 (parent) to 5.95 (no contact). A group of females yielded mean scores of 5.58 (parent) to 5.79 (no contact). Closer contact with children appears to produce lower scores and more liberal expressed opinions.

Norms: The 2-form reliability study was based on a general adult group ($N = 233$). Subjects (232 women and 127 men) from scattered parts of the country provided other normative data.

Administration and Scoring: This instrument is self-administering. Directions are printed on each form. The subject responds to all items indicating either agreement or disagreement. The computed score is the median of the scale values of items with which the subject agrees. Scale values range from .55 to 10.43. A low score indicates a more liberal attitude toward freedom of children.

Comments: The Attitude Toward the Freedom of Children Scale appears to possess good psychometric properties, although data are rather limited. Available reliability estimates are adequate, but test/retest figures are needed. While validity studies are extensive, they all employ the same approach (i.e., group comparisons). Accordingly, the authors of this instrument suggest that it be used for uncovering group differences rather than for individual diagnosis (Koch, Dentler, Dysart, and Streit, 1934).

References: Koch, H. L., M. Dentler, B. Dysart, and H. Streit, "A scale for measuring attitude toward the question of children's freedom." *Child Development,* 1934, **5**, 253–266.

Shaw, M. E., and J. M. Wright, *Scales for the measurement of attitudes.* New York: McGraw-Hill, 1967.

Name: ATTITUDE TOWARD TEACHING AS A CAREER

Authors: Jack C. Merwin and Francis J. DiVesta

Type of Measure: Rating scale

Availability: A copy of this instrument appears in: Shaw, M. E., and J. M. Wright, *Scales for the measurement of attitudes*. New York: McGraw-Hill, 1967.

Description: This instrument is designed to measure an adult's attitude toward teaching as a career. The theoretical basis of the inventory is the attitude/concept view of attitude structure (Rhine, 1958; Woodruff, 1942). According to this view, attitudes are a manifestation of an individual's belief/value matrix. Favorable attitudes result from perceptions that the attitude object facilitates need satisfaction, while unfavorable attitudes derive from perceptions that the attitude object hinders need satisfaction. Thus, the degree of acceptance or rejection of a career choice depends on whether that career is perceived to facilitate or hinder satisfaction of important needs. The Attitude Toward Teaching as a Career Scale was developed, along with 2 other measures, in accordance with this theory. It was designed to yield an expression of the subject's feeling about teaching as a career, while the other 2 measures assessed, respectively, the strength of 4 needs related to teaching and the individual's perception of the degree to which teaching would facilitate or inhibit satisfaction of these needs (perceived instrumentality). Scores on the attitude scale were correlated with subscale scores. The obtained coefficients ranged from .14 to .29. These low correlations indicated that the 2 scales were measuring different dimensions, the attitude scale tapping the individual's feeling of acceptance or rejection of teaching as a career.

Sample Items: This inventory is an 11-item Likert scale. The items are designed to have maximum affective and minimum cognitive content. Four items are stated in an unfavorable direction, while 7 items are presented in a favorable direction. From among 6 response categories, the subject selects a response which best describes his or her feeling toward each item: (1) strongly agree, (2) moderately agree, (3) slightly agree, (4) slightly disagree, (5) moderately disagree, or (6) strongly disagree. Favorable or unfavorable attitudes toward teaching as a career are represented in items of the following type.

(favorable)	Teaching is the best job for me.
(favorable)	Teaching offers a lot of benefits.
(unfavorable)	Teaching requires too much academic preparation and offers too little financial reward.
(unfavorable)	Working as a teacher doesn't interest me.
(unfavorable)	Teaching isn't right for me, though it may be all right for other people.

Reliability: Reliability was investigated on 2 groups of college freshmen (Merwin and DiVesta, 1959). Corrected split-half reliability on a group of 300 was .71. Another sample ($N = 218$), retested after a 4-month interval, yielded a test-retest correlation of .79. No item analysis data have been reported.

Validity: Validity was approached by comparing the scores of students who had chosen teaching as a career ($N = 67$) to those of students who had selected other occupations ($N = 151$) (Merwin and DiVesta, 1959). The inventory differentiated teaching and nonteaching groups. The mean scores earned by the teaching group on two administrations of the test were 26.57 and 26.30, as compared with means of 41.85 and 40.49 for the nonteaching group. These differences between mean scores of teachers and nonteachers were significant at better than the .01 level of confidence.

Norms: Normative data were based on high school and college populations, including 518 freshmen at Syracuse University, 87 students from the School of Education at that university, and 155 high school juniors and seniors.

Administration and Scoring: This instrument is self-administering, with instructions printed on a single form. An answer sheet is provided, and there is no time limit. Before the total score is computed, the direction of scores is reversed for unfavorable items. The attitude score is the sum of the item scores. There is a theoretical range of scores from 11 to 66, the lower scores representing favorable attitudes toward teaching as a career.

Comments: The Attitude Toward Teaching as a Career Scale demonstrates adequate reliability for an instrument with so few items. Validity data, however, are limited to group differences, and norms are based only on student groups. Due to its brevity, the scale can be administered in a short period of time.

References: DiVesta, F. J., and J. C. Merwin, "The effects of need-oriented communications on attitude change." *Journal of Abnormal and Social Psychology,* 1960, **60**, 80–85.

Merwin, J. C., and F. J. DiVesta, "A study of need theory and career choice." *Journal of Counseling Psychology,* 1959, **6**, 302–308.

Rhine, R. J., "A concept-formation approach to attitude acquisition." *Pyschological Review,* 1958, **65**, 362–370.

Shaw, M. E., and J. M. Wright, *Scales for the measurement of attitudes.* New York: McGraw-Hill, 1967.

Woodruff, A. D., "Personal values and the direction of behavior." *School Review,* 1942, **50**, 32–42.

Name: DEPRESSION ADJECTIVE CHECK LISTS

Author: Bernard Lubin

Type of Measure: Checklist

Availability: Lubin, B., *Depression adjective check lists.* San Diego, California: Educational and Industrial Testing Service, 1967.

Description: The Depression Adjective Check Lists (DACL) measure depressive mood and affect. The DACL was developed to meet the need for a quick, reliable, and objective measure to use in assessing depression among medical and psychiatric patients. However, it is also appropriate for noninstitution-alized and nonclinical groups.

In developing the DACL, 171 adjectives relating to depression and elation were arranged into 7 balanced lists (Forms A, B, C, D, E, F, and G). These adjectives were administered to normal females and to depressed female psychiatric patients. An item analysis was then performed, yielding 128 adjectives, in 4 lists (A, B, C, and D), which significantly differentiated ($p < .01$) the 2 criterion groups. This same procedure was applied to the responses of male subjects, normal and depressed. In this case, 108 adjectives were selected and assigned by 3 lists (forms E, F, and G). The lists for females compose Set 1 and the lists for males, Set 2. An eighth-grade reading level or higher is required for all forms except A and E, which require a seventh-grade reading level, and D, which requires a sixth-grade reading level.

Sample Items: Each form in Set 1 contains 22 positive and 10 negative items, while each form in Set 2 contains 22 positive and 12 negative items. The subject is asked to check only those adjectives which describe how he or she presently feels. Adjectives of the following type are included on the DACL:

1. happy
2. tired
3. hopeful
4. successful
5. wanted

Reliability: The reliability of the DACL has been estimated using internal consistency and split-half methods. Internal consistency coefficients, computed through a 2-way analysis of variance method, range from .79 to .88 for males ($N = 105$), and from .85 to .90 for females ($N = 156$). Split-half reliabilities computed for each list range from .82 to .93 for normal subjects ($N = 156$ males, 469 females), and from .86 to .93 for psychiatric patients ($N = 84$ males, 218 females) (Lubin, 1967).

Validity: The DACL has been extensively tested for the purpose of validation. After the lists were developed, they were administered to a new sample of normal subjects, nondepressed psychiatric patients, and depressed psychiatric patients. Cross validation and analysis of variance procedures yielded expected group differences, significant at the .01 level for lists A through D, and significant beyond the .001 level for lists E through G.

Fogel, Curtis, Kordasz, and Smith (1966) correlated judges' ratings and patients' self-ratings of depression with DACL scores. They obtained coefficients of .71 and .95 between total DACL scores and the evaluations of judges and patients, respectively. These coefficients were significant at the .01 level. DACL scores also correlated significantly and predictably with the clinical scales of the MMPI, the Interpersonal Check List, the D scale of the MAACL Depression Scale, and the Beck Inventory of Depression.

Further evidence of validity is presented in the DACL manual (Lubin, 1967).

Norms: Means and standard deviations are reported for 851 high school, college, and graduate students; 61 senior citizens; 78 adolescent delinquents; and several groups of depressed and nondepressed psychiatric patients (Lubin, 1967).

Administration and Scoring: The DACL is self-administering. Each of the 7 lists contains standardized instructions printed at the top of the page and requires 3 to 5 minutes to complete. A scoring key is provided for each list. Scores are computed by adding up the negative (depressed) items which the subject has checked and adding that figure to the number of positive items not checked.

Comments: The Depression Adjective Check Lists are among the best measures of depression available. Considerable effort has been made to determine the reliability and validity of the DACL, and both appear satisfactory. The instrument's quick and relatively easy administration offers an added advantage. While the DACL may be criticized for a normative sample dominated by students, it remains one of the most sophisticated measures of depression available.

References: Fogel, M. I., G. C. Curtis, F. Kordasz, and W. G. Smith, "Judges' ratings, self-ratings and checklist report of affects." *Psychological Reports*, 1966, **19**, 299–307.

Lubin, B. *Manual for the Depression Adjective Check List.* San Diego, California: Educational and Industrial Testing Service, 1967.

Lubin, B., V. A. Dupre, and A. W. Lubin, "Comparability and sensitivity of Set 2 (lists E, F, and G) of the Depression Adjective Check Lists." *Psychological Reports*, 1967, **20**, 756–758.

Marone, J., and B. Lubin: "Relationship between Set 2 of the Depression Adjective Checklist (DACL) and Zung Self-Rating Depression Scale (SDS). *Psychological Reports*, 1968, **22**, 333–334.

Name: DIFFERENTIAL VALUES INVENTORY

Author: Richard Prince

Type of Measure: Forced-choice inventory

Availability: Prince, R., *A study of the relationship between individual values and administrative effectiveness in the school situation.* Unpublished doctoral dissertation, University of Chicago, 1967.

Description: The Differential Values Inventory (DVI) is a forced-choice instrument designed to measure the respondent's values. Based on the work of Spindler (1955) and Getzels (1957), the DVI classifies values as either emergent or traditional. The 4 emergent value categories represented on the DVI are relativistic moral attitudes, conformity, sociability, and present-time orientation. The 4 traditional value categories are Puritan morality, individualism, work-success ethic, and future-time orientation. In constructing the instrument, items were placed in these 8 value categories according to the judgment of 10 administrators on the staff of the Midwest Administration Center. The items were then administered, in pilot studies, to high school students and teachers, and the results were subjected to item analysis. The 64 items which best met the tests of internal consistency and discrimination between criterion groups were retained and labeled the Differential Values Inventory.

The DVI has been used to relate value orientation to education, age, sex, occupation, income, educational viewpoint (McPhee, 1959), and administrative effectiveness (Prince, 1957a, 1957b). It is appropriate for high school and adult populations.

Sample Items: The 64 items on the DVI are presented in pairs, each of which contains 1 emergent and 1 traditional statement for a particular value category. The respondent is asked to select the item in each pair which best describes his or her own feelings or behavior. Items of the following type appear on the instrument:

1. A. I feel that the main purpose of attending school is to gain knowledge that I can use in the future.
   B. I feel that the main purpose of attending school is to learn how to cooperate with others.
2. A. I work hard so that I will become a success.
   B. I work hard so that I can enjoy some of the luxuries which life offers.

Reliability: Bentley (1963) reports that Leymann and Payne administered the DVI to 2,219 college freshmen and obtained a test/retest coefficient, over a 7-month interval, of .60, and an internal consistency coefficient of .75.

Validity: Validity has been approached primarily through the known-group method. Mean scores of various groups holding known values and attitudes have been compared. For example, Prince (1957a, 1957b, 1960) found that older teachers were significantly more traditional than younger teachers. Administering the DVI to 100 teachers, Prince (1959) compared the scores of those over 50 years old and those under 30, and found the difference in mean value scores significant at the .05 level. The mean score for teachers over 50 ($N = 18$) was 36.61, and for teachers under 30 ($N = 18$), 30.56. He found similar value differences between older and younger principals. Ten principals over age 47 produced a mean value score of 39.00, while 10 under age 47 had a mean score of 32.10. These findings were supported by McPhee (1959) and Wannamaker and Tennyson (1970), who administered the DVI to several populations and found older subjects more traditional than younger subjects.

The DVI has also been shown to discriminate between the populations of 3 types of schools. Prince (1960) administered the instrument to teachers, seniors, and freshmen at 16 public, 2 private, and 4 religious high schools. He found that religious schools had the most traditional and private schools the most emergent scores, for all 3 groups of subjects. The differences between mean value scores were all statistically significant at the .01 level, except for those between public and private school seniors, which were significant at the .05 level, and that between public and private school freshmen, which was not significant.

Norms: The DVI has been administered to teachers and students from public, private, religious (Prince, 1959), suburban, and industrial (Getzels, 1958) high schools. It has also been given to college freshmen (Bentley, 1963), school principals (Prince, 1957a, 1957b), school superintendents (Abbott, 1960), and elementary education students (Wannamaker and Tennyson, 1970).

Administration and Scoring: The DVI is easily administered and scored. The respondent simply selects his or her preference in each of 64 pairs of items. One point is given for each traditional choice. Subjects scoring above 32 are considered traditional in value orientation, while those scoring below 32 are considered emergent.

Comments: The DVI, reportedly the first instrument designed to measure traditional/emergent value patterns, is well constructed and easy to administer. While available data suggest adequate validity, an approach to validation other than the known-group method would be helpful in determining the usefulness of this instrument.

References: Abbott, M. G., "Values and value-perceptions in superintendent-school board relationships." *Administrator's Notebook*, 1960, **9**, 1–4.

Bentley, J. C., *Relationships between traditional-emerging values and vocational choice variables.* Unpublished doctoral dissertation, University of Minnesota, 1963.

Getzels, J. W., "The acquisition of values in school and society," in Chase and Anderson (eds.), *The high school in a new era.* Chicago: University of Chicago Press, 1958.

Getzels, J. W., Changing values challenge the schools. *School Review*, 1957, **65**, 92–102.

McPhee, R. F., "Individual values, educational viewpoint, and local school approval." *Administrator's Notebook*, 1959, **7**, 1–4.

Prince, R., "Individual values and administrative effectiveness." *Administrator's Notebook*, 1957, **6**, 1–4. (a)

Prince, R., *A study of the relationships between individual values and administrative effectiveness in the school situation.* Unpublished doctoral dissertation, University of Chicago, 1957. (b)

Prince, R., "Values, grades, achievement, and career choice of high-school students." *Elementary School Journal*, 1960, **60**, 376–384.

Spindler, G. D., "Education in a transforming American culture." *Harvard Educational Review*, 1955, **25**, 145–156.

Wannamaker, M., and W. W. Tennyson, "The value orientation of beginning elementary teacher education students." *Journal of Teacher Education*, 1970, **21**, 544–550.

Name: EDUCATION SCALE

Author: Fred N. Kerlinger and Esin Kaya

Type of Measure: Rating scale

Availability: A copy of the scale may be found in: Shaw, M. E., and J. M. Wright, *Scales for the measurement of attitudes.* New York: McGraw-Hill, 1967.

Description: The Education Scale was developed in a study of educational attitudes. The authors attempted to isolate the major dimensions of educational attitudes by using 2 previous Q studies which had produced 2 major factors: Progressivism (A) and Traditionalism (B). Twenty "A" statements and 20 "B" statements were chosen according to their degree of saturation with the 2 factors. The 40 statements were arranged into a Likert-type scale and were administered to approximately 200 subjects. The results were factor analyzed, and the 10 progressive and 10 traditional statements which had the highest factor saturations and highest discriminatory power were selected for the final scale. The scale is designed for use in both research and administrative contexts.

Sample Items: Twenty statements are listed relating to educational ideas and problems about which people have beliefs, opinions, and attitudes. The individual responds to each of the items according to the following scale: Agree Very Strongly = +3, Agree Strongly = +2, Agree = +1, Disagree Very Strongly = −3, Disagree Strongly = −2, Disagree = −1.

Items of the following type appear on the Education Scale:

1. There is no subject which is more important than the personalities of the pupils.
2. Our current schools are neglecting the three R's.
3. Teachers should have the freedom to teach what they think is right and best.
4. The curriculum is composed of subject matter to be learned and skills to be acquired.

Reliability: For the progressive scale, corrected split-half reliabilities ranged from .54 to .77, with a value of .75 for a combination of the samples. Reliabilities for the traditional scale ranged from .68 to .79, with a value of .83 for a combination of the samples. Total scale reliabilities ranged from .68 to .81, with a combined value of .83. Test/retest reliability coefficients from a sample of 106 education students, with an interval of 3 to 4 months, were .70 for the progressive scale, .71 for the traditional scale, and .76 for the total scale (Shaw and Wright, 1967).

Validity: Kerlinger and Kaya (1959) demonstrated that education students revealed more progressive attitudes than did other respondents ($p < .001$). Other studies based on samples of 131 undergraduates, 93 graduates, and 229 noncollege subjects yielded similar results. However, Wheeler (1960) analyzed responses item by item and concluded that group differences were not as great as the total score indicated.

Intercorrelations of all scale items were computed and a factor analysis performed (Kerlinger and Kaya, 1959). The two major factors emerged with clear, independent clusterings of A and B items. Commonalities between item types were very low, ranging from .142 to .433.

Product-moment correlations were also determined. The A items were shown to correlate positively and significantly with total A scores, the range being from .42 to .63. The B items showed similar relationships to total B scores, with a range of .46 to .68.

Norms: Half of the approximately 200 subjects used for the original item analysis were graduate education students in a large Eastern university, and half were individuals outside the university. The later samples consisted of 157 graduate education students at a large Eastern university, 136 undergraduate education students at the same institution, and 305 persons outside the university.

Administration and Scoring: The scale is self-administering. A 20-item list is presented to which the subject responds either $+3$, $+2$, $+1$, -1, -2, or -3, according to a rating scale. The following values are assigned in scoring: $+3 = 7$; $+2 = 6$; $+1 = 5$; no response $= 4$; $-1 = 3$; $-2 = 2$; $-3 = 1$. To find separate scores for traditional and progressive attitudes toward education, the 10 items constituting each scale are summed. The total score is computed by subtracting the traditional score from the progressive score.

Comments: The Education Scale is a well constructed instrument with moderate reliability and validity. However, the scale may be appropriate for research purposes only since the response format implies a single continuum of attitudes toward 2 different educational practices—progressive and traditional—while at the same time suggesting that each end of the continuum be considered a separate attitude in scoring.

References: Kerlinger, F. N., and E. Kaya, "The construction and factor analytic validation of scales to measure attitudes toward education." *Educational and Psychological Measurement*, 1959, **19**, 13–29.

Shaw, M. E., and J. M. Wright, *Scales for the measurement of attitudes*. New York: McGraw-Hill, 1967.

Name: THE EMBEDDED FIGURES TEST

Author: Herman A. Witkin

Type of Measure: Perceptual performance test

Availability: Witkin, H. A., *The embedded figures test*. Palo Alto, California: Consulting Psychologists Press, 1971.

Description: The Embedded Figures Test (EFT) is a perceptual measure, which assesses, according to its author, "ability to break up an organized visual field in order to keep a part of it separate from that field (Witkin, Oltman, Raskin, and Karp, 1971, p. 4)." This ability, referred to as "field-independence," is a mode of perceiving in which objects are experienced as discrete from their backgrounds. "Field-dependence," on the other hand, is a perceptual style characterized by a tendency to see the overall picture, in a relatively global manner, viewing the individual parts as "fused." Although the EFT is clearly a measure of perceptual style, differences in EFT scores have been related to differences in other areas of psychological functioning (Witkin et al., 1971).

The long form of the EFT consists of 24 complex and 8 simple figures modified from those used by Gottschaldt (1926) in his studies of contextual factors and past experience in perception. The 8 simple figures are printed separately on individual cards and are also embedded within the more complex 24, which are selectively colored in such a way to make disembedding more difficult. The subject's task is to locate the simple figure within the complex figure. A shortened version, using only the first 12 items on the original EFT and correlating in the mid .90's with the total test, and a 16-item group form are also available. The short form has, in fact, virtually replaced the long one. Besides reducing administration time, the short form yields a distribution of scores with a less extended tail at the high-score end. It is the short form which is described in the manual. All 3 forms are designed for use with persons at or above the age of 10. The Children's Embedded Figure Test (CEFT) is available for use with individuals from 5 to 10 years old.

Sample Items: The figures used in the EFT are geometric. They are graded so that they become increasingly difficult. Representative of the easier items is a small triangle embedded within a more complex, multicolored, cube-like figure. A cross hidden within a highly complex, patterned, octagonal design is typical of the more difficult items.

Reliability: The EFT manual reports split-half reliabilities for ages 10 through 17, for college students and for adults, ranging from .61 to .92. Several independent investigators have obtained split-half reliabilities of .90, .92, and .95 for college students. Corrected odd-even reliability of the short form is .88. A test-retest coefficient of .89, with a 3-year interval, has also been reported.

Validity: The construct validity of the EFT has been questioned in several studies which have attempted to distinguish between embedding fields and merely distracting fields. Longnecker (1956), for example, compared performance on the EFT to that on 2 forms of the Holtzman Form-Recognition Test, one requiring identification of incomplete line drawings, the other, identification of figures within a distracting, chromatic field. Correlations between the EFT and the Holtzman tests were .54 and .46. This study, and another conducted by Jackson (1955) which showed a correlation of .46 between men's EFT scores and ability to distinguish words against a background of noise, suggest that ability to disembed figures is just one aspect of the more general ability to overcome distracting fields. Karp (1963), however, found the EFT to load and define different factors than did distraction tests. The EFT manual defends the construct validity of the test by citing numerous studies which relate ability to overcome an embedding context in the EFT to more differentiated perceptual functioning in other psychological areas. These areas include social behavior, body concept, nature of defenses, forms of pathology, physiological reactivity, and differences in family and cultural experience. Studies relating performance on the EFT to that on other perceptual tests requiring the ability to disembed are also cited, in an attempt to validate the concept that the EFT is a test of field-dependence/independence.

Evidence for concurrent validity is provided by correlations of .46, .77, and .69 between EFT scores and performance on the Thurstone Gottschaldt test of flexibility and closure.

Norms: The manual provides a norm table giving means and standard deviations for the EFT for a number of different age/sex groups.

Administration and Scoring: The EFT is administered individually. The examiner presents each complex figure to the subject, exposing the design for 15 seconds, covering it for 10 seconds with the corresponding simple form, and finally removing the latter from sight. At this point the subject begins his search for the simple figure within the complex field, and the examiner begins timing the performance. Three minutes are allowed for each test item on the short form. As soon as the subject reports that he has located the simple figure, the examiner notes the time elapsed but does not reset his watch. If the subject can accurately trace the simple figure within the complex one, his score is the number of seconds elapsed. If he cannot, his attempt is marked incorrect, the time is noted, and timing is resumed. The subject continues his efforts until 3 (or, using the long form, 5) minutes are up. The group form is administered using somewhat different procedures.

Comments: The EFT apparently taps important cognitive and perceptual dimensions. However, there has been some controversy about the validity of field-independence as a construct separate from ability to resist distraction. Vernon (1972) has questioned field-independence as a distinct factor, suggesting that it is related to general intelligence. Furthermore, use of the EFT as a nonclinical personality measure has been discouraged (Dana and Goocher, 1959). The EFT, however, has been used in a great number of studies and appears to be a valuable research tool.

References: Dana, R. H., and B. Goocher, Embedded figures and personality. *Perceptual and Motor Skills,* 1959, **9**, 99–102.

Gottschaldt, K., "Über den einfluss der erfahrung auf die wahrnehmung von figuren I; über den einfluss gehäufter einprägung von figuren auf ihre sichtbarkeit in unfassenden konfigurationen." *Psychol. Forsch.,* 1926, **8**, 261–317.

Jackson, D. N., *Stability in resistance to field forces.* Unpublished doctoral dissertation, Purdue University, 1955.

Karp, S. A., "Field independence and overcoming embeddedness." *Journal of Consulting Psychology,* 1963, **27**, 294–302.

Longnecker, E. D., *Form perception as a function of anxiety, motivation, and the testing situation.* Unpublished doctoral dissertation, The University of Texas, 1956.

Vernon, P. E., "The distinctiveness of field independence." *Journal of Personality,* 1972, **40**, 366–391.

Witkin, H. A., R. Dyk, H. F. Faterson, D. R. Goodenough, and S. A. Karp, *Psychological differentiation.* New York: John Wiley & Sons, 1962.

Witkin, H. A., P. K. Oltman, E. Raskin, and S. A. Karp. *A manual for the Embedded Figures Tests.* Palo Alto, California: Consulting Psychologists Press, 1971.

Name: EXPERIMENTAL MEASURE OF MOTIVATION

Author: Harry J. Caughren, Jr.

Type of Measure: Self-report questionnaire

Availability: A copy of this instrument appears in the appendices of: Caughren, H. J., Jr., *Construction of an experimental measure of motivation.* Washington, D.C.: Bureau of Research, Office of Education, 1972. (ERIC Document Reproduction Service No. ED 062 374)

Description: Caughren (1972) proposed that motivation is dependent upon the interactions of sublimation, person orientation, and socioeconomic status. He designed the Experimental Measure of Motivation to measure these 3 variables. The instrument consists of 4 relatively independent scales, identified as Intrinsic Motivation (IM), Self-Enhancement (SE), Person Orientation (PO) and Goal Deficiency (GD). Scale items were originally extracted from the autobiographies of 176 college students who had participated in an earlier study by Caughren (1965). From an initial pool of 450 items, 300 were selected to be given to judges for initial categorization. Six judges, working independently, divided the items into preliminary clusters. Two-thirds agreement among the judges was required for placing items into particular scales. The original scales were administered to 346 males enrolled in community colleges, and results were subjected to item analyses. In all, the scales were reconstructed 5 times, the final revision involving purification of the scales on each of 2 separate samples (185 males and 195 females). The final, 200-item form is appropriate for older adolescents and adults.

Sample Items: The subject responds to each item on the Experimental Measure of Motivation by marking "T" if the item describes him, or "F" if it does not describe him. Each of the 4 scales contains items of the following type:

Scale	*Item*
I. Intrinsic Motivation	1. I enjoy creative writing.
	2. I like the theatre.
II. Self-Enhancement	1. I hope to accomplish something which will make others proud of me.
	2. Eventually, I hope to be a respected and responsible member of the community.
III. Person Orientation	1. I rarely miss an important social event.
	2. I like being in a group of people.
IV. Goal Deficiency	1. I have a hard time saying "no," even when it is in my interest to do so.
	2. It is hard for me to forget embarrassing experiences.

Reliability: In order to determine test/retest reliability, the scales were administered to 56 subjects in 2 psychology classes at Merritt College, who had not been used in the construction of the instrument. The time interval between the 2 test administrations was 6 weeks. Product-moment correlation coefficients, uncorrected for attenuation, ranged from .88 to .92 for the 4 scales.

Validity: Construct validity is suggested by the clinical judgment phase of the test's construction. The mean percent of interjudge agreement on item selection was 52.2%, significantly different from chance (12.5%), thus providing some evidence for construct validity.

Concurrent validity was approached by correlating scores on each of the 4 scales with scores on the California Psychological Inventory (CPI), the Omnibus Personality Inventory (OPI), the Minnesota Multiphasic Personality Inventory (MMPI) and the Edwards Personal Preference Schedule (EPPS).

Overall, the 280 correlations obtained were in the expected direction. For example, Scale I (Intrinsic Motivation), which has a scholarly and artistic orientation, correlated highly with the following OPI scales: Thinking Introversion (.79), Theoretical Orientation (.56), and Estheticism (.75). Similarly, Scale II (Self-Enhancement), which was constructed to measure status motivation, correlated significantly with the Socialization (.38) and Achievement via Conformity (.41) scales of the CPI. Scale III (Person Orientation) had positive and significant correlations with the following CPI scales: Sociability (.66), Social Presence (.56), Self-Acceptance (.60), Socialization (.40), and Dominance (.54). Scale IV (Goal Deficiency), which reflects the self-defeating aspects of human motivation, showed negative relationships to all but one of the CPI scales, the exception being Femininity (.01). The CPI scales showing very high, significant correlations with Scale IV were Sense of Well Being $(-.70)$, Social Presence $(-.60)$, Sociability $(-.51)$, and Achievement via Conformity $(-.54)$.

Norms: The scales were standardized, separately, on 650 males and 649 females, predominately college-age. Norms are provided as standard ("T") scores, with a mean of 50, and a standard deviation of 10.

Administration and Scoring: The Experimental Measure of Motivation is easily administered and scored. The subject simply reads each item and marks it true (T) or false (F). There is no time limit. The direction of scoring is shown for each item, and tables are provided for converting raw scores to standard scores.

Comments: The Experimental Measure of Motivation, a fairly new instrument, has been carefully designed. The 4 component scales are relatively independent of one another and show high test/retest reliability. Though more diverse normative and validity data are needed, this instrument shows promise for description and analysis of motivation in occupational and educational settings.

References: Caughren, H. J., Jr., *Construction of an experimental measure of motivation.* Washington, D.C.: Bureau of Research, Office of Education, 1972.

(ERIC Document Reproduction Service No. ED 062 374)

Caughren, H. J., Jr., "The relationship of stimulus-structure and selected personality variables to the discomfort-relief quotient in autobiographies." *Journal of Counseling Psychology*, 1965, **12**, 74–80.

Name: FUNDAMENTAL INTERPERSONAL RELATIONS
ORIENTATION—BEHAVIOR (FIRO-B)

Author: William C. Schutz

Type of Measure: Rating scale

Availability: Schutz, W. C., *The FIRO scales.* Palo Alto, California: Consulting
Psychologists Press, 1967. The FIRO-B scales are reproduced in: Schutz, W. C.,
FIRO: A three-dimensional theory of interpersonal behavior. New York: Holt,
Rinehart & Winston, 1958. (Republished as *The interpersonal underworld.* Palo
Alto, California: Science and Behavior Books, 1966).

Description: The Fundamental Interpersonal Relations Orientation (FIRO)
Scales are derived from a theory developed by Schutz (1958, 1966) stating that
each person has a relatively invariant orientation in interpersonal situations.
This orientation is determined by the individual's need for Inclusion, Control,
and Affection. Inclusion refers to the desire to interact with people; Control
involves a need for power and influence; and Affection concerns the need for
close, emotional relations with people. Each of these 3 need areas has 2 dimensions: express and want. That is, people need to express behaviors and to
receive them as well. If the want and express aspects of an individual's needs are
known, it is then theoretically possible to determine the compatibility with
another individual whose needs are similarly known. The 6 FIRO scales are
designed to uncover these needs by assessing the individual's: (1) reported
behavior towards others (FIRO-Behavior); (2) feelings toward others (FIRO-
Feeling); (3) feelings about past needs (Life Interpersonal History Enquiry); (4)
feelings desired of spouse (Marital Attitudes Evaluation); (5) feelings about how
educators should behave (Educational Values); and (6) preference for particular
defense mechanisms (Coping Operations Preference Enquiry). Among these 6
scales, only the FIRO-Behavior, or FIRO-B, is well enough developed for use in
systematic research. This form of the FIRO concentrates on how an individual
behaves, rather than how he or she feels. Since one of the aims of the FIRO-B is
to predict interaction, the instrument assesses both the individual's behavior
toward others and the behavior he wants from others. These behaviors are
measured for each of the 3 need areas, leading to 6 scores: expressed inclusion
behavior; wanted inclusion behavior; expressed control behavior; wanted control behavior; expressed affection behavior; and wanted affection behavior.

Sample Items: The FIRO-B contains 54 multiple-choice items, arranged in six
9-item Guttman scales, each measuring one of the interpersonal needs in its
want and express forms. Response alternatives are on a 1-to-6 scale, from
"nobody" to "most people" for some items, and from "never" to "usually" for
others. The FIRO-B scales contain items of the following type:

Scale	Item
Express Inclusion	I usually join group activities.
Want Inclusion	I like people to invite me to take part in their discussions.
Express Control	I am the one to take charge of people in a group.
Want Control	I allow others to influence my behavior.

Reliability: Internal consistency of the FIRO-B was determined by computing a reproducibility index. Reproducibility generally requires that 90% of all responses be predictable from scale scores. The FIRO-B was administered to approximately 1,543 subjects (college students and a limited number of Air Force personnel), and mean reproducibility for all scales was .94 (Schutz, 1958). However, a subsequent administration of the test to 144 noncollege adults (salesmen, policemen, and service volunteers) yielded reproducibility coefficients ranging from .80 to .91, with only 2 scales, Express Affection and Want Affection, achieving the .90 criterion (Ryan, Maguire, and Ryan, 1970).

Test/retest reliability of the FIRO-B was computed on college student samples, with 1-month or 1-week intervals between test administrations. Correlation coefficients ranged from .71 to .82, averaging .76 (Schutz, 1958).

Validity: Efforts to validate the FIRO-B have focused primarily on its relationship to external criteria. Scale scores have been shown to correlate with: rated creativity, freshman grades, the diagnosis of schizophrenia, rated effectiveness of supervisors, and the production of good ideas in problem-solving groups. Gard (1964) administered the FIRO-B to subjects manifesting various personality disorders and found that the lowest scores on the Inclusion Scale were obtained by those subjects demonstrating withdrawal symptoms. Kramer (1967) reported a significant relationship between psychology students' scores on all 6 scales and self-ratings on the same 6 dimensions.

Less encouraging results were obtained by Ryan, Maguire, and Ryan (1970), who investigated the construct validity of the FIRO-B on a sample of 144 salesmen, policemen, and service volunteers. Their findings supported none of the expectations regarding the construct validity (substantive, structural, and external) of the FIRO-B. For example, policemen and service volunteers did not differ significantly on any of the 6 scales. The investigators concluded that the FIRO-B is not a valid measure of interpersonal needs, as outlined by Schutz (1966).

Norms: Subscale means and standard deviations are provided for a number of student and occupational groups. Norm group means (without standard deviations) are also supplied for combinations of subscale scores.

Administration and Scoring: The FIRO-B may be administered to large or small groups within 15 minutes. Generally, no instructions are provided. Scale scores are computed by adding the number of items "accepted" on each scale. (The first 3 categories on the 1-to-6 response scale are scored as "accepting.") Therefore, scale scores range from 0 to 9. The total FIRO-B score is expressed as a set of 6 single-digit numbers. A computer program for scoring the FIRO-B is available (Borich, 1971).

Comments: While the FIRO-B has achieved some popularity among researchers, it has also received its share of criticism. The scales have been described as too narrow, and the items as too repetitious, to adequately cover the constructs under consideration (Affection, Inclusion, and Control). Also, some concern has been expressed that the items are transparent (Ryan, Maguire, and Ryan, 1970), though Kramer (1967) found that psychology students, unfamiliar with FIRO theory, could not name the variables being measured from mere exposure to the items. The validity of the FIRO-B has also been questioned by those who feel that the instrument is primarily a measure of the amount of interpersonal behavior a person exhibits (Ryan, Maguire, and Ryan, 1970). Evidence for validity is indeed not strong enough to support use of the FIRO-B in counseling and guidance. However, the instrument is suitable for research.

References: Borich, G. D., "A Fortran IV program to compute interchange, originator and reciprocal compatibility from Schutz's FIRO-B." *Behavioral Science*, 1971, **11**, 21–23.

Gard, J. G., "Interpersonal orientation in clinical groups." *Journal of Abnormal and Social Psychology*, 1964, **69**, 516–521.

Kramer, E., "A contribution toward the validation of the FIRO-B questionnaire." *Journal of Projective Techniques and Personality Assessment*, 1967, **31**, 80–81.

Ryan, B. A., T. O. Maguire, and T. M. Ryan. An examination of the construct validity of the FIRO-B. *Journal of Projective Techniques*, 1970, **34**, 419–425.

Schutz, W. C., *FIRO: A three-dimensional theory of interpersonal behavior*. New York: Holt, Rinehart & Winston, 1958. (Republished as *The interpersonal underworld*. Palo Alto, California: Science and Behavior Books, 1966).

Schutz, W. C., *The FIRO scales*. Palo Alto, California: Consulting Psychologists Press, 1967.

Name: GORDON PERSONAL PROFILE

Author: Leonard V. Gordon

Type of Measure: Forced-choice inventory

Availability: Gordon L. V. *Gordon personal profile.* New York: Harcourt, Brace & World, 1953.

Description: The Gordon Personal Profile (GPP) measures 4 personality traits on 4 separate scales: Ascendancy (A), Responsibility (R), Emotional Stability (E), and Sociability (S). It was developed on the basis of an extensive series of investigations. Six personality traits were initially drawn from the studies of Cattell (1947) and Mosier (1937), and in a series of factor analyses (Gordon, 1963) the 4 factors mentioned above emerged. There have been 5 revisions of the Profile, each one improving the discriminating power of the 4 scales. The GPP is a companion instrument to the Gordon Personal Inventory, which measures 4 additional personality traits: Cautiousness (C), Original Thinking (O), Personal Relations (P), and Vigor (V). When used together, they provide economical coverage of 8 important factors in the personality domain.

The Profile was designed primarily for the adult population. However, it has been used successfully with high school and selected seventh- and eighth-grade groups. Furthermore, the GPP has been shown to have applications in industrial selection, vocational guidance, classroom appraisal, personal counseling, and basic research.

Sample Items: The Profile consists of 18 sets of 4 descriptive phrases, each set known as a "tetrad." Each trait (A, R, E, and S) is represented by one of the items in a tetrad. The subject selects 1 item in each tetrad as "Most" like himself and 1 as "Least" like himself. This forced-choice technique prevents individuals from responding favorably to all items and, in effect, produces a 3-level ranking within each tetrad. The GPP contains items of the following type:

Scale	*Item*	*M*	*L*
(A)	Is confident in relationships with others	☐	☐
(E)	Gets feelings hurt easily	☐	☐
(R)	Has developed good work habits	☐	☐
(S)	Prefers to stay with a small group of friends	☐	☐

Reliability: While long-term stability of the trait scores has not been extensively investigated, correlations obtained over a 3-month interval suggest satisfactory stability over longer periods. Reliability coefficients were obtained from various groups of college and high school students. Split-half reliabilities (corrected by Spearman-Brown) for all 4 scales ranged from .84 to .88; Kuder-Richardson from .74 to .85; and test/retest, with a 1-week interval, from .84 to .87 and with a 3-month interval from .80 to .87. Standard deviations are from 5 to 6 points, reliability coefficients average around .80, and the error of measurement for an individual Profile is approximately 2.5 score points.

Validity: As previously noted, the GPP employs the forced-choice technique. This approach forces the subject to choose items most like himself and least like himself, even though the presented items may not be particularly descriptive of him. For this reason, the subject may resort to guessing. However, psychological experiments show that guesses usually fall in the direction of the true value (Gordon, 1963).

The GPP manual (Gordon, 1963) documents the test's correlation with personality ratings. After taking the GPP, a group of 118 college students rated every other member of the group on each of the 4 traits. Product-moment correlations (significant at the .01 level) between peer ratings and GPP scores were: Men—A, .50; R, .57; E, .61; S. .49; and Women—A, .47; R, .47; E, .73; S, .61. In another study, the GPP was administered to 27 clients prior to counseling. After the final interview and without knowledge of scores, each counselor rated his or her clients on a 9-point scale for each trait on the Profile. The following product-moment correlations between the counselor's ratings and the client's earlier score were obtained: A, .54 and E, .58 (significant at the .01 level) and R, .36 and S, .53 (significant at the .05 level). Similarly, the GPP scales correlate satisfactorily with their corresponding scales on the Guilford-Zimmerman Temperament Survey, the Survey of Interpersonal Values, the Edwards Personal Preference Schedule, and the California Psychological Inventory.

The GPP has also been correlated with measures of success. As part of a battery, the Profile was administered to a group of 146 salesmen in an oil company. In this study, conducted by Munger and cited by Gordon (1963), criterion rankings were obtained for each subject from a minimum of 5 district managers. Product-moment correlations between GPP scores and a high-middle-low trichotomous criterion were: A, .16 and R, .19 (significant at the .05 level) and E, .04 and S, .13. Other studies have shown similar correlations between GPP scores and measures of success. However, the magnitude of the relationships obtained in these studies may be somewhat greater than reported, since none of the validity coefficients were corrected for criterion unreliability.

Norms: Norms are provided for college and high school populations as well as selected occupational groups. There are no "general adult" norms. The student norms were derived from composite groups throughout the country at various institutions. The occupational data, however, were obtained from cases within 1 company only; no combinations across companies have been made. All normative data are separated by sex, since significant sex differences have been found on all traits.

Administration and Scoring: The GPP, consisting of 18 tetrads, is self-administering. No timing is necessary; the instrument can be completed in 7 to 15 minutes. The profile can be hand computed with a perforated stencil key. This key contains 4 sections (A, R, E, S) from which are derived 4 separate scale scores. These 4 scores are translated to percentile ranks and plotted on a Profile Chart. Generally, the further the subject's score from the 50th percentile, the more likely it is that his or her true score lies in the indicated direction.

Comments: The GPP appears to be carefully constructed, and it demonstrates good reliability and validity. The lack of "general adult" norms, however, might limit the usefulness of this test to groups which are young, fairly well educated, or in certain occupational areas. Furthermore, the validity findings suggest that *any* relationship between a scale and a performance rating indicates validity. For instance, it is not specified why Ascendance should relate to one criterion and Emotional Stability to another. Clarification of the problem is desirable, yet the structure, apparent reliability and validity, and interpretative projections of the Gordon Personal Profile make it a well designed and useful instrument.

References: Braun, J. R., "Stereotypes of the scientist as seen with the Gordon Personal Profile and Gordon Personal Inventory." *Journal of Psychology*, 1962, **53**, 453–455.

Cattell, R. B., "Confirmation and clarification of primary personality factor." *Psychometrika*, 1947, **12**, 197–220.

Gordon, L. V., *Gordon Personal Profile. Manual.* New York: Harcourt, Brace & World, 1963.

Greenberg, H., R. Guerino, M. Lashen, D. Mayer, and D. Piskowski. "Order of birth as a determinant of personality and attitudinal characteristics." *Journal of Social Psychology*, 1963, **60**, 221–230.

Mosier, C. I. "A factor analysis of certain neurotic symptoms." *Psychometrika*, 1937, **2**, 263–286.

Name: HOW I TEACH

Authors: Ida B. Kelly and Keith J. Perkins

Type of Measure: Rating scale

Availability: Kelley, I. B., and K. J. Perkins, *How I teach.* Minneapolis, Minnesota: Educational Test Bureau, 1942.

Description: How I Teach was designed to measure a teacher's knowledge about child and adolescent psychology and development. Accordingly, the scale is appropriate for both elementary and secondary teachers.

  The test has 2 forms, A and B, which include 75 items each. Drawing from literature on child and adolescent psychology, case histories of problem children, children's descriptions of teachers most liked and disliked, and observations of classrooms, the authors devised the items and then grouped them according to teaching practices, opinions, and factual results of experimental studies. Scoring standards were based on judgments of 84 classroom teachers and 10 recognized authorities in the fields of psychology, psychiatry, and mental hygiene.

  The authors recommend that the scale be used in teacher training and selection. However, it may also be employed as a self-appraisal instrument for teachers who wish to evaluate their understanding of the principles of mental hygiene.

Sample Items: Each subject is asked to rate a number of actions or practices in terms of what his or her own behavior is, or would be, in dealing with the problem or situation described. The rating scale reads: 1 = decidedly harmful, 2 = probably harmful; 3 = doubtful value, 4 = probably good, 5 = decidedly good. Items of the following type appear on the scale:

1. Requiring an additional assignment from a pupil who is disruptive in class.
2. Warning the pupil who tells lies that he or she will be punished.

Reliability: Two studies of alternate form reliability have been conducted, yielding different results. One study (reported in Buros, 1949) of forms A and B, based on 845 cases, yielded a correlation coefficient of .88. Another (reported in Buros, 1953) obtained a correlation of .77. The authors suggest that Form A be used at the beginning of a course in teacher preparation and Form B at the end. However, the 2 forms may not cover the same content. An examination of the list of areas covered by the items showed that of the 94 areas named, 20 were represented in both forms and 65 were represented by a single item in 1 form only. Therefore, the fairly high reliability coefficients may simply show that the respondent who knows one part of his field probably knows another part, or that the areas were not accurately defined (Buros, 1953).

Validity: Validity was approached through the comparison of various criterion groups. Significantly higher scores were obtained by the following groups:

teachers from school systems known to emphasize progressive, as opposed to traditional, mental hygiene attitudes; elementary and secondary teachers rated "plus" by their principals or superintendents (indicating that they were perceived to be the teachers who understood children best and to whom the administrators would send their own children); teachers who held positions of leadership in their schools; and teachers who had held their present positions for 5 or more years (Buros, 1949).

Items which elicited markedly different average responses from elementary and secondary teachers were eliminated or revised. The scale could then be used with both groups (Remmers and Gage, 1955).

Content validity was considered in the method of choosing and scoring the items.

Norms: Normative data were based on studies using elementary and secondary school teacher populations. The manual provides percentile norms based on 1,000 cases. Also in the manual are detailed reports of many statistical analyses of scores of teachers from different schools, subject areas, and educational backgrounds. Norms are reported for 2 different scoring methods.

Administration and Scoring: The instrument is self-administering. A 75-item list is presented to the subject, who responds to a 1–5 basis. There is no time limit. The test sheet may be either hand or machine scored, according to 1 of 2 procedures available. The first procedure allows 1 point for each correct answer, with no correction for guessing. The second gives 2 points for each correct answer and 1 point for the next best answer. The second method is recommended when individual teachers are being studied.

Comments: Items on How I Teach are carefully chosen and worded, and validity appears to be good. However, comparability of the 2 forms is questionable. Investigation of this problem would provide further information on the reliability of the instrument, and, perhaps, more consistent findings. The inventory has value as a teaching device in education courses.

References: Buros, O. K., *The third mental measurement yearbook*. Highland Park, New Jersey: The Gryphon Press, 1949.

Buros, O. K., *The fourth mental measurement yearbook*. Highland Park, New Jersey: The Gryphon Press, 1953.

Remmers, H. H., and N. L. Gage, *Educational measurement and evaluation*. New York: Harper & Brothers, 1955.

Wrightstone, J. W., J. Justman, and I. Robbins, *Evaluation in modern education*. New York: American Book Company, 1956.

Name: INTER-PERSON PERCEPTION TEST

Author: F. K. Heussenstamm and R. Hoepfner

Type of Measure: Perceptual test

Availability: Heussenstamm, F. K., and R. Hoepfner, *Inter-person perception test.* Hollywood, California: Monitor, 1969.

Description: The Inter-Person Perception Test (IPPT) measures ability to read the underlying emotional state of people through their facial expressions. The IPPT, originally designed as a training instrument for the Teacher Corps, was based on the work of O'Sullivan, Guilford, and deMille (1965), who demonstrated the existence of a separate intelligence involved in understanding people.

The IPPT is available in 2 forms: AA, for adults, and AC, for children. Both contain 40 items, each of which present 5 photographs of people's faces. The subject is required to choose from the last 4 faces the 1 expressing the same thought or feeling as the first face. The AA form includes pictures of adults while the AC form uses pictures of 11- and 13-year-old children. The photographs picture males and females, Caucasians, Blacks, Mexican-Americans, and Oriental-Americans. These photographs are systematically arranged within each form of the test. During test construction, sex was alternated, race was varied, and items within each age/race/sex group were arranged in order of difficulty.

The final form of the IPPT contains 40 items drawn from an original pool of 224, which were pilot tested. Item selection was based on difficulty level and internal consistency.

The authors maintain that the IPPT is valuable in: assessing change in sensitivity training over time; developing norms for selection of personnel who must deal with people; evaluating success of counseling or psychotheraphy; training teachers; and conducting cross-cultural sociological research (Heussenstamm and Hoepfner, 1969).

Sample Items: Each test item consists of a series of 5 photographs. The first photograph, the stimulus, shows the face of 1 individual. The 4 response photographs present another individual showing various facial expressions. The 2 people in each item are of the same sex, age, and ethnic group. The facial expressions represent happiness, thoughtfulness, anger, sadness, and other feelings.

Reliability: The test manual reports several reliability studies. Estimates of the reliability of the total forms were obtained from standardization data. The average internal consistency (alpha) coefficient for each of the AC subtests was .35, and that for the AA subtests was .36. Assuming that the subtests within each form were parallel, total test reliabilities were estimated by .81 for the AC and at .83 for the AA. The authors point out, however, that the subtests may not be parallel at all. Empirically determined estimates of internal consistency were in fact much lower, being computed at .50 (Form AA) and .41 (Form AC) on a sample of 1,058 subjects.

Validity: Validity studies employing the IPPT have documented the test's relationship to race/ethnicity, sex, age, and area of academic study. These studies were based on the responses of 1,056 students at a state college in Southern California, who were administered both forms AC and AA. Results indicated that the IPPT is unbiased on racial/ethnic and academic grounds. Test scores across both variables were very similar. Though slight sex and age differences were found, they were not considered meaningful.

 The manual reports that no validity studies have yet been performed to determine the usefulness of the IPPT in predicting, diagnosing, or prognosing (Heussenstamm and Hoepfner, 1969).

Norms: The manual presents normed centile conversions for Forms AA and AC of the IPPT, based on the responses of 1,056 college students. No norms for children are reported.

Administration and Scoring: The IPPT is easily administered. The authors suggest that the instrument be introduced as a kind of exercise, rather than as a traditional test. Instructions are read out loud by the examiner while the subjects read silently. Responses are recorded on a separate answer sheet, and 15 minutes are allowed for test completion. Scoring is performed manually, using a stencil.

Comments: The Inter-Person Perception Test is easy to administer and score and its content generally interests the subjects. However, validity studies and normative data for children are needed. This instrument merits further research in order to determine its utility.

References: Heussenstamm, F. K., and R. Hoepfner, *Manual. Inter-Person Perception Test.* Hollywood, California: Monitor, 1969.

O'Sullivan, M., J. P. Guilford, and R. deMille, "The measurement of social intelligence." *Report from the Psychological Laboratory*, No. 34. Los Angeles: University of Southern California, 1965.

Name: MANIFEST ANXIETY SCALE

Author: Janet Taylor

Type of Measure: Self-report questionnaire

Availability: A copy of the scale may be found in: Taylor, J. A., "A personality scale of manifest anxiety." *Journal of Abnormal and Social Psychology*, 1953, **48**, 285–290.

Description: The Manifest Anxiety Scale (MAS) was originally constructed for use in a study of eyelid conditioning. Items from the Minnesota Multiphasic Personality Inventory (MMPI) were submitted to judges, who were to designate those indicative of manifest anxiety according to a specified definition (Cameron, 1947). Sixty-five items on which there was at least 80% agreement were selected. These were supplemented by 135 additional " buffer " items which had been consistently classified by the judges as nonindicative of anxiety. This scale was then administered to 352 students in a course in introductory psychology. Scores ranged from 1 to 36, with a median of 14. After several further modifications, the present scale was devised. It consists of 50 of the original 65 items showing a high correlation with total anxiety scores in the initial subject group. The buffer items (175) have been modified somewhat, so that the test now includes most of the items from the L, K, and F scales of the MMPI and 41 items from a rigidity scale developed by Wesley (1950). These buffer items are not relevant, but are included to disguise the intent of the scale. The final scale includes 225 items and is given under the title, "The Biographical Inventory."

Sample Items: The MAS is presented as 225 statements to which the subject responds with True or False. An anxiety score is determined from these responses. Items similar to those on the scale, along with the responses considered "anxious," appear below:

I do not have many headaches (False).

I rarely blush (False).

I have nightmares two or three times a week (True).

I am hungry almost all of the time (True).

Reliability: Test/retest reliability was measured on a group of 59 students after an interval of 3 weeks, yielding a Pearson product-moment coefficient of .89 (Taylor and Spence, 1952). In another test/retest study (Ahana, 1952), the scale was given to 162 students in an advanced undergraduate psychology course who had previously taken the test as introductory students. For 113 of the students, 5 months had elapsed since the first testing, and for 50 of them 9–17 months had intervened. The first group yielded a coefficient of .82, the second group, .81. In both groups, each individual's relative position and absolute score tended to remain constant over these periods of time.

   In a subsequent revision of the scale, 28 items were rewritten for further clarity. Scores from 59 students showed a Pearson product-moment correlation of .85 between the old and new forms, and a correlation of .80, considering only the 28 rewritten items (Taylor, 1953).

Test/retest scores were also determined on 179 students in introductory psychology, using only the revised form of the scale. A product-moment correlation of .88 was found after a lapse of 4 weeks (Ahana, 1952).

Validity: Concurrent validity was investigated in an attempt to determine the relationship between the anxiety scale scores and manifest anxiety as defined and observed by clinicians. Anxiety scores from a group of 103 psychiatric patients were compared to those from a group of normal individuals. The score distributions for these 2 groups were markedly different, with the median score of the patient group being equivalent to about the 99th percentile of the normal group (Taylor, 1953).

It was also found that the MAS correlated with other measures of anxiety. In a study by Korchin and Heath (1961), the MAS was shown to be positively correlated to the Anxiety scale, and negatively correlated to the Ego Strength scale, of the Autonomic Perception Questionnaire (APQ), both of these correlations being at significant levels. The APQ is an instrument which allows self-description of somatic symptoms characteristics of the subject's anxiety experience. The population used in this study was composed of 139 male and 37 female college students.

Norms: In its original form, the MAS has been administered to 1,971 students in introductory psychology classes at the State University of Iowa, from 1948 to 1951. Scores are also available for 683 airmen in training at Lackland Air Force Base and for 201 Northwestern University students.

Norms for the new scale are based on 229 students in introductory psychology at Northwestern University.

Administration and Scoring: This instrument is self-administering. The subject simply reads the items and records his or her responses. A scorer then checks these responses to see if they correspond to those which have been labeled "anxious."

Comments: The MAS is a carefully constructed instrument. Reliability appears to be good, but more validity information would be useful. Normative data from more varied populations would also be desirable. The instrument can be valuable in selecting subjects for experimental purposes, but its use, alone, for clinical prediction and individual interpretation should be questioned.

References: Ahana, E., *A study on the reliability and internal consistency of a manifest anxiety scale.* Unpublished master's thesis, Northwestern University, 1952.

Cameron, N. *The psychology of behavior disorders: A bio-social interpretation.* Boston: Houghton-Mifflin, 1947.

Korchin, S. J., and H. A. Heath, "Somatic experience in the anxiety state: Some sex and personality correlates of 'autonomic feedback'." *Journal of Consulting Psychology*, 1961, **25**, 398–404.

Taylor, J. A., "A personality scale of manifest anxiety." *Journal of Abnormal and Social Psychology*, 1953, **48**, 285–290.

Taylor, J. A., and K. W. Spence, "The relationship anxiety to performance in serial learning." *Journal of Experimental Psychology*, 1952, **44**, 61–64.

Wesley, E. L. *Perseverative behavior in a concept formation task*. Unpublished doctoral dissertation, State University of Iowa, 1950.

Name: MINNESOTA TEACHER ATTITUDE INVENTORY

Authors: Walter W. Cook, Carroll H. Leeds, and Robert Callis

Type of Measure: Rating scale

Availability: Cook, W. W., C. H. Leeds, and R. Callis. *Minnesota teacher attitude inventory.* New York, New York: Psychological Corporation, 1951.

Description: The Minnesota Teacher Attitude Inventory (MTAI) measures attitudes indicative of a teacher's effectiveness in interpersonal relationships with pupils. After reviewing the literature on teacher/pupil relationships, the authors wrote 378 opinion statements and classified them into 5 categories. Two forms—A and B—of the inventory were constructed, with the items in Form B stated differently (usually in reversed form) from the corresponding items in Form A. All items were tested on two groups of 100 teachers, who had been classified by their principals as "superior" or "inferior" according to 3 criteria: ability to win the affection of pupils; fondness for, and understanding of, children; and ability to maintain a desirable form of discipline. Form A was administered first, and then, at a later date, Form B was given. After extensive item analyses, 164 items were selected which differentiated the 2 groups of teachers. Further modifications resulted in a final instrument composed of 150 items.

Sample Items: The 150 items on the MTAI are written as opinion statements to which a subject responds according to whether he or she strongly agrees (SA), agrees (A), is undecided (U), disagrees (D), or strongly disagrees (SD). Items similar to those on the inventory appear below:

Most pupils do not appreciate a teacher's efforts.

Children have a natural tendency to be disruptive.

Grading is given too much emphasis.

Often children act more civilized than adults.

Reliability: The reliability of the instrument was determined by the split-half method (Leeds, 1952). The scores on the odd-numbered items were correlated with those on the even-numbered items, and a reliability coefficient of .93 (corrected by the Spearman-Brown formula) was obtained.

Validity: Validity investigations were approached in several different ways. Leeds (1950) administered the MTAI to a sample of 100 fourth- through sixth-grade teachers in South Carolina. Ratings of the teachers were then obtained from 3 sources: the principal, the investigator (from classroom observations), and the pupils. These were correlated with scores on the MTAI, and the resulting validity coefficients were .43, .48, and .45 for the principal, investigator, and pupil ratings respectively. The combined results for the 3 ratings correlated .59 with MTAI scores. A multiple correlation of .59 was obtained between the Inventory and the 3 criteria. All of these correlations were significant at the .01 level.

A second study was conducted, using the same procedures described above, to reaffirm these findings (Leeds, 1952). Validity coefficients were .46, .57, and .31 between the test and principal, investigator, and pupil ratings respectively. The correlation between the combined criteria and the test was .59, and the multiple correlation was .63. The difference in pupils' ratings from the first to the second study was the only significant difference found between the 2 studies.

In another study, Sandgren and Schmidt (1956) found no relationship between MTAI scores and teachers' ratings of the effectiveness of 393 student teachers who had been divided into 3 categories based on their test scores.

Della Piana and Gage (1955) correlated MTAI scores with pupils' ratings of their teachers. The pupils came from classrooms designated either "most cognitively oriented" or "least cognitively oriented." Test scores correlated significantly with the ratings of pupils in the least cognitively oriented sample, but not with those of pupils in the other sample. The results suggest that the validity of the MTAI may be influenced by pupils' values.

Stein and Hardy (1957) investigated "fake-ability" of the MTAI. They compared test scores of 3 samples, each composed of 24 education students. All 3 groups were given the standard instructions at the first administration of the MTAI. At the second administration, 2 of the groups were given modified instructions, which suggested faking response patterns in a specified manner. The results from these 2 groups showed significant differences in mean scores (in the predicted direction) on the 2 administrations.

Norms: Norms are available for high school and college students, teacher trainees, and elementary and secondary school teachers.

Administration and Scoring: The MTAI is easy to administer, with instructions printed on the test booklets. There is no time limit, but most subjects finish in less than 1 hour. Each response is scored $+1, 0$, or -1 according to prior item analysis results. Scores can range from -150 to $+150$, with a high score indicating a "progressive" orientation.

Comments: The MTAI appears to be a well constructed instrument. The reliability and validity are moderate, though results from investigations of validity have been variable. Precautions should be taken to ensure the authenticity of responses, since faking is possible if respondents are advised of the intended use of their scores. In general, the MTAI seems to be an economical and valuable tool for predicting the social/emotional climate in a teacher's classroom.

References: Della Piana, G. M., and N. L. Gage, "Pupils' values and the validity of the Minnesota Teacher Attitude Inventory." *Journal of Educational Psychology*, 1955, **46**, 167–178.

Leeds, C. H., "A scale for measuring teacher-pupil attitudes and teacher-pupil rapport." *Psychological Monographs, General and Applied.* 1950, **64**(6, Whole No. 312).

Leeds, C. H., "A second validity study of the Minnesota Teacher Attitude Inventory." *Elementary School Journal*, 1952, **52**, 398–405.

Sandgren, D. L., and L. G. Schmidt, "Does practice teaching change attitudes toward teaching?" *Journal of Educational Research*, 1956, **49**, 673–680.

Stein, H. L., and J. A. Hardy, "A validation study of the MTAI in Manitoba." *Journal of Educational Research*, 1957, **50**, 321–338.

Name: ONE-WORD SENTENCE COMPLETION

Authors: Robert F. Peck and Donald J. Veldman—Form 4-A. Robert F. Peck, Donald J. Veldman, and Shirley L. Menaker—Form 62.

Type of Measure: Projective test

Availability: Peck, R. F., and D. J. Veldman, *One-word sentence completion, form 4-A.* Austin, Texas: Research and Development Center for Teacher Education, University of Texas, 1963. A modified version of the instrument, Form 62, is available in: Menaker, S. L., and C. L. Lewis, *Clinical interpretation of the One-Word Sentence Completion.* Austin, Texas: Research and Development Center for Teacher Education, University of Texas, 1970.

Description: The One-Word Sentence Completion (OWSC), developed by the University of Texas Research and Development Center for Teacher Education and intended primarily for female undergraduates majoring in education, is a projective instrument which taps motivational, emotional, and attitudinal reactions. It requires the respondent to complete a number of unfinished sentences, using only 1 word to do so. Item stems for the original 90-item form (4-A) were derived from incomplete sentences used in the Prairie City Study of Character Development (Peck, Havighurst, et al., 1960), the Kansas City Study of Adult Life (Peck, 1959), and the Mental Health in Teacher Education Project (Peck, Bown, and Veldman, 1964). These stems measure 25 psychological variables.

Form 62, a more recent (1970) version of the OWSC, contains 62 items representing the following categories and subdivisions.

  I. Intrapersonal Characteristics
   A. Self-Esteem
       1. Physical Well-Being
       2. General Self-Esteem
   B. Self-Ability
   C. Emotional Self
   D. Causes of Anxiety

 II. Interpersonal Attitudes
   A. Attitude to Parents
   B. Attitude to Children
   C. Attitude to Others (Men, Women, Peers)
   D. Sociability

III. Job-related Characteristics
   A. Autonomy
       1. Independence
       2. Acceptance of Responsibility
   B. Goals and Sources of Satisfaction
   C. Commitment to Teaching

Sample Items: The OWSC contains items of the following type:

Category	Subdivision	Item
I. Intrapersonal Characteristics	C. Emotional Self	1. I generally _____ my feelings. 2. I take _____ chances.
II. Interpersonal Attitudes	D. Sociability	1. I fear _____. 2. When I need help, I rely on _____.
III. Job-Related Characteristics	C. Commitment to Teaching	1. If I were a teacher, I would be _____. 2. The secret of effective teaching is _____.

Reliability: Since highly objective computer scoring methods have been developed for this test (Peck, Menaker, and Veldman, 1966; Veldman, Menaker, and Peck, 1969), OWSC protocols may be scored either by raters or by computer. Therefore, both interrater and rater vs. computer reliabilities are provided (Peck, Menaker, and Veldman, 1966). For a sample of 79 female elementary education students who had completed Form 4-A of the OWSC, correlations between 2 raters ranged from .38 to .95 and averaged .66, while correlations between the average of these raters and the computer scoring ranged from .45 to .94, with a mean of .66.

Validity: Published evidence of validity is limited, though a preliminary estimate of concurrent validity is reported by Peck, Menaker, and Veldman (1966). The 25 variables on OWSC Form 4-A were correlated with the 9 scales of the Self-Report Inventory (SRI) for 79 subjects. Significant correlations tending to support the validity of the machine scored OWSC were obtained. For example, the OWSC Attitude Toward Mother and Attitude Toward Father variables correlated .44 and .47, respectively, with the SRI Parent Scale. Extraversion correlated .33 with the SRI Others Scale, and Persistence .37 with the SRI Work Scale. Similarly, Overall Mental Health correlated .51 with the SRI Total Scale.

Further evidence of validity is provided by the relationship (.55) between adjustment scores derived from computer-scored OWSC data and a general adjustment score obtained from a clinical rating of an extensive assessment battery. When grade-point averages were added to the OWSC adjustment variables, this relationship increased to .73 (Menaker and Lewis, 1970).

Norms: For the 90-item form, a normative distribution of the machine scored responses of 1,000 female education students is available. For the 62-item form, more complete normative data, based on the responses of 851 juniors (male and female) majoring in education, are provided by Menaker and Lewis (1970). All 62 stems are listed along with the total number of different responses, the number of "blank" responses, and the 10 most common responses for each stem. The percentage of the population giving each listed response is also supplied. Finally, 5 unusual or low frequency responses are specified.

Administration and Scoring: The OWSC is essentially self-administering and requires about 20 minutes to complete. Scoring may be done by trained raters or by computer. Detailed instructions are provided for machine scoring (Peck, Menaker, and Veldman, 1966; Veldman, Menaker, and Peck, 1969), as well as hand scoring (Peck, Menaker, and Veldman, 1966). Menaker and Lewis (1970) provide several sample protocols along with clinical interpretations for Form 62.

Comments: The One-Word Sentence Completion retains the advantages of a free-response format and the richness of a projective device while at the same time restricting the subjects' verbal input and thus permitting computer scoring. The advantages of computer scoring include savings in time and cost and elimination of rater variability and bias. With the OWSC one can economically obtain and objectively score a wealth of projective data from preservice or inservice teachers. These data may be used in research or counseling.

References: Menaker, S. L., and C. L. Lewis, *Clinical interpretation of the One-Word Sentence Completion.* Austin, Texas: Research and Development Center for Teacher Education, University of Texas, 1970.

Peck, R. F., "Measuring the mental health of normal adults." *Genetic Psychology Monographs,* 1959, **60**, 197–255.

Peck, R. F., O. H. Bown, and D. J. Veldman, "Mental Health in teacher education." *Journal of Teacher Education,* 1964, **15**, 319–327.

Peck, R. F., R. J. Havighurst, et al., *The psychology of character development.* New York: John Wiley, 1960.

Peck, R. F., S. L. Menaker, and D. J. Veldman, *Computer analysis of sentence completion data.* Austin, Texas: Research and Development Center for Teacher Education, University of Texas, 1966.

Veldman, D. J., S. L. Menaker, and R. F. Peck. "Computer scoring of sentence completion data." *Behavioral Science,* 1969, **14**, 501–507.

Name: OPINIONNAIRE ON ATTITUDES TOWARD EDUCATION

Authors: Henry C. Lindgren and Gladys May Patton

Type of Measure: Forced-choice inventory

Availability: A copy of the scale may be found in: Shaw, M. E., and J. M. Wright, *Scales for the measurement of attitudes.* New York: McGraw-Hill, 1967.

Description: The Opinionnaire on Attitudes toward Education is a 50-item scale constructed to measure attitudes toward theories and practices in education which are basically child centered. The instrument was developed according to the Likert technique. Approximately half of the items were taken directly from an attitudinal questionnaire used in a study by Kelley (1941). The statements are related to the value of understanding pupils' behavior, the desirability of the teacher's use of authoritarian methods to control behavior of pupils, and the appropriateness of a subject-matter concentration as opposed to a student-centered concentration. The subject has a choice of two responses: "Agree" or "Disagree." The scale is designed for use with teachers from kindergarten through twelfth grade.

Sample Items: Fifty statements are listed, along with the explanation that the subject is to circle "A" if he is "more or less in agreement" with the statement, and "B" if he is "more or less in disagreement" with it. Items similar to those on the scale appear below:

A D 1. Children who are delinquent are really basically good.

A D 2. For children to do an adequate job of learning in school, their need for love must be met.

A D 3. It is reasonable for teachers to require an additional assignment from a pupil who misbehaves in class.

A D 4. A pupil's feelings about what he learns are as important as what he learns.

A D 5. It is appropriate to threaten and punish a pupil who tells lies.

A D 6. High school students who are not interested in dating should be commended.

A D 7. Education is unsuccessful unless it has helped pupils to understand and express their own feelings and experiences.

Reliability: The instrument was administered in 14 inservice teacher education courses at San Francisco State College. The total population consisted of 216 teachers: 63 male and 98 female elementary and junior high teachers, and 45 male and 10 female high school teachers. The corrected split-half reliability was .82 (Lindgren and Patton, 1958).

Validity: The validity of the scale was investigated on the same population of 216 teachers described above. The differences between the scores of high school and non-high school teachers and between males and females were assessed (Lindgren and Patton, 1958). The results showed that non-high school teachers scored higher than high school teachers and that females scored higher than males, with a high score indicating a preference for child-centered practices in education. Differences in both cases were significant.

Further evidence of validity was derived from later studies by Lindgren, who compared the Opinionnaire to several criteria. He reported negative correlations with the F-scale using a population of 81 nonacademic men and 69 nonacademic women, with a coefficient of $-.28$ for the first group and $-.51$ for the second group. He also reported positive correlations with Barron's "independence" scale, the coefficients being .36 for men and .57 for women. However, these studies were based upon a 30-item revision of the scale, which was constructed by eliminating from the original scale the 20 items that had the lowest correlations with the total scores. This form yielded a corrected split-half reliability of .64.

Norms: Normative data are available for teachers from kindergarten through grade 12.

Administration and Scoring: The scale is self-administering. Instructions are printed on the form, and there is no time limit. The attitude score is determined by adding the number of positive items with which the subject agrees to the number of negative items with which he or she disagrees. Positive items are those favoring child-centered practices. The theoretical range of scores is from 0 to 50, with higher scores indicating favorable attitudes toward more child-centered theories and practices in education.

Comments: The Opinionnaire on Attitudes toward Education appears to be a well constructed instrument. The evidence presented for reliability is good, though limited, but further investigation of validity is needed. The scale seems to have value for economical assessment of educational attitudes.

References: Kelley, I. B., "An investigation of teacher's knowledge of and attitudes toward child and adolescent behavior in everyday school situations." *Further studies in attitudes, Series IV*. Lafayette, Indiana: Purdue University, 1941.

Lindgren, H. C., and G. M. Patton, "Attitudes of high school and other teachers toward children and current educational methodology." *California Journal of Educational Research*, 1958, **9**(3), 80–85.

Shaw, M. E., and J. M. Wright, *Scales for the measurement of attitudes*. New York: McGraw-Hill, 1967.

Name: THE PUPIL CONTROL IDEOLOGY FORM

Authors: Donald J. Willower, Terry L. Eidell, and Wayne K. Hoy

Type of Measure: Rating scale

Availability: Willower, D. J., T. L. Eidell, and W. K. Hoy, *The school and pupil control ideology*. The Pennsylvania State University Studies, No. 24. University Park, Pennsylvania: Pennsylvania State University, 1967.

Description: The Pupil Control Ideology Form (PCI) was developed for use in schools as a measure of control ideology, a concept adapted from Gilbert and Levinson's work (1957). The terms "custodial" and "humanistic" were adopted to identify contrasting ideologies and school organizations. The former term describes a rigidly traditional school, while the latter refers to an educational community in which students learn by interacting and experiencing. Construction of the PCI began with 57 statements concerning pupil control which were drawn from the literature, the author's experience in public schools, previous studies, and a specialized conceptualization of control. This initial form was administered to 58 subjects, some of whom were graduate students in education and some of whom were teachers. After item analyses and an examination of comments elicited from subjects, the original form was modified and reduced to 38 items. This second form was then administered in 7 schools in Pennsylvania and New York. Elementary and secondary, urban, suburban, and rural schools were included. Two of the schools (one elementary and one secondary) were included because they were known to be "humanistic." From an item analysis based on this administration of the test, a final, 20-item form emerged. While the PCI is aimed primarily at teachers, it is appropriate for all school personnel.

Sample Items: The PCI includes statements about schools, teachers, and pupils. The subject reacts to each statement by choosing 1 of 5 response categories, ranging from "strongly agree" to "strongly disagree." Items of the following type appear on the scale:

1. Using sarcasm with a disobedient student is a good disciplinary technique.

2. Beginning teachers usually are not strict enough with their pupils.

3. It is a moral offense when a pupil uses obscene or profane language at school.

Reliability: Reliability was investigated by Willower, Eidell, and Hoy (1967), using 2 different populations. From the PCI scores of 170 teachers in the 7 schools described above, split-half reliability was calculated by correlating even-item subscores with odd-item subscores. Application of the Pearson product-moment formula yielded a coefficient of .91, corrected by the Spearman-Brown formula to .95. Data were also gathered from a second sample of 55 teachers from 2 schools, 1 elementary and 1 secondary. The resulting split-half reliability coefficient was .83, corrected by the Spearman-Brown formula to .91.

Validity: Validity was also investigated by the authors. Principals of the 7 schools mentioned above were asked to name a specified number of teachers in their schools whom they judged to be most "custodial" and most "humanistic," according to the PCI definitions. The number of each type to be identified was equal to about 15% of the faculty of the school. Using a *t*-test, the authors found that teachers judged to be most custodial had significantly higher PCI scores than those judged to be most humanistic. These same procedures were used on a second sample, drawn from another 7 schools (5 elementary and 2 secondary). This cross-validation also produced significant differences between the 2 groups of teachers.

In another investigation by the authors, mean scores of personnel in 2 schools known to be humanistic were compared with mean scores of personnel in other schools, at the same grade levels. Although statistical analyses were not performed, scores from the two schools identified as humanistic were clearly lower than those from other schools in the sample.

The PCI has also been correlated with a number of other instruments, one of which was the Pupil Attitude Questionnaire (PAQ), a measure of student alienation. The results showed custodial orientation to be positively correlated with student alienation. (Rafalides and Hoy, 1971).

The relationship between pupil control ideology and a broad set of personality characteristics was measured by comparing scores from the PCI and the Activities Index (AI). None of the individual factors of the AI was strongly correlated to custodialism, yet a multiple regression analysis indicated that certain personality factors, combined with demographic information, correlated significantly with PCI scores (Leppert and Hoy, 1972).

The PCI and the Organizational Climate Description Questionnaire (OCDQ) were administered to personnel of 45 elementary schools. According to PCI scores, 15 schools were identified as custodial, and 15 as humanistic. Significant differences between the two types of schools were found on 4 of the 8 dimensions of the OCDQ. Also, humanistic schools were found to be significantly more "open" than custodial schools (Hoy and Appleberry, 1970).

Norms: Normative data are given in the form of mean PCI scores for a sample of 1,306 educators, consisting of 945 teachers (468 elementary and 477 secondary), 181 principals (84 elementary and 97 secondary), and 180 counselors.

Administration and Scoring: The PCI is self-administering, with instructions printed on the form. There is no time limit. Response categories are scored as follows: strongly agree = 5, agree = 4, undecided = 3, disagree = 2, and strongly disagree = 1. Scoring is reversed, however, for the 2 items designated as characteristic of the humanistic viewpoint. Item scores are summed to provide a single test score. The higher the total score, the more custodial the subject's viewpoint.

Comments: The Pupil Control Ideology Form has proved valuable as a research tool. Reliability and validity are satisfactory. However, the scale might be better balanced, and its intent less obvious, if more "humanistic" items were included. Also, more complete and descriptive normative data would be useful.

References: Gilbert, D. C., and D. J. Levinson, "'Custodialism' and 'humanism' in mental hospital structure and in staff ideology," in D. Greenblat, D. Levinson, and R. Williams (eds.), *The patient and the mental hospital*. Glenco, Illinois: Free Press, 1957.

Hoy, W. K., "Organizational socialization: The student teacher and pupil control ideology." *Journal of Educational Research*, 1967, **61**, 153–155.

Hoy, W. K., "The influence of experience on the beginning teacher." *School Review*, 1968, **76**, 313–323.

Hoy, W. K., and J. B. Appleberry, "Teacher-principal relationships in 'humanistic' and 'custodial' elementary schools." *Journal of Experimental Education*, 1970, **39**(2), 27–31.

Leppert, E., and W. K. Hoy, "Teacher personality and pupil control ideology." *Journal of Experimental Education*, 1972, **40**(3), 57–59.

Rafalides, M., and W. K. Hoy, "Student sense of alienation and pupil control orientation of high schools." *High School Journal*, 1971, 101–111.

Willower, D. J., T. L. Eidell, and W. K. Hoy, *The school and pupil control ideology*. The Pennsylvania State University Studies, No. 24. University Park, Pennsylvania: Pennsylvania State University, 1967.

Name: PURDUE TEACHER OPINIONAIRE

Authors: Ralph R. Bentley and Averno M. Rempel

Type of Measure: Rating scale

Availability: Bentley, R. R., and A. M. Rempel, *Purdue teacher opinionaire.* West Lafayette, Indiana: Measurement and Research Center, Purdue University, 1970.

Description: The Purdue Teacher Opinionaire is designed to measure teacher morale. It yields a general score and subscores which separate morale into the following component dimensions: (1) Teacher Rapport with Principal; (2) Satisfaction with Teaching; (3) Rapport among Teachers; (4) Teacher Salary; (5) Teacher Load; (6) Curriculum Issue; (7) Teacher Status; (8) Community Support of Education; (9) School Facilities and Services; and (10) Community Pressures. The instrument originally consisted of 145 items grouped into 8 categories. Using a representative sample of 570 teachers, factor analyses were applied to the group as a whole and then to 3 teacher morale groups identified as "high," "middle," and "low." The 10 factors in the present 100-item instrument were extracted using these procedures.

    The instrument may be administered to teachers within a specific school, or school system, to produce an index of teacher morale and also to provide specific information about problems which adversely affect morale. This type of information can be useful to researchers, school administrators, and teachers.

Sample Items: The Opinionaire consists of 100 statements of the type below, to which a teacher responds by indicating whether he or she agrees (A), probably agrees (PA), probably disagrees (PD), or disagrees (D).

My school provides me with sufficient supplies and equipment.

Other teachers in my school have high professional ethics.

Community expectations about the personal standards of teachers are unreasonable.

Reliability: Reliability data are presented in the manual (Bentley and Rempel, 1970). Test/retest reliability coefficients were obtained from 3,023 high school teachers from 76 schools (60 in Indiana, 16 in Oregon), using a 4-week interval. The correlation for total scores was .87, while correlations for the 10 factors ranged from .62 to .88, with most being in the .80's.

    The interfactor correlations were also computed from the above sample. These ranged from .18 to .61, with a median of .38, which is sufficient to imply factor independence.

Validity: Little information on validity is available. However, some evidence for construct validity is reported in the manual. In a single school system, teachers selected from 3 to 10 of their peers whom they considered to have the highest morale, and the same number considered to have the lowest morale. The exact number selected depended on the size of the faculty. From these ratings, "high," "middle," and "low" teacher moral groups were identified, and their mean scores on the Opinionaire were computed. The results showed that differences between the groups were significant and in the expected direction.

In another study, principals in Oregon and Indiana schools were asked to respond to the Opinionaire as they believed their faculty would respond. There were no significant differences between the median scores for teachers and principals.

In a study by Bentley and Rempel (1963) marked differences were found in the morale levels of different schools.

Further evidence for validity was suggested in a study by Brinkman (1966), which showed that school conditions were often reflected in teachers' and principals' reponses to the instrument.

Norms: Median scores for individual items and for the 10 factors, derived from the responses of 3,023 high school teachers in Indiana and Oregon, are provided in the manual. Stanine norms are also given, based on a representative sample of 250 school faculties, including elementary, junior high, and senior high schools.

Administration and Scoring: The instrument is self-administering, with directions printed on the form. There is no time limit, but most teachers complete it in 20 to 30 minutes. It is available in folder form for hand scoring, or in a 2-part form for machine scoring, with a separate IBM card on which to record responses. From 3 to 5 days are required for computer scoring. For hand scoring, a key is provided. The appropriate factor number as shown on the key is written to the right of the response weight. Factor scores are obtained by summing the weights of all items belonging to a single factor. Total scores are obtained by summing the factor scores.

Comments: The Purdue Teacher Opinionaire is a well constructed instrument. The evidence for reliability is satisfactory, but evidence for validity, particularly predictive validity, is meager, and further investigation in this area is warranted. More complete descriptions of the normative samples would be useful, also. The Opinionaire can be valuable as a research tool or a diagnostic instrument for school staffs and administrators who desire information about teacher morale in their schools or school systems.

References: Bentley, R. R., and A. M. Rempel, "Peer-selection vs. expert judgment as a means of validating a teacher morale measuring instrument." *Journal of Experimental Education,* 1963, **31**(3), 233–240.

Bentley, R. R., and A. M. Rempel, *Manual for the Purdue Teacher Opinionaire.* Lafayette, Indiana: Purdue Research Foundation, Purdue University, 1970.

Brinkman, M. J., *Factors related to teacher morale in three junior high schools.* Unpublished thesis, D. Ed., Library, Wayne State University, Detroit, Michigan, 1966.

Name: SELF-REPORT INVENTORY

Author: Oliver H. Bown

Type of Measure: Rating scale

Availability: Bown, O. H., and D. J. Veldman, *Scoring procedures and college freshman norms for the Self-Report Inventory.* Austin, Texas: Research and Development Center for Teacher Education, The University of Texas at Austin, 1967.

Description: The Self-Report Inventory (SRI) measures attitudes toward 8 logically distinct areas of the phenomenological world. These areas are represented by the following scales: Self, Others, Children, Authority, Work, Reality, Parents, and Hope. Each scale contains 6 items and produces its own scale score. Thus, the instrument yields 8 scale scores, a total score, and an Intensity score, which reflects the subject's preference for extremes on the response continuum.

Since its initial construction in 1958, the SRI has been subjected to a series of item analyses, which have resulted in 3 major revisions. The current form, R-3, was printed in 1961. Although usually administered to college samples, the SRI is also appropriate for general adult populations.

Sample Items: Each of the 48 items on the SRI is followed by a 1-to-5 response scale, ranging from " very much like me " to " very much unlike me." The subject selects the reponse which best indicates how well the item expresses his own feelings and attitudes. Items of the following type appear on the scale:

Scale	*Item*
Self	I'd like to be a very different sort of person than I am.
Others	I don't expect to have many close friends who are my own age.
Children	I have no trouble being affectionate toward young children.
Authority	I feel ill at ease and affected around people who are considerably older than I.

Reliability: Alpha coefficients for the 8 scales of the SRI are as follows: Self = .78; Others = .65; Children = .85; Authority = .53; Work = .70; Reality = .28; Parents = .84; and Hope = .66. Internal consistency coefficients for the Total Score and the Intensity Score are both .87.

Validity: SRI Scale, Total and Intensity scores from a sample of 1,362 males and 959 females were correlated with a number of variables, including verbal ability, numerical ability, high school grades, high school activities, confidence about college, physical factors, and family background (Bown and Veldman, 1967). Correlation coefficients ranged from −.29 to .31, with the majority falling between $-.10$ and $.10$. High school grade average was related to the Work scale in the expected positive direction ($.31$ for males and females). Confidence about ability to obtain a college degree correlated positively with scores on the Self, Work, and Total scales ($.24$, $.29$, and $.24$ for females; $.21$, $.19$, and $.24$ for males). In both the male and female groups a history of ill health correlated in the expected direction with Self and Total scores ($-.16$ and $-.13$ for females; $-.08$ and $-.07$ for males). Also, the dichotomous variable, "parents separated" related to the Parents scale ($-.16$ for females and $-.17$ for males).

SRI scores have also been related to extroversion/introversion (Bown and Richek, 1969). Prospective teachers ($N = 149$), who had been classified as extroverts and introverts according to direction of preference scores on the Myers-Briggs Type Indicator, were administered the SRI. Results indicated that extroverts differed significantly from introverts on the Total scale and on all SRI subscales, except Work and Reality. On 3 of the scales (Self, Others, and Total), results were significant at less than the .001 level.

Norms: The SRI is regularly administered to all students enrolled in the introductory course in Educational Psychology at the University of Texas. Means, standard deviations, and standard errors of the mean, based on samples of male and female education students, are provided for the Total score, the Intensity score, and each of the 8 subscales. Percentile equivalents, separated by sex, are also supplied for all of the scales.

Administration and Scoring: The SRI is essentially self-administering. In scoring the inventory, numerical scaling is reversed on 24 positively phased items, and scores within each of 8 areas are then summed. A computer program, which automatically reverses scaling and computes area totals, is provided to facilitate scoring. This procedure yields 10 scores: 8 subscores which represent positiveness of attitude in each area; a Total score (the sum of all subscores) which reflects overall perception of the phenomenological world; and an Intensity score, which indicates the subject's tendency to select the ends of the response continuum.

Comments: The Self-Report Inventory provides an economical means of personality assessment. Although test/retest reliability estimates and more varied normative data are needed, this instrument effectively measures several dimensions of attitude. The SRI was developed for research, and its primary use has been in that area.

References: Bown, O. H., "The development of a self-report inventory and its function in a mental health assessment battery." *American Psychologist*, 1961, **16**, 402.

Bown, O. H., and H. G. Richek, "The Bown Self-Report Inventory (SRI): A quick screening instrument for mental health professionals." *Comprehensive Psychiatry*, 1967, **8**(1), 45–52.

Bown, O. H., and H. G. Richek, "Teachers-to-be: Extroversion/introversion and self-perceptions." *Elementary School Journal*, 1969, **70**(3), 164–170.

Bown, O. H., and D. J. Veldman, *Scoring procedure and college freshman norms for the Self-Report Inventory.* Austin, Texas: Research and Development Center for Teacher Education, The University of Texas, 1967.

Name: SIXTEEN PERSONALITY FACTOR QUESTIONNAIRE, FORMS A AND B

Author: Raymond B. Cattell

Type of Measure: Self-report questionnaire

Availability: Cattell, R. B. *The sixteen personality factor questionnaire*. Champaign, Illinois: Institute for Personality and Ability Testing, 1967.

Description: The Sixteen Personality Factor Questionnaire (16PF) is a personality inventory which, depending on the scoring procedure used, yields scores on 16 specific traits or on 4 broader, more general traits. Cattell selected the trait names after reviewing the psychiatric and psychological literature as well as a dictionary of 18,000 adjectives describing personality characteristics. He then edited and combined them to produce a list of 171 traits. A group of 100 adults was then rated on these traits, and ratings were correlated and eventually factor analyzed, reducing the list of trait names to 12. Four additional traits were derived from subsequent factor analyses of questionnaires. These 16 dimensions form the basis of Cattell's questionnaire: Reserved vs. Outgoing; Less Intelligent vs. More Intelligent; Affected by Feelings vs. Emotionally Stable; Humble vs. Assertive; Sober vs. Happy-go-Lucky; Expedient vs. Conscientious; Shy vs. Venturesome; Tough-minded vs. Tender-minded; Trusting vs. Suspicious; Practical vs. Imaginative; Forthright vs. Shrewd; Placid vs. Apprehensive; Conservative vs. Experimenting; Group-Dependent vs. Self-Sufficient; Undisciplined Self-Conflict vs. Controlled; Relaxed vs. Tense.

The 16PF is designed for use with individuals aged 17 or older. It is available in 6 forms (A, B, C, D, E, and F), 2 of which are equivalent at each of 3 reading levels. It is recommended that both equivalent forms be used to insure accuracy. Forms A and B, which are appropriate for fully literate individuals (average high school graduates), both contain 187 items—10 to 13 on each factor.

The 16PF can be used for prediction and classification and may be administered either individually or in groups.

Sample Items: Three alternatives are provided for each statement or stem of the following type:

Item	*Response Alternatives*
1. When something makes me very angry, I calm down again quite quickly.	a. yes b. in between c. no
2. At social events, I:	a. readily involve myself. b. in between c. prefer to remain quietly in the background.

Item	*Response Alternatives*
3. I would prefer to stop in the street	a. true
to watch an artist paint than to	b. uncertain
listen to people arguing:	c. false

Reliability: Several investigations of the reliability of the 16PF scales have been conducted. For forms A and B combined, stability coefficients range from .63 to .88 over a 2-month interval, and from .76 to .93 over a 6-day interval (in the latter case on a sample of 146 adults). Estimates of internal consistency, derived by correlating factor scores across forms A and B, fall between .34 and .76 for a group of 230 male college students. For form A alone, coefficients of internal consistency range from .06 to .78. Corresponding estimates for form B are from .12 to .81 (Cattell and Eber, undated). Buros (1972) reports that 4 of the 16 scales correlate more highly with other scales than with themselves.

Validity: The evidence of construct validity for the 16PF is demonstrated by a mean correlation of .85 between each group of items and the factor it represents. Direct validities (the combined, averaged validities of A and B) corrected by the Spearman-Brown formula, range from .74 to .86. Circumstantial validities (the rank-difference correlations between corresponding theoretical and actual correlations of a factor with all other factors) fall between .42 and .99, with the average being .81.

    Cattell and Eber (undated) acknowledge that correlations with specific outside criteria are of limited value in the case of a multiple-purpose test, since test results relate to so many different criteria. Nevertheless, several correlations with individual criteria are reported in the *Handbook* (Cattell and Eber, 1957). For example, enthusiasm, represented on Factor F, Sober vs. Happy-go-Lucky, declines quickly between the ages of 20 and 30. The *Handbook* also presents regression equations (using all 16 factors) which predicted academic achievement (grades) for 4 different samples. The multiple r's were .55, .63, .37, and .56.

    A study by Golightly and Reinehr (1969), demonstrated that alcoholic patients can be identified by their 16PF profiles. These results replicated previous findings of this type. If the technique used in this study were refined, the 16PF could function as a screening device for the psychiatric classification of alcoholic patients and as an aid in planning treatment programs.

    Lebovits and Ostfeld (1970) found test-taking attitudes significantly associated with 6 16PF scales, and educational level significantly related to 4 scales.

Norms: Normative data, separated by sex and subsample, are reported for the general adult population. Norms are also provided for college undergraduates and high school juniors and seniors (both male and female).

Administration and Scoring: Instructions for completing the 16PF are presented on the test booklet, but it is advised that the administrator read these aloud.

The administrator should also establish good rapport with examinees in order to create a favorable test-taking attitude among them. The test is untimed, but it usually takes from 45 to 60 minutes to complete each form.

The scale can be either hand scored, using keys which are provided, or machine scored by the National Computer Systems Scoring Service. Most items are scored from 0 to 2. Raw score totals for each factor are converted to standard scores and placed on a profile. Usually, a high score indicates the positive aspect of each factor and a low score indicates the negative (Greene, 1952).

Comments: The 16PF has been criticized in the past for the relatively low reliabilities of scale scores, the lack of evidence for the factorial homogeneity of items in each scale, and the questionable factorial independence of the scales (Anastasi, 1968). Its various forms may not be as comparable as they purport to be, making most empirical or predictive validity data collected on the earlier forms of limited applicability (Buros, 1972). Yet, the test has been well accepted and widely used, and it continues to be of value as a comprehensive personality inventory.

References: Anastasi, A., *Psychological testing* (3rd ed.). London: The Macmillan Co., 1968.

Buros, O. K., *Seventh mental measurements yearbook.* Highland Park, New Jersey: Gryphon Press, 1972.

Cattell, R. B., and H. W. Eber, *Manual for forms A and B: Sixteen Personality Factor Questionnaire.* Champaign, Illinois: Institute for Personality and Ability Testing, undated.

Cattell, R. B., and H. W. Eber, *Handbook for the Sixteen Personality Factor Questionnaire.* Champaign, Illinois: Institute for Personality and Ability Testing, 1957.

Golightly, C., and R. C. Reinehr, "16PF profiles of hospitalized alcoholic patients: Replication and extension." *Psychological Reports,* 1969, **24**, 543–545.

Kleinmutz, B., *Personality measurement: An introduction.* Homewood, Illinois: Dorsey Press, 1967.

Lebovits, B. Z., and A. M. Ostfeld. "Personality, defensiveness and educational achievement: II. The Cattell 16PF Questionnaire." *Journal of Clinical Psychology,* 1970, **26**, 183–188.

Name: SOCIAL INSIGHT TEST

Author: F. Stuart Chapin

Type of Measure: Questionnaire

Availability: Chaplin, F. S. *The social insight test.* Palo Alto, Calif.: Consulting Psychologists Press, 1967.

Description: The Social Insight Test, which may be administered to populations aged 13 and over, is designed to measure an individual's perception and accuracy in evaluating outcomes of interpersonal situations. This instrument stresses the diagnostic capacity of an individual to appraise others and forecast what they might do in various situations. Introduced in 1942, the questionnaire originally contained 45 items on social insight. Item analyses were conducted using 2 groups—1 ranking high on social participation, the other ranking low. The high-ranking group was active in political, professional, and social areas, while the low scorers came from industrial, religious, and youth organizations. From the 45-item format, 25 items were then selected which best differentiated between the 2 groups.

These 25 short paragraphs each describe a situational problem involving interpersonal relations or personality dynamics. From among 4 multiple-choice options, the subject selects the one offering the wisest or most satisfactory course of action. Generally, the correct response supplies the most probable reason for, or the most likely consequence of, the behavior described.

Sample Items: This instrument is a 2-part, multiple-choice questionnaire. Part I, containing 16 questions, requires selection of the most logical response. Part II, containing 9 questions, requires selection of the response yielding the most satisfaction or least embarrassment to the person described in the paragraph. Items similar to those on the test are:

Part I. Joan, a girl of 19 years, is given to self-analysis. She is overly conscientious and always concerned about what other people think of her. Joan often analyzes the motives of others and also has difficulty initiating conversations with strangers. Another trait of Joan's behavior is:
   a. Concern over possible misfortunes.
   b. Desire for excitement.
   c. Consideration of others' feelings.
   d. Inclination to read about things rather than experience them.

Part II. During a meeting, the discussion is so heated and argumentative that everyone appears to be angry at each other. Finally, one person, who is receiving the worst end of the argument, angrily leaves the room. The chairman of the meeting should:
   a. Immediately adjourn the meeting.
   b. Send someone after the departed person.
   c. Ask for a vote on whether or not to adjourn the meeting.
   d. Ignore the departure and continue with the business at hand.

Reliability: For the original 45-item format, a corrected odd/even reliability coefficient of .75 was obtained. For the revised 25-item format, an odd/even check on a sample of 100 adult males yielded a corrected coefficient of .78. Item vs. total-score correlations (point-biserial) for the long form have been obtained for groups of 494 males and 215 females with median coefficients of .30 for men and .28 for women. When projected by the Guilford method (to correct for reducing the length of the test from 45 to 25 items), these reliabilities were .71 and .68. Test/retest coefficients have not been computed (Gough, 1968).

Validity: The validity of the Social Insight Test has been investigated using a variety of criteria. Gough (1968) suggests that in evaluating the validity of this instrument these criteria be considered in combination.

Ratings by psychologists on a sample of 100 commissioned military officers served as the criterion in a study by MacKinnon (1958). When these ratings were correlated with the officers' scores on the Social Insight Test, the following coefficients emerged: .31 with "ability to communicate;" .29 with "ability to evaluate ideas;" .27 with "good judgment;" and .26 with "leadership." In a similar study, mean Q-sort descriptions of 66 students, done by 3 psychologists, were correlated with the students' scores on the Social Insight Test (Gough, 1968). This procedure yielded 50 correlations, ranging from .43 to −.45. The Q-sort items having high positive correlations with test scores stressed ability to elicit cooperation from others, ability to lead and to listen, and responsiveness to the nuances of others' behavior. The most negatively related items, on the other hand, emphasized inflexibility, resistance to change, need for routine, and lack of perception.

Standings of various occupational groups on the test provide another source of evidence for validity. For males, the mean scores range from 28.15 for bank managers to 15.47 for high school students. For females, the range is from 29.25 for graduate students in psychology to 15.90 for high school students.

Finally, relationships between the Social Insight Test and other measures supply further validity data. Correlations with 8 standard tests of ability and aptitude ranged from .24 to .40 with a mean of .34. Presumably social insight relates to the cognitive component common to these 8 measures. Correlations with personality tests (the California Psychology Inventory, the Minnesota Multiphasic Personality Inventory, and the Study of Values) offer indirect evidence of validity. Since these correlations are low (mostly under .30), it appears that the Social Insight Test is measuring a specific personality trait related to social functioning.

Norms: Interpretive aids are not provided. Means and standard variations for a variety of subject groups are given, but there are no norms in either percentile or standard score form.

Administration and Scoring: Administration of this instrument involves a reusable Situations Booklet, in which the 25 situations are presented, and a Response

Booklet, which contains 4 choices for each situation. The test is self-administering. Generally, it takes about 30 minutes to complete. There is no time limit. Scoring may be done by hand, using a key which is provided. Differential scoring weights of 3, 2, or 1 are assigned to the test items. These scoring weights, ascertained by item analysis, indicate the relative discriminating power of each item. A high total score is recognized as evidence of social insight.

Comments: The Social Insight Test is still in research status. Reliability is too low to warrant use of the instrument for individual diagnosis, yet it is acceptable for group work. Also, there is no indication of stability of scores over periods of time. The experimental data presented in the manual are characterized by validity coefficients which are invariably low. This may be explained by the item/test correlations, which were not given individually but instead were given as medians of .30 for men and .28 for women. These data, and a look at the items themselves, suggest that the instrument does not measure a unitary dimension, but rather a multifaceted, heterogeneous dimension. If the items were more homogeneous, perhaps the validity coefficients would be higher. At present, however, relationships established are moderate and highly tentative. More evidence on reliability and validity should be obtained before the Social Insight Test is accepted as a diagnostic instrument. Moreover, adequate norms should be provided. Nonetheless, this instrument may be recommended for experimental use. Its weaknesses and omissions are identified in the manual, and with continued use of the test they may be corrected.

References: Chapin, F. S., *The social insight test.* Palo Alto, California: Consulting Psychologists Press, 1967.

Gough, H. G. *Manual, The Chaplin social insight test.* Palo Alto, California: Consulting Psychologists Press, 1968.

Lake, D. B., M. B. Miles, and R. B. Earle, Jr. (eds.), *Measuring human behavior.* New York: Columbia University, Teachers College Press, 1973.

MacKinnon, D. W., et al., *An assessment study of Air Force officers. Part I: Design of the study and description of variables.* (Technical Report WADC-TR-58-91 (1), ASTIA Document No. AD 151-040). Lackland Air Force Base, Texas: Wright Air Development Center, Personnel Laboratory, 1958.

McDermid, C. D., "Some correlates of creativity in engineering personnel." *Journal of Applied Psychology,* 1965, **49**, 14–19.

Name: STATE-TRAIT ANXIETY INVENTORY

Authors: Charles D. Spielberger, Richard L. Gorsuch, and Robert E. Lushene

Type of Measure: Rating scale

Availability: Spielberger, C. D., R. L. Gorsuch, and R. E. Lushene, *State-trait anxiety inventory.* Palo Alto, California: Consulting Psychologists Press, 1968.

Description: The State-Trait Anxiety Inventory (STAI) consists of 2 separate self-report scales for measuring state (A-State) and trait (A-Trait) anxiety. It was originally designed as a research instrument to be used for investigating anxiety in normal adults, but it has also been found useful in measuring anxiety in junior and senior high school students, and in neuropsychiatric, medical, and surgical patients.

When the STAI was developed, items which demonstrated relationship to other measures of anxiety were included for assessing both A-State and A-Trait. A single form was developed which could be administered with different instructions to measure either A-State or A-Trait.

It was discovered that some of the items in this form had ambiguous connotations, which interfered with their use as measures of both types of anxiety. Therefore, 1 set of items was selected to measure A-State, and another set to measure A-Trait. The resulting form consists of 20 statements that ask subjects to indicate how they "generally" feel (A-Trait), and 20 statements that ask subjects to indicate how they feel "at a particular moment in time" (A-State). Only 5 items were found to be equally useful as measures of both types of anxiety and consequently were included on both scales. The two scales are printed on a single test form, 1 on each side.

Sample Items: This instrument consists of 2 scales (Forms X-1 and X-2), which can be administered separately or together. The examinee responds by blackening the appropriate response to the right of each item. The following items are similar to those on the inventory:

	Not at all	Somewhat	Moderately So	Very Much So
Form X-1.				
I feel satisfied.	1	2	3	4
I am fidgety.	1	2	3	4
Form X-2.				
I feel sad.	1	2	3	4
I am a stable person.	1	2	3	4

Reliability: Reliability of the STAI is reported in the test manual (Speilberger, Gorsuch, and Lushene, 1970). Test/retest reliability data for individuals included in the normative sample (484 undergraduate students) showed correlations for the A-Trait scale ranging from .73 to .86, and for the A-State scale ranging from .16 to .54. Three subject groups were used: the first was retested after 1 hour, during which time the group members were exposed to a brief period of relaxation training, a difficult IQ test, and a film that depicted accidents resulting in serious injury or death; the second group was retested after 20 days; and the third group was retested after 104 days. The low correlations for the A-State scale were anticipated, since a valid measure of A-State should reflect the influence of unique situational factors at the time of testing.

Alpha coefficients for the scales were also determined using the samples above. These coefficients ranged from .83 to .92 for A-State and from .86 to .92 for A-Trait.

Item-remainder coefficients were computed for normative samples of high school and college students. For the high school students, the median A-State correlation was .55 and A-Trait, .54. For the college freshmen, the A-State correlation was .45 and the A-Trait, .46. For the college undergraduates, the median correlation was .55 for A-State and .53 for A-Trait. Over half of the items on each scale yielded item-remainder correlations of .50 or higher.

Validity: Several approaches to validity are reported in the manual. In the construction of the STAI, items were required to meet certain A-State and A-Trait validity criteria at each stage of the development process in order to be retained for further evaluation and validation. (See Appendix B of the manual.)

Concurrent validity was investigated for the A-Trait scale by correlating it with the IPAT Anxiety Scale, the Taylor Manifest Anxiety Scale (TMAS), and the Zuckerman Affect Adjective Check List (AACL), General Form, using college students and patients. The correlations between the STAI and the IPAT and TMAS were moderately high for both populations (.76 and .77 for IPAT, .80 and .83 for TMAS). In contrast, correlations with the AACL were lower: .55 for students and .83 for patients.

Construct validity was investigated using a sample of 977 undergraduate students at Florida State University. These students were first administered the A-State scale according to the standard instructions, then asked to respond to it again, this time imagining how they would feel just prior to the final examination in an important course. The mean score was considerably higher on the second administration (the critical ratio being 24.14 for males and 42.13 for females, and the point-biserial correlation being .60 for males and .73 for females).

Additional validity data for the STAI A-State Scale were obtained in a study using 197 undergraduate students at Florida State University under 4 different experimental conditions (Lazarus and Opton, 1966). The mean scores were lowest in the least stressful situation and highest in the most stressful situation.

The STAI scale was also correlated with 4 anxiety factors determined in a study by Hodges and Felling (1970). The A-Trait scale did not correlate with the physical danger or pain factors but did correlate with factors involving speech, classroom participation, social and academic failure, and dating. This is consistent with Spielberger's contention that A-Trait is a measure of the predisposition to respond with heightened A-State anxiety to situations regarding failure or loss of self-esteem.

Norms: Normative data are available for large samples of college undergraduates and high school students. They are also available for male psychiatric patients, general medical and surgical patients, and young prisoners.

Administration and Scoring: The STAI is self-administering. Instructions are printed on the test form, and there is no time limit. The instrument is given under the title of the Self-Evaluation Questionnaire. It is recommended that the A-State scale be given first when both scales are administered. The STAI may be given in an alternate form, multiple-choice format, in order to permit machine scoring. In hand scoring, 10 items from the A-State scale and 7 from the A-Trait scale are scored in reverse, and the rest are scored directly. The scoring weights are 1, 2, 3, and 4, corresponding to the blackened numbers on the scale for high anxiety items.

Comments: The STAI appears to be a carefully constructed instrument. Reliability and validity are high, and normative data are sufficient for most purposes. It can be useful in measuring state and trait anxiety for a variety of purposes.

References: Hodges, W. F., and J. P. Felling, "Types of stressful situations and their relation to trait anxiety and sex." *Journal of Consulting and Clinical Psychology*, 1970, **34**, 333–337.

Lazarus, R. S., and E. M. Opton, "The study of psychological stress: A summary of theoretical formulations and experimental findings," in C. D. Spielberger (ed.), *Anxiety and behavior*. New York: Academic Press, 1966, 225–262.

Spielberger, C. D., R. L. Gorsuch, and R. E. Lushene. *STAI manual*. Palo Alto California: Consulting Psychologists Press, 1970.

Name: STUDY OF VALUES

Authors: Gordon W. Allport, Phillip E. Vernon, and Gardner Lindzey

Type of Measure: Rating scale

Availability: Allport, G. W., P. E. Vernon, and G. Lindzey, *Study of values* (3rd ed.). Boston: Houghton-Mifflin, 1960. A copy of the instrument also appears in: Robinson, J. P., and P. R. Shaver, *Measures of social psychological attitudes.* Ann Arbor, Michigan: Institute for Social Research, University of Michigan, 1969.

Description: The Study of Values measures the relative strength of 6 basic evaluative attitudes, which are, according to Spranger (1928), the most revealing aspects of personality. These are: Theoretical, Economic, Aesthetic, Social, Political, and Religious. This 45-item instrument contains 2 sections. Part I presents 30 forced-choice items with 2 alternative responses, while Part II consists of 15 items offering 4 alternatives to be rank-ordered. The criterion used for item selection was internal consistency within each of the 6 attitude areas.

The scale may be administered to high school, college, and adult populations. It is commonly used in research and in educational and vocational guidance.

Sample Items: In Part I of the Study of Values, the subject indicates strength of preference for an alternative by the manner in which he distributes 3 points. For instance, if the subject strongly prefers one alternative over the other, he indicates this by marking the preferred alternative " 3 " and the other " 0 "; however, if one alternative is preferred only slightly more than the other, the subject labels his choices with the numbers " 2 " and " 1 ". In Part II, statements are ranked from 1 to 4, with 4 indicating highest preference. Items of the following type appears on the Study of Values:

Part I. Which of the following fields of study will eventually prove to be more important to mankind? (a) mathematics; (b) theology.

Part II. Usually, at the theater you enjoy most:
   a. plays about the lives of great men;
   b. ballet or imaginative performances;
   c. plays with a theme of love and pain;
   d. problem plays that support a certain point of view.

Reliability: Reliability has been investigated in several different studies. Anastasi (1968) reports split-half reliabilities for the 6 areas ranging from .73 to .90 and test/retest reliabilities, with 1- or 2-month intervals, ranging from .77 to .93.

Robinson and Shaver (1969) supply reliability data from several sources. They report split-half reliabilities ranging from .84 to .95, on a sample of 100. Further evidence of internal consistency is provided by an item analysis performed on the scores of 780 male and female college students, which yielded significant positive correlations between every item and the appropriate total area score.

In a study by Hilton and Korn (1964), the test was administered 7 times to 30 subjects at monthly intervals. Retest reliabilities ranged from .74 to .89. Additional test/retest data are provided for the Economic and Religious scales. After 1-month ($N = 34$) and 2-month ($N = 53$) intervals, correlations ranging from .84 to .93 were obtained.

Validity: The authors of the Study of Values demonstrated its criterion-related validity by the method of contrasted groups (Allport, Vernon, and Lindzey, 1960). For example, art and design students were shown to score highest in the Aesthetic area, theological students and clergymen in the Religious area, and personnel and guidance workers in the Social area.

Further evidence of validity is reported in Anastasi's review of the test (1968). She notes that value profiles are related to academic achievement, to associates' ratings, and to other tests, such as the Strong Vocational Interest Blank and the Thurstone Attitude Scale.

Simon (1970) reported a positive relationship between scores on the Study of Values and individuals' perceptions of their own values. Seventy-nine subjects were asked to rate personality descriptions according to similarity to self. The descriptions to be rated were either very similar or very dissimilar to each subject's own value system, which was determined by his or her past scores on the Study of Values. Descriptions consistent with the subject's value system were rated significantly more similar to self than were inconsistent descriptions.

Norms: Norms for the original edition of the test consist of scores from 1,400 college students. Norms for the 1960 edition are based on the scores of 1,816 college students and over 1,400 high school students, separated by sex.

Administration and Scoring: The Study of Values is self-administering and can be completed in 20 minutes. The test may be hand or machine scored. Hand scoring, which may be done by the subject, involves summing item scores and adding or subtracting correction figures. The 6 values are measured on an ipsative basis: as a subject's score on 1 value increases, his or her score on 1 or more of the other values must decrease. Therefore, the subject who is moderately interested in aesthetic pursuits but disinterested in the other 5 areas might score higher on the Aesthetic Scale than the very artistic subject with strong interests in the other areas.

Comments: The Study of Values is a standard among personality measures. Since its introduction in 1931, the test has been widely used, and its weaknesses have been well documented. The instrument has been criticized for its vague theoretical base (confusion of "values" with "interests"), its sophisticated vocabulary (though a less complex version is available), and its norms (which are college-based and oriented toward the liberal arts). The ipsative scoring which characterizes the test is not necessarily a weakness, though it can complicate interpretation by yielding negative correlations. In spite of these considerations, however, the Study of Values continues to be widely used. It is easy to administer, and the subjects can score their own tests and plot their profiles. The wealth of data on this instrument which has accumulated over the years adds to its value as a research and counseling tool.

References: Allport, G. W., P. E. Vernon, and G. Lindzey, *Study of values* (3rd ed.). Boston: Houghton-Mifflin, 1960.

Anastasi, A., *Psychological testing* (3rd ed.). London: The Macmillan Co., 1968.

Hilton, T., and J. Korn, "Measured change in personal values." *Educational and Psychological Measurement*, 1964, **24**, 609–622.

Newcomb, T., *Personality and social change: Attitude formation in a student community*. New York: Dryden Press, 1943.

Robinson, J. P., and P. R. Shaver, *Measures of social psychological attitudes*. Ann Arbor, Michigan: Institute for Social Research, University of Michigan, 1969.

Simon, W. E., "Self-concept and the validity of the Allport-Vernon-Lindzey Study of Values." *Perceptual and Motor Skills*, 1970, **31**, 263–266.

Spranger, E., *Types of men*. Translated from the 5th German edition of *Lebens-formen* by P. J. Pigors. Halle: Max Niemeyer Verlag, 1928. American Agent: Stechert-Hafner, Inc., New York.

Name: TAV SELECTION SYSTEM

Author: R. R. Morman

Type of Measure: Battery, including checklists, questionnaires, rating scales, and interpretive items

Availability: R. R. Morman. *TAV selection system*. North Hollywood, California: John P. Smith Press, 1968.

Description: The TAV Selection System is a battery of checklists and tests designed for use in counseling and personnel selection. The letters T, A, and V represent 3 interpersonal orientations originally described by Horney (1945): (1) moving *toward* people; (2) moving *away* from people; and (3) moving *versus* (against) people. A T-person typically moves toward people through dependency, sociability, and agreeability, while an A-person is quiet, asocial, and reflective, and a V-person is assertive, status-conscious, and competitive. Though Horney developed her theory working with disturbed individuals, the TAV Selection System is designed for normal adults. The battery is composed of 7 tests, described below, all of which measure the 3 modes of relating to others.

Sample Items: The 7 TAV tests are listed below. The response mode varies according to the nature of the item.

1. Adjective Check List
2. Personal Data
3. Proverbs and Sayings
4. Preferences
5. Sales Reactions
6. Judgment
7. Mental Agility
   Subtests
   (a) Following Directions and Carefulness
   (b) Verbal Comprehension
   (c) Weights and Balances

Reliability: Kuder-Richardson (formula 21) estimates of internal consistency are reported for the various tests of an early form of the TAV (Morman, Liddle, Heywood, Hankey, and Duvlick, 1965). These range from .54 to .88, the majority being in the .80s and the lowest being for the Personal Data test. Kuder-Richardson reliabilities reported in the manual are all at acceptable levels (Crites, 1969), though Personal Data, Following Directions and Carefulness, and Verbal Comprehension are less homogeneous than the other tests.

Validity: The TAV has been validated with on-the-job performance criteria. The manual reports 13 validity investigations, all using multiple correlation methods which indicate that the TAV tests are related (.53 to .90) to job success in a variety of occupations. The samples used in these studies, however, were small, the N's ranging from 26 to 62.

The manual also reports that test efficiency indices (percentage correct predictions and utility/cost ratios) provide support for the TAV as a selection device.

Norms: Means and standard deviations are provided in the manual for the following occupational groups: state traffic officers; municipal patrolmen; female high school teachers; male high school teachers; life insurance claims adjusters; life insurance salesmen; deputy sheriff cadets; and female probation counselors. These data are not grouped by age or educational level.

Administration and Scoring: Since the average reading difficulty of the TAV is at the ninth-grade level, the test is appropriate for most adults. However, administration of the entire battery requires about $3\frac{1}{2}$ hours. Directions and scoring procedures vary from test to test, though each test produces one of 3 scores: T (toward people), A (away from people), or V (versus people). The battery may be scored by hand or machine. Scoring stencils are provided on request.

Comments: The TAV Selection System represents a unique approach to the measurement of personality. Although the battery would benefit from further refinement of the subtests and additional evidence of relationship to relevant and well defined external criteria, it shows promise for counseling and personal selection. Use of the TAV, however, may be limited by its length.

References: Crites, J. O., "Test reviews." *Journal of Counseling Psychology*, 1969, **16**(2), 181–184.

Hankey, R. O., R. R. Morman, H. L. Heywood, and P. K. Kennedy, "Evaluating patrolman performance: A new test method." *Police Chief*, 1967, **34**, 33–35.

Horney, K., *Our inner conflicts: A constructive theory of neurosis.* New York: W. W. Norton, 1945.

Morman, R. R., *TAV selection system.* North Hollywood, California: John P. Smith Press, 1968.

Morman, R. R., L. R. Liddle, H. L. Heywood, R. O. Hankey, and J. Duvlick, "High school teaching effectiveness." *Journal of Secondary Education*, 1965, **40**(6), 270–274.

Name: TEACHER CHARACTERISTICS SCHEDULE

Author: David G. Ryans

Type of Measure: Self-report questionnaire

Availability: Ryans, D. G. *Teacher characteristics schedule. Revised form G-70/2.* Honolulu, Hawaii: Teacher Characteristics Study, University of Hawaii, 1970. Earlier forms of the test appear in: Ryans, D. G. *Characteristics of teachers.* Washington, D. C.: American Council on Education, 1960.

Description: The Teacher Characteristics Schedule assesses the experiences, activities, preferences, and values of teachers. The current form, G-70/2, is an updated and extended revision of the original Teacher Characteristics Schedule, which was developed during the 1950s. While the original form was the product of extensive classroom observations, item analyses, and validity checks, the revision was based primarily on factor analyses of the responses of 2,000 teachers. The 2 versions, however, are similar. The addition to the new form of 9 scales reflecting "life views" or "values" is the major difference between the 2 instruments.

Form G-70/2 consists of 450 items and 20 scales, examples of which are: Kindly Teaching Behavior; Organized Teaching Behavior; Traditional Educational Viewpoints; Permissive Educational Viewpoints; General Adjustment; Altruism/Benevolence; Work/Conformance; and Competition. One scale, Valid Response, is intended to identify individuals with a strong tendency to give socially acceptable responses.

Sample Items: For every item on the Teacher Characteristics Schedule, the respondent selects 1 of several response alternatives. The nature of the items, however, varies considerably. Some items ask questions; others require the subject to express his or her preference for 1 of 2 drawings; and still others present statements with which the subject must agree or disagree on a 4-point scale. The following items and response alternatives are similar to those on the Schedule:

Item

1. Suppose a pupil approached you at the beginning of class and said, "I wrote an essay. Can you look at it now?" How would you respond?

  A. "I'll accept it now and read it in a little while."
  B. "I can't accept it now. Class is starting."
  C. "Thank you. I'd like to read it."

2. Which of the following best describes you?

  A. Creative
  B. Agreeable
  C. Productive

Item

3. Approximately what proportion
   of high school classes are
   extremely hard to control?

   A. 0%
   B. 5–10%
   C. 10–20%
   D. 20–30%

4. Who influenced your decision to
   become a teacher?

   A. Nobody
   B. Relatives
   C. A former teacher
   D. Guidance counselor
   E. Acquaintances

5. I hope that any children I have
   are not interested or active
   in athletics.

   A. Strongly Disagree
   B. Tend to Disagree
   C. Tend to Agree
   D. Strongly Agree

Reliabilities: Alpha reliabilities for the scales of the revised Teacher Characteristics Schedule, based on 3 samples of teachers and student teachers (total $N = 3,963$), ranged from .43 to .81, with most being in the .70s. The Friends and Social Contacts scale produced the lowest alpha coefficients (.50, .43, and .60), while the Traditional Educational Viewpoints and Dedication to Teaching scales yielded the highest (.81, .79, .76, .81 and .77, .78, respectively). Stability and equivalence estimates for the original Teacher Characteristics Schedule fell between .70 and .80.

Validity: Little validity information is available for the revised form of the Schedule. However, since the old and new scales are similar, some validity for the new form may be inferred from statistics derived with the original form. Scores on the original form were obtained for a variety of teacher samples and correlated with observations of teacher classroom behavior and inquiries relating to certain traits, such as attitudes and verbal ability. Concurrent validity coefficients ranged from .20 to .50; cross-validity coefficients fell between .40 and .60; and coefficients of predictive validity exceeded .20 in only 3 instances (Ryans, 1961).

Norms: For form G-70/2, means and standard deviations are provided for 441 student teachers at the University of Hawaii and 3,248 inservice teachers in public schools throughout the United States. These samples include males and females from both elementary and secondary teaching levels (Ryans, 1972).

Administration and Scoring: The Teacher Characteristics Schedule is presented in a 46-page, reusable booklet, which is accompanied by 2 response sheets. Directions are printed inside the test booklet, and keys are provided for scoring.

Comments: The Teacher Characteristics Schedule is a carefully constructed instrument, which yields a wealth of information about teachers. The Schedule is long, but item content is varied and interesting. Although validity data are needed for the revised form, this instrument is a valuable research tool.

References: Ryans, D. G. *Characteristics of teachers.* Washington, D.C.: American Council on Education, 1960.

Ryans, D. G., "Inventory estimated teacher characteristics as covariants of observer assessed pupil behavior." *Journal of Educational Psychology,* 1961, **52**(2), 91–97.

Ryans, D. G., *Notes on Teacher Characteristics Schedule scores of (1) University of Hawaii student teachers (1972), (2) 1972 national (U.S.) sample of in-service teachers, (3) 1972 Hawaii in-service teacher sample.* Mimeo, University of Hawaii, 1972.

Ryans, D. G., *Teacher characteristics schedule. Revised form G-70/2.* Honolulu, Hawaii: Teacher Characteristics Study, University of Hawaii, 1970.

Name: TEACHER CONCERNS CHECKLIST

Authors: Frances Fuller and Gary Borich

Type of Measure: Self-report questionnaire

Availability: Fuller, F. F., and G. D. Borich, *Teacher Concerns Checklist*. Austin, Texas: Research and Development Center for Teacher Education, University of Texas, 1974.

Description: The Teacher Concerns Checklist (TCC) assesses the concerns of teachers at different points in their careers. This self-report, multiple-choice instrument consists of 50 items classified into the following 3 subscales: (1) Teacher Self-Concerns; (2) Situational Concerns (focused on the teaching task and the learning environment); and (3) Student Concerns (focused on the impact of one's teaching). The conceptual basis of this instrument is Fuller's (1969) Concerns Theory, which views the learning process as a natural flow from concerns about Self to concerns about Task (teaching) and then Impact (pupil). The Checklist can be used to relate level of concerns to other teacher behaviors. Responses can be examined in terms of: (1) the respondent's level of training; (2) the degree of inference from the measured behavior to classroom performance; and (3) the relationship of the measured behavior to the affective or cognitive objectives of the respondent.

Sample Items: Sample items from each of the 3 subscales appear below. The teacher indicates on a 5-point scale the degree to which each item reflects his or her current concerns.

Self Concerns
  Getting a favorable evaluation of my teaching
  Being accepted and respected by professional persons
  Doing well when a supervisor is present

Situational (Task) Concerns
  Frustrated by the routine and inflexibility of the situation
  Lack of instructional materials
  Too many noninstructional duties

Student Needs (Impact) Concerns
  Whether each student is getting what he or she needs
  Guiding students toward intellectual and emotional growth
  Whether students can apply what they learn

Reliability: The internal consistency of the 3 subscales of the Teacher Concerns Checklist is indicated by alpha coefficients of .86, .79, and .91 for Factor 1 (Self Concerns), Factor 2 (Situational Concerns) and Factor 3 (Student Needs Concerns), respectively. Test/retest correlations over a 1-week interval were .87, .80 and .77 for the 3 factors. Both analyses were based on a sample of 680 preservice and inservice teachers.

Validity: The TCC is behaviorally based, having been derived from analyses of recorded typescripts of student teaching seminars and interviews with student teachers. These records, collected over an extended period of time, were used in the identification and classification of problems and concerns of student teachers. These expressed concerns were grouped into developmental and sequential stages. The early concerns of student teachers were characterized by a preoccupation with self and self-protection, while the later concerns of student and inservice teachers involved the needs of others, relationships with others, and pupil learning.

Intercorrelations among the 3 scales of an early form of the TCC, computed on a sample of 335 preservice teachers, yielded coefficients of .23 between Factors 1 and 2, .48 between Factors 1 and 3, and .55 between Factors 2 and 3, indicating moderate scale independence.

The TCC has revealed differences between preservice and inservice samples for each of the 3 factors. Preservice teachers showed significantly greater self-concerns ($p < .001$) and significantly fewer situational concerns ($p < .001$) than inservice teachers. Group differences were expected between inservice and preservice teachers on Factor 3, concern for student needs, but these did not occur. This was due in part to the fact that both groups responded at the high end of the scale, producing a negatively skewed distribution. Modifications have been incorporated within the revised instrument in order to sharpen distinctions between preservice and inservice teachers on the student needs dimension.

Norms: The TCC has been used in several studies of preservice and inservice teachers, all of which are reported in George, Borich, and Fuller (1974). Subscale and item means are provided for both groups.

Procedures for Use: The TCC consists of 50 Likert-scaled items which require about 10 minutes to complete and can be hand or machine scored. Each statement is scored from 1 ("not concerned") to 5 ("totally preoccupied with this concern"). Subscales are scored by adding individual item scores within each of the factors. A computer program is available (though not necessary) for scoring the instrument.

Comments: The Teacher Concerns Checklist is an easily administered, quickly scored instrument which can tap major areas of teacher concerns. The instrument has high reliability and indications of validity, and can be used effectively with both inservice and preservice teachers. The framework for analyzing teacher responses permits score interpretation not only in relation to self, task, and student concerns, but also with respect to cognitive and affective objectives.

References: Borich, G. D., and F. F. Fuller, *Teacher Concerns Checklist: An instrument for measuring concerns for self, task, and impact.* Austin, Texas: Research and Development Center for Teacher Education, University of Texas, 1975.

Fuller, F. F., "Concerns of teachers: A developmental conceptualization." *American Educational Research Journal*, 1969, **6**(2), 207–226.

George, A., G. D. Borich, and F. F. Fuller, *Progress report on research on the Teacher Concerns Checklist*. Austin, Texas: Research and Development Center for Teacher Education, University of Texas, 1974.

Name: TEACHER PRACTICES QUESTIONNAIRE

Authors: A. Garth Sorenson, T. R. Husek, and Constance Yu

Type of Measure: Rating scale

Availability: Sorenson, A. G., T. R. Husek, and C. Yu. "Divergent concepts of teacher role: An approach to the measurement of teacher effectiveness." *Journal of Educational Psychology*, 1963, **54**(6), 287–294. A copy of the instrument may also be obtained from the American Documentation Institute by requesting Document No. 7707 from the ADI Auxiliary Publication Project, Photoduplication Service, Library of Congress, Washington, D.C., 20540.

Description: The Teacher Practices Questionnaire (TPQ) is designed to assess teacher role expectations. The initial form of the instrument was based on a review of the literature pertaining to teacher behavior and on discussions with teachers, administrators, and teacher educators. From these 2 sources, 6 teacher roles were postulated: Advisor, Counselor, Disciplinarian, Information Giver, Motivator, and Referrer. A preliminary form, designed to measure these 6 dimensions, was administered to 284 education students. A factor analysis confirmed these 6 teacher roles but showed that many of the individual items did not load highly on the predicted factors. Therefore, 51 of the 120 items were rewritten for a second version of the questionnaire. This form was administered to 94 education students, and results were again factor analyzed. On the basis of this second factor analysis, a revised set of items was developed, and 2 of the scales, Advisor and Information Giver, were combined to form a single dimension, thus reducing the number of scales from 6 to 5. The final form consists of 30 problem situations, typical of those encountered by teachers daily, and a number of alternative solutions ("items") representing different role dimensions. This arrangement allows the subject to select among a variety of role behaviors, thereby providing a picture of his role expectations.

Sample Items: The subject's task is to respond to each of the 30 problem situations by rating the alternative solutions on a 5-step scale, ranging from "Very Appropriate" to "Very Inappropriate." Problems and response items similar to those on the TPQ appear on the following page.

Reliability: Split-half reliabilities for each of the role dimensions on the original scale fell between .75 and .92. For the final form split-half reliabilities ranged from .77 to .93. These estimates, however, should be interpreted with caution since they were computed on data which were used in part to select the scales. The authors of the TPQ suggest that these coefficients be treated as upper limits for the reliabilities (Sorenson, Husek, and Yu, 1963).

Validity: Evidence for the validity of the TPQ is scarce. Content validity is suggested by the comments of randomly selected subjects, who consistently reported that the problem situations presented in the test were realistic and

Problem	*Items*	*Scale*
I. Lately a number of fourth-grade pupils have complained that their pencils and erasers have been disappearing. Mary is discovered to have taken the missing items. She comes from a middle-class home and apparently has no need to steal.	1. Tell Mary's parents about her behavior and leave the problem in their hands.	Referrer
	2. Talk to Mary and help her understand why the other students are annoyed about losing their pencils and erasers.	Motivator
	3. Tell Mary that if she steals again, she will be suspended from school.	Disciplinarian
II. Mike, a sophomore student in computer science, is uncertain about his career choice. He likes computer science, makes good grades, and foresees a financially profitable future in this field. However, he is also very interested in journalism. He is altruistic and wonders if he can contribute more to society in the field of journalism.	1. Supply Mike with information about career opportunities and pay scales in both professions.	Motivator
	2. Tell him that there is a great demand for computer scientists in business, education and the space industry, and that he will be challenged by such a career.	Advisor/ Information-Giver
	3. Help him discover and analyze the causes of his vocational uncertainty.	Counselor

relevant. Some construct validity may be inferred from the procedures used in developing the TPQ. In no case was an item included on the test unless its loading on the appropriate factor was at least .40. Furthermore, the 5 revised scales showed low to moderate intercorrelations, though no attempt was made to obtain items as pure as possible, since the dimensions were not assumed to be entirely unrelated.

Norms: Means and standard deviations are provided for each of the 5 revised scales. These data were obtained from 94 education students (60 females and 34 males) at the University of California at Los Angeles. Most of the students in this sample were graduates, half of whom had 1 or more years of teaching experience.

Administration and Scoring: The TPQ is easily administered and scored. Each alternative is scored 1, 2, 3, 4, or 5, depending on how it is ranked by the respondent. All the items on each scale are summed yielding 5 scores, 1 for each role dimension.

Comments: The Teacher Practices Questionnaire appears to be a useful measure of teacher role expectations. While the reliability coefficients provided are adequate, considerably more evidence of validity, particularly criterion-related validity, is needed.

Reference: Sorenson, A. G., T. R. Husek, and C. Yu, "Divergent concepts of teacher role: An approach to the measurement of teacher effectiveness." *Journal of Educational Psychology*, 1963, **54**(6), 287–294.

Name: TEACHER PREFERENCE SCHEDULES

Authors: George G. Stern, Joseph Masling, Barnett Denton, John Henderson, and Rachel Levin

Type of measure: Rating scale

Availability: This instrument is described in: Stern, G. G., J. Masling, B. Denton, J. Henderson, and R. Levin. "Two scales for the assessment of unconscious motivations for teaching." *Educational and Psychological Measurement*, 1960, **20**, 9–29.

Description: The Teacher Preference Schedules (TPS) contain two scales: Form G, which assesses personal gratifications derived from teaching; and Form A, which assesses the attitudes supporting and justifying these gratifications. Together, the 2 forms measure unconscious motivations for teaching.

   The TPS underwent a long development process, the first stage of which involved the preparation of 18 teacher role descriptions, which were subsequently used by a panel of educators to identify 29 teachers representing each role type. These 29 teachers were then individually interviewed and administered 10 TAT cards, an 80-item Q sort, and the Stern Activities Index. Data collected from these sources were compiled to form a comprehensive case study of each teacher. Case studies were examined in turn, and unconscious motives for teaching were inferred from expressed gratifications, each of which was buttressed by an appropriate attitude and needs system. The 10 motives selected proved consistent with the role categories to which the teachers had originally been nominated.

   These motives are represented on the 10 scales of each TPS form: Practical, Status-Striving, Nurturant, Nondirective, Critical, Preadult-Fixated, Orderly, Dependent, Exhibitionistic, and Dominant. Material in the teachers' case studies provided a basic pool of items for constructing both the Attitude and Gratification scales.

Sample Items: Both forms of the TPS consist of 100 items. The Gratification form requires the teacher to respond on a 6-point scale, ranging from "strong dislike, disapproval" to "strong liking, preference, approval." The Attitude form also includes a 6-point response scale, ranging from "strong disagreement" to "strong agreement." Items of the following type appear on the TPS:

Scale	Form	Item
Nurturant	Gratification	1. Having a pupil respond to me as if I were his or her parent.
	Attitude	2. A pupil's primary need is for acceptance and warmth.

Scale	Form	Item
Preadult-Fixated	Gratification	1. Being included in the pupils' games and activities.
	Attitude	2. The ability to recall the nature of childhood helps a teacher in dealing with children.

Reliability: Test/retest reliabilities were computed over a 3- to 4-week interval on a sample of 53 teachers enrolled in summer session graduate education courses at Syracuse University. Coefficients for the 10 TPS scales ranged from .65 to .83 for Form A and from .68 to .86 for Form G.

Estimates of the internal consistency of each scale were derived by comparing the upper and lower 27% of score distributions obtained from 3 samples: 105 freshmen at Cortland State Teachers College; 42 seniors in the School of Education at Syracuse University; and 98 teachers enrolled in summer session graduate courses at Syracuse University. Using a procedure described by Ebel (1954), the average item discrimination was determined for each scale. The lowest scale average was .26—higher than the value of .20 suggested by Ebel as indicating significant discriminating power. Most of the remaining averages were above .40 (Stern, Masling, Denton, Henderson, and Levin, 1960).

Validity: Scale intercorrelations revealed that the TPS contains 2 groups of 4 related scales, 1 of which can be described as child-centered and the other as teacher-centered. Although means for both undergraduate samples (the Cortland freshmen and the Syracuse seniors) were higher on the student-centered than the teacher-centered scales, the TPS did differentiate the two populations. Syracuse practice teachers, for example, rejected the teacher-centered scales to a greater extent than the Cortland freshmen did. Also, Syracuse means were consistently lower on the Practical, Dominant, and Orderly scales and higher on the Nondirective and Nurturant scales of both TPS forms (Stern et al., 1960).

The TPS has also differentiated between elementary and secondary teaching candidates (Davis and Yamamoto, 1968). Prospective elementary and early childhood teachers scored significantly higher than secondary candidates on 4 of the TPS Gratification scales (i.e., Orderly, Dependent, Exhibitionistic, and Preadult-Fixated) and on 2 of the Attitude scales (Orderly and Dependent). In addition, elementary students scored significantly higher than secondary candidates on the Preadult-Fixated scale, while early childhood students were significantly higher on the Exhibitionistic scale.

Norms: Means and standard deviations are provided for 105 freshmen (30 males, 75 females) at Cortland State Teachers College and 42 seniors (all female) enrolled in the School of Education at Syracuse University (Stern et al., 1960).

Administration and Scoring: The two forms of the TPS are self-administering, each requiring 25 to 40 minutes to complete. Responses are recorded on a special answer sheet and are assigned numerical values for scoring. The answer sheet is arranged so that the 10 scales on each form can be machine scored.

Comments: Stern and his associates exercised care in developing the Teacher Preference Schedules, and in so doing produced a useful measure of two components (gratification and attitude) of unconscious motivation for teaching. Although more extensive normative and validity data are needed, the TPS appears to be a valuable research tool.

References: Davis, O. L., Jr., and K. Yamamoto, "Teachers in preparation: II. Professional attitudes and motivations." *Journal of Teacher Education*, 1968, **19**, 365–369.

Ebel, R. L., Procedures for analysis of classroom tests. *Educational and Psychological Measurement*, 1954, **14**, 352–364.

Stern, G. G., J. Masling, B. Denton, J. Henderson, and R. Levin. "Two scales for the assessment of unconscious motivations for teaching." *Educational and Psychological Measurement*, 1960, **20**, 9–29.

Name: TEACHING ANXIETY SCALE

Author: Jane S. Parsons

Type of Measure: Rating scale

Availability: Parsons, J. S., *Assessment of anxiety about teaching using the Teaching Anxiety Scale: Manual and research report.* Austin, Texas: Research and Development Center for Teacher Education, The University of Texas, 1972.

Description: The Teaching Anxiety Scale (TCHAS) was designed to measure anxiety specifically related to teaching. Initially, 2 equivalent forms— TCHAS(1)–25 and TCHAS(2)–25—were developed for use with preservice, intern teachers. Subsequently, several slightly modified versions of the instrument—TCHAS(1)–24, TCHAS(1)–28, and TCHAS(1)–29—were made available for use with inservice teachers. The TCHAS(1)–29 is the form preferred by Parsons (1972), since it can be scored in a number of ways depending upon the kind of teachers being studied. This version consists of 25 items from 1 of the 2 original forms, plus 4 additional items. Approximately half of the items are negatively phrased and half are positively phrased. The statements are of 2 different types, some involving emotional reactions to various teaching situations and some involving attitudes toward the teaching profession.

Sample Items: The Teaching Anxiety Scale (1)–29 contains statements concerning reactions to teaching. Items of the following type are rated from 1 ("never") to 5 ("always"):

I feel confident about my ability to maintain control over a class.
I am not as happy teaching as I thought I would be.
I feel ill at ease speaking before a group.

Reliability: Both internal consistency and stability of the TCHAS are reported in the test manual (Parsons, 1972). The alpha coefficients for form (1)–29 are .90 ($N = 36$), and .94 ($N = 14$) for a sample of undergraduate preservice secondary education teachers, and .92 ($N = 30$) and .90 ($N = 20$) for a group of undergraduate preservice elementary education teachers. Alpha coefficients for other forms of the test range from .87 to .94. Form (1)–29 was also administered to 30 female undergraduates attending the University of Texas, and after an interval of 1 to 3 days, a test/retest coefficient of .95 was obtained.

Validity: Validity of the scale was determined by several different methods. First, the TCHAS was correlated with two other measures of anxiety, the Taylor Manifest Anxiety Scale (MAS) (Taylor, 1953) and the Test Anxiety Scale (TAS) (Sarason, 1957). Correlations between several forms of the TCHAS and the Manifest Anxiety Scale (administered concurrently to 55 preservice intern teachers) ranged from .30 to .45 and were significant at the .05 level. Correlations between the TCHAS and the Test Anxiety Scale (which were administered

1 month apart to the same 55 subjects) ranged from .25 to .34 (Parsons, 1972). These results indicate that the TCHAS shares common variance with both the MAS and the TAS. However, the TCHAS also has a unique component related to the construct of teaching anxiety. Using a procedure suggested by Cronbach (1960), Parsons (1972) found that 86% and 76% of what the TCHAS measures is reliable (error-free) and independent of what is measured by the TAS and the MAS, respectively.

The TCHAS was also correlated with the Anxiety Self Report (ASR), another test which measures anxiety specific to the task of teaching. A correlation of .62 was obtained, which is considerably higher than the correlation between TCHAS and the MAS or the TAS. According to Campbell and Fiske (1959), the high correlation between the TCHAS and the ASR, in combination with the moderate correlations between TCHAS and the general anxiety measures, indicates that the scale's validity coefficients are not unduly influenced by peripheral variables, such as the tendency of respondents to answer in a socially desirable way.

Also reported in the manual is the relationship between preservice teachers' responses on the TCHAS and supervisors' judgments of the teachers. Twenty-five teaching supervisors completed 19 TCHAS items about each of their preservice interns, and each intern then completed the same items about himself or herself. Correlations between the 2 sets of responses ranged from .24 to .54, with 11 out of 19 being significant.

In a study by Parsons (1970), teaching supervisors selected 31 "most anxious" and 49 "least anxious" graduate preservice interns. The "most anxious" group had a significantly higher mean score on the TCHAS than did the "least anxious" group.

The results of two factor analyses, reported in the manual, suggest that the original form of the scale, TCHAS (1)–25, and the preferred form, TCHAS (1)–29, are not pure, single-factor measures of teaching anxiety. When such a measure is needed, Parsons recommends that form (1)–22 of the TCHAS be used. This form eliminates the 3 items on the original form which represent a second factor.

Norms: Norms are provided for 200 preservice teachers from Stanford University and the University of Texas at Austin, including males and females, graduates and undergraduates, elementary and secondary education majors. Normative data are also supplied for 407 inservice teachers, both elementary and secondary, males and females, from Austin and San Francisco.

Administration and Scoring: The TCHAS can be self-administered. Approximately half of the items on each form are positively phrased, and half are negatively phrased. High agreement with 1 type of item suggests high anxiety, while agreement with the other suggests low anxiety. Positively phrased items are scored in reverse in order to produce item scores with consistent meaning. This scoring procedure cancels out the effects of an acquiescent response set (the tendency to agree to the same extent with all items). The total score is calculated by summing the item scores. A high score reflects a high degree of admitted anxiety.

Comments: The Teaching Anxiety Scale is a sufficiently reliable and valid instrument for research use. The author suggests that it be used to gather information about the relationship of anxiety to the acquisition of teaching skills, or about changes in anxiety level during teacher training. She also indicates that the scale should not at this point be used for selection, diagnosis, or evaluation of individual teachers (Parsons, 1972).

References: Campbell, D. T., and D. W. Fiske, Convergent and discriminant validation by the multitrait-multimethod matrix. *Psychological Bulletin,* 1959, **56**, 81–105.

Cronbach, L. J., *Essentials of psychological testing* (2nd ed.). New York: Harper and Row, 1960.

Parsons, J. S., *Anxiety and teaching competence.* Unpublished doctoral dissertation, Stanford University, 1970.

Parsons, J. S., *Assessment of anxiety about teaching using the Teaching Anxiety Scale: Manual and research report.* Austin, Texas: Research and Development Center for Teacher Education, The University of Texas, 1972.

Sarason, I., "Test anxiety, general anxiety, and intellectual performance." *Journal of Consulting Psychology,* 1957, **221**, 485–490.

Taylor, J. A., "A personality scale of manifest anxiety." *Journal of Abnormal and Social Psychology,* 1953, **48**, 285–290.

Name: TEACHING SITUATION REACTION TEST

Authors: John B. Hough and James K. Duncan

Type of Measure: Rating scale

Availability: Duncan, J. K., and J. B. Hough, *Technical review of the Teaching Situation Reaction Test.* Morgantown, West Virginia: College of Education, West Virginia University, undated.

Description: The Teaching Situation Reaction Test (TSRT) was designed to measure teacher attitudes toward classroom situations and to assess the effectiveness of student teaching programs. The original 36-item instrument was based on no clear theoretical framework; therefore, factors affecting total performance were not defined by the authors. The revised 48-item scale contains 9 clusters, each of which is represented by several classroom situations, covering planning, classroom management, and teacher/pupil relationships. For each of these 48 situations, the respondent is provided with 4 possible courses of action. He or she must rank these according to their appropriateness.

Sample Item: The subject ranks the TSRT alternatives by labeling the "most desirable choice" 1, and the "least desirable choice" 4. Situations and responses similar to the following are included on the TSRT:

The school system you work for is carrying out a research program, which includes the establishment of a class designed to improve pupils' general adjustment to their environment. A group of 25 students from 13 to 14 years old, heterogeneous as to physical, mental, and social characteristics, have enrolled in the class, which is entitled "Teen Topics."

The class is to meet during the last period on Tuesdays and Thursdays of the second semester. Class trips and informal discussions will be possible.

You have accepted the principal's invitation to teach the class. You have quite a lot of freedom in developing the course, with a teacher/counselor and plenty of instructional materials available to help you. The adjustment gains made by your pupils will be evaluated during and after the course.

Tomorrow is the first day of the class. It is important that you have planned for:
 (a) the pupils to get acquainted.
 (b) a clear explanation of your grading system.
 (c) activities to increase student interest.
 (d) a comprehensive explanation of your plans for the entire semester.

Reliability: Test/retest reliability has been investigated by the authors (Hough and Duncan, 1965). Eighty-four preservice teachers took the TSRT for the second time after an interval of 8 days; the reliability coefficient obtained on this group was .84.

Validity: Predictive validity of the TSRT was demonstrated in a study comparing student teaching grades and TSRT scores. A significant relationship was found ($r = .51$) between the two (Hough and Duncan, 1965). Similarly, TSRT scores of 10 student teachers ranked "best" by their supervisors were compared to those of 11 ranked "poorest" out of a group of 48, and a significant difference ($p < .05$) was obtained between the 2 sets of scores. Using the same procedure, the scores of inservice teachers rated "best" and "poorest" by administrators were compared. Again, a significant difference emerged between groups (Hough and Duncan, 1965).

Five studies of concurrent validity are reported by the authors (Hough and Duncan, 1965), who correlated TSRT scores with scores obtained on the Minnesota Teacher Attitude Inventory, the Barrett-Lennard Relationship Inventory, the California Test of Mental Maturity, and the Rokeach Dogmatism Scale. Significant but low correlations (.28 and .31) were found between the TSRT and the CTMM and MTAI, respectively. The meaning of these correlations is not explained by the authors.

Construct validity was studied by Murray (1969), who, after examining TSRT items, determined that 6 factors were present: Objectivity, Sociability, Control, Confidence, Reflectiveness, and Empathy. The factored TSRT scores of 238 preservice education students were related to the scores of the same subjects on the following measures: the Objectivity and Sociability scales of the Guilford-Zimmerman Temperament Survey; the California F Scale; the Confidence scale of the Sixteen Personality Factor Questionnaire; the Reflective scale of the Thurstone Temperament Schedule; and the Intraception (empathy) scale of the Edwards Personal Preference Schedule. Results indicated that TSRT scores correlated positively with measures of objectivity and empathy and negatively with measures of control. Duncan concluded that increased skill in reacting to classroom situations (reflected by high TSRT scores) is associated with greater concern for empathy and less for control.

The TSRT has also proved to be fake-resistant in 2 studies (Hough and Duncan, undated). A group of 35 subjects was told to respond to test items according to their actual feelings, while a second group was instructed to respond in a way which would ensure a "good" score. The 2 sets of scores did not differ significantly. When the same directions were given to 2 groups of 27 student teachers, again no significant differences were found.

Norms: Though no norms are provided for the third and most recent form of the TSRT, means and standard deviations are reported for four samples who completed the second revision.

Administration and Scoring: Directions for responding to the TSRT are printed on the form. The test is scored by comparing the respondent's rankings to a key, which is provided. Low scores indicate better performance and suggest behavior characterized by acceptance and empathy. High scores are indicative of rejecting, punitive, and controlling behavior.

Comments: The main weakness of the Teaching Situation Reaction Test is the absence of a theoretical foundation. In spite of the one factor analysis which has been performed on the test, there is still some question about what the instrument is measuring. This, however, could be clarified by further research. This instrument has potential as a pre- and posttest of student teacher performance, but since it is still in an experimental stage, it should be used only for research purposes at present.

References: Hough, J. B., and J. K. Duncan, *Exploratory studies of a Teaching Situation Reaction Test.* Paper read at the annual meeting of the American Educational Research Association, February, 1965.

Hough, J. B., and J. K. Duncan, *Technical review of the Teaching Situation Reaction Test.* Morgantown, West Virginia: College of Education, West Virginia University, undated.

Murray, K. C., "The construct validity of the Teaching Situation Reaction Test." *The Journal of Educational Research,* 1969, **62**, 323–328.

Name: TEST OF DIRECTED IMAGINATION

Authors: Donald J. Veldman and Shirley L. Menaker

Type of Measure: Projective test

Availability: Veldman, D. J., and S. L. Menaker, *Directed imagination.* Austin, Texas: Authors, 1962. This instrument is also available in: Lewis, C. L., and S. L. Menaker, *Clinical interpretation of the Test of Directed Imagination.* Austin, Texas: Personal-Professional Development Systems, The Research and Development Center for Teacher Education, The University of Texas, 1970.

Description: The Test of Directed Imagination (DI) was developed as 1 instrument in a battery designed to help professors and counselors in the teacher education program at The University of Texas to understand their students. It requires the examinee to compose 4 fictional stories about "teachers and their experiences." The examinee's own interests and characteristics are thereby projected in the stories, as they are in the Thematic Apperception Test. The individual's general personality characteristics can be assessed by interpreting these stories according to the following specified indicators: (1) Coherence and Handwriting; (2) Teacher Characteristics, including role identification, self-ability, empathy, and coping activities; (3) Children Characteristics; (4) Other Persons introduced; (5) Interaction Characteristics, including affect and activity; and (6) Themes. Although the authors intended the DI for use with prospective teachers, it can, with modification, be applied to other populations. DI protocols can be used for individual assessment and counseling.

Sample Items: Examinees respond to the DI by writing 4 fictional stories. Subject matter is limited to "teachers and their experiences," and 4 minutes are allowed for composing each story.

Reliability: The reliability of DI interpretations was examined by correlating ratings (1) across stories within protocols, (2) across raters of the same protocols, and (3) between 2 protocols from each subject. The first set of computations, based on 500 protocols, yielded intraclass correlations among the 4 story ratings, which ranged from .62 to .84. Intraclass correlations between 2 raters of the same protocol, based on 250 protocols (2 from each subject), ranged from .53 to .82. The third set of calculations—Pearson correlations between rater-sum scores derived from 2 testings of 125 subjects, over an 18-month interval—ranged from .05 to .49. Because the experiences of the subjects during the interval between testings were varied, these coefficients were not considered an adequate representation of retest stability.

These reliability studies were based on the original scoring system, which utilized 6 broad criteria (Structural Features, Interest Qualities, Emotional Features, Characteristics and Activity Level, Role Identity, and Self-Ability and Confidence) each subsuming separate scales (Veldman and Menaker, 1969).

This scoring system is similar to the one presently recommended. There is not yet enough evidence to determine which scoring procedure is the more reliable.

Validity: Four validity studies are reported by Veldman and Menaker (1969). The first demonstrated that the DI yields information which differentiates elementary and secondary teachers. The second indicated that DI ratings can be effectively used to help prospective teachers maintain and perhaps improve their perceptions of teaching. One hundred and twenty-five students in the College of Education at The University of Texas were administered the DI and other personality assessment instruments at the beginning and at the end of their coursework. Ninety-five of these subjects (the experimental group) received feedback counseling on their personality assessment data, while the remaining 30 did not. Results of the second DI administration indicated that the stories of experimental subjects changed very little (except to become more imaginative), while those of control subjects became less organized, less imaginative, and less student-centered.

The third validity study involved a follow-up of elementary education majors 2 years after their graduation from The University of Texas. Their retrospective views of training and their professional activities and plans were collected. Based on these data, the sample was divided into two groups, 1 showing a relatively weak commitment to teaching and the other a strong commitment. DI data on these subjects (which had been collected 2 years earlier) were then analyzed, and it was found that the strong commitment group had written stories higher in optimism, coherence, self-confidence, and educational content. These stories also dealt more actively with problems, indicated more appropriate actions, resolved more completely the problems raised, and demonstrated a higher level of general adjustment.

The final validity study cited compared the DI stories of experimental subjects who sought additional counseling and those who did not. Those who sought additional counseling had written less coherent stories, demonstrating more pessimism, less confidence in personal ability, more passive coping behavior, less appropriate action, less effective problem resolution, and lower levels of general adjustment.

Norms: Norms are composed of 2 protocols, completed over an 18-month interval, from each of 125 education majors at The University of Texas. The authors plan to provide additional norms by collecting protocols from education students at The University of Texas at the beginning of a junior-year course in educational psychology (Veldman and Menaker, 1969).

Administration and Scoring: Each examinee is given 4 blank sheets of paper and instructed "to write 4 fictional stories about teachers and their experiences." Four minutes are allowed for completion of each story.

There are several procedures for scoring, the latest of which is described by Menaker and Lewis (1970) and illustrated with several sample protocols. The scorer uses a Story Rating Form on which to summarize his or her impressions under each of 6 interpretative areas. He or she then completes a Protocol Rating Form, evaluating the protocol as a whole.

For those who prefer a research-oriented rather than a clinical scoring procedure, a manual describing instructions for rating the DI on 11 variables is available (Veldman, Menaker, and Williams, 1970).

Comments: The Test of Directed Imagination shares the deficiencies common to most projective instruments, including inadequate standardization, lack of objectivity in administration and scoring, and incomplete information on reliability, validity and norms. Yet, when included as part of a battery of tests, the DI can be profitably used by skilled clinicians for individual assessment, prediction, counseling, and research.

References: Lewis, C. L., and S. L. Menaker, *Clinical interpretation of the Test of Directed Imagination.* Austin, Texas: Personal-Professional Development Systems, The Research and Development Center for Teacher Education, The University of Texas, 1970.

Veldman, D. J., and S. L. Menaker, "Directed imagination method for projective assessment of teacher candidates." *Journal of Educational Psychology,* 1969, **60**(3), 178–187.

Veldman, D. J., S. L. Menaker, and D. L. Williams, *Manual for scoring the Test of Directed Imagination (Adult).* Austin, Texas: Research and Development Center for Teacher Education, The University of Texas, 1970.

Name: A TEST OF TEACHER'S ABILITY TO JUDGE INTERPUPIL PREFERENCES

Authors: N. L. Gage, George S. Leavitt, and George C. Stone

Type of Measure: Sociometric questionnaire

Availability: Gage, N. L., G. S. Leavitt, and G. C. Stone, "Teachers' understanding of their pupils and pupils' ratings of their teachers." *Psychological Monographs*, 1955, **69** (21, Whole No. 406).

Description: The Test of Teacher's Ability to Judge Interpupil Preferences (TTAJIP), as described in Gage, Leavitt, and Stone (1955), consists of a sociometric questionnaire completed by pupils and an attempt by the teacher to predict the results of that questionnaire. The score obtained is a correlational accuracy score.

   The test has no specific length. It varies according to class size. However, since class size may have some bearing on a teacher's ability to perceive interpupil relationships, it is recommended that groups tested fall within the size range used by Gage, Leavitt, and Stone, which was 19 to 40 pupils.

   The TTAJIP procedure seems appropriate for almost any age group, as long as the instructions are modified according to the reading and comprehension level of the subjects.

Sample Items: The TTAJIP does not contain items, per se. The teacher is simply given a set of instructions similar to the following:

We are trying to measure your ability to perceive pupils' preferences for each other.

The pupils in your class are going to name 5 classmates whom they would most like to have in their class. You are to predict what their preferences will be. You are to: (1) write the names of your students in alphabetical order, and (2) after each name, indicate 2 of the pupils he or she will choose as preferred classmates.

Students are also provided with instructions. They are told to list, in order of preference, the 5 pupils with whom they would most like to be in a classroom group. They are assured that answers are confidential.

Reliability: The test authors could not find a statistical method appropriate for assessing the reliability of the kind of data produced by the TTAJIP. Therefore, no reliability data are available.

Validity: Gage, Leavitt, and Stone (1955) report a correlation of .28 between TTAJIP scores and students' responses to: "(Teacher) knows whom I like best in this class." This correlation was based on 103 cases and was considered significantly greater than zero. The test authors also report that this correlation was significantly higher for teachers who had previously obtained sociometric data from their children than for those who had not solicited such information.

The correlation between socioeconomic status of pupils measured by a 5-item inventory reported in Gage, Leavitt, and Stone (1955), and TTAJIP scores of teachers was .27. The authors provided 3 alternative explanations of this finding: (1) high SES pupils are more socially active; (2) high SES pupils demonstrate more group cleavage; and (3) the preferences of high SES pupils are more similar to those of the teachers.

Gage, Leavitt, and Stone (1955) also found that TTAJIP scores did not correlate significantly with the pupils' overall evaluation of the teacher.

Norms: No norms are available for the TTAJIP, and none are needed for this kind of measure, other than to emphasize differences related to class, race, sex, or region.

Administration and Scoring: The instructions supplied in Gage, Leavitt, and Stone (1955) are self-explanatory; the test user need only present a copy to the teacher and the students. For some pupils, however, it may be necessary for the examiner to read the instructions aloud.

Scoring is fairly complicated. "Specific" accuracy is assessed by giving a point for each correct prediction made by the teacher and dividing the sum of these points by the number of pupils in the class, in order to correct for different class sizes. To correct for the smaller probability of chance accuracy in larger classes, the test authors also correlated the number-right/class-size ratio with class size and used the resulting coefficient to obtain a "regression-corrected ratio score."

Overall correlational accuracy is measured by counting the number of nominations the teacher predicted each student would receive. This number is then correlated with the number of nominations each student actually did receive.

Comments: The Test of Teacher's Ability to Judge Interpupil Preferences provides a good measure of the teacher's awareness of interpersonal relationships among students. Although the reliability of this procedure will be difficult to establish, further efforts at validation should present no problem. Although scoring is somewhat cumbersome, it could be simplified through revision of the scoring procedure or use of a computer.

Reference: Gage, N. L., G. S. Leavitt, and G. C. Stone, "Teacher's understanding of their pupils and pupils' ratings of their teachers." *Psychological Monographs*, 1955, **69** (21, Whole No. 406).

Name: WHICH QUESTION IS HARDER?

Authors: N. L. Gage, G. S. Leavitt, and G. C. Stone

Type of Measure: Rating scale

Availability: The measure is described in Gage, N. L., G. S. Leavitt, and G. C. Stone, "Teachers' understanding of their pupils and pupils' rating of their teachers." *Psychological Monographs*, 1955, **69** (21, Whole No. 406).

Description: The Which Question is Harder Test (WQHT) consists of 60 pairs of items drawn from a nationally standardized achievement test appropriate for children in grades 4 through 6. The subject, usually a teacher, selects the question in each pair which he or she considers the harder of the two. This answer is then compared to the absolute difficulty level of each item, determined during the standardization of the achievement test from which the questions were drawn.

    The WQHT was constructed for use with undergraduate elementary education students. Two developmental versions preceded the third and final form of the test. The first form presented items in sets of 10, rather than in pairs. The teacher was required to rank-order the items in each set in terms of relative difficulty. When this first form was administered to undergraduate elementary education majors, however, its reliability was so low that a second form was constructed, containing item pairs rather than 10-item sets. Items in each pair differed in absolute difficulty level from about 70% passing to 20% passing (i.e., the *difference* in percentage of students passing each item ranged from 20 to 70). Again the instrument demonstrated low reliability, so a third form was constructed, reducing the difference in difficulty level within each pair of items to 23 to 47% passing. This revision became the final form of the test.

Sample Items: A set of instructions, describing the purpose of the test and the nature of the task required, is presented to the teacher or education student. Subjects are instructed to read the entire item, including directions to the pupil and all possible response alternatives, before making a choice. The following pair of items is similar to those which appear on the test:

Which question is harder for fourth- to sixth-grade children?

A. Look at the following arithmetic problem and decide which operation to perform first.

$$\frac{1 - 5X[3 + (2 \times 6)]}{4} = N$$

    1. add   2. subtract   3. multiply   4. divide

B. Choose the correct answer to the following arithmetic problem.

    Al gets in a train going south at 50 miles per hour. Joe walks north from the train station at 5 miles per hour. In 1 hour and 30 minutes, how far apart will they be?

    1. 55 miles   2. 75.2 miles   3. 80 miles   4. 82.5 miles

Reliability: Gage, Leavitt, and Stone (1955) administered the final form of the WQHT to 103 undergraduate elementary education majors and obtained a Kuder-Richardson (formula 20) reliability coefficient of .45.

Validity: Empirical validity is established primarily through group differences. Gage et al. (1955) administered the WQHT to 103 teachers-in-training and to 103 inservice teachers. The mean scores of these two groups differed significantly ($p < .01$), with experienced teachers showing greater accuracy in predicting the difficulty of cognitive questions. The biserial correlation between the WQHT scores and teaching experience was .32. Among experienced teachers, group differences also emerged in regard to sex and grade level taught. Male teachers scored significantly ($p < .05$) lower than female teachers on the WQHT, and fourth-grade teachers scored significantly higher ($p < .05$) than fifth- and sixth-grade teachers.

   The authors (Gage et al., 1955) point out that while the WQHT has logical validity, its validity as a correlate of teaching effectiveness might be improved if (1) it measured knowledge of absolute rather than relative difficulty of cognitive tasks, and if (2) it were scored in relation to the achievement test scores of the teacher's own students rather than those of a national sample.

Norms: Gage et al. (1955) present means and standard deviations, by total group, by sex, and by grade level taught, for 103 inservice teachers.

Administration and Scoring: The WQHT is self-administering. Directions are read by the subject prior to completing the test. Scoring involves comparing the subject's choice with item difficulty levels determined by standardization data. When the 2 agree, 1 point is scored; when they differ, a 0 is given. Points are totalled to achieve a final score.

Comments: The Which Question is Harder Test appears to be a logical measure of teachers' accuracy in perceiving the intellectual abilities and skills of pupils. However, before this instrument is used as a practical device in teacher training, its reliability should be improved. This can perhaps be accomplished by using local data and absolute difficulty levels rather than relative difficulty levels and national data. Such an adjustment would also increase the test's validity, since teachers in various parts of the country encounter different training procedures and different students.

Reference: Gage, N. L., G. S. Leavitt, and G. C. Stone, "Teachers' understanding of their pupils and pupils' ratings of their teachers." *Psychological Monographs*, 1955, **69** (21, Whole No. 406).

IB

About the teacher from the pupil

Name: DIAGNOSTIC TEACHER-RATING SCALE

Author: Sister Mary Amatora

Type of Measure: Rating scale

Availability: Amatora, M., *Diagnostic teacher-rating scale*. Cincinnati, Ohio: Educators'-Employers' Tests and Services Associates, 1938.

Description: The Diagnostic Teacher-Rating Scale measures students' attitudes toward their teachers. The instrument was originally based on a list of teacher characteristics "liked" and "disliked" by a group of 200 children in grades 4 through 8. Three hundred teacher qualities were selected from this list. Items were written to represent these qualities and were organized on 7 scales: Liking for the Teacher; Ability to Explain; Kindliness, Friendliness, and Understanding; Fairness in Grading; Discipline; Amount of Work Required; and Liking for Lessons. Further revision reduced the number of items to 200, which were then sorted into 11 graduated categories, according to their estimated value. The 98 items determined most valuable were retained and arranged on 2 parallel forms (A and B), each containing 49 items, 7 on each scale. These 2 forms constitute the Diagnostic Check List, which is the major component of the Diagnostic Teacher-Rating Scale. The minor component is the Area Scale, a list of 7 questions corresponding to the 7 scales on the Check List.

Sample Items: The Area Scale contains questions which the student answers on a 5-point scale, ranging from "best" to "worst." The Diagnostic Check List, on the other hand, presents a series of qualities which may or may not apply to the teacher. The student simply checks those characteristics which he feels are typical of his teacher. The rating scale contains items of the following type:

Area Scale   *Best*   *Worst*

1. How clear are your teacher's explanations?	1	2	3	4	5
2. How much do you like your teacher?	1	2	3	4	5
3. How well does your teacher manage children in the classroom?	1	2	3	4	5

Diagnostic Check List

Scale I. Liking the Teacher

———1. Best teacher I've had.

———2. Smiles.

———3. Polite.

———4. Nice-looking.

———5. Doesn't keep the room neat.

———6. Doesn't have good sense of humor.

———7. Mean.

Reliability: The reliability of the Area Scale was investigated by Tschechtelin, Hipskind, and Remmers (1940). Using the split-half procedure on a group of 31 teachers and 610 students, they obtained coefficients ranging from .86 to .96.

The reliability of the Diagnostic Check List was estimated by correlating forms A and B. Data from a sample of 300 children produced coefficients ranging from .72 to .81 (reported in Buros, 1959).

Validity: Validity of the Diagnostic Teacher-Rating Scale can be approached in several ways (Remmers and Gage, 1955). First, since the instrument is designed to measure pupil attitudes, its validity may be assumed from its reliability. Or, if verbalized opinions are considered measures of attitude, the scale achieves construct validity to the extent to which it assesses verbalized opinions.

More concrete evidence of validity is provided by the scale's ability to differentiate between groups. A study by Tschechtelin, Hipskind, and Remmers (1940) indicates that scores discriminate between teachers selected by students as "best" and "poorest."

Correlations among the scales on the Diagnostic Check List and between the Area Scale and Diagnostic Check List also suggest validity. Correlations among the Check List scales are low (.06 to .33), while those between the Area Scale and the Check List are high (.74 to .90 for Form A, .75 to .91 for Form B).

Norms: Tentative norms are reported as percentile equivalents of the average ratings on each of the 7 scales.

Administration and Scoring: The Diagnostic Teacher-Rating Scale may be administered to students in grades 4 through 12 by principals, superintendents, supervisors, researchers, or teachers. When administered by the teacher being rated, suggestions are provided (Amatora, 1952) to insure honest responses from pupils. Though the scale is not timed, it usually takes about 30 minutes to complete.

The Area Scale is scored by adding the values of all responses to each of the 7 questions and then dividing each total by the number of pupils responding. Thus 7 scores are produced for the Area Scale. If a total score is desired, the 7 raw scores may be averaged.

The Diagnostic Check List is scored by computing the median number of items marked on each scale. The score for each scale is then found on a table. A total score for the Check List may be determined by finding the median value of these 7 scale scores.

The 2 parts of the instrument may be compared to find strengths, weaknesses, and areas needing improvement.

Comments: Although developed in 1938, the Diagnostic Teacher-Rating Scale remains a useful measure of students' attitudes toward the teacher, since item content is not at all dated. This scale has been frequently used in spite of insufficient validity and normative data. Evidence of criterion-related validity, along with updated norms, would increase the value of this instrument.

References: Amatora, M., "Can elementary school children discriminate traits in their teachers?" *Child Development*, 1952, **23**, 75–79.

Amatora, M., "A diagnostic teacher-rating scale." *Journal of Psychology*, 1950, **80**, 395–399.

Amatora, M., *"Manual of directions for Diagnostic Teacher-Rating Scale."* Cincinnati, Ohio: Educators'-Employers' Tests and Services Associates, 1952.

Buros, O. K., *The fifth mental measurements yearbook.* Highland Park, New Jersey: The Gryphon Press, 1959.

Remmers, H. H., and N. L. Gage, *Educational measurement and evaluation.* New York: Harper & Brothers, 1955.

Tschechtelin, M. A., M. J. F. Hipskind, and H. H. Remmers, "Measuring the attitudes of elementary-school children toward their teachers." *Journal of Educational Psychology*, 1940, **31**(3), 195–203.

Wrightsone, J. W., J. Justman, and I. Robbins, *"Evaluation in modern education."* New York: American Book Co., 1956.

Name: THE ILLINOIS COURSE EVALUATION QUESTIONNAIRE

Author: Lawrence M. Aleamoni

Type of Measure: Questionnaire

Availability: Aleamoni, L. M., *The Illinois course evaluation questionnaire.* Urbana, Illinois: Measurement and Research Division, Office of Instructional Resources, University of Illinois, 1972. A copy of Form 66 can also be found in: Aleamoni, L. M., and R. E. Spencer, "The Illinois Course Evaluation Questionnaire: A description of its development and a report of some of its results." *Educational and Psychological Measurement,* 1973, **33**, 669–684.

Description: The Illinois Course Evaluation Questionnaire (CEQ) provides for student evaluation of courses and instructors. The original 1,000 items were based on criteria of effective instruction which were derived from an extensive review of the literature and suggestions from student and faculty committees at Pennsylvania State University. Following a trial administration of the instrument and factor analysis of the results obtained, 450 items were selected. Experimental forms of the test were readministered to 2 undergraduate samples at Pennsylvania State University. Results were analyzed, 28 items were retained, and 22 new items were added. This 50-item questionnaire (Form 66) was subjected to factor analysis, which produced 6 subscores.

A final revision of the CEQ, Form 73, was developed in 1973 to eliminate redundancy in the first form. It contains 23 items and yields 5 subscores: General Course Attitude, Course Content, Method of Instruction, Interest and Attention of the Students, and the Instructor. In addition, the teacher may include optional items which he has devised or selected from a catalogue of supplementary items.

The CEQ was designed for use with college-level students, although its content appears appropriate for high school seniors and juniors. A variation of the scale, the Illinois Teacher Evaluation Questionnaire (Mahan, 1970), has been constructed specifically for use in high school classrooms, but limited psychometric information is available on this form.

The CEQ can be used to provide information to both administrators and instructors in an effort to improve the quality of teaching.

Sample Items: The 23 items of Form 73 of the CEQ are followed by 4 response alternatives: Strongly Agree, Agree, Disagree, and Strongly Disagree. The instrument contains items of the following type:

1. I do not want to take another course from this instructor.
2. I would have preferred a different method of teaching in this course.
3. The instructor seemed to have an excellent knowledge of the subject matter.

Reliability: The reliability of the CEQ (Form 66) has been investigated in several different studies. Using split-half methods, 2 of these studies reported reliabilities of .92 and .93, corrected for length by the Spearman-Brown formula. The first study correlated negative and positive items, while the second correlated both halves of the negative items and both halves of positive items (reported in

Aleamoni, 1972). Reliabilities for each of the subscore areas were computed using the Kuder-Richardson formula 21 on the responses of students from 7 different courses. These ranged from .40 to .92, with Content being the least reliable subscale (Aleamoni and Spencer, 1973).

Gillmore (1972) also conducted several reliability studies. On a sample of 5,346 students, he obtained CEQ item reliabilities ranging from .73 to .94; subscale reliabilities ranged from .80 to .98. In a second study, using ratings of 103 instructors teaching 2 sections of the same course, he obtained item reliabilities ranging from .53 to .82. Dividing these sections into 2 groups and correlating odd and even items within each group, Gillmore found that coefficients ranged from .54 to .91 for Group I and from .67 to .91 for Group II.

Validity: Many different studies have investigated the validity of the CEQ (Form 66). Spencer and Dick (1965) related CEQ subscores to sex, term, curriculum, and final grade. Only final grade was significantly correlated with CEQ scores, a finding which is consistent with previous research.

Stallings and Spencer (1967) asked 10 measurement specialists and teaching assistants from the Speech Department of the University of Illinois to rate nine instructors. Their evaluations were correlated with student ratings, and a significant coefficient of .70 was obtained.

In a study by Swanson and Sisson (1971), a rank-order correlation of .70 was found between peer and student ratings of 12 instructors at Bowling Green State University. Aleamoni and Yimer (1972) found that colleague and student ratings on the CEQ were not significantly related to an instructor's research productivity. Yet, colleague ratings were significantly and positively related to an instructor's academic rank. This suggests that an instructor's reputation may also influence the ratings given him.

Finally, Aleamoni and Hexner (1973) found that students gave instructors higher ratings when they were told that their evaluations would be used in making salary and promotion decisions. These results suggest that information given preceding a course evaluation is an important variable to consider when administering the CEQ.

Norms: Normative data have been derived from the ratings of approximately 750 courses containing 2,784 sections and over 100,000 students at the University of Illinois. Additional normative information is provided on 5,346 course sections taught throughout the United States. These norms are continually updated.

Administration and Scoring: The CEQ is usually administered in the classroom over a 10-minute period. It is machine scored, and results are returned to the instructor. Average subscores and total scores with norm deciles are provided, along with specific item responses and their means and norm deciles. Pooled results for a number of sections of the same course may also be obtained.

Comments: The Illinois Course Evaluation Questionnaire is a well constructed instrument with adequate reliability, validity, and normative data provided for Form 66. The CEQ is an economical means of supplying feedback to individual instructors or evaluating the teaching process on a larger scale. The high school version, The Illinois Teacher Evaluation Questionnaire, should become equally useful with the accumulation of relevant psychometric data.

References: Aleamoni, L. M., *A review of recent reliability and validity studies of the Illinois Course Evaluation Questionnaire (CEQ).* Research Memorandum No. 127. Urbana, Illinois: Measurement and Research Division, Office of Instructional Resources, University of Illinois, 1972.

Aleamoni, L. M., *Evaluation by students to identify general instructional problems.* Urbana, Illinois: Measurement and Research Division, Office of Instructional Resources, University of Illinois, 1973.

Aleamoni, L. M., *The evaluation of instruction and the use of CEQ, Form 73.* Research Memorandum No. 152. Urbana, Illinois: Measurement and Research Division, Office of Instructional Resources, University of Illinois, 1974.

Aleamoni, L. M., and P. Z. Hexner, *The effect of different sets of instructions on student course and instructor evaluation.* Research Report 339. Urbana, Illinois: Measurement and Research Division, Office of Instructional Resources, University of Illinois, 1973.

Aleamoni, L. M., and R. E. Spencer, "The Illinois Course Evaluation Questionnaire: A description of its development and a report of some of its results." *Educational and Psychological Measurement,* 1973, **33**, 669–684.

Aleamoni, L. M., and M. Yimer, "An investigation of the relationship between colleague rating, student rating, research productivity, and academic rank in rating instructional effectiveness." *Journal of Educational Psychology,* 1973, **64**(3), 274–277.

Gillmore, G. M., *Estimates of reliability coefficients for items and subscales of the Illinois Course Evaluation Questionnaire.* Report No. 341. Urbana, Illinois: Measurement and Research Division, Office of Instructional Resources, University of Illinois, 1972.

Mahan, J. M., *Manual of interpretation for the Illinois Teacher Evaluation Questionnaire.* Research Report No. 316. Urbana, Illinois: Measurement and Research Division, Office of Instructional Resources, University of Illinois, 1970.

Spencer, R. E., and W. Dick, *Course evaluation questionnaire: Manual of interpretation.* Research Report No. 200. Urbana, Illinois: Measurement and Research Division, Office of Instructional Resources, University of Illinois, 1965.

Stallings, W. M., and R. E. Spencer, *Ratings of instructors in Accountancy 101 from video-tape clips.* Research Report No. 265. Urbana, Illinois: Measurement and Research Division, Office of Instructional Resources, University of Illinois, 1967.

Swanson, R. A., and D. J. Sisson, "The development, evaluation, and utilization of a departmental faculty appraisal system." *Journal of Industrial Teacher Education,* 1971, **1**, 64–79.

Name: LEADER BEHAVIOR DESCRIPTION QUESTIONNAIRE

Authors: John K. Hemphill and Alvin E. Coons

Type of Measure: Rating scale

Availability: This instrument may be obtained from the Bureau of Business Research, Ohio State University, Columbus, Ohio, 43210. A form adapted for educational use with administrators is available in: Halpin, A. W. *The leadership behavior of school superintendents.* Columbus, Ohio: Ohio State University, 1956.

Description: The Leader Behavior Description Questionnaire (LBDQ) is a Likert scale which contains 40 items representing 2 components of leadership behavior: Initiating Structure and Consideration. The former refers to behavior which clarifies the leader's role, establishes organizational patterns, and defines channels of communication, methods of goal attainment, and other task dimensions. Consideration, on the other hand, concerns the leader's interpersonal or socioemotional behavior.

The original version of the LBDQ was developed by Hemphill and Coons (1957) to provide a means for employees to rate supervisors. Subsequently, a modified 80-item form was developed on Air Force personnel (Halpin and Winer, 1952), and Halpin (1956) devised another version to be used in rating educational administrators.

Sample Items: Each item on the LBDQ is followed by 5 response alternatives ranging from "always" to "never." Fifteen items deal with Consideration, another 15 measure Initiating Structure, and an additional 10 are included as buffer items. The questionnaire contains items of the following type:

Scale	*Items*
Consideration	1. He favors certain staff members.
	2. He remains aloof from the staff.
	3. He accepts staff suggestions.
Initiating Structure	1. He promotes the use of standard procedures.
	2. He speaks in a way which discourages questions.
	3. He clarifies his expectations to the staff.

Reliability: Halpin (1956) provides estimates of split-half reliability for his version of the LBDQ. He reports coefficients of .83 for Initiating Structure and .92 for Consideration. The corresponding figures for "ideal self" ratings of leaders are .69 and .66.

Further reliability information is presented by Mitchell (1970). Using LBDQ ratings of the same leader from 3 different sources (the leader himself, group members, and outside observers), Mitchell obtained interrater reliability coefficients ranging from .35 to .46 for Consideration and from .38 to .60 for Initiating Structure. He also estimated internal consistency at .30 for Consideration and .75 for Initiating Structure.

Validity: Evidence for construct validity is provided by Hemphill (1955), who reports that college department heads ($N = 11$) reputed to be good administrators scored high on both Initiating Structure and Consideration. Mitchell (1970), however, questions the construct validity of the LBDQ, noting differences among leader, member, and observer ratings. He warns against assuming that a leader's self-report represents the same constructs as a group member's rating of leader behavior. Evidence suggests that the traits measured by the LBDQ may be perceived differently by leaders and members. Furthermore, the instrument is easily faked.

Norms: The LBDQ has been administered to a total of 395 aircraft commanders and 280 crewmen as well as 64 educational administrators. Mitchell (1970) used 105 male university students in his study.

Administration and Scoring: The LBDQ is self-administering and can be completed by leaders, their subordinates, or outside observers in 10 to 20 minutes. Respondents can be asked to describe actual or ideal behavior. Leadership scores are computed by averaging the ratings completed by subordinates. A scoring key is provided to facilitate this process. The authors recommend leadership scores be based on the responses of at least 4 subordinates.

The 5 responses for each item are scored 4, 3, 2, 1, and 0 for positive items and reversed for negative items.

Comments: Though not originally designed for use in educational settings, the LBDQ has been effectively adapted for that purpose. Because it can be easily faked, the LBDQ should probably be used in conjunction with other measures of leader behavior. Since interrater reliability is low and construct validity questionable, care should be exercised in interpreting LBDQ results.

References: Halpin, A. W., *The leadership behavior of school superintendents*. Columbus, Ohio: Ohio State University, 1956.

Halpin, A. W., and B. J. Winer, *The leadership behavior of the airplane commander*. Washington, D.C.: Human Research Laboratories, Department of the Air Force, 1952.

Hemphill, J. K., and A. E. Coons, *Development of the Leader Behavior Description Questionnaire*. Bureau of Business Research Monograph No. 88. Columbus, Ohio: Ohio State University, 1957.

Mitchell, T. R., "The construct validity of three dimensions of leadership research." *The Journal of Social Psychology*, 1970, **80**, 87–94.

Name: PUPIL OBSERVATION SURVEY REPORT

Authors: Donald J. Veldman and Robert F. Peck

Type of Measure: Rating scale

Availability: The Pupil Observation Survey Report can be obtained from the Research and Development Center for Teacher Education, The University of Texas, Austin, Texas 78712. A copy of this instrument also appears in: Veldman, D. J., and R. F. Peck, "Student teacher characteristics from the pupils' viewpoint." *Journal of Educational Psychology,* 1963, **54,** 346–355; and in White, W. F., and O. T. Dekle, "Effect of teacher's motivational cues on achievement level in elementary grades." *Psychological Reports,* 1966, **18,** 351–356.

Description: The Pupil Observation Survey Report (POSR) is a 38-item rating scale used to measure pupils' perceptions of their student teacher. Though originally designed for use in grades 7 through 12, the POSR has been successfully employed by White and Dekle (1966) in grades 5 and 6 as well.

Items on the POSR represent 5 factors: (1) Friendly, Cheerful, Admired; (2) Knowledgeable, Poised; (3) Interesting, Preferred; (4) Strict Control; and (5) Democratic Procedure. Factor 1 has been shown to differentiate ($p < .01$) overachievers, underachievers, and average achievers (White and Dekle, 1966). On Factors, 2, 4, and 5, cooperating teachers received higher ratings than student teachers, while the reverse was true on Factors 1 and 3 (Veldman, 1970).

Sample Items: All of the items on the POSR are positively phrased statements describing the student teacher. The pupils respond to these statements in 1 of 4 ways: "T" = completely true; "t" = more true than false; "f" = more false than true; and "F" = totally false. Items of the following type appear on the scale:

Factor	Item
1. Friendly, Cheerful, Admired	She is very easy to get along with.
2. Knowledgeable, Poised	She knows a lot about the subject she teaches.
3. Interesting, Preferred	With her, learning is more fun than it is work.
4. Strict Control	Her students can't get away with anything.
5. Democratic Procedure	She often asks the students how they feel about proposed projects before assigning them.

Reliability: Veldman and Peck (1963) report factor score reliabilities for the POSR. These were computed on 50 student teachers (selected from a sample of 554) whose classes were the largest. Each class was randomly divided in half, and each of these halves completed the POSR. Factor scores were obtained for each half-class. The two comparable factor scores for each teacher were then correlated to yield "split-class" reliabilities of: .92 for Factor 1; .72 for Factor 2; .91 for Factor 3; .81 for Factor 4; and .89 for Factor 5. These estimates were not corrected for size since they were computed on the largest classes in the sample.

Validity: Veldman and Peck (1963) approached construct validity by checking the stability of POSR factors across different samples. They compared factor structures based on the scores of three separate groups of student teachers and obtained coefficients ranging from .89 to .99 (median = .98).

In an attempt to establish criterion-related validity, POSR factor scores were correlated with scale scores on the California Personality Inventory (CPI) and the Self-Report Inventory (SRI). Correlations between POSR and CPI scores never exceeded .30, although 34 out of 180 were statistically significant. Those between the POSR and the SRI did not exceed .24. These correlations indicated minor, but indistinct, relationships between the measures. Correlations between the POSR scores and supervisor ratings of student teachers yielded more interpretable results. Factors 1, 2, and 4 (Friendliness, Knowledge, and Control) were all significantly related to the supervisory ratings of teaching effectiveness (Veldman and Peck, 1963).

In a later study, Veldman and Peck (1969) investigated the effect of content and other variables on POSR scores. Their data clearly indicated that the subject matter being taught strongly affected POSR scores, while grade level and socioeconomic status of the respondents exerted only minor influence on ratings given to teachers.

Norms: Veldman and Peck (1963) present no normative data for the POSR. However, use of local norms is recommended for this instrument.

Administration and Scoring: Administering the POSR is fairly easy. Pupils are given a set of instructions and an explanation of the test, assuring them that their responses will not be used to give the student teacher a grade. It is preferable that the POSR be answered anonymously and administered by someone other than the student teacher.

Scores on the POSR are determined by assigning numerical values (1 through 4) to the various response categories. Since all items are positively stated, scoring is never reversed. Factor scores are computed by summing the scores of items representing each factor.

Comments: As a research instrument, the Pupil Observation Survey Report has considerable utility. It can also be used in teacher training to help student teachers assess their performances and identify problems in pupil/teacher relationships. Users of the POSR, however, must recall that subject matter being taught may affect POSR scores, causing certain groups of student teachers to obtain consistently lower ratings.

References: Veldman, D. J., "Pupil evaluation of student teachers and their supervisors." *Journal of Teacher Education*, 1970, **21**, 165–167.

Veldman, D. J., and R. F. Peck, "Student teacher characteristics from the pupils' viewpoint." *Journal of Educational Psychology*, 1963, **54**, 346–355.

Veldman, D. J., and R. F. Peck, "Influences on pupil evaluations of student teachers." *Journal of Educational Psychology*, 1969, **60**, 103–108.

White, W. F., and O. T. Dekle, "Effects of teacher motivational cues on achievement level in elementary grades." *Psychological Reports*, 1966, **18**, 351–356.

Name: THE PURDUE RATING SCALE FOR INSTRUCTION

Authors: H. H. Remmers and D. N. Elliott

Type of Measure: Rating scale

Availability: Remmers, H. H., *Manual for instruction for the Purdue Rating Scale for Instruction* (Rev. ed.). Lafayette, Indiana: Purdue Research Foundation, Purdue University, 1960. This instrument may be obtained from the University Book Store, 360 State Street, West Lafayette, Indiana 47906. A copy may also be found in: Remmers, H. H., and N. L. Gage, *Educational measurement and evaluation*. New York: Harper & Brothers, 1955.

Description: The Purdue Rating Scale for Instruction (PRSI) allows students to rate their teachers on 10 traits: Interest in the Subject; Sympathy toward Students; Fairness in Grading; Liberal and Progressive Attitudes; Presentation of Subject Matter; Sense of Proportion and Humor; Self-Reliance and Confidence; Personal Peculiarities; Personal Appearance; and Ability to Stimulate Intellectual Curiosity. In addition, the teacher is given an overall rating, and 15 aspects of the classroom situation are evaluated. Although the rating scale is most often applied in college or university classrooms, it can easily be adapted for use at the high school level.

Sample Items: Subjects respond to items on the first part of the scale by darkening the portion of a continuum which best describes the teacher in reference to a specified trait. Items on the second part are answered by darkening 1 of 5 spaces designated 1, 2, 3, 4, or 5 (from "very poor" to "superior"). Items of the following type appear on Parts I and II.

Part I:

1. Interest in Subject

Always shows high interest	Seems moderately interested	Seems annoyed with subject

2. Personal Appearance

Always neat and well-groomed	Less emphasis on appearance and tidiness	Untidy and unclean

Part II:

	5	4	3	2	1
Adequacy of textbook used					
Adequacy of the load and nature of assigned outside work	5	4	3	2	1

Reliability: The reliability of the instrument depends on the number of students rating the teacher. For the 10 teacher traits, classes of 20 students, rating 205 instructors, produced reliabilities ranging from .84 (Fairness in Grading) to .93

(Interest in Subject). The overall teacher rating yielded a reliability coefficient of .91, and the evaluation of course characteristics produced a median coefficient of .82 (*Purdue Measurement and Evaluation Instruments,* undated).

Validity: Several studies have provided evidence of the validity of ratings made on the Purdue Scale. Using an early version of the scale, Remmers, Martin, and Elliott (1949) found that teachers who give their students grades higher than those predicted by placement tests are rated "superior" by those students. Similarly, it has been shown that instructors who grade leniently receive high ratings (Anikeef, 1953) and that the better students in a class give higher ratings to their teachers (Stewart and Malpass, 1966).

In a study by Elliott (reported in Remmers, 1960), instructors with at least 5 years of teaching experience received higher ratings than those with less experience. Miklich (1969) obtained similar results comparing ratings predicted by psychologists with those given by students to 2 different courses taught by the same instructor. In one of these courses, the instructor was experienced and interested, while in the other he was inexperienced and disinterested. Results provided moderate support for the validity of the PRSI.

A study by Brookover (1940) showed no correlations between students' and administrators' ratings of the same instructor. Bowman (1934) found little agreement between students' and teachers' ratings of the same instructor. These results, however, may have been due to differences in interpretation of items on the scale.

Norms: Extensive norms are available in the PRSI manual (Remmers, 1960). Local norms, comparing the instructor to his colleagues in the department, school, or institution, are also specified by the computer scoring service if desired.

Administration and Scoring: Instructions for completing the PRSI are printed on each form. There is no time limit, but the scale is usually completed in 5 to 10 minutes.

Ratings may be either hand or machine scored. Computerized scoring is recommended in order to guarantee the validity of the ratings. The computer processing service also provides local norms, profile reports (comparing an instructor's ranking on each trait to the norm group used), and confidentiality.

Comments: The Purdue Rating Scale for Instruction is a popular means of measuring teaching style and effectiveness from the students' point of view. Reliability data are satisfactory, and norms are extensive and varied.

References: Anikeef, A. M., "Factors affecting student evaluation of college faculty members." *Journal of Applied Psychology,* 1953, **37,** 458–460.

Bowman, E. C., "Pupils' ratings of student-teachers." *Educational Administration and Supervision,* 1934, **20,** 141–146.

Brookover, W. B., "Person-person interaction between teachers and pupils and teaching effectiveness." *Journal of Educational Research,* 1940, **34,** 272–287.

Miklich, D. R., "An experimental validation study of the Purdue Rating Scale for Instruction. *Educational and Psychological Measurement*, 1969, **29**, 1963–1967.

Purdue measurement and evaluation instruments. Lafayette, Indiana: Purdue Research Foundation, Purdue University, undated.

Remmers, H. H., *Manual for instruction for the Purdue Rating Scale for Instruction* (Rev. ed.). Lafayette, Indiana: Purdue Research Foundation, Purdue University, 1960.

Remmers, H. H., and N. L. Gage, *Educational measurement and evaluation.* New York: Harper & Brothers, 1955.

Remmers, H. H., F. D. Martin, and D. N. Elliott, "Are students' ratings of instructors related to their grades?" *Purdue University Studies in Higher Education*, 1949, **66**, 17–26.

Stewart, C. T., and L. F. Malpass, Estimates of achievement and ratings of instructors. *Journal of Educational Research*, 1966, **59**, 347–350.

Wrightstone, J. W., J. Justman, and I. Robbins, *Evaluation in modern education.* New York: American Book Co., 1956.

Name: THE PURDUE TEACHER EVALUATION SCALE

Authors: Ralph R. Bentley and Allan R. Starry

Type of Measure: Rating scale

Availability: Bentley, R. R., and A. R. Starry, *The Purdue teacher evaluation scale, form A.* Lafayette, Indiana: Purdue Research Foundation, Purdue University, 1970. *The Purdue Teacher Evaluation Scale* and the *Manual for the Purdue Teacher Evaluation Scale* may be obtained from the University Book Store, 360 State Street, West Lafayette, Indiana 47906.

Description: The Purdue Teacher Evaluation Scale (PTES) was designed to provide the junior or senior high school teacher with an evaluation of his performance as seen through the eyes of his students. The PTES contains 60 questions which are grouped into 6 scales identified by a composite principal components analysis. These scales are: (1) Ability to Motivate Students; (2) Ability to Control Students; (3) Subject Matter Orientation of Teacher; (4) Student-Teacher Communication; (5) Teaching Methods and Procedures; and (6) Teacher Fairness.

    The PTES was developed to aid teachers in their efforts at self-improvement. Accordingly, students are asked to assess specific, rather than general, behavioral characteristics. Scale items were originally drawn from a collection of short statements about teacher behaviors, written by educators and researchers. These statements were administered to approximately 60 classes of students, and were then analyzed and revised to make up the present form of the PTES.

Sample Items: Students respond to PTES items by selecting and checking 1 of 4 alternatives, ranging from "very much like my teacher" to "very much unlike my teacher." Items of the following type are included on the scale.

My teacher . . .
1. speaks clearly.
2. knows when we do not understand.
3. has pet students.
4. gives homework which helps in understanding the lessons.

Reliability: Bentley and Starry (1970) maintain that test/retest reliabilities are most meaningful for a rating scale of this type. However, since test/retest data are not available, they report an estimate of stability obtained using a modified split-half technique. Twenty evaluations for each of 128 teachers were selected and divided into random halves. For each random half, a median score for each scale was computed. These 128 median scores were then correlated, producing reliability coefficients ranging from .83 for Teacher Fairness to .91 for Ability to Motivate Students.

Validity: Bently and Starry (1970) report that there are no relevant criteria by which to judge the validity of the PTES. They do note, however, that students tend to agree with one another in rating a particular teacher.

Correlations among the six PTES scales, computed on a sample of 198 teachers, range from .47 to .89.

Norms: Norms are based on a sample of 198 teachers, evaluated on the PTES by approximately 5,000 students. These teachers were from middle- and upper-class junior and senior high schools located in the midwestern United States.

Administration and Scoring: The PTES is self-administering, though the instructions, printed on a separate sheet, must be read to the students, preferably by someone other than the teacher being evaluated. Approximately 20 minutes are required to complete the PTES.

Scoring may be done either by hand or by computer. Sixty median item scores and 6 scale scores are produced for each class. For positive statements the response "Very much like my teacher" is weighted 4 and the response "Very much unlike my teacher" is weighted 1. For negatively worded items the weights are reversed. While a scoring key is provided, a more comprehensive scoring and reporting service is offered by Purdue University's Measurement and Research Center. If the teacher desires, PTES results are treated confidentially.

Comments: The Purdue Teacher Evaluation Scale is an excellent aid for the teacher interested in improving his performance. Though the value of scale scores is questionable (due to high scale intercorrelations), the PTES does provide valuable information via 60 item scores. It also offers adequate normative data (a rarity among teacher evaluation questionnaires) and a confidential scoring service.

References: Bentley, R. R., and A. R. Starry, *Manual for the Purdue Teacher Evaluation Scale.* Lafayette, Indiana: Purdue Research Foundation, Purdue University, 1970.

Purdue measurement and evaluation instruments. Lafayette, Indiana: Purdue Research Foundation, Purdue University, undated.

Woolfold, T. V., *Teacher perception of organizational inducement and student assessment of teacher performance.* Unpublished doctoral dissertation, Purdue University, 1970.

Name: RATING   SCALE   FOR   PERSON-PERSON   INTERACTION
APPLIED TO TEACHER-PUPIL RELATIONSHIPS

Author: Wilbur B. Brookover

Type of Measure: Rating scale

Availability: A copy of the instrument may be found in Brookover, W. B.,
"Person-person interaction between teachers and pupils and teaching effectiveness." *Journal of Educational Research*, 1940, **34**(4), 272–287.

Description: The Rating Scale for Person-Person Interaction Applied to Teacher-
Pupil Relationships was developed to assess the effect of personal relationships
between teachers and pupils on the quality of high school teaching. Since it is
primarily a measure of interaction between people, rather than an attitude scale,
this test distinguishes between personal and role relationships.

The Rating Scale was developed according to the Likert method. It contains 9 items, each of which has 5 response alternatives. Scoring values were
assigned to these alternatives according to the degree of person/person interaction represented in each, as determined by graduate students and high school
teachers. Response choices indicating the highest degree of interaction are
scored "5," and those indicating the lowest, "1."

Sample Items: For each item, the student indicates with a check which of the 5
response alternatives best describes his or her relationship with the teacher.
Each item is designed to measure a different aspect of that relationship. The
instrument contains items of the following type:

1. When I see this teacher outside of school, she
   a. is generally friendly.
   b. seldom speaks.
   c. speaks briefly.
   d. snubs me.
   e. always acts friendly.
2. Because of my associations with this teacher, I
   a. have decided I'd like to be like her.
   b. have tried to imitate some of her traits.
   c. have become indifferent toward her.
   d. sometimes make fun of her.
   e. often make fun of her.
3. In my associations with this teacher, I find her
   a. somewhat warm and congenial.
   b. usually not warm and congenial.
   c. never warm and congenial.
   d. generally warm and congenial.
   e. always warm and congenial.

Reliability: Reliability has been established only by the test/retest method. Over an interval of 2 weeks, 2 sets of scores obtained from teachers showed a high degree of agreement, according to Brookover (1940), though a coefficient is not reported.

Validity: Few investigations of this instrument's validity are reported (Brookover, 1940). Some validity, however, may be assumed from the test's reliability, since it is student opinions which serve as the index of person/person interaction. The scale has been correlated with the Purdue Rating Scale for Instruction, a measure on which students evaluate a teacher's ability (Remmers, 1960). The mean pupil ratings of 39 Indiana high school teachers were obtained on both scales and correlated, yielding an r of .64. Teachers who have a high degree of person/person interaction with their pupils tend to be rated favorably as instructors.

The instrument has also demonstrated that teachers in smaller, rural schools have a higher degree of person/person interaction with their students than do teachers in larger, urban schools. This finding suggests some validity for the scale.

Administration and Scoring: The scale can be self-administered, since the instructions are printed on the test form. Each student responds anonymously to avoid personal repercussions. He or she chooses 1 of 5 possible alternatives which best describes his or her relationship with the teacher. Response alternatives are valued differentially. High scores indicate a high degree of person/person interaction, low scores, a low degree of interaction.

Norms: No normative data are reported.

Comments: Although very little information is available about the Rating Scale for Person-Person Interaction Applied to Teacher-Pupil Relationships, it may have value as a research tool. The correlation between this measure and the Purdue Rating Scale for Instruction suggests, but does not firmly establish, validity. Though reliability is reportedly high, a coefficient should accompany the author's report. Furthermore, normative data are badly needed.

References: Brookover, W. B., "Person-person interaction between teachers and pupils and teaching effectiveness." *Journal of Educational Research,* 1940, **34**(4), 272–287.

Remmers, H. H., *Manual for instruction for the Purdue Rating Scale for Instruction* (rev. ed). West Lafayette, Indiana: University Book Store, 1960.

Name: STUDENT EVALUATION OF TEACHING I

Authors: Donald J. Veldman and Robert F. Peck

Type of Measure: Rating scale

Availability: Requests should be sent to SET I Order, Dissemination Department, Research and Development Center for Teacher Education, The University of Texas, Austin, Texas 78712.

Description: The Student Evaluation of Teaching (SET) I is a 10-item scale designed to measure the way in which students in fifth grade or above perceive their teachers. The SET I was derived from a factor analysis of the Pupil Observation Survey Report (POSR) (Veldman and Peck, 1967), which yielded 5 major dimensions describing student perceptions of teacher style. These were: Friendly and Cheerful; Knowledgeable and Poised; Lively and Interesting; Firm Control (Discipline); and Nondirective (Democratic). The two items loading highest on each factor were selected for inclusion on the SET I. Data used in developing the SET I were collected only on the POSR and then applied to SET I items.

    The authors suggest that this instrument be used in evaluating student teachers, as a source of information concerning pupil/teacher interaction. A companion instrument, the SET II (included in this volume), may be used to evaluate kindergarten through third-grade teachers.

Sample Items: The 10 items on the SET I are divided into 5 scales, each containing 2 items. The student responds to each item by marking F for "always false," f for "often false," t for "often true," and T for "always true," depending on the degree to which the statement applies to the teacher in question.

    The following items are similar to those on the SET I:

            This teacher:

1. F f t T   is always kind to students.
2. F f t T   is very interesting.
3. F f t T   does not let students misbehave.

Reliability: Since the research report describing the SET I presents no data collected specifically on the SET I, no reliability figures are available. Veldman (1970) does report intercorrelations between the 2 items on each scale, ranging from .56 to .86. These data were obtained by deriving SET scores from POSR data.

Validity: Validity studies on the SET I are also scarce. However, the items clearly relate to the student's perception of the teacher. Therefore, the instrument seems to have face validity.

    A factor analytic study reported by Veldman (1970) attempted to confirm that the SET I factor structure corresponded to that of the POSR. Each item loaded highest on the expected factor. Unfortunately, the SET I data used in this study were simulated from the POSR data to which they were compared.

Norms: No norms are provided for the SET I. The nature and purposes of this instrument preclude normative expectations. Veldman and Peck (1970) report several tendencies in the way in which particular kinds of teachers are perceived. These should be considered when one is interpreting SET I results. Variables that are apparently related to SET I scores are teacher and pupil sex, subject matter area, grade, and socioeconomic level.

Administration and Scoring: Administration of the SET I is not explicitly discussed in the research report describing the instrument. However, it appears that administration is quite easy. Instructions are printed on the test sheets, which may be given to an entire class of pupils at once.

Scoring the SET I is also fairly easy. All items are stated in a positive direction: $F = 1$; $f = 2$; $t = 3$; and $T = 4$. A computer is useful in processing group data. Student responses can be punched onto computer cards according to a program recommended by Veldman (1970), which produces item means and scale scores, giving a verbal interpretation of both. Finally, the average of all item means is computed as an index of overall evaluation. All of this can be done by hand, but it would be a laborious procedure.

Veldman (1970) emphasizes the importance of interpreting scale scores as complete profiles. For example, a high score on Firm Control would mean different things depending on the level of other scale scores.

Comments: Though the SET I lacks adequate psychometric data, it is probably an appropriate instrument for the purposes suggested by its authors. It does yield a summary measure of students' perceptions of a teacher. Such an assessment can provide useful information to the teacher concerning his or her impact on students. Users of the SET I, however, should be careful not to over-interpret the results, since so few psychometric data are available.

References: Veldman, D. J., *Student evaluation of teaching*. Research Methodology Monograph No. 10. Austin, Texas: Research and Development Center for Teacher Education, University of Texas, 1970.

Veldman, D. J., and R. F. Peck, *Information about Student Evaluation of Teaching*. Austin, Texas: Research and Development Center for Teacher Education, University of Texas, undated.

Veldman, D. J., and R. F. Peck, *The Pupil Observation Survey: Teacher behavior from the pupils' viewpoint*. Austin, Texas: Research and Development Center for Teacher Education, University of Texas, 1967.

Name: STUDENT EVALUATION OF TEACHER INSTRUMENT II

Authors: Ruth Adolf Haak, Douglas A. Kleiber, and Robert F. Peck

Type of Measure: Rating scale

Availability: Requests should be sent to: SET II Order, Dissemination Department, Research and Development Center for Teacher Education, University of Texas, Austin, Texas 78712.

Description: The Student Evaluation of Teacher Instrument II (SET II) contains 20 items, each of which is a simple statement about the teacher or the teacher's attitude toward the student. It incorporates 3 dimensions, derived through factor analysis of an early form of the instrument. These are: Unreasonable Negativity; Fosterance of Self-Esteem; and Stimulating, Interactive Style, which has two subscales, Rapport and Interactional Competence.

The SET II was designed to assess the way in which children in kindergarten through third grade (or disadvantaged children through grade 6) view their teachers. Its predecessor, the SET I (included in this volume), is used with older children, in grades 5 and above. In developing the initial form of SET II, the authors attempted to construct items that would measure either students' perceptions of teacher competency or their feeling ("love") toward the teacher. Items were originally classified as either direct assessments of the teacher or estimates of the teacher's attitude toward students. Under each classification were the dimensions of "love," "competency," and "diagnostic information." Factor analysis of the pilot data failed to substantially support these classifications, and they were abandoned in favor of the factor structure mentioned above.

Sample Items: The SET II contains items of the following type:

Factor	*Item*
I. Stimulating, Interactive Style	
Subscale 1: Rapport (5 items)	1. My teacher makes school a lot of fun.
	2. My teacher thinks kids are good.
Subscale 2: Interactional Competence (4 items)	1. My teacher listens to what we say.

Factor	*Item*
II. Unreasonable Negativity (5 items)	1. My teacher thinks I am lazy.
	2. My teacher is always "picking on" me.
III. Fosterance of Self-Esteem (6 items)	1. My teacher thinks I can do a lot by myself.
	2. My teacher thinks I have good ideas.

Each item is printed on a separate card and is read to the student who then places the card in either a "true" or "false" pile.

Reliability: Haak, Kleiber, and Peck (1972) report test/retest reliability data collected during the pilot study of the SET II. Since item format calls for a true-false answer, the authors chose a percentage of agreement (PA) statistic as a measure of reliability. The sample was taken from children in kindergarten through grade 6 in the Austin (Texas) Independent School District. An attempt was made to choose a stratified sample in terms of grade level and cultural background. Percentages of agreement among children in kindergarten ranged from 59.3 to 89.5, with 8 items achieving PAs greater than 75. PAs for first-grade children ranged from 69.7 to 92.2, with 15 being greater than 80. The range for second- and third-grade children was 68.3 to 89.4, with 16 PAs at 75 or above. An additional sample composed of fourth- through sixth-grade Mexican-American children yielded PAs ranging from 66.9 to 94, with 19 over 75. The authors also report percentage of agreement from first to second testing on a sample divided in terms of cultural group (black, Mexican-American, and white), ability level (low, medium, and high), and a combination of cultural group and ability level. Except at the kindergarten level, PAs for each item were generally between 70 and 90.

Validity: No validity data are reported in the SET II manual (Haak, Kleiber, and Peck, 1972). However, factor analytic data for grades 1 through 3 in the pilot study are presented. Factor loadings are fairly high: those on Factor 1 ranged from .60 to .94; those on Factor 2 from .61 to .81; and those on Factor 3 from .59 to .78. Most items did not load substantially in the same direction on more than 1 factor, the only exception being item 19 ("She likes for me to help her"), which loaded $-.45$ on Factor 2 and $-.59$ on Factor 3. A factor analysis of data collected from all elementary grades produced similar factor loadings. Items on Factor 1, however, split into 2 groups: Rapport and Interactional Competence. These 2 item groupings were incorporated as subscales of Factor 1.

Norms: The norms presented in the SET II manual are based on only 36 teachers in the public schools of Austin, Texas. The SET II authors do not recommend their use in other settings; instead they encourage local norming.

Administration and Scoring: The procedure for administering the SET II is uncomplicated and requires no special training. On each card an item is printed, along with a picture which is placed in the upper right-hand corner. The administrator identifies the card to the children by calling attention to the picture. He or she then reads the item to the children, who respond to it by placing the card in either a "true" envelope, identified by a picture of a post-office box, or a "false" envelope, identified by a picture of a trash can.

A tally sheet is used to score each student's responses. The scorer checks "true" or "false" beside each item listed. Responses are weighted as indicated on the scoring sheet, and then summed to obtain a scale score.

Teacher tally sheets and profile sheets may be used to record the entire class' perception of the teacher.

Comments: The SET II is a carefully constructed instrument with a great deal of face validity. However, there are as yet no real validity or reliability studies relating to scale or subscale scores. With more developmental research in these 2 areas, the SET II may become a useful instrument for helping teachers in grades 1 through 3 to develop interpersonal skills and more positive relationships with their pupils.

References: Haak, R., D. Kleiber, and R. Peck, *Manual: Student Evaluation of Teacher Instrument, II.* Austin, Texas: The Research and Development Center for Teacher Education, The University of Texas, 1972.

Borich, G. D., R. C. Godbout, R. F. Peck, M. M. Kash, and L. H. Poynor, *An evaluation of the personalized model of reacher training. Final report.* Austin, Texas: Research and Development Center for Teacher Education, The University of Texas, 1974.

Name: STUDENT PERCEPTION OF TEACHER STYLE

Author: Bruce W. Tuckman

Type of Measure: Rating scale

Availability: A copy of the scale may be found in: Tuckman, B. W., "A technique for the assessment of teacher directiveness." *Journal of Educational Research,* 1970, **63**, 398–400.

Description: The 17-item Student Perception of Teacher Style (SPOTS) rating scale was designed to measure student perception of teacher directiveness. The instrument is based on concepts of directive teaching which were determined by the author from a review of the literature and from classroom observation. These concepts emphasize the structure and quality of interpersonal relationships within junior high and secondary school classrooms. The original SPOTS consisted of 32 items. Two other instruments, the Observer Rating Scale (ORS) and the Teacher Style Checklist (TSC), were developed to refine and determine the construct validity of the SPOTS. Two trained observers rated 22 11th- and 12th-grade teachers on the ORS and the TSC. These teachers were concurrently rated by their students on the SPOTS. Based on intercorrelations between the 3 tests, item analysis, and factor analysis, the original 32 items were reduced to the present 17, yielding a more efficient instrument.

Sample Items: Each SPOTS item consists of a stem followed by a response scale. The student marks one of the 9 points on the scale which best describes his perception of the teacher or classroom. The instrument contains items of the following type:

1. Your instructor is mainly concerned with

1 2 3	4 5 6	7 8 9
The number of facts you know.	Getting an idea across to you.	Your ability to think for yourself.

2. Students in our classroom

1 2 3	4 5 6	7 8 9
Only talk if the instructor asks them a question.	Sometimes volunteer information.	Frequently initiate discussion.

3. For group projects or class committees the teacher

1 2 3	4 5 6	7 8 9
Gives us exact instructions on what to do.	Makes suggestions about the project	Allows the group members to make the decisions.

Reliability: Reliability of the SPOTS was investigated as the instrument was revised (Tuckman, 1970). The mean SPOTS score on each item of the 32-item scale was correlated with the total mean score for each of 22 teachers. Seventy-eight percent of the item scores correlated significantly with total scores, the coefficients ranging from .45 to .91. The 7 items demonstrating the lowest item-total correlations were omitted from the final scale.

Interrater reliability was determined by ranking each student according to the agreement between his SPOTS score and the mean SPOTS score for each of 22 teachers, and then correlating these agreement figures with each teacher's average SPOTS rating. The ratings of students ranking 1 through 4 correlated approximately .95 with the class average; those of students ranking 5 through 8 correlated approximately .84 with the class average; and those of students ranking 9 and 10 correlated .77 and .69, respectively. The ratings of students ranked below 10 did not show high agreement with the class average.

Validity: A significant ($p < .01$) correlation (.53) was obtained between the mean SPOTS rating for each teacher and his corresponding ORS rating. Similarly, a correlation of .31 ($p < .01$) was obtained between the SPOTS mean for each teacher and his mean TSC score. The TSC and ORS correlated .75 ($p < .01$), indicating that they are comparable measures.

Administration and Scoring: The SPOTS is easy to administer. The average high school student should be able to complete the instrument in a short time with minimal instruction. The teacher's rating is obtained by computing the mean score for each item as well as a mean for all of the items combined.

Norms: Item and total means are available on ratings given by 363 male students at 2 vocational/technical high schools to 22 11th- and 12th-grade male teachers, each of whom had at least 5 years of teaching experience.

Comments: Remmers (1963) suggested 5 criteria for evaluating student rating scales, and the Student Perception of Teacher Style appears to meet all 5. The instrument demonstrates sufficient (1) objectivity, (2) reliability, (3) sensitivity in discriminating between instructors, (4) utility and (5) relevance, in this case to the construct of directiveness.

Because the instrument is fairly new, and psychometric data still somewhat limited, its use should be restricted to research at present.

References: Remmers, H. H., "Rating methods in research on teaching." In N. L. Gage (ed.), *Handbook of research on teaching.* Chicago: Rand McNally, 1963. Tuckman, B. W., "A technique for the assessment of teacher directiveness." *Journal of Educational Research,* 1970, **63**, 395–400.

Name: TEACHER IMAGE QUESTIONNAIRE

Author: Roy C. Bryan

Type of Measure: Rating scale

Availability: Bryan, R. C., *Some observations concerning written student reactions to high school teachers.* Kalamazoo, Michigan: Student Reaction Center, Western Michigan University, 1968. A copy of the instrument may also be obtained from the Education Feedback Center, Western Michigan University, Kalamazoo, Michigan 49001.

Description: The Teacher Image Questionnaire (TIQ) contains 16 questions designed to obtain the opinions of students in grades 7 through 12 about their teachers, as well as 2 optional items which allow students to comment upon the teacher's strengths and weaknesses. Although the TIQ was initially designed to provide feedback for improving teacher effectiveness, it has also been used in studies of teacher image.

This instrument was developed on the theory that there are 3 kinds of criteria for judging teacher effectiveness: product criteria, presage criteria, and process criteria. Since product criteria (long-term outcomes) are difficult to measure, and presage criteria (teacher experience variables) do not provide feedback which can help the teacher improve his or her effectiveness, process criteria were chosen as the basis of the TIQ. Process criteria include variables such as teacher attitude, teacher behavior, and student perceptions of teacher performance. Student perceptions were considered the most important factor in determining teacher effectiveness since they reflect the other 2 process variables, and therefore were selected as the assessment technique for the TIQ.

Sample Item: The TIQ measures the student's reaction to questions about his or her teacher. Responses vary from "poor" to "excellent" on a 5-point scale. Items of the following type are included on the questionnaire:

1. *Knowledge of Subject Matter:* (Does your teacher seem to have a good grasp of the subject matter?)

poor	fair	average	good	excellent

2. *Homework:* (Does your teacher give homework assignments which are interesting and appropriate?)

poor	fair	average	good	excellent

3. *Openness:* (Can your teacher see things from a variety of perspectives?)

poor	fair	average	good	excellent

Reliability: Bryan (1968) reports reliability data collected in 50 randomly selected secondary school classes, each composed of 24 to 32 students. Classes were split into chance halves, and estimates of internal consistency were computed for the first 12 TIQ items and corrected with the Spearman-Brown formula. These estimates ranged from .82 to .95.

Validity: Bryan (1968b) correlated TIQ ratings completed by students with those completed by administrators on a group of 114 teachers and obtained a coefficient of .61. In a similar study, involving 38 teachers, student and administrator ratings correlated .68.

Bryan (1966) also reported that teacher image, which is normally resistant to change, can be modified with the help of TIQ profiles. In periods up to 2 years, 57% of a group of teachers who had access to their TIQ ratings were able to produce significant gains on 1 or more of the TIQ variables.

A factor analysis of the TIQ (Coats, 1970) produced no meaningful or clearcut item clusters. While student-centered items tended to cluster together, as did structure-related items, one single factor, labeled teacher charisma, accounted for 61.5% of the variance. Coats also found that correlations among items ranged from .32 to .85.

Norms: The TIQ has been administered to students in the 7th through 12th grades. Means and standard deviations computed on the responses of these students are available for 1,630 teachers who were rated on the TIQ from 1970 to 1973.

Administration and Scoring: The TIQ can be administered to an entire class in about 15 minutes. After the instrument has been administered, completed questionnaires are placed in an envelope (along with class and teacher ID forms) and mailed to the Student Reaction Center (Western Michigan University), where answers are analyzed and a report is prepared and sent to the teacher. Confidentiality is assured, and the teacher may request letters of recommendation based on his TIQ profile.

Comments: The TIQ is an inexpensive and useful tool for determining student attitudes toward the teacher. For a nominal fee, the teacher receives a report and profile of his students' reactions. There is some danger, however, that this instrument may measure teacher charisma or popularity rather than actual teaching effectiveness.

References: Bryan, R. C., "The teacher's image is stubbornly stable." *Clearing House*, 1966, **40**, 459–460.

Bryan, R. C., "High school students view classroom control." *Clearing House*, 1968, **42**, 345–346. (a)

Bryan, R. C., *Some observations concerning written student reactions to high school teachers.* Kalamazoo, Michigan: Student Reaction Center, Western Michigan University, 1968. (b)

Coats, W. D., *Students' perceptions of teachers: A factor analytic study.* Paper presented at annual meeting of the American Educational Research Association, Minneapolis, Minnesota, March, 1970.

Name: THE UNFORCED TEACHER RATING SCALE ("OUR TEACHER")

Authors: N. L. Gage, G. S. Leavitt, and G. C. Stone

Type of Measure: Rating scale

Availability: Gage, N. L., G. S. Leavitt, and G. C. Stone, "Teachers' understanding of their pupils and pupils' ratings of their teachers." *Psychological Monographs*, 1959, **69** (21, Whole No. 406).

Description: The Unforced Teacher Rating Scale ("Our Teacher") is a 12-item scale designed to measure pupils' general attitude (favorable vs. unfavorable) toward the teacher. In constructing Our Teacher (OT), the authors focused on teacher behaviors which, according to research, promote cognitive, social, or emotional adjustment among students. Four items representing each adjustment category are included on the final scale. Though intended for use with children in grades 4 through 6, this measure can, with appropriate modifications in vocabulary, be used at almost any grade level.

The OT scale was developed in a study of the relationship between the teacher's capacity to correctly perceive his or her students' problems, social behaviors, and abilities, and the students' perception of the teacher's ability to do this. As a part of this project, Gage, Leavitt, and Stone (1959) required a measure of pupil favorability toward the teacher which would incorporate the "halo effect." The unforced response format of the OT scale, in which each question is answered independently, was intended to encourage the halo effect. To ensure that the OT was in fact promoting the halo effect, the authors, for comparative purposes, arranged the 12 OT items on a forced-choice instrument which required students to choose which of 2 statements most applied to the teacher. Responses to both measures indicated that the unforced OT scale was indeed yielding a generalized index of favorability.

Sample Items: Each of the 12 OT items asks the student a question about the teacher. The student responds by underlining the most appropriate of the following responses: (1) always; (2) usually; (3) sometimes; and (4) never. Responses are arranged so that choice (1) is always the most favorable response. The other alternatives follow in order of decreasing favorability. Items similar to the following appear on the scale:

Category	*Item*
I. Promoting Cognitive Adjustment	1. Does your teacher explain your school work so that you know how to do it?
II. Promoting Social Adjustment	2. Does your teacher know who your friends are in this class?
III. Promoting Emotional Adjustment	3. Is your teacher careful not to scare you or hurt your feelings?

Reliability: Gage et al. (1959) used Cronbach's coefficient alpha to establish the internal consistency of the OT scale. They obtained a value of .92, from which they concluded that only 1 factor is involved in the test. In addition, they computed Horst coefficients for each item and for the total scale in order to determine stability across samples. These ranged from .43 to .76 (median = .66) for scale items. For the total score, the Horst coefficient was .79. The authors concluded that the OT yields teacher descriptions which possess substantial nonerror variance and reliability from one class to another.

Validity: A principal components analysis of OT item intercorrelations produced a first-order factor which accounted for 63.9% of the common variance. This was interpreted as a " halo effect " factor and cited as evidence that the OT scale, at least to some extent, validly measures pupils' general favorability toward their teachers (Gage et al., 1959).

Correlations between OT scores and those on Leeds' " My Teacher " Inventory (1950) were used to establish evidence of criterion-related validity. The coefficient between total scores was .25, while correlations between OT items and Leeds' total scores ranged from .03 to .39, with a median around .17.

Rank-difference correlations were also computed between item-total correlational patterns on the OT and those on the Leeds' Inventory. A *rho* of .54 was obtained, indicating some agreement between the two instruments in respect to the degree to which items measure favorability.

Norms: Gage et al. (1959) present no normative data for the OT scale.

Administration and Scoring: In administering the OT scale, printed tests, including directions for responding, are distributed to the students. It is emphasized that test results are completely anonymous. The scale is scored by assigning numerical values to response alternatives and summing those of the choices underlined by the subject.

Comments: Our Teacher is a useful research instrument for measuring pupil favorability toward the teacher. Since it apparently assesses something rather different from what is measured by the Leeds' Inventory, the OT should probably be used as 1 of several instruments. More reliability and validity studies are needed in order to fully determine the value of this scale. Estimates of retest reliability would be particularly interesting since attitudes of favorability might be related to pupil moods, experience with the teacher, or classroom setting.

References: Gage, N. L., G. S. Leavitt, and G. C. Stone, Teachers' understanding of their pupils and pupils' ratings of their teachers. *Psychological Monographs,* 1959, **69**, (21, Whole No. 406).

Leeds, C. H., "A scale for measuring teacher-pupil attitudes and teacher-pupil rapport." *Psychological Monographs,* 1950, **64** (6, Whole No. 312).

IC

About the teacher from an observer

Name: CLASSROOM BEHAVIOR TAPE ANALYSIS FORM

Author: Daniel Solomon

Type of Measure: Observation coding system

Availability: Solomon, D. *Teaching styles and learning*. Chicago: Center for the Study of Liberal Education for Adults, 1963.

Description: The Classroom Behavior Tape Analysis Form (CBTAF) employs tape recordings of classroom interaction to yield indices of teacher and student behavior. Developed in a study of teacher style and student outcomes (Solomon, 1963), the CBTAF requires raters to tape and then classify verbal behaviors occurring in the classroom, using categories derived from: (1) a review of the literature; (2) theoretical and intuitive expectations; and (3) the results of an exploratory study by Solomon and Miller (1961). These categories, listed below, encompass 3 aspects of teacher behavior and 2 aspects of student participation.

I. Teacher Behavior

    A. Statements
- 1. Providing Organization, Orientation
- 2. Providing Hypothesis
- 3. Providing Opinion
- 4. Providing Factual
- 5. Providing Interpretation
- 6. Providing Personal Reference

    B. Questions
- 7. Requesting Organization, Orientation
- 8. Requesting Hypothesis
- 9. Requesting Opinion
- 10. Requesting Factual
- 11. Requesting Interpretation
- 12. Requesting, Nonspecific
- 13. Requesting Clarification

    C. Feedback
- 14. Positive Reinforcement
- 15. Negative Reinforcement
- 16. No Reinforcement
- 17. High Information
- 18. Low Information
- 19. No Information
- 20. Residual

II. Student Behavior

    A. Statements
- 21. Providing Organization, Orientation
- 22. Providing Hypothesis
- 23. Providing Opinion
- 24. Providing Factual
- 25. Providing Interpretation
- 26. Providing Personal Reference

    B. Questions
- 27. Requesting Organization, Orientation
- 28. Requesting Hypothesis
- 29. Requesting Opinion
- 30. Requesting Factual
- 31. Providing Interpretation
- 32. Providing, Nonspecific
- 33. Providing Clarification
- 34. Residual
- 35. Tension Release

Sample Items: Solomon (1963) provides examples of the kinds of behaviors classified under each CBTAF category. " Requesting, Nonspecific," for example, includes any "unstructured invitation to participate (p. 138)," any comment which encourages group discussion. " No Reinforcement " refers to the teacher's " dispassionate reiteration of student's communication, silence, shift to another topic (p. 138)."

Reliability: Interrater reliability of the Tape Analysis Form was checked by Solomon (1963) on two occasions—at the end of the rater training period and midway through the actual tape analyses. On each of these occasions, 4 raters classified approximately 45 minutes of a tape to which they had not yet listened. The categories recorded by each rater were ranked according to their relative frequencies. The similarity among these rankings was computed using Kendall's coefficient of concordance. The first reliability check yielded a coefficient of .97 and the second, .84, each significant beyond the .001 level.

Intervisit correlations were also computed for each CBTAF category. The majority of these were above .50, and many exceeded .60, indicating a fair degree of stability in teacher behavior across class sessions (Solomon, 1963).

Validity: Solomon (1963) investigated concurrent validity by correlating CBTAF dimensions with similar variables measured by other instruments employed in his study. Amount of Teacher Speech on the CBTAF correlated significantly ($p < .05$) with the following items on the Student Questionnaire: Teacher Provides Main Directing Force (.80); Amount of Teacher Lecturing (.48); Instructor's Loss of Control ($-.52$); and Inter-Student Discussion ($-.62$). The CBTAF variable, Teacher's Personal References, correlated .54 with Expressed Opinions About Material and .65 with References to Self. Similarly, Teacher's Use of Negative Reinforcement was positively related (.71) to the Student Questionnaire item, Teacher's Use of Challenging, Embarrassing Techniques. Comparable correlations between CBTAF scores and observers' ratings of teacher behavior provide further evidence of validity.

Norms: The sample used in the Solomon (1963) study was composed of 24 college instructors teaching evening courses in Introductory American Government at 13 schools. All of the schools were located in the Midwest, except 1, which was in a large Eastern city. Class size ranged from 11 to 38. Students were predominantly male, "working full time," and from 16 to 60 years old (median age $= 20$).

Procedures for Use: In using the CBTAF, the entire class session is recorded. Statements and questions of the teacher and students are coded as they occur on the tape, all student speech being scored together rather than separately for individual students.

A number of indices can be derived from the tape, including: (1) the proportion of teacher and student talk falling into each of the speech categories; (2)

the ratio of each category of teacher talk to the same category of student talk; and (3) the percentage of total talk contributed by the teacher.

Comments: The Classroom Behavior Tape Analysis Form attempts to assign every statement made in the classroom to a meaningful category. The CBTAF focuses on relatively small units of behavior, which are scored immediately. The tape recording provides a permanent record of classroom activity; thus there is no reliance on the observer's memory. Because this instrument considers only the verbal behavior of students and teachers, it is perhaps best used in conjunction with other measures of classroom interaction. This is, in fact, how Solomon has employed the CBTAF in the past.

References: Solomon, D., *Teaching styles and learning*. Chicago: Center for the Study of Liberal Education for Adults, 1963.

Solomon, D., W. E. Bezdek, Rosenberg, L., " Dimensions of teacher behavior." *Journal of Experimental Education*, 1964, **33**(1), 23–40.

Solomon, D., and H. L. Miller, *Exploration in teaching styles*. Chicago: Center for the Study of Liberal Education for Adults, 1961.

Name: CONNERS-EISENBERG OBSERVATION SYSTEM

Authors: C. Keith Conners and Leon Eisenberg

Type of Measure: Observation coding system

Availability: Conners, C. K., and L. Eisenberg, *The effect of teacher behavior on verbal intelligence in Operation Headstart children.* Baltimore, Maryland: School of Medicine, Johns Hopkins University, 1966. (ERIC Document Reproduction Service No. 010 782)

Description: This observation system is designed to measure 3 sets of teacher and classroom variables. First, observers classify teacher behavior *episodes* according to Communication, Management, and Encouragement. Second, they record the degree to which teacher *activities* promote the following "values":

1. Development of an adequate self-concept, emotional stability, and a sense of security;
2. Intellectual growth;
3. Personal responsibility for private or community property;
4. Cultural habit training;
5. Consideration for others;
6. Achievement orientation;
7. Development of physical abilities and skills;
8. Creativity; and
9. Obedience and self-control.

Third, observers make *overall judgments* of teacher performance on four 6-point scales: Warmth vs. Coldness; Permissiveness vs. Restrictiveness; Active vs. Passive; and Variety vs. Non-Variety.

Sample Items: Observations of teacher behavior are recorded as discrete episodes, as suggested by Baldwin (1960) and Reichenberg-Hackett (1962). An episode is defined as "a change in the triangular relationship between teacher, child, and environment, no matter how small this change might be (Conners and Eisenberg, 1966, p. 4)." A change of subject, for example, or a shift of the teacher's attention, signals the end of one episode and the beginning of another. Each statement made by the teacher is recorded verbatim.

Related episodes are grouped to form teacher activities, which are then scored according to the values listed in the previous section.

Reliability: To determine interobserver agreement, 2 raters independently scored sample protocols for all categories. Spearman rank-order correlation coefficients ranged from .79 (promotion of obedience and self-control) to .97 (promotion of physical abilities and skills), with a mean of .87.

Data collected by all 8 observers on 6 teachers indicated that the greatest variation from one observer to another occurred in the overall teacher ratings. Since the 4 global ratings were highly intercorrelated, they were combined to form a single "good vs. bad" score. An analysis of variance was then performed on the data, and an intraclass correlation of .82 was computed. This coefficient, which is equivalent to the average intercorrelation among all 8 observers, may be considered a measure of the reliability of individual scores (Conners and Eisenberg, 1966).

No data on the reliability of episode definition were collected. However, according to Conners and Eisenberg (1966), training sessions conducted prior to the observations indicated that raters generally agreed in determining episode boundaries.

Validity: Validity is suggested by correlations between teacher characteristics, as recorded on the Conners-Eisenberg system, and the intellectual growth of pupils, as measured by the Peabody Picture Vocabulary Test (PPVT). For example, teacher activities judged as promoting intellectual growth were strongly associated with increased PPVT scores. Similarly, teacher behavior which placed a high value on property rights and care of materials produced little change in PPVT scores. Teachers rated as warm, active, permissive, and varied produced more intellectual growth than those judged low on these traits (Conners and Eisenberg, 1966).

Norms: Subjects in the Conners and Eisenberg study were 38 teachers (32 from public schools and 6 from a privately operated church nursery school) and 500 children participating in a Headstart program in Baltimore City in the summer of 1965.

Procedures for Use: In using this system, observers take general notes on an entire day's activities, but record a 1-hour period in great detail. As unobtrusively as possible, they record teacher behavior as discrete episodes. When the observation interval is over, these episodes are scored in 2 ways. According to the first procedure, each episode is scored for 1 or more of the following variables: (1) Communication (to the child, the group, or an adult); (2) Management (altering a child's activity, either positively, by suggesting a substitute activity, or negatively, by simply interrupting or stopping the activity); and (3) Encouragement. The second scoring procedure groups related, consecutive episodes to form teacher activities, which are then scored according to the degree to which they foster 9 specific "values." A teacher is classified as being "high," "medium," or "low" on each value, relative to other teachers.

Finally, each teacher is given an overall score on Warmth, Permissiveness, Activity, and Variety.

Comments: The Conners-Eisenberg Observation System is appropriate for use in assessing elementary or nursery school teachers. It yields 3 sets of scores from 1 set of data and, therefore, is an economical research tool. Although the categories appear to require considerable inference on the observer's part, indices of interrater agreement are high.

References: Baldwin, A. L., "The study of child behavior and development," in P.

Mussen (ed.), *Handbook of research methods in child development*. New York: Wiley, 1960.

Conners, C. K., and L. Eisenberg, *The effect of teacher behavior on verbal intelligence in Operation Headstart children*. Baltimore, Maryland: School of Medicine, Johns Hopkins University, 1966. (ERIC Document Reproduction Service No. ED 010 782)

Reichenberg-Hackett, W., "Practices, attitudes, and values in nursery group education." *Psychological Reports*, 1962, **10**, 151–172.

Name: OBSERVATION SCHEDULE AND RECORD FORM No. 4 (OScAR 4V)

Authors: Donald M. Medley, J. T. Impellitteri, and L. H. Smith

Type of Measure: Observation coding system

Availability: Dr. D. M. Medley, Chairman, Department of Research Methodology, Ruffner Hall, University of Virginia, Charlottesville, Virginia 22903.

Description: OScAR 4V is a system for classifying teacher verbal behaviors observed in the classroom. The focus of this recording system is on the teacher rather than the student. Content of teacher verbal behaviors is coded, while student verbalizations are merely tallied. OScAR 4V is primarily a research tool, consisting of 50 interrelated categories which are presented in flow-chart form. The flow chart guides the observer in classifying teacher statements. Tallies are placed on a separate recording form which contains all end points represented on the flow chart.

Sample Items: OScAR 4V codes classroom behavior under 3 major categories: (1) Teacher Statements; (2) Substantive Interchanges (teacher/student interaction focused on lesson content); and (3) Non-Substantive Interchanges (teacher/student interaction involving subjects other than lesson content). Each of these categories is further subdivided so that behaviors may be more specifically identified. Teacher Statements, for example, subsumes the following codes:

Teacher Statements

I. Affective	II. Procedural	III. Substantive
A. Considering (CSN)	A. Directing (DRC)	A. Informing (INF)
B. Rebuking (RBK)	B. Describing (DSC)	B. Problem Structuring (PRB)

Additional categories are used to indicate whether a verbalization is an Initial Statement (I) or a Continuing (C) remark.

Reliability: Reliability estimates are provided in a study described by Medley and Hill (undated), based on a sample of 72 intern teachers who were observed on OScAR 4V by 6 university supervisors. A reliability coefficient was calculated from an analysis of variance design for each OScAR 4V frequency count and contrast score. (A raw OScAR record is comprised of 42 frequency counts, while a scored record consists of 42 contrast scores, which are linear functions of these frequencies.) Estimated stability coefficients for contrast scores ranged from .00 to .85, with a median of .59. The range for frequencies was .00 to .84, with a median of .50. In general, the categories which proved least reliable were those with low frequencies, suggesting that instability may have been caused by the fact that certain behaviors were rarely observed.

Validity: No data indicating validity could be found. However, the flow chart which serves as a framework for OScAR 4V suggests logical category construction.

Norms: No normative data are available.

Procedures for Use: OScAR 4V requires no special equipment and can be easily learned. The observer uses the flow chart in categorizing classroom verbalizations. For example, in classifying a Teacher Statement, the observer refers to the flow chart, which asks if the statement called for a response. If the answer is no, the flow chart then asks if the statement had affective content. If the answer is no, the observer is guided to the next cell which asks if the statement had substantive content. If the answer is yes, the observer asks if it was a problem structuring statement. If so, he then determines whether it was an initiating or continuing remark.

Behaviors are tallied as they occur on the form provided. For research purposes, the observation period usually lasts between 5 and 10 minutes. However, there is no set time limit. Because only teacher verbalizations are coded for content, the observer's task is not difficult.

Comments: The OScAR 4V is a sophisticated instrument which is easy to use. It requires only 1 person to collect and code data. However, because validity information is unavailable, it is difficult to determine whether this system actually measures what it intends to measure. Nevertheless, OScAR 4V is a well organized and widely used instrument.

References: Medley, D. M., and R. A. Hill, *Measurement properties of Observation Schedule and Record, Form 4V*, undated. (mimeo)

Simon, A., and E. G. Boyer, *Mirrors for behavior. An anthology of observation instruments. Volume 3.* Philadelphia: Research for Better Schools, 1970.

Name: PERFORMANCE ASSESSMENT RECORD FOR TEACHERS

Author: Bob Burton Brown

Type of Measure: Observation coding system

Availability: Brown, B. B. *Performance assessment record for teachers.* Gainesville, Florida: Institute for Development of Human Resources, College of Education, University of Florida, 1970.

Description: The Performance Assessment Record for Teachers (PART) provides a framework for systematically observing, describing, and assessing the classroom performance of teachers and pupils. Though this instrument codes a number of pupil behaviors, it is designed primarily for teacher self-assessment. Audio or video tape recordings or live observation of classroom performance may serve as the basis of this assessment.

PART consists of 22 items which describe what does and does not happen in classrooms. The observer records the presence or absence of a given behavior during a brief (usually 6-minute) working period, without indicating the number of times it may have occurred. PART items are drawn from several other observation instruments. The first 4 are borrowed from the Teacher Practices Observation Record, which measures the extent to which classroom activity promotes inquiry or reflective thinking. Items 5 through 15 are adapted from the Florida Taxonomy of Cognitive Behavior, which assesses the level of cognitive operations overtly used by pupils in the classroom. Items 16 through 19, extracted from the Taxonomy of Affective Behavior, represent higher affective processes, particularly valuing. The remaining 3 items, drawn from the research of Soar (1970), deal with classroom control. Brown (1970) points out that these 22 items represent only a limited cross section of several alternative approaches to the analysis of teaching/learning situations in the classroom. PART items are not intended to represent universally "good" or "bad" behaviors. They should be used only as a means of gaining insight into classroom processes and effective teaching procedures.

Sample Items: The 22 PART items include teacher and pupil behaviors of the following type:

1. Teacher initiates a learning activity focusing on a question or problem which is of real concern to the student.

2. Teacher initiates a learning activity which addresses a question or problem arising from textbook or class discussion.

3. Student interprets, explains, tells why, compares, or points out causal relationships.

4. Student alters judgment in light of new information.

Brown (1970) lists specific statements or behaviors which indicate the occurrence of each item. For example, item 3, above, is coded when the student makes a statement similar to any of the following:

a. A campfire goes out when you cover it with dirt because fire needs oxygen in order to burn.

b. These 3 words sound alike, but they are spelled differently.

c. The plants on the window sill are dead because the window was left open last night and the temperature fell below freezing.

Reliability, Validity, and Norms: Because PART items were extracted from several other observation systems, no reliability, validity, or normative data are provided by Brown (1970).

Procedures for Use: Brown (1970) gives clear instructions for recording observations. Each 30-minute observation period is composed of 5 separate 7-minute working intervals, each of which corresponds to one of 5 columns on the coding sheet. During working period 1, the rater places a check in column 1 alongside the behavior observed. This procedure is repeated for each of the 6-minute working periods. When the entire observation is over, the number of checks recorded in columns 1 through 5 are totalled for each item. Therefore, the score for each item reflects frequency of occurrence.

Comments: The Performance Assessment Record for Teachers offers a method of evaluating teachers on an everyday basis. According to the author, this test is not intended for research purposes, but instead for use in the field as a self-assessment tool. Although PART covers limited content, such a restriction is necessary in an instrument designed for practical use by teachers. The absence of psychometric information, however, does weaken this measure in spite of the fact that its items are drawn from other, established observation systems.

References: Brown, B. B., *The experimental mind in education.* New York: Harper & Row, 1968.

Brown, B. B., *Instructional guide for the Performance Assessment Record for Teachers (PART).* Gainesville, Florida: Institute for Development of Human Resources, College of Education, University of Florida, 1970.

Soar, R. S., *Interim report, evaluation of Follow-Through model implementation.* Gainesville, Florida: Institute for Development of Human Resources, College of Education, University of Florida, 1970.

Name: REICHENBERG-HACKETT TEACHER BEHAVIOR OBSERVATION SYSTEM

Author: Wally Reichenberg-Hackett

Type of Measure: Observation coding system

Availability: This instrument is described in: Reichenberg-Hackett, W., "Practices, attitudes, and values in nursery group education." *Psychological Reports*, 1962, **10**, 151–172.

Description: The Reichenberg-Hackett Teacher Behavior Observation System uses trained observers to measure the practices and attitudes of nursery school teachers as expressed in action. Teacher behavior is coded according to the following categories and subdivisions.

I. Teacher Approach

    A. Communicative
       1. Verbal
       2. Nonverbal
       3. With an individual
       4. With a group
       5. With a child
       6. With an adult

    B. Noncommunicative
       1. Child-centered
       2. Neutral
       3. Subjective
       4. Silent supervision

II. Teacher's Motivating Techniques

    A. Encouragement
    B. Management
    C. Discouragement

III. Activities

IV. Lessons Taught

V. Values Promoted

Because the last 3 categories are closely related, they are considered sequentially for each behavioral episode observed.

Sample Items: Reichenberg-Hackett (1962) provides examples of behavior typically coded under each category. Under Discouragement, for instance, the observer records teacher behaviors which suppress spontaneity, promote regimentation, or criticize with no attempt to correct. Statements such as, "You are not a good leader, Mary" are considered discouraging to the child.

Reliability: To determine interrater agreement, 2 teams of observers worked independently over a 3-month period in 4 of the same nursery groups, with the same teacher in charge. According to the author, these observations demonstrated "enough consistency to permit comparisons of teacher behavior (Reichenberg-Hackett, 1962, p. 154)." Furthermore, when 3 or 4 teams analyzed the same record of teacher behavior, they achieved 96% agreement on Teacher Approach, 85% on Teacher's Motivating Behavior, and 100% on Activities. Figures were not provided for the last 2 categories.

Validity: Data supporting the validity of this system are scarce. Reichenberg-Hackett (1962) does, however, report group differences uncovered by the instrument. Four nursery school groups, for example, were differentiated according to socioeconomic status, the upper-middle-class groups being characterized by an encouraging climate, more independence on the children's part, and frequent conversations, dealing with activities, interests, and alternatives, between the teacher and small groups of children. In lower-middle-class groups, on the other hand, there prevailed a restless atmosphere, in which the teacher frequently turned away from responsibilities, addressed the entire group rather individual children or small groups, and devoted a greater proportion of time to "neutral activities." Furthermore, nursery school groups which varied according to the degree of Encouragement vs. Discouragement showed a corresponding variation in the type of child behavior recorded.

An attempt to correlate observed teacher behavior with attitudes as expressed on the PARI Scale produced nonsignificant results (Reichenberg-Hackett, 1962).

Norms: The 11 nursery school groups studied by Reichenberg-Hackett (1962) were each composed of 15 to 20 4-year-old children. Six of the schools enrolled white children only, while 4 served black children. The teachers were of the same race as the pupils. The socioeconomic level of the pupils, determined by a modified version of the Henry Warner Occupational Prestige Scale, was judged upper-middle at 4 schools, middle at 2, and lower-middle at 5.

Procedures for Use: This system is used in 2 stages: observation and analysis. First, data are collected by trained observers working in teams of 2. Using a combination of shorthand and checkmarking, the 2 observers take 10-minute turns recording behavior in detail. Attention is always focused on the teacher in charge. Both communicative and noncommunicative behaviors are coded. These observations form a running account of teacher behavior which is broken into small units, or "episodes," for analysis. These episodes are reviewed and classified according to the 6 categories represented on the system. An individual episode may be analyzed repeatedly if it applies to several different categories.

Comments: Although developed for use with nursery school classes, the Reichenberg-Hackett Teacher Behavior Observation System is also appropriate for other age groups. It provides a picture of the teacher's interaction with individual children and with the group as a whole. Though psychometric data are limited, this instrument appears to be carefully and thoughtfully constructed. Behavioral categories are well defined and coding procedures are explicitly described.

References: Reichenberg-Hackett, W., *Children's attitudes, happiness and social values in nursery schools.* Paper presented at the 4th meeting of the Inter-American Society of Psychology, San Juan, Puerto Rico, December, 1956.

Reichenberg-Hackett, W., "Practices, attitudes, and values in nursery group education." *Psychological Reports,* 1962, **10**, 151–172.

Name: RUBOVITS AND MAEHR OBSERVATION SYSTEM

Authors: Pamela C. Rubovits and Martin L. Maehr

Type of Measure: Observation coding system

Availability: Rubovits, P. C., *Teacher interaction with students labeled gifted and nongifted in a micro-teaching situation.* Unpublished master's thesis, University of Illinois, 1970.

Description: The Rubovits and Maehr Observation System was developed in a study relating teacher expectations to teacher/student interaction (Rubovits, 1970; Rubovits and Maehr, 1971). Focusing specifically on the quality and quantity of teacher/student interaction, this instrument requires a trained observer to record the incidence of the following teacher behaviors:

1. *Attention* to students' statements
   a) to requested statements
   b) to spontaneous statements
2. *Encouragement* of students' statements
3. *Elaboration* of students' statements
4. *Ignoring* students' statements
5. *Praise* of students' statements
6. *Criticism* of students' statements

Although originally used to assess transactions in a micro-teaching situation, this observation system can be employed in regular elementary or secondary classrooms.

Sample Items: Though the dimensions included on this system are fairly explicit and self-explanatory, Rubovits (1970) provides examples of behavior typically coded under each category.

Reliability: In a preliminary reliability check, 2 raters achieved interobserver agreement of 90% or above for all categories (Rubovits and Maehr, 1971).

Validity: Evidence of validity is quite limited, though the authors maintain that the instrument is "reasonably objective in nature, allowing for minimal judgment on the part of the observer (Rubovits and Maehr, 1973, p. 217)." It has successfully revealed differences in teacher interaction with students labeled gifted and nongifted. For example, inexperienced teachers observed on this system were found to request significantly more statements from "gifted" than "nongifted" students, and to praise the former group significantly more than the latter (Rubovits and Maehr, 1971). In a similar study (Rubovits and Maehr, 1973), this instrument revealed that inexperienced teachers gave black students significantly less attention, less praise, and more criticism.

Norms: This coding system has been employed in a number of studies (Rubovits,

1970; Rubovits and Maehr, 1971; Rubovits and Maehr, 1973), though samples used have been quite similar. In an early study, Rubovits and Maehr (1971) observed 26 white female undergraduates, none of whom had completed student teaching, and 104 white sixth and seventh graders from a middle school in a small midwestern city. In a more recent investigation (Rubovits and Maehr, 1973), they observed 66 white female undergraduates, none of whom were enrolled in an education curriculum and none of whom had teaching experience, and 264 seventh and eighth graders (blacks as well as whites) attending 3 junior high schools in a small midwestern city. Both of these samples were observed in micro-teaching situations.

Procedures for Use: In using the Rubovits and Maehr Observation System, the observer sits in the classroom, about 2 rows behind the students. He or she begins categorizing teacher behavior when the class starts and continues doing so for 40 minutes.

When the observations are completed, frequency counts are tabulated on each teacher for all 8 categories.

Comments: The psychometric data published on this instrument are very limited, and those which are available are derived from a somewhat atypical population (undergraduates with no teaching experience, many of whom were not even enrolled in an education curriculum), teaching under atypical circumstances (micro-teaching). However, this instrument may be useful to researchers studying teacher-child interaction since it is easy to use, has a relatively narrow focus, and is applicable to almost any teaching situation or environment.

References: Rubovits, P. C., *Teacher interaction with students labeled gifted and nongifted in a micro-teaching situation.* Unpublished master's thesis, University of Illinois, 1970.

Rubovits, P. C., and M. L. Maehr, *The effect of the labels gifted and nongifted on teacher's interaction with black and white students.* Urbana, Illinois: Center for Instructional Research and Curriculum Evaluation, University of Illinois, 1970.

Rubovits, P. C., and M. L. Maehr, "Pygmalion analyzed: Toward an explanation of the Rosenthal-Jacobson findings." *Journal of Personality and Social Psychology,* 1971, **19**(2), 197–203.

Rubovits, P. C., and M. L. Maehr, "Pygmalion black and white." *Journal of Personality and Social Psychology,* 1973, **25**(2), 210–218.

Name: SCALE FOR RATING EFFECTIVE TEACHER BEHAVIOR

Author: Dwight E. Beecher

Type of Measure: Observer rating form

Availability: Beecher, D. E., *The evaluation of teaching: Backgrounds and concepts.* New York: Syracuse University Press, 1949.

Description: The Scale for Rating Effective Teacher Behavior (SRETB) is a 38-item device intended to measure vital aspects of the student/teacher relationship. Scale development began with a review of studies concerning pupil evaluation of teachers. This review produced 6 teacher rating categories: Fairness; Cheerfulness; Sympathetic Understanding; Control; Ability to Stimulate Response; and Knowledge. Under these categories were classified the specific, observable teacher behaviors which, according to the author, most frequently provoke a reaction among high school students. These behaviors are the scale's items. The observer, after rating the teacher on each of these items, may clarify his ratings with anecdotal comments, space for which is provided on the record sheet.

After several preliminary administrations, Beecher decided to leave the scale in its original form. He suggests (1949) that it be used by teachers for self-evaluation and by student teachers for supplemental training information.

Sample Items: Each item on the SRETB describes an observable teacher behavior. If the behavior described is observed, the item is marked with a plus sign; if its opposite is observed, the item is marked with a minus sign. From 5 to 8 items of the following type appear in each category:

Category	*Item*
Fairness	1. Shows no favorites.
Cheerfulness	2. Is not crabby or cross. Does not nag.
Sympathetic Understanding	3. Always tries to show approval of effort. Encouraging.
Control	4. Maintains good pupil conduct without reprimanding frequently.
Ability to Stimulate Response	5. Elicits responses, enthusiasm from students. Many pupils contribute.
Knowledge	6. Knows subject area well. Can answer students' questions.

Reliability: Beecher (1949) reports 2 reliability coefficients. Interrater agreement between 2 judges of the same teacher was estimated at .79. Also, 2 ratings of the same teacher, taken by the same observer on 2 different occasions, correlated .90.

Validity: Because it was developed directly from research findings related to pupil/teacher relationships and the variables affecting those relationships, the SRETB can claim some content validity. Evidence of concurrent validity is provided by Beecher (1949), who had a panel of "experts" rate 50 teachers as superior, average, or poor. The same 50 teachers were, at the same time, rated on the SRETB by an observer. Scores on the scale were used to divide the teachers into upper, middle, and lower groups. A contingency coefficient for these data was computed and found to be .72. Beecher, using Yule's Formula, corrected this contingency coefficient to estimate the product-moment correlation between the 2 ratings. The corrected value was .88.

Norms: Norms consist of percentile ranks, divided into 9 deciles, which correspond to computed scores. However, information regarding the number, kind, and location of teachers on which these norms are based is not reported.

Administration and Scoring: Beecher (1949) presents only a page of directions for administering the SRETB. Procedures for training observers are not mentioned, although it seems reasonable to assume that such training would be necessary. Because it takes a good deal of time to rate a single teacher on all 38 items, Beecher suggests that only 25 items be used at a time, thus requiring 2 classroom visits for a complete observation.

Scoring the SRETB involves computing the percentage of items marked positively. Thus, if 38 items are rated, and 34 of these ratings are positive, the teacher's score is $\frac{34}{38} \times 100$, or 89.

Comments: The Scale for Rating Effective Teacher Behavior is a logically developed instrument which can be useful in teacher evaluation or student teacher training. However, its value is limited by poorly defined norms and an absence of instructions for training observers. Furthermore, the "either/or" response format of the SRETB has been questioned (in Buros, 1953) since it allows no room for teacher behavior which falls in between the positive and negative extremes implied in Beecher's items.

References: Beecher, E., *The evaluation of teaching: Backgrounds and concepts.* New York: Syracuse University Press, 1949.

Buros, O. K., *The fourth mental measurements yearbook.* Highland Park, New Jersey: The Gryphon Press, 1953.

Name: SPAULDING TEACHER ACTIVITY RATING SCHEDULE (STARS)

Author: Robert L. Spaulding

Type of Measure: Observation coding system

Availability: This instrument may be ordered from: Robert L. Spaulding, Institute for Research in Child Development, Room 200, School of Education, San Jose State University, 125 South 7th Street, San Jose, California 95192.

Description: The Spaulding Teacher Activity Rating Schedule (STARS) is an observation coding system designed to assess the cognitive instructional methods and affective and control strategies of teachers. The current form is a 1975 revision of an earlier edition reviewed in *Mirrors for Behavior* (Simon and Boyer, 1970). Both forms have been used in teacher training to provide feedback to prospective teachers about their cognitive and affective styles. The revised form has also been used, along with its companion instrument, Coping Analysis Schedule for Educational Settings (CASES), in a study relating teacher behaviors and student outcomes (Spaulding, 1975b).

Sample Items: STARS consists of several molar categories, under which are subsumed a number of subcategories. These categories, listed below, are defined by Spaulding (1975b):

1. General
   a. Nontransactional behavior
   b. Disapproval with aversive stimuli
   c. Disapproval without aversive stimuli
   d. Withholding reinforcers when a student bids for attention
   e. Approval with positive affect present

2. Social and/or Motor Structuring and Restructuring
   a. Social and/or motor structuring
   b. Social and/or motor restructuring

3. Cognitive Structuring and Restructuring—unrelated to academic task

4. Concept Formation, Attainment, or Development by Discovery Methods
   a. Simple
   b. Complex

5. Concept Formation, Attainment, or Development by Deductive Methods
   a. Simple
   b. Complex

6. Concept Formation, Attainment, or Development by Transductive Methods
   a. Simple
   b. Complex

7. Concept Formation, Attainment, or Development by Expository Methods
   a. Telling—Simple
   b. Telling—Complex
   c. Rote Process—Simple
   d. Rote Process—Complex

8. Cognitive Structuring or Restructuring by Focusing Attention on Data

9. Concept Checking, Testing, Strengthening
   a. Asking for or eliciting recall—Simple
   b. Asking for or eliciting recall—Complex
   c. Asking for use or application—Simple
   d. Asking for use or application—Complex

10. Valuing
    a. Expressing
    b. Eliciting

11. Listening and/or Observing

Reliability: Preliminary work by Spaulding (1975a) indicates that split-half reliability is highly variable for some categories and more consistent for others. Routine recordings of interobserver agreement fall in the .80s and .90s.

Validity: STARS is based on a factor analytic study of 113 categories of teacher/student interaction observed in 21 elementary school classrooms. Three types of teacher variables recorded on STARS were significantly related to student performance and self-concept: (1) supportive teacher behaviors which served as rewards; (2) aversive behaviors which served as punishment; and (3) goal setting behaviors which served to clarify or structure the environment for the student. Other researchers have also found these variables to be significantly related to change in student behaviors (Sibley, Abbott, and Cooper, 1967, as cited by Simon and Boyer, 1970).

Norms: Norms can be derived by summing frequencies over several observation periods. An example of norm setting is provided by Simon and Boyer (1970).

Procedures for Use: STARS is generally used in conjunction with CASES. Together, the measures yield a picture of student/teacher interaction. Data are gathered by time sampling techniques, using 10-second intervals.

STARS yields a total score derived from a weighted interaction matrix using CASES and STARS. Frequencies from each cell of the matrix are weighted, added, and divided by the total number of tallies to produce an Overall STARS Coefficient.

Comments: STARS appears to be a relatively reliable and valid measure of the teacher's cognitive, affective, and control behaviors. STARS is a versatile system which can be used in conjunction with a variety of instruments, in a variety of settings, for both research and teacher training.

References: Simon, A., and E. G. Boyer, *Mirrors for behavior. An anthology of observation instruments.* Philadelphia: Research for Better Schools, 1970.

Spaulding, R. L., Personal communication, November 26, 1975. (a)

Spaulding R. L., *The Spaulding Teacher Activity Rating Schedule (STARS).* San Jose, California: Institute for Research in Child Development, School of Education, San Jose State University, 1975. (mimeo) (b)

Name: TEACHER PRACTICES OBSERVATION RECORD (TPOR)

Author: Bob Burton Brown

Type of Measure: Observation coding system

Availability: Brown, B. B., "Experimentalism in teaching practice." *Journal of Research and Development in Education,* 1970, **4**(1), 14–22.

Description: The Teacher Practices Observation Record (TPOR) is a companion instrument to the Personal Beliefs Inventory (PBI) and the Teacher Practices Inventory (TPI). The TPOR is designed to measure congruence between a teacher's observed behavior and his beliefs in relation to Dewey's "experimentalism" (Brown, 1970; Simon and Boyer, 1970). However, agreement or disagreement with Dewey's philosophy is not the primary focus of the TPOR. Instead, this instrument uses "experimentalism" as a theoretical framework within which to compare teacher practices with teacher beliefs (Brown, 1970).

　　This system consists of 62 items (31 positive and 31 negative), grouped into 7 categories. Even-numbered items are positive and pro-Dewey, while odd-numbered items are negative and anti-Dewey. The first 10 items focus on the "Nature of the (classroom) Situation." Items 11 through 20 concern questions or topics around which student activity is centered ("Nature of the Problem"), and items 21 through 30 involve "Development of Ideas." The fourth section (items 31 through 40) focuses on "Use of Subject Matter," while the next section centers on "Evaluation." Items 51 through 56 involve the extent to which the teacher provides for "Differentiation" of tasks to meet the needs of the students; and, a final section (items 57–62) focuses on "Motivation and Control" (Brown, 1970).

Sample Items: Sample items for each of the 7 sections appear below (Brown, 1970, pp. 17–18):

A. Nature of the Situation
   1. Teacher occupies center of attention.
   2. Teacher joins in pupil's activities.

B. Nature of the Problem
   1. Teacher organizes learning around question posed by teacher.
   2. Teacher emphasizes realistic, disconcerting, or "ugly" aspects of topic.

C. Development of Ideas
   1. Teacher accepts only one answer as being correct.
   2. Teacher encourages pupil to guess or hypothesize about the unknown or untested.

D. Use of Subject Matter
   1. Teacher collects and analyzes subject matter for pupil.
   2. Teacher questions misconceptions, faulty logic, unwarranted conclusions.

E. Evaluation
  1. Teacher passes judgment on pupil's behavior or work.
  2. Teacher gives pupil time to sit and think, mull things over.
F. Differentiation
  1. Teacher has all pupils working at same task at same time.
  2. Teacher evaluates work of different pupils by different standards.
G. Motivation, Control
  1. Teacher motivates pupil with privileges, prizes, grades.
  2. Teacher approaches subject matter in indirect, informal way.

Reliability: Internal consistency reliability coefficients for the TPOR range from .85 to .93 (Brown, 1970). Between-observer reliability coefficients for homogeneous groups of observers average .80 (Steele, 1969; Webb, 1969). Also, interobserver agreement of .57 is reported in a study which encouraged variability in ratings by selecting observers from a wide range of backgrounds (Brown, 1968).

Validity: Items on the TPOR meet high standards in regard to both content and predictive validity (Brown, 1970). In a study by Steele (1969), untrained observers demonstrated high agreement among themselves, but lower agreement with experts. After 10 hours of training, novice observers moved from 43 to 67% agreement with experts. Ten weeks later, observers obtained a validity coefficient rating of .58. Techniques for training have since been improved so that selected observers can now achieve validity coefficients of up to .80 and .90.

    TPOR's discriminating powers are illustrated in a study by Soar (1970) in which the instrument differentiated classroom behavior in seven diverse Follow-Through program models.

Norms: The maximum score on the TPOR is 186, which indicates complete experimentalism. The minimum score of 0 indicates complete nonexperimentalism. A score of 94 or above indicates that the teacher is more experimental than nonexperimental, while a score below 94 indicates the reverse. The highest score recorded at the time of this report was 153, and the lowest, 9. Mean scores ranged from 85 to 100 (Brown, 1970).

Procedures for Use: Trained, experienced observers record behavior every 2 to 3 minutes. Check marks are placed in a column next to the appropriate item as it occurs. At the close of an observing period (45 minutes), the observer reviews the rating sheet and makes any needed additions. He then sums the number of marks placed next to each item and records this number next to the item. Scores are reversed for odd-numbered items. Finally, all numbers are added to obtain a total score (Brown, 1970).

Comments: The TPOR has impressive reliability, validity, and normative data. It is easy to use, and the interpretation of results is clearly defined. Coders can be easily trained, and no special equipment is necessary to obtain accurate results.

References: Brown, B. B., *The experimental mind in education*. New York: Harper and Row, 1968.

Brown, B. B., "Experimentalism in teaching practice." *Journal of Research and Development in Education,* 1970, **4**(1), 14–22.

Brown, B. B., *Handbook for Teacher Practices Observation Record (TPOR).* Gainesville, Florida: University of Florida, undated.

Simon, A., and E. G. Boyer, *Mirrors for behavior. An anthology of observation instruments.* Philadelphia: Research for Better Schools, 1970.

Soar, R. S., *Interim report. Evaluation of Follow-Through model implementation.* Gainesville, Florida: Institute for Development of Human Resources, 1969.

Steele, K. R. L., *A comparison of two methods of preparing observers to make systematic classroom observations.* Unpublished doctoral dissertation, University of Florida, 1969.

Webb, J. N., *Improving reliability estimates for systematic classroom observations with the Teacher Practices Observation Record.* Unpublished doctoral dissertation, University of Florida, 1969.

Name: WALLEN'S MODIFICATION OF FLANDERS' INTERACTION ANALYSIS

Author: Norman E. Wallen

Type of Measure: Observation coding system

Availability: Wallen, N. E. *Relationships between teacher characteristics and student behavior—Part III.* Salt Lake City, Utah: Department of Educational Psychology, University of Utah, 1966. (ERIC Document Reproduction Service No. ED 010 390)

Description: This observation procedure was developed in a study of teacher behavior and pupil change (Wallen, 1966). In designing this system, the author modified Flanders' Interaction Analysis (1962) in regard to focus, recording procedures, and number and nature of behavioral categories observed. The focus, for example, was limited to teacher behavior only. Also, the continuous, sequential recording which characterizes the Flanders system was abandoned in favor of a simple frequency approach. Finally, some of Flanders' categories which were inapplicable to or inappropriate for the first- and third-grade samples used by Wallen were altered, producing the behavioral classifications listed below.

  1. Acknowledges student's raised hand

  2. Praise and encouragement

2a. Nonverbal affiliation

  3. Minimal reinforcement

  4. Asking questions with the intent that the student answer.

  5. Explaining or problem structuring

  6. Academic control

  7. Personal control

7m. Moralizing by teacher

  8. Hostility and reprimands

8x. Ignores child's behavior when child is attempting to get teacher's attention.

In using the system, the observer may record a given teacher behavior in more than one category. For example, if the teacher praises a pupil in an attempt to control the others, the action would be tallied as both a 7 (personal control) and then as either a 2 or a 3, depending on the strength of the reinforcement given.

Sample Items: While many of Wallen's categories are self-explanatory, he provides examples of specific behaviors which are coded under each area. "Nonverbal affiliation," for example, includes physical contact with the student, such as putting an arm around him or her. "Minimal reinforcement" refers to comments such as, "uh huh," "okay," "right," etc.

Reliability: The records of 4 raters who had observed the same teachers at the same time, shortly before and midway through the major data collection period, where compared by Wallen (1966). Descriptive profiles for 2 teachers showed adequate agreement among observers. Correlations between observations recorded simultaneously by the 2 members of each recording team also showed good correspondence. These ranged from .85 to .96 for Team I ($N = 33$ teachers) and from .65 to .94 for Team II ($N = 34$ teachers).

The 2 observation teams were also compared with regard to overall mean frequencies in each category. They showed close agreement in all areas except problem structuring (Wallen, 1968).

Validity: Validity may be inferred from correlations between teacher behavior observed on this system and (1) other assessments of teacher classroom behavior and (2) measures of pupil behavior.

After all observations had been completed, Wallen (1966) instructed observers to Q-sort the sample of teachers according to 10 categories analogous to those on the observation system. Results of these Q-sorts were correlated with observational data, revealing a satisfactory and expected relationship between the two. For example, "praise, and encouragement" on the observation scale correlated positively with the Q-sort dimensions, "warmth" and "supportive behavior." Coefficients were .67 and .60, respectively, for the first grade, and .47 and .42 for the third grade. Similarly, "praise and encouragement" correlated negatively with "punitive behavior" on the Q-sort.

Relationships between teacher behavior and pupil behavior also generally supported the validity of the observation system. Measures of pupil behavior included the following: California Achievement Tests; Circles Test from the Torrance Tests of Creative Thinking; the Barron-Welsh Art Scales; a sociometric device; and a Pupil Questionnaire composed of items from the Sarason Test Anxiety Scale and Medley and Kline's Liking for School Test (Wallen, 1966).

Norms: Wallen (1966) presents observational data collected on 36 first-grade and 40 third-grade teachers in a large metropolitan school district in Salt Lake City.

Procedures for Use: In using this system, the observer sits in the classroom for five 30-minute periods and records teacher behaviors in the appropriate categories. No attempt is made to indicate the sequence of these behaviors. Both frequency and proportion (percentage) scores are derived from the data obtained.

Comments: Wallen's observation system offers an uncomplicated, easy-to-use procedure for assessing the affective behavior of teachers. It requires low inference and relatively limited training on the coders' part and demonstrates adequate agreement among observers.

Reference: Wallen, N. E., *Relationships between teacher characteristics and student behavior—Part III*. Salt Lake City, Utah: Department of Educational Psychology, University of Utah, 1966. (ERIC Document Reproduction Service No. ED 010 390)

Name: WRIGHTSTONE OBSERVATION SYSTEM FOR MEASURING TEACHER CONDUCT OF CLASS DISCUSSION

Author: J. Wayne Wrightstone

Type to Measure: Observation coding system

Availability: Wrightstone, J. W., "Measuring teacher conduct of class discussion." *Elementary School Journal*, 1934, **34**, 454–460.

Description: In an early attempt to use controlled observation in the study of classroom processes, Wrightstone (1934b) developed this instrument to assess the teacher's management of class discussion. After visiting a number of classrooms, Wrightstone devised tentative categories of teacher behavior. He then applied these categories in several classrooms, revised them according to data obtained from these applications, and included those listed below on a final coding system.

A. Allows pupil to make a voluntary contribution.

B. Encourages pupil to make a contribution.

C. Proposes a question or thesis for pupil or class.

D. Refers pupil or pupils to sources of data or information.

E. Suggests (explains) means, method, activity, or solution.

F. Discourages or prohibits a pupil contribution.

G. Recalls pupil's attention by direct word, look, or gesture.

H. Assignment by teacher of specific subject matter or tasks.

I. Question and answer on assigned textbook subject matter.

Each time the teacher interacts with a pupil, the observer codes the behavior on a tally sheet, opposite the name of the pupil involved.

Sample Items: Wrightstone defines the above categories in an attempt to clarify for the observer the kinds of behavior to be recorded under each heading. Since the categories themselves are self-explanatory, these definitions are brief. Encouragement, for example, occurs when the teacher names a pupil, points to him, or otherwise designates him.

Reliability: Interobserver agreement, computed on records taken by 2 raters independently observing the same situation at the same time, reached 90% for pupil scores and 88% for category scores.

   To obtain split-half reliability, the observation system was applied in 12 elementary school classes, each of which was observed for a total of 180 minutes. Each record was divided in half, half scores were correlated, and the coefficients obtained were corrected by the Spearman-Brown formula. These coefficients ranged from .51 to .91, with a median of .83 (Wrightstone, 1934b).

Validity: Wrightstone (1934b) provides no data to support the validity of this instrument.

Norms: Percentage frequencies for each behavior category are reported for first-through sixth-grade classrooms in 2 elementary schools (Wrightstone, 1934b).

Procedures for Use: In using this instrument, the observer, as unobtrusively as possible, enters each teacher behavior opposite the name of the pupil who caused the teacher's response or received the teacher's attention. Wrightstone suggests that this entry be made on a standard form which lists pupils' names in alphabetical order.

Each teacher behavior is represented by a code, and the code is recorded each time that behavior is observed. The total number of codes which appears opposite a given pupil's name is regarded as that pupil's score. Scores for each pupil or for each class may be expressed as frequencies for individual code items or for the total of all items.

Comments: Like many of the early attempts at systematic classroom observation, Wrightstone's method requires a great deal of attention and speed on the observer's part. Since the pupil must be identified and the behavior categorized at the same time, this system is not easy to use. However, with some modification (e.g., the elimination of pupil names in favor of a blank seating chart), this instrument could serve as a model for the development of other observational measures of teacher behavior or classroom interaction.

References: Medley, D. M., and H. E. Mitzel, "Measuring classroom behavior by systematic observation," in N. L. Gage (ed.), *Handbook of research on teaching.* Chicago: Rand-McNally, 1963.

Wrightstone, J. W., "Analyzing and measuring democracy in the classroom." *Nation's Schools,* 1933, **11**, 31–35.

Wrightstone, J. W., "An instrument for measuring group discussion and planning." *Journal of Educational Research,* 1934, **27**, 641–650. (a)

Wrightstone, J. W., "Measuring teacher conduct of class discussion." *Elementary School Journal,* 1934, **34**, 454–460. (b)

Wrightstone, J. W., "Constructing an observational technique." *Teachers College Record,* 1935, **37**, 1–9.

Section II

IIA

About the pupil from the teacher

Name: BEHAVIOR CHECKLIST

Authors: Eli Rubin, Clyde B. Simson, and Marcus L. Betwee

Type of Measure: Rating scale

Availability: A copy of the instrument may be found in: Rubin, E. Z., C. B. Simson, and M. L. Betwee, *Emotionally handicapped children and the elementary schools.* Detroit, Michigan: Wayne State University Press, 1966.

Description: The Behavior Checklist is an instrument on which the teacher reports symptomatic behaviors exhibited by a child in the classroom. The items, representing behavioral and academic symptoms most frequently reported by teachers, were developed from previously used referral and screening forms. Seven scales were derived from a factor analysis of the 39 items making up the Checklist. These scales represent 7 distinct clusters, or factors: Disorientation and Maladaptation to the Environment; Antisocial Behavior; Unassertive, Overconforming Behavior; Neglect; Infantile Behavior; Immature Social Behavior; and Irresponsible Behavior.

    The Behavior Checklist has been employed as an initial referral form and as a means of assessing change in behavioral symptoms (Rubin, Simson, and Betwee, 1966). It is appropriate for use with children in kindergarten through fifth grade.

Sample Items: The 39 items are presented as descriptions of behavior. A rating is completed by the teacher or by another individual who is familiar with the child's classroom behavior over a period of time. The checklist contains items of the following type:

	Factor	*Item*
Factor I	Disorientation and Maladaptation to the Environment	Makes peculiar noises
Factor II	Antisocial Behavior	Tends toward primitive anger, tantrums, or wild damage
Factor III	Unassertive, Over-conforming Behavior	Considered a loner in class
Factor IV	Neglect	Frequently sick
Factor V	Infantile Behavior	Reacts badly to criticism
Factor VI	Immature Social Behavior	Will not share, or "take turns"
Factor VII	Irresponsible Behavior	Is aggressive in a roundabout way

Reliability: The factor analysis of the Checklist, based on ratings of 73 elementary school children referred by teachers for potential placement in a special education program, yielded 7 clusters (Rubin, Simson, and Betwee, 1966). Factor loadings for the items in each behavior cluster ranged from .41 to .78, with most loadings at .60 or higher. An additional factor analysis, based upon 2,600 children in 4 elementary grades, produced the same clusters. These data comprise the only evidence supporting internal consistency. At present, no other reliability information is available.

Validity: From 251 variables assessed in several diagnostic examinations, 100 were selected as criteria against which to validate the Behavior Checklist. These were classified into 3 groups: current diagnostic status information; current environmental influences; and antecedent factors in a child's early life. Diagnostic information included scores from physiological and neurological tests, projective tests, Frostig tests, the Metropolitan Achievement Test, and the Wide Range Achievement Test. The environmental information concerned parental age, occupation, and education as well as the nature of parent-child relations and disciplinary methods used in the home. Antecedent variables ranged over early childhood development.

Individual items and the 7 major factors of the Behavior Checklist were intercorrelated with the above variables based on data from 83 elementary school children (68 boys and 15 girls; mean age, 7 years) who had been referred for diagnostic screening (Rubin, Simson, and Betwee, 1966). The majority of the intercorrelations were low, failing to reach a level suggesting prediction. However, some of the correlations, especially those with physiological and neurological measures, supported the validity of the behavior clusters. The internal consistency of the scale, based upon factor analysis, serves as an index of its construct validity. No further validity data are reported.

Norms: The Behavior Checklist was developed on normal elementary school students, as well as pupils needing special services, from kindergarten, first, second, third, and fifth grades (Rubin, Simson, and Betwee, 1966).

Administration and Scoring: Children are rated by teachers or knowledgeable others on the 39 behavioral items. One check is placed beside items which are typical of the child; 2 checks indicate behavior very common to the child. The score for the entire Checklist, as well as for each individual factor, consists of the total number of checks. In individual diagnosis, the items are considered according to their weight and appropriateness for the child in question.

Comments: The reasonably high factor loadings characterizing the Behavior Checklist indicate adequate internal consistency. However, additional indices of internal consistency and data on other forms of reliability are needed. Construct validity is supported by the high factor loadings and to some extent by intercorrelations with other measures.

Further testing and use of the Checklist with different groups should generate more extensive norms. At this time, the Behavior Checklist is appropriate for diagnostic purposes only when it is used in conjunction with other instruments.

References: Rubin, E. Z., C. B. Simson and M. L. Betwee, *Emotionally handicapped children and the elementary schools.* Detroit, Michigan: Wayne State University Press, 1966.

Johnson, O. G., and J. W. Bommarito, *Tests and measurements in child development.* San Francisco, California: Jossey-Bass, 1971.

Name: THE BELLER CHILD DEPENDENCY AND INDEPENDENCE SCALES

Author: Emanuel K. Beller

Type of Measure: Rating scale

Availability: Beller, E. K., "Dependency and autonomous achievement striving related to orality and anality in early childhood." *Child Development*, 1957, **28**, 287–315.

Description: Beller's Child Dependency and Independence Scales include 2 separate measures: 1 assessing dependent behavior in children, and the other assessing independent or autonomous behavior. The former consists of 5 subscales which measure the frequency at which a child seeks help, recognition, physical contact, and proximity to adults, and his persistence in doing so. The latter, which also includes 5 subscales, measures the child's initiative, satisfaction in work, independence in performing routine tasks, success in overcoming obstacles in his environment, and ability to complete activities.

   Though these rating scales are based on the author's theoretical analysis of the relationships between children and parents, they can be used to measure the child's dependency on the teacher, and are therefore often completed by the teacher. They are appropriate for rating children aged $2\frac{1}{2}$ to 6 years old.

Sample Items: Each question on the 10 subscales is followed by a 7-point response range, from "very often and very persistent" to "very rarely and without persistence." When both frequency and persistence apply equally, the teacher uses the values 7, 5, 3, and 1 to rate the child. If, however, the child's dependent behavior is more frequent than it is persistent, or vice versa, the teacher indicates this by using the even-numbered values, 6, 4, and 2. The scales include items of the following type:

Dependency Scale

How often does the child seek approval from others?

   This refers to any request, direct or indirect, for praise or acknowledgement. For example, the child might let an adult know that he had carried out a task requested of him. Or he might show an adult something he had made or accomplished, or ask someone to watch him perform.

Independence Scale

How often does the child finish an activity?

   The child carries to completion an assigned or selected activity. This behavior contrasts to that of a child who gives up easily, becomes distracted, disinterested, or adheres to rigid perseveration.

Reliability: The reliability of the scales has been investigated by the author in 2 separate studies. The first (Beller, 1955) produced coefficients of agreement between the ratings of 4 pairs of nursery school teachers who had received intensive training in observation techniques. These teachers rated 43 children from $3\frac{1}{2}$ to 5 years of age attending preschools in Iowa. Ratings were correlated, and the coefficients obtained ranged from .66 to .98, with 53% being at or above .90, and 88% at or above .80.

Beller's second study (1957) compared teachers' ratings of 52 middle- and lower-class children from 28 to 74 months of age, most of whom were emotionally disturbed and all of whom attended therapeutic nurseries in New York City. Product-moment coefficients ranged from .62 to .84, with a median of .78, for the Dependency Scales, and from .67 to .80, with a median of .75, for the Independence Scales. *Rho* reliability coefficients for summed ratings of teacher pairs fell between .67 and .91, with a median of .84, for the Dependency Scales, and between .69 and .93, with a median of .83, for the Independence Scales. An analysis of variance demonstrated that a child's relative position in the group did not change significantly over time according to the ratings of different teacher pairs.

Validity: The validity of these scales has also been investigated by Beller (1955, 1957). Using a sample of 43 children from 42 to 67 months of age, he obtained a correlation of $-.53$ between the Dependency and Independence scales. On a sample of 49 children, aged 28 to 74 months, Beller found a correlation of $-.01$ between the two scales. He also reported significant positive relationships (.30 and .15, respectively), between dependency and orality and dependency and anality. Independence was negatively correlated with orality ($-.15$) and anality ($-.30$). Also, correlations between dimensions within each scale were significant and positive, while most of those between scales were neither positive nor significant. This finding supports the internal consistency and construct validity of the scales.

Norms: Normative data are not available. The ratings of children in the reliability and validity studies are not presented in detail.

Administration and Scoring: The Beller Scales are completed by adults (usually teachers) who are familiar with the children they are rating. In his studies, Beller has given raters extensive training prior to their final use of the scales. Scoring is fairly straightforward, with each dimension or behavior manifestation being scored separately, by simple summing.

Comments: The Beller Child Dependency and Independence Scales are useful measures for investigating drive tendencies in young children. They would be more useful, however, if norms, and more psychometric data in general, were provided. The information which is currently available on this instrument is, for the most part, positive.

References: Beller, E. K., "Dependency and independence in young children." *The Journal of Genetic Psychology*, 1955, **87**, 25–35.

Beller, E. K., "Dependency and autonomous achievement striving related to orality and anality in early childhood." *Child Development*, 1957, **28**, 289–315.

Beller, E. K., "Exploratory studies of dependency." *Transaction of the New York Academy of Science*, 1959, **21**, 414–426.

Emmerich, W., "Continuity and stability in early social development: II. Teacher rating." *Child Development*, 1966, **37**, 17–27.

Name: CLASSROOM BEHAVIOR INVENTORY

Authors: Earl S. Schaefer, May R. Aaronson, and Victor H. Small

Type of Measure: Rating scale

Availability: The 15-item form used in the Head Start Planned Variation Study may be obtained by requesting ERIC PN # 002801 from ERIC Document Reproduction Service, Leasco Information Products, 4827 Rugby Avenue, Bethesda, Maryland 20014. Other versions may be obtained from M. R. Aaronson, Center for Studies of Child and Family Mental Health, National Institute of Mental Health, 5600 Fishers Lane, Rockville, Maryland 20852.

Description: The Classroom Behavior Inventory (CBI) is designed to measure 3 behavior traits in the socioemotional domain: task orientation, extraversion, and hostility. The CBI consists of 15 items on which a teacher rates a preschool or elementary school child according to a 7-point scale.

   This instrument was developed from a factor analysis of Schaefer and Droppleman's Classroom Behavior Checklist, which was based on Schaefer's circumplex model of behavior (Schaefer, 1961). Three bipolar factors emerged, which served as the basis for a new 25-item instrument. Further factor analyses of the scores of over 5,000 children produced a condensed and revised final form of the CBI. Several other forms are available, however, along with a number of companion instruments.

Sample Items: Each of the 3 traits measured by the CBI are represented by 5 items. The teacher circles the number of the response which best describes the child in relation to a specific characteristic. Items of the following type appear on the inventory.

	Never	Almost never	Occasionally	Half the time	Frequently	Almost always	Always
Completes most jobs he starts.	1	2	3	4	5	6	7
Enjoys participating in activities with others.	1	2	3	4	5	6	7
Slow to forgive others.	1	2	3	4	5	6	7

Reliability: Several studies have investigated the reliability of the CBI. One of these (Walker, Bane, and Bryk, 1973) obtained retest reliability coefficients in the .70s, after a 3-week interval, on a sample of 464 Head Start children. Interrater reliability coefficients derived from the ratings of classroom aides and other paraprofessionals were highest for Task-Orientation scores (medians of .60 and .62). Median coefficients for Extraversion scores were .46 and .49 and for Hostility scores, .39 and .44. Large discrepancies were found between mean scores for the various raters.

Internal consistency coefficients obtained on the Home Start evaluation (Hi-Scope, 1973) sample of 180 children were .72 for Task Orientation, .72 for Extraversion, and .67 for Hostility. Correlations between items and total test scores showed that every item correlated higher with its assigned scale than with the other 2 scales.

Validity: Validity of the CBI has been approached in several different ways. Construct validity was established through factor analytic methods. A principal components analysis was performed on the scores of 464 Head Start children, yielding the same 3 factors that were used in developing the scale (Walker, Bane, and Bryk, 1973). These 3 factors also emerged in an analysis of the scores of 173 children in the Home Start pilot study (Hi-Scope, 1973).

Correlations between CBI subtest scores and scores obtained on other tests (cognitive and noncognitive) administered as part of the Head Start Planned Variation battery give evidence of the instrument's concurrent validity. As was expected, all correlations were low, ranging from −.10 to .29 (Walker, Bane and Bryk, 1973).

Datta, Schaefer and Davis (1968) found that both ethnic group and sex were significantly related to teachers' CBI ratings of 153 seventh-grade students. The effect of ethnic group was contingent on scholastic aptitude, but not on sex. Higher IQ blacks were rated as favorably as other subjects with higher IQs, but lower IQ blacks received less favorable reports than other lower IQ subjects. Boys, regardless of IQ or ethnic group, were scored less favorably than girls.

Norms: Normative data in the form of means and standard deviations are provided for each of the 3 subtests for 4,943 children who were in the 1971 Head Start Planned Variation Program. These data are grouped into following sub-samples: males, females, black children, white children, Mexican–American children, children with previous school experience, and children without previous school experience.

Administration and Scoring: The CBI is completed by a teacher or an observer. Instructions are printed on each form. For each of the 3 traits being measured, the child receives a separate score, which is computed by summing the points on the 5 items representing each trait.

Comments: The content validity of the Classroom Behavior Inventory is well supported by the factor analyses of the instrument. The 3 subscales appear to be measuring independent traits. Test/retest and internal consistency reliabilities are adequate, but more information is needed about the validity and profile interpretation of CBI scores. Since the CBI is a relatively new measure, still in a developmental stage, it should be used in formative rather than summative evaluation of children.

References: Datta, L., E. Schaefer, and M. Davis, "Sex and scholastic aptitude as variables in teachers' ratings of the adjustment and classroom behavior of

Negro and other seventh-grade students." *Journal of Educational Psychology,* 1968, **59**(2), 94–101.

Hi-Scope Foundation/Abt Associates, *Home Start evaluation study.* Draft interim report to the Office of Child Development, Department of Health, Education, and Welfare, No. HEW-OS-72-127. Ypsilanti, Michigan: Hi-Scope/Abt, 1973.

Schaefer, E. S., "Converging conceptual models for maternal behavior and child behavior," in J. C. Glidewell (ed.), *Parental attitudes and child behavior.* Springfield, Illinois: Thomas, 1961.

Walker, D. K., *Socioemotional measures for preschool and kindergarten children.* San Francisco: Jossey-Bass, 1973.

Walker, D. K., J. M. Bane, and A. S. Bryk, *The quality of the Head Start Planned Variation Data.* Report for the Office of Child Development under Grant No. H-1926. Cambridge, Massachusetts: Huron Institute, 1973.

Name: KOHN PROBLEM CHECKLIST

Authors: Martin Kohn and Bernice L. Rosman

Type of Measure: Checklist

Availability: Kohn, M., B. Parnes, and B. L. Rosman, *A rating and scoring manual for the Kohn Problem Checklist and Kohn Social Competence Scale.* New York: The William A. White Institute of Psychiatry, Psychoanalysis, and Psychology, 1972.

Description: The Kohn Problem Checklist (KPC) was designed to determine the presence or absence of the major clinical symptoms of emotional disturbance in children aged 3 through 6. The scale was developed from an initial list of 90 items which was administered to 150 children. Results of this administration were used in selecting 49 items for inclusion in the final scale. Factor analysis revealed 2 dimensions: Apathy-Withdrawal (Factor I) and Anger-Defiance (Factor II).

The KPC is completed by teachers or trained observers and is often used in conjunction with the Social Competence Scale, another measure developed by Kohn and Rosman and reviewed in this volume.

Sample Items: Teachers or observers rate the child according to a 3-point scale on 49 items of the following type:

	Not at all Typical	*Somewhat Typical*	*Very Typical*
1. Acts jealous of teacher's attention toward classmates.	0	1	2
2. Seldom talks.	0	1	2
3. Seems to be in a daze, bewildered.	0	1	2
4. Yells at people or hits things when angry.	0	1	2

Reliability: Several investigations of reliability have been conducted by the authors. Each of 407 children from 6 day care centers (3 with primarily white populations and 3 with primarily black) in New York City was rated independently by 2 full-time teachers. An interrater reliability coefficient of .57 was obtained for both factor scores. The reliability estimate for pooled teacher ratings of each child was .73 for both factors. The two factors correlated .18, indicating that they are relatively independent.

The stability of KPC scores was determined in a study of 486 children from day care centers in New York City. These children were rated on the KPC on 4 different occasions separated by intervals of 6, 12, and 18 months. After a 6-month interval, ratings computed by the same teacher correlated .60 for

Factor I and .73 for Factor II. Those done by different teachers correlated .46 (Factor I) and .54 (Factor II). After a 12-month period, the ratings of different teachers correlated .43 (Factor I) and .52 (Factor II). The corresponding figures for an 18-month interval were .35 and .47. The cross-factor correlations over these time intervals were much lower, ranging from −.08 to .11 (Kohn and Rosman, 1972b).

Validity: The KPC has been correlated with a number of external criteria. The authors (1971) found that children rated high in Anger-Defiance on the KPC had mothers that rejected or neglected them and those rated high in Apathy-Withdrawal had mothers who were overprotective and overcontrolling.

In another study (Kohn and Rosman, 1972a), they found that Factor I, Apathy-Withdrawal, was negatively correlated with scores on readiness and achievement tests given to children in the first and second grades. Factor II, Anger-Defiance, was not related to the achievement test scores of boys but was negatively correlated with the achievement scores of second-grade girls. The authors explain this finding by noting the cultural tolerance of anger and defiance in boys, but not in girls.

Results from another study by the authors (1973) indicated that cognitive functioning in a group of 287 5-year-old boys was related to social-emotional functioning, as measured on the KPC.

Norms: True normative data are not provided, though a table for converting raw factor scores to standard scores is available (Kohn, Parnes, and Rosman, 1972). This table is based on the scores of 604 girls and 628 boys representing a 20% random sample of children attending 90 day care centers in New York City in September of 1967. These children ranged in age from 35 to 70 months and came from lower- or lower-middle-class homes. The sample included blacks (56%), whites (27%), and Puerto Ricans (16%).

Administration and Scoring: An introductory page explaining rating procedures is included with the test form. The rater is to consider each item in reference to behavior which has occurred during "the most recent week." A child's score on each item corresponds to the number (0, 1, or 2) which has been circled. A list of the items representing each of the 2 factors is provided. A score is computed for each factor by summing responses to the appropriate items according to a special key which is provided to simplify scoring. A high score suggests the presence of many symptoms of emotional disturbance. Explanations and tables are supplied so that the user can determine standard scores and (when both the KPC and its companion measure, the Social Competence Scale, are used) pooled scores.

Comments: The Kohn Problem Checklist, like the Social Competence Scale, has been used primarily for research purposes. Though reliabilities are somewhat low, validity is adequate. The provision of normative data would enhance the value of this instrument.

References: Kohn, M., B. Parnes, and B. L. Rosman, *A rating and scoring manual for the Kohn Problem Checklist and Kohn Social Competence Scale.* New York: The William A. White Institute of Psychiatry, Psychoanalysis, and Psychology, 1972.

Kohn, M., and B. Rosman, "Therapeutic intervention with disturbed children in day care: Implications of the deprivation hypothesis." *Child Care Quarterly,* 1971, **1**(1), 21–45.

Kohn, M., and B. Rosman, "Relationship of preschool social-emotional functioning to later intellectual achievement." *Developmental Psychology,* 1972, **6**, 445–452. (a)

Kohn, M., and B. Rosman, "A social competence scale and symptom checklist for the preschool child: Factor dimensions, their cross-instrument generality, and longitudinal persistence." *Developmental Psychology,* 1972, **6**, 430–444. (b)

Kohn, M., and B. Rosman, "Cognitive functioning in five-year-old boys as related to social-emotional and background-demographic variables." *Developmental Psychology,* 1973, **8**, 277–294.

Kohn, M., and B. Rosman, "Social-emotional, cognitive, and demographic determinants of poor school achievement: Implications for a strategy of intervention." *Journal of Educational Psychology,* 1974, **66**(2), 267–276.

Name: KOHN SOCIAL COMPETENCE SCALE

Authors: Martin Kohn and Bernice Rosman

Type of Measure: Rating scale

Availability: Kohn, J., B. Parnes, and B. Rosman, *A rating and scoring manual for the Kohn Problem Checklist and Kohn Social Competence Scale.* New York: The William A. White Institute of Psychiatry, Psychoanalysis, and Psychology, 1972.

Description: The Social Competence Scale is designed to assess the social-emotional functioning of 3- to 6-year-old children, in relation to mastery of the environment. It is completed by teachers or trained observers, who rate children on 1 of 2 forms: (1) a 73-item version for use in full-day nurseries and kindergartens; or (2) a 64-item scale appropriate for half-day settings.

In developing the scale, the work of Chance (1959) was used to define high and low social competence. Coping behavior was categorized as Active or Passive and Friendly or Hostile (i.e., Positive or Negative), thus producing 4 dimensions of interpersonal functioning: Positive/Active, Negative/Active, Negative/Passive, and Positive/Passive. Among these dimensions, only Positive/Active represented competent functioning. Within this theoretical framework, 200 items were written, screened, and finally tested on 45 children. Those showing adequate interrater reliability were retained. A factor analysis of the scale revealed 2 factors: Interest-Participation vs. Apathy-Withdrawal (I) and Cooperation-Compliance vs. Anger-Defiance (II).

Sample Items: In completing the 73-item Social Competence Scale, the teacher or observer rates the child on items similar to those below.

	Always	Very often	Often	Sometimes	Hardly	Hardly ever	Never
1. The child strikes the teacher.	1	2	3	4	5	6	7
2. The child is willing to try new things.	1	2	3	4	5	6	7
3. The child follows instructions and requests.	1	2	3	4	5	6	7
4. The child is imitated by the other children.	1	2	3	4	5	6	7

Reliability: The reliability of the instrument has been investigated by the authors (Kohn and Rosman, 1972b). Children (N = 407) from predominantly lower- and lower-middle-class families in New York City were rated by 2 full-time teachers. These ratings correlated .62 (Factor I scores) and .66 (Factor II scores). The reliability coefficients for the pooled ratings of head and assistant teachers, corrected by the Spearman-Brown formula, were .77 and .80 for Factors I and II, respectively.

Another sample of 486 children from New York City day care centers was used to compare teacher ratings completed on 4 different occasions. After a 6-month interval, ratings completed by the same teacher correlated .66 for Factor I and .75 for Factor II. Those done by different teachers correlated .50 (Factor I) and .57 (Factor II). After a 12-month interval the ratings of different teachers correlated .41 (Factor I) and .52 (Factor II). The corresponding figures for an 18-month interval were .35 and .48 (Kohn and Rosman, 1972b).

Validity: The authors have conducted several studies investigating the validity of the scale. They found Interest-Participation positively correlated to school readiness and first- and second-grade achievement test scores, with coefficients ranging from .23 to .41. Anger-Defiance was not correlated with achievement for boys, but was negatively correlated with second-grade achievement measures for girls. The authors explain this finding by noting the cultural tolerance of anger and defiance in boys but not in girls (Kohn and Rosman, 1972a). In a similar study Kohn and Rosman (1974) found that the preschool scores of 209 boys on Factor I of the Social Competence Scale significantly predicted their second-grade achievement test scores.

Using a sample of 287 boys attending public kindergartens and day care centers in New York City, Kohn and Rosman (1973) also found preschool social-emotional functioning, as measured on the Social Competence Scale, related to preschool cognitive functioning. Social competence, in fact, accounted for as much variance in cognitive functioning as did background demographic variables.

Norms: True normative data are not provided, though a table for converting raw factor scores to standard scores is available (Kohn, Parnes, and Rosman, 1972). This table is based on the scores of 604 girls and 628 boys representing a 20% random sample of children attending 90 day care centers in New York City in September of 1967. These children ranged in age from 35 to 70 months and came from lower- or lower-middle-class homes. The sample included blacks (56%), whites (27%) and Puerto Ricans (16%).

Administration and Scoring: Rating instructions accompany each test form. The rater is to consider each item in reference to the behavior during "the most recent week." A child's score on each item corresponds to the number (1 to 7 on the full-day form, 1 to 5 on the half-day form) which has been circled. A score is computed for each factor by summing the scores on items representing that factor. Since the factors are bipolar, some items have negative values while others have positive values. This difference is taken into account on the scoring form which is provided. Explanations and tables are also supplied so that the user can determine standard scores and (when both the Social Competence Scale and its companion measure, the Problem Checklist, are used) pooled scores.

Comments: The Social Competence Scale has been used primarily as a research tool. It has potential value, however, in evaluation, prediction, and therapeutic intervention. Though reliabilities are somewhat low, validity information is satisfactory. The provision of normative data would make this instrument more useful.

References: Chance, E. *Families in treatment.* New York: Basic Books, 1959.

Kohn, M., B. Parnes, and B. Rosman, *A rating and scoring manual for the Kohn Problem Checklist and Kohn Social Competence Scale.* New York: The William A. White Institute of Psychiatry, Psychoanalysis, and Psychology, 1972.

Kohn, M., and B. Rosman, "Relationship of preschool social-emotional functioning to later intellectual achievement." *Developmental Psychology,* 1972, **6**, 445–452. (a)

Kohn, M., and B. Rosman, "A social competence scale and symptom checklist for the preschool child: Factor dimensions, their cross-instrument generality, and longitudinal persistance." *Developmental Psychology,* 1972, **6**, 430–444. (b)

Kohn, M., and B. Rosman, "Cognitive functioning in five-year-old boys as related to social-emotional and background-demographic variables." *Developmental Psychology,* 1973, **8**, 277–294.

Kohn, M., and B. Rosman, "Social-emotional, cognitive, and demographic determinants of poor school achievement: Implications for a strategy of intervention." *Journal of Educational Psychology,* 1974, **66**(2), 267–276.

Name: TEACHER RATING SCALE

Authors: Judith A. Agard and Sandra M. Harrison

Type of Measure: Rating scale

Availability: Agard, J. A., and S. M. Harrison, *Teacher Rating Scale* (*developmental stage*). *Teacher's instructions*. Austin, Texas: Project PRIME, undated.

Description: The Teacher Rating Scale (TRS) allows the teacher to evaluate individual pupils on 4 dimensions: Academic Concentration; Misbehavior; Outgoing-Expressive; and Anxious-Depressed. These dimensions were identified through separate factor analyses of data from 3 subsamples (640 mentally retarded, 286 learning disabled, and 928 normal children) and a total, combined sample. Analyses of the normal and total samples yielded only 2 common factors, but data from the learning disabled group produced a 4-factor structure which was selected as the basis for scaling. Although minor in terms of item representation, the 2 additional factors (Outgoing-Expressive and Anxious-Depressed) were included for reasons of psychological interest.

While originally developed for Project PRIME (Programmed Re-Entry Into Mainstream Education) and designed for teachers of elementary school children, this instrument could, with a few minor alterations, be used to rate secondary pupils as well.

Sample Items: The teacher responds to each of the 85 TRS items by rating the child on a 5-point response continuum ("Always" to "Never"). Items of the following type appear on the instrument.

Scale	Item
I. Academic Concentration	1. Requires continual supervision to finish his/her assignment.
	2. Can stick to a task for a long period of time.
II. Misbehavior	1. Is rowdy and disruptive in class.
	2. Breaks the rules.
III. Outgoing-Expressive	1. Voluntarily offers ideas in class discussion.
	2. Is comfortable and at ease with other pupils.
IV. Anxious-Depressed	1. Responds to criticism or reprimand by withdrawing.
	2. Gets discouraged when makes a mistake.

Reliability: Alpha coefficients for each TRS factor were computed separately for 3 subsamples and the total sample (Veldman, undated). These ranged from .69 to .98 for the mentally retarded group, from .73 to .98 for the learning disabled children, and .75 to .98 for the normal and total samples. In each case, the 2 short scales (Outgoing-Expressive and Anxious-Depressed, containing 5 and 6 items, respectively) were least reliable.

Validity: Analyses of variance revealed expected differences (significant beyond the .01 level) among the TRS ratings of MR, LD, and normal groups. Normal children, for example, were rated much higher than the MR and LD pupils on Academic Concentration and Outgoing-Expressive behavior, and lower on Misbehavior and Anxiety. The MR sample was rated lower than the LD group on all factors except Anxiety (Veldman, undated).

Norms: Normative data (means, standard deviations, and quartiles) are provided for each TRS scale on a sample of 2,031 children (Veldman, undated).

Administration and Scoring: The TRS is self-administering. The teacher can complete 1 rating in about 15 minutes, using a separate, machine-scorable answer sheet for each child.

   Response alternatives are assigned numerical values, and scale scores are computed by simple summing. Low scores are associated with scale names.

Comments: Like other Project PRIME measures, the Teacher Rating Scale is still in a developmental stage. Its 2 major factors, however, appear to reliably assess 2 fundamental aspects of classroom behavior, while its 2 second-order factors measure 2 well established dimensions of personality.

References: Agard, J. A., and S. M. Harrison, *Teacher Rating Scale* (*developmental stage*). *Teacher's instructions.* Austin, Texas: Project PRIME, Undated.

Veldman, D. J., *Scale structure of Teacher Rating Scale.* Austin, Texas: Project PRIME Data Analysis Center, University of Texas, undated.

Name: TEACHER'S RATING SCALE

Author: Eli Rubin

Type of Measure: Rating scale

Availability: Rubin, E., *Rating guide for Teacher's Rating Scales*. Detroit, Michigan: Northeast Guidance Center, 1962.

Description: The Teacher's Rating Scale (TRS) is designed to measure the social and emotional adjustment of emotionally disturbed children in kindergarten through second-grade classrooms. The nature of the items indicates, however, that this test applies to children in general. Containing 79 separate scales, the TRS assesses many different characteristics, including mood, curiosity, aggressiveness, concentration, sulking, stealing, nervous habits, anxiety, popularity, attention-seeking, and shyness. The teacher rates the child on each item, using a 9-point scale.

The TRS was initially used in a study by Rubin, Simson, and Betwee (1966), in which 28 experimental subjects in special classrooms and 28 control subjects in regular classrooms were compared. The author maintains that the scale is useful in evaluating gains in social and emotional adjustment resulting from placement in special education classrooms for the emotionally disturbed.

Sample Items: Each 9-point response scale is punctuated with rating cues to guide the examiner. Usually the first, fifth, and ninth scale points are described. Though the second, fourth, sixth, and eighth points are omitted, they may be used when greater precision is needed. Items of the following type appear on the scale:

Scale	*Item*
Anger	1. Child rarely gets angry.
	3.
	5. Child sometimes gets angry, about as often as other children his age.
	7.
	9. Child is angry very often.
Impulse Control	1. Child rarely acts impulsively.
	3.
	5. Child sometimes acts impulsively, but has some control of his impulses.
	7.
	9. Child is very impulsive and rarely considers the consequences of his actions.

Reliability: Interrater reliability coefficients between 2 judges rating 12 subjects ranged from .26 to .94. Two-thirds of the coefficients were above .75. Only 4 scales yielded coefficients lower than .50 (Rubin et al., 1966).

Validity: The TRS was used to evaluate changes in classroom behavior among emotionally disturbed children placed in special classes. Subjects were 56 emotionally immature children, half of whom received the treatment. The experimental children showed greater improvement than the control subjects on 64 of the 79 items. However, significant discrimination between the groups was found for 8 items: mood, academic achievement, quarrelsomeness, day-dreaming, impulse control, popularity, intensity of overt anger, and friendly approach (Rubin et al., 1966).

A follow-up study using 35 children from the original sample indicated that the experimental group maintained superiority over the control group. On 81% of the 79 variables, the experimental group showed a higher level of adjustment than the control group. On 16%, the control group was rated higher.

Norms: Group pre- and posttreatment means for the 56 emotionally immature children used in the validity and reliability studies are available for all 79 TRS scales (Rubin et al., 1966).

Administration and Scoring: In completing the TRS, the teacher should consider the child's usual behavior and not one or two unusual incidents. The manual points out that the numbering of scale points does not reflect a value judgment and that point 5 does not always represent average behavior. Alongside each item, space is provided for remarks and anecdotal behavior descriptions.

The TRS scoring sheet provides boxes representing 2 different settings: the teacher's sphere and independent seatwork. On some items, the teacher rates the child in each setting. On others, he or she records a general impression of the child, regardless of setting. For example, 2 ratings are required on the first item below, and 1 on the second.

	Teacher's sphere	*General*	*Independent work*
1. Patience	☐		☐
2. Popularity		☐	

Comments: The Teacher's Rating Scale should be administered to larger samples of children in order to gain more precise validity information. Preliminary work indicates that the scale is useful in measuring changes in the classroom behavior of emotionally disturbed children who have received special education. It can also serve as an assessment device in the evaluation of experimental programs.

References: Rubin, E. A., *Rating guide for Teacher's Rating Scales.* Detroit, Michigan: Northeast Guidance Center, 1962.

Rubin, E. A., C. B. Simson, and M. C. Betwee, *Emotionally handicapped children and the elementary school.* Detroit, Michigan: Wayne State University Press, 1966.

IIB

About the pupil from the pupil

Name: ABOUT ME

Author: James Parker

Type of Measure: Rating scale

Availability: Parker, J., "The relationship of self report to inferred self concept. *Educational and Psychological Measurement*, 1966, **26**, 691–700.

Description: About Me was developed in a study examining differences between the self-reports of children and their self-concepts as inferred from their behavior (Parker, 1966). It contains 30 items measuring 5 areas of self-concept: the Self; the Self in Relation to Others; the Self as Achieving; the Self in School; and the Physical Self. The items are arranged in such a way that any 5 in sequence will tap each of the areas of self-concept.

Although About Me was developed for use with sixth-grade children, its content seems appropriate for other elementary grade levels as well.

Sample Items: Each item is represented on a continuum at the ends of which are positive and negative statements relating to a particular aspect of self. Six items of the following type are included for each of the 5 self-concept areas:

Area A: The Self

(1)　　　　(2)　　　　(3)　　　　(4)　　　　(5)

I'm a nice person.　　　　　　　　　I'm not a nice person.

Area B: The Self in Relation to Others

(1)　　　　(2)　　　　(3)　　　　(4)　　　　(5)

Most of the kids like me.　　　　Most of the kids don't like me.

Area C: The Self as Achieving

(1)　　　　(2)　　　　(3)　　　　(4)　　　　(5)

I'm good at most things　　　　I'm not good at most things.

Area D: The Self in School

(1)　　　　(2)　　　　(3)　　　　(4)　　　　(5)

I get good grades in school.　　　　I get poor grades in school.

Area E: The Physical Self

(1)　　　　(2)　　　　(3)　　　　(4)　　　　(5)

I'm good at sports and games　　　　I'm not very good at sports and games.

Reliability: About Me was administered to 31 sixth-grade pupils on 2 occasions, separated by an unspecified interval. An agreement of 64.2% was obtained between the 2 administrations (Parker, undated).

Validity: Data on the validity of this instrument are scarce. Correlations between

About Me and another measure devised by Parker (1966), the Picture Story Test, reveal more about what the instrument does *not* measure than what it does measure. About Me and the Picture Story Test, a projective measure from which self-concept ratings are inferred, were administered to 31 sixth-graders under 2 conditions. On the first administration children were assured anonymity; on the second, they were required to sign their names to both tests. Under confidential conditions, About Me scores correlated .14 (Self in Relation to Others) to .36 (Physical Self) with the inferred ratings of self-concept. Under nonconfidential conditions, the corresponding figures were −.12 (Physical Self) to .03 (Self in Relation to Others). Even under nonthreatening conditions, then, correlations between the self-report and the inferred self-concept were low, indicating that the 2 measures do not furnish the same insight into personality (Parker, 1966). Teachers recognized children more often (70%) from the inferred ratings than from the children's self-reports.

Correlations between signed and unsigned responses to About Me ranged from .65 (Self in School) to .80 (the Self), suggesting that scores are not greatly affected by social desirability.

Norms: The test was originally administered to 31 sixth-grade children enrolled in an urban public school, but normative data are not provided for this sample.

Administration and Scoring: Clear and concise instructions are printed on the test form. The respondent is advised that there are no right or wrong answers and is encouraged to work quickly, without dwelling on any particular item. Although there is no time limit, most children complete the instrument in 15 minutes or less.

The scoring procedure suggested involves summing the numerical values of the subjects' ratings. Low scores indicate positive self-concepts and high scores suggest relatively negative self-concepts. Area scores can also be computed using the same procedure.

Comments: Parker (undated, p. 7) admits that "this device is informal in that it was not rigorously standardized." It is also informal in that it was apparently devised without reference to any theoretical rationale. This particular shortcoming makes it difficult to determine exactly what the instrument is measuring. On the one hand, Parker (undated, p. 7) claims that "low scores indicate positive self concepts," thus leading us to believe that this is indeed a measure of self-concept. Yet, on the other hand, he maintains that "there is no basis for concluding that the self report accurately reflects children's perceptions of self (Parker, 1966, p. 699)." Without more definite evidence of validity, this measure should be used for research purposes only. Since it has good face validity and is easy to administer, it may be of value in that context.

References: Parker, J., *About me.* Clearwater, Florida: Author, undated.

Parker, J., "The relationship of self report to inferred self concept." *Educational and Psychological Measurement*, 1966, **26**, 691–700.

Name: ABOUT YOU AND YOUR FRIENDS

Authors: Judith A. Agard and Sandra M. Harrison

Type of Measure: Self-report questionnaire

Availability: Agard, J. A., and S. M. Harrison, *About You and Your Friends* (*developmental stage*). *Test administrator's instructions.* Austin, Texas: Project PRIME, undated.

Description: About You and Your Friends is a measure of self-perception developed for Project PRIME (Programmed Re-Entry Into Mainstream Education) and intended for use with elementary school children. Its 96 items represent 4 factors derived from analyses performed separately on the scores of 620 mentally retarded children, 317 learning disabled children, and 1,023 normal children, and the 3 samples combined (Veldman, 1973a). Although 3 of the 4 analyses indicated a 3-factor solution, the 4-factor solution obtained on the normal population was selected as the basis for the scale since it clearly revealed 2 separate types of negative-affect item content. The 4 factor scales which emerged from these analyses are: Loneliness and Rejection (19 items); Enjoys School (30 items); Does Well in School (21 items); and Misbehavior (13 items).

Sample Items: This scale contains 96 questions of the following type, to which the child responds by writing "yes" or "no" on his answer sheet:

1. Are you afraid of making mistakes at school?

2. Do you sometimes give up on your school work because it is so difficult?

3. Does the teacher scold you a lot?

4. Do you enjoy playing with younger children rather than children your own age?

Reliability: Alpha coefficients of internal consistency are reported for each of the instrument's 4 scales (Veldman, 1973a). These range from .69 to .82 for a sample of mentally retarded children; from .75 to .88 for a learning disabled sample; from .77 to .83 for a normal sample; and from .76 to .84 for the 3 samples combined. Alpha reliabilities ranging from .68 to .92 are also reported for the following subgroups: mentally retarded (MR) children in segregated classrooms; MR children in integrated classrooms; learning disabled (LD) children in segregated classrooms; LD children in integrated classrooms; and normal children in grades 3, 4, and 5 (Veldman, 1973b).

Validity: Some construct validity may be inferred from scale intercorrelations obtained for mentally retarded ($N = 626$), learning disabled ($N = 319$), and normal ($N = 978$) children. These revealed 2 expected scale relationships: Loneliness-Rejection and Misbehavior were positively correlated at .40, .42, and .37; Enjoys School and Does Well in School were related at .42, .44, and .46.

Further analyses provided additional evidence of the instrument's validity.

For example, among the 3 samples, normal children indicated the least loneliness and rejection, while mentally retarded children, especially girls, reported the most. Scores also showed that normal children enjoyed school more than the other 2 groups and that, in general, girls reported more enjoyment than boys. Similarly, normal children scored higher on the Does Well in School scale, while MR and LD children, especially those in integrated classrooms, scored low. On Misbehavior, boys scored higher than girls, except among integrated MR and LD students, and normal children scored the lowest (Veldman, 1973b).

Norms: Sample size, mean, standard deviation, standard error of the mean, and percentile equivalents of all possible raw scores are provided by Veldman (1973b) for each of the 4 scales, for each of 6 subgroups (MR, LD, and normal, by sex).

Administration and Scoring: In administering About You and Your Friends, the examiner reads each item aloud to the children, who respond on an answer sheet which encloses every 5 items in a separate box. The administrator may refer to these boxes in assuring that pupils are responding in the appropriate spaces.

For scoring, item responses are transferred from the answer sheets to an optical-scan form. An answer of "yes" is assigned a value of 1, "no" a value of 2.

Comments: About You and Your Friends is a well constructed and reasonably reliable scale. While there are indications of construct validity, the user is advised to exercise caution in interpreting scores in absolute terms (Veldman, 1973a). Reluctance or inability to give an accurate self-report (or subjective differences in interpreting questions) could invalidate scores in relation to external criteria. As a measure of self-perception, however, this scale appears to be valid. Because it is still in a developmental stage, About You and Your Friends should be used for research purposes only.

References: Veldman, D. J., *Scale structure of About You and Your Friends.* Austin, Texas: Project PRIME Data Analysis Center, University of Texas, 1973. (a)

Veldman, D. J., *Scale structure of About You and Your Friends. Supplementary analyses.* Austin, Texas: Project PRIME Data Analysis Center, University of Texas, 1973. (b)

Name: ADJECTIVE CHECK LIST

Authors: Helen Davidson and Gerhard Lang

Type of Measure: Checklist

Availability: Davidson, H. H., and G. Lang, "Children's perceptions of their teachers' feelings toward them related to self-perception, school achievement, and behavior." *Journal of Experimental Education*, 1960, **29**, 107–118.

Description: The Adjective Check List is designed to measure a child's self-perception and his perception of teachers' attitudes toward him. It is composed of 35 words, describing behavioral and personality traits. The Check List is intended for use with fourth-grade through junior high school students.

Adjectives to be included on the Check List were selected according to their suitability for 10- to 16-year-old children. To ensure that the final list would include an equal number of words having positive and negative connotations, the adjectives being considered were rated as "favorable," "unfavorable," or "neutral" by 35 teachers and 50 junior high school students. Only those words on which teachers and students reached at least 80% agreement were retained. Adjectives rated as "neutral" were discarded.

Sample Items: The 35 items are presented in a list. Each is rated on a 3-point scale ("Most of the Time," "Half of the Time," and "Seldom or Almost Never") depending on the respondent's perception of his teacher's view of him. Adjectives of the following type are included on the Check List.

Intelligent

Reasonable

Tidy

Mannerly

Trustworthy

Reliability: The Adjective Check List was administered to 4 junior high school classes ($N = 105$) on 2 different occasions, separated by an interval of 4 to 6 weeks. A rank-difference correlation coefficient of .85 was obtained (Davidson and Lang, 1960).

Validity: The empirical and concurrent validity of the instrument was established by administering the Adjective Check List and a modified version of the Teacher Approval and Disapproval Scale to 93 junior high school children. The latter instrument measures students' perceptions of the teacher's attitude toward class members. Each student was asked to indicate on the Check List those adjectives which described his *teacher's* feelings toward him. Thus, the student's own perception of his teacher's appraisal of him (obtained on the Adjective Check List) was correlated with his classmates' perceptions of the teacher's feelings toward him (as indicated by scores on the Teacher Approval and Disapproval Scale). The rank-difference ($p < .001$) correlation between Check List and Scale scores was .51 (Davidson and Lang, 1960).

Some evidence of content validity is provided by techniques, already mentioned, which were used in constructing the Check List.

Norms: No normative data are reported (Davidson and Lang, 1960).

Administration and Scoring: In administering the instrument, children are instructed to rate each trait name on a 3-point scale according to how their teacher feels toward them. On "favorable" items, the response "Most of the Time" is scored 3 points; "Half the Time" is scored 2 points; and "Seldom or Almost Never" is scored 1 point. For items judged "unfavorable," the scoring procedure is reversed. The total score, or Index of Favorability, is obtained by summing the scores of all adjectives and dividing this sum by the number of words checked. The higher the index, the more favorable is the student's perception of his teacher's appraisal of him. Index values range from 1.00 to 3.00.

Comments: Judging from the limited data that are available, reliability and validity appear to be satisfactory. The instrument is presently most appropriate as a research tool. The inclusion of normative data would broaden the scale's applicability.

References: Davidson, H. H., and G. Lang, "Children's perceptions of their teachers' feelings toward them related to self-perception, school achievement, and behavior." *Journal of Experimental Education*, 1960, **29**, 107–118.

Johnson, O. G., and J. W. Bommarito, *Tests and measurements in child development*. San Francisco: Jossey-Bass, 1971.

Name: THE ADJUSTMENT INVENTORY (STUDENT FORM)

Author: Hugh M. Bell

Type of Measure: Self-report questionnaire

Availability: Bell, H. M., *The adjustment inventory, student form* (revised). Palo Alto, California: Consulting Psychologists Press, 1962.

Description: The Adjustment Inventory provides separate measures of personal and social adjustment as well as a total adjustment score. Scales on the original (1934) version are: Home, Health, Social, and Emotional Adjustment. The more recent version (1962) consists of 200 questions designed to supply information about a student's adjustment in 6 areas: Home, Health, Submissiveness, Emotionality, Hostility, and Masculinity. Questions are labeled for quick identification of the problem area involved. Results can be used as an aid in individual diagnosis, an index of total adjustment, or a means of comparing 2 individuals. The manual suggests that the inventory offers a unique contribution by providing information regarding maladjustment in several areas.

The instrument is appropriate for males and females of high school and college age.

Sample Items: The inventory requires the respondent to circle "yes," "no," or "?" for each item. Both versions contain items of the following type.

Scale	Response Alternatives	Items
Home Adjustment	Yes No ?	Have you ever intensely felt like running away from home?
	Yes No ?	Does your mother control things at home?
Health Adjustment	Yes No ?	Do you catch cold from others easily?
	Yes No ?	Have you ever been in surgery?
Social Adjustment	Yes No ?	Do you often not know just what to say in a group?
	Yes No ?	Is it easy for you to request aid from others?
Emotional Adjustment	Yes No ?	Do things easily discourage you?
	Yes No ?	Do you often feel low because of poor grades in school?

Reliability: According to the original manual (Bell, 1934), reliability coefficients were estimated by correlating the odd and even items of the inventory, and correcting by the Spearman-Brown formula. The coefficients obtained from 258 college juniors and freshmen were relatively high, at .89 for Home and Social Adjustment, .80 for Health Adjustment, .85 for Emotional Adjustment, and .93 for the total score. Odd/even reliabilities for the more recent version are all in the .80s (reported in Buros, 1965).

Validity: Content validity of the Adjustment Inventory was established through a 3-step process. First, items which seemed appropriate were written. Then those which failed to correlate highly with the test as a whole were eliminated. Items remaining on the preliminary instrument were validated against a number of external criteria. Only those which differentiated between the upper and lower 15% of a distribution of scores were retained. Furthermore, several sections of the Inventory were evaluated in interviews with 400 college students over a 2-year period.

The Inventory was tested for concurrent validity by correlating its scale scores with other measures. Social Adjustment was correlated with the Allport Ascendance-Submission Test ($N = 46$ men, 50 women), yielding coefficients of .72 for men, and .81 for women, and with the Bernreuter Personality Inventory ($N = 39$), yielding a coefficient of .90. Emotional Adjustment and the Total Inventory score were correlated with the Thurstone Personality Schedule, yielding validity coefficients of .93 and .94, respectively. Scales on the revised form, except Masculinity, correlated highly with a number of measures. Masculinity-Feminity correlated only .13 for men and .38 for women with the MF score on the MMPI.

The Bell scales have also been correlated with various outside criteria. Home Adjustment, for example, was validated on high school students in California and New Jersey. Counselors and school administrators selected "very well" and "very poorly" adjusted groups. The Inventory detected a .80 sigma difference between these groups. To validate Health Adjustment, high school students from 3 towns were chosen. Those absent from school 3 or more times because of illness were placed in the "poorly adjusted" group, while those not absent at all were classified "well adjusted." When the Health Adjustment scales of these 2 groups were compared, a .93 sigma difference emerged. In the case of Social Adjustment, a 1.52 sigma difference was found between freshman and sophomore junior college students who were either leaders or followers in school activities. The Emotional Adjustment Scale was validated against groups selected by counselors as "well adjusted" and "poorly adjusted"; the scale differentiated between these groups at a level of 1.41 sigmas.

Norms: Norms are presented for high school and college students of both sexes. Scores for high school freshmen through seniors (161 males and 190 females) were obtained in Redwood City and Chico, California. Scores for college men ($N = 171$) and women (243) at 3 different colleges were also obtained. Tentative norms, separated by sex, are provided in the original manual for each of the scales and for the total score. These are presented as score ranges and descriptive statements ("very unsatisfactory" to "excellent"). The more recent manual (1962) presents percentile norms for 577 high school students (205 males and 372 females) and for 663 college students (316 males and 347 females).

Administration and Scoring: This 4-page instrument is self-administrating. Conditions for administration are described in the manual. Though there is no time limit, the test generally requires less than 25 minutes to complete.

Scoring may be done by stencil or machine. Generally, low scores indicate more satisfactory adjustment in all areas. The total score is the sum of all subscale scores.

Comments: The Adjustment Inventory appears to be valid and reliable. Coefficients of concurrent validity are particularly high, and intercorrelations among the scales (median .24) indicate that they are relatively independent.

The Adjustment Inventory is helpful in providing information on specific kinds of maladjustment. Its format allows quick diagnosis of the problem area. If corroborated by other evidence and interpreted according to local norms, this instrument could be used by teachers and counselors to identify the source of students' difficulty in the classroom.

References: Bell, H. M., *Manual for The Adjustment Inventory, Student Form.* Stanford, California: Stanford University Press, 1934.

Bell, H. M., *Manual for The Adjustment Inventory, Student Form* (rev. ed.). Palo Alto, California: Consulting Psychologists Press, 1962.

Buros, O. K., *The sixth mental measurements yearbook.* Highland Park, New Jersey: The Gryphon Press, 1965.

Dana, R. H., and D. H. Baker, "High school achievement and the Bell Adjustment Inventory." *Psychological Reports,* 1961, **8**, 353–356.

Name: ANIMAL CRACKERS: A TEST OF MOTIVATION TO ACHIEVE

Authors: Dorothy C. Adkins and Bonnie L. Ballif

Type of Measure: Objective-projective questionnaire

Availability: Adkins D. C., and B. L. Ballif, *Animal crackers: A test of motivation to achieve* (research ed.). Monterey, California: CTB/McGraw-Hill, 1973.

Description: Animal Crackers assesses motivation to achieve in learning. Designed for use with preschool, kindergarten, and first-grade children, this measure is based on the premise that a young child's success in school depends on *both* his intellectual ability and his motivation to learn. Animal Crackers focuses on 5 aspects of achievement-oriented behavior which are not attributable to intellectual ability: (1) School Enjoyment; (2) Self-Confidence; (3) Purposiveness; (4) Instrumental Activity; and (5) Self-Evaluation. The test authors hypothesize that achievement-oriented behavior is a product of the dynamic interaction of these 5 variables. That is, a child is motivated to achieve in school only when: (1) he expects that such behavior will be pleasurable; (2) he believes he can achieve; (3) he can determine his own purposes for achieving; (4) he knows how to achieve; and (5) he can evaluate his performance (Adkins and Ballif, 1973).

Animal Crackers and its forerunner, Gumpgookies, an experimental measure of achievement motivation developed at the University of Hawaii's Education Research and Development Center, underwent careful construction and extensive revision, based on a series of item and factor analyses. While Gumpgookies employed as item stimuli amorphous figures depicted in different stances, Animal Crackers instead uses pairs of identical animals. (This change was made in order to eliminate possible confounding effects of response sets.) Each animal within a pair is described by the test administrator as behaving in a certain way. The child is asked to choose the animal which "does what he does" or "likes what he likes." The alternative behaviors attributed to the 2 animals are intended to reveal differences in achievement motivation. Twelve separate animals are used an equal number of times to represent the 5 variables measured. To control for response bias, the keyed answers are counterbalanced with respect to position and order of presentation.

Sample Items: Animal Crackers contains 60 items, 12 for each variable measured. Each item presents a picture of 2 identical animals, which are separately described by the test administrator. The child identifies on his answer sheet which of the 2 animals is "his own" (i.e., which behaves as he behaves). The following items are similar to those that appear on the test:

1. This rabbit tries to play a new game.
   This rabbit keeps on playing an old game.
2. This kitten likes to come to school.
   This kitten likes to stay home.

3. This bear shows his school work to the others.
   This bear hides his school work from the others.

Reliability: Kuder-Richardson (formula 20) reliability coefficients are reported for the Animal Crackers 12-item component scores (Adkins and Ballif, 1973). These range from .65 to .76 for a kindergarten sample ($N = 624$), and from .69 to .82 for a first-grade population ($N = 588$). For the total test, KR_{20} reliability coefficients fall at .90 for both samples. Intercorrelations among the 5 components range from .43 to .60 for the kindergarten group and from .34 to .64 for the first-graders.

Validity: Animal Crackers claims content validity on the basis of methods used in test construction. The original items from Gumpgookies, some revised items, and some new items were pilot tested on several national samples, which included children from various socioeconomic and ethnic backgrounds. Data obtained from these trial administrations were subjected to item difficulty studies, item-test correlations, and factor and cluster analyses. Furthermore, opinions were collected from test administrators regarding the face validity and clarity of items and the feasibility of test format. Item content and assignment of items to hypothesized factors were determined by the comprehensive work on Gump-gookies (Adkins and Ballif, 1970a). Further item refinement for Animal Crackers was based on these theoretical and empirical foundations.

Evidence of construct validity is provided by factor analyses. Ninety-six items were administered to kindergarten and first-grade children, and the data obtained from these administrations were used in selecting the best 12 items for each of the 5 motivation components. These selections were made according to the following statistical criteria: biserial correlation coefficient; item difficulty level; item reliability; and factor loading (Adkins and Ballif, 1973).

Since Animal Crackers retains the theoretical basis of Gumpgookies, the authors maintain that it assumes some of the criterion-related validity demonstrated by the earlier instrument. Low positive correlations (.20 to .35) were obtained between Gumpgookies and Stanford-Binet IQ's, and statistically significant relationships were found between test scores and teacher ratings of motivation (Adkins and Ballif, 1970a).

Norms: Preliminary normative data (subgroup distributions, means, and standard deviations) are reported for kindergarten and first-grade samples, including black, Spanish-speaking, and "other" children. More complete standardization data, obtained from a national sample tested in November, 1973, and retested in April, 1974, are currently being prepared. These data are being analyzed according to grade, sex, ethnic group, and age. It is expected that normative distributions computed by age will allow more definitive performance comparisons (Adkins and Ballif, 1973).

Administration and Scoring: Animal Crackers may be given individually or in groups, though individual administration is recommended for preschool or very immature children. For group administrations, the assistance of proctors is required and a 10-minute practice exercise is conducted. The test can usually be completed in one 20-to-45-minute session. However, for younger children with limited attention spans, 2 sessions may be necessary.

In scoring Animal Crackers, the choice indicating the greater degree of motivation is considered the correct response. A scoring key is provided with both the group and the individual answer sheets. While the individual forms are generally scored by hand, group answer sheets may be hand or machine scored. Procedures for hand or machine scoring are outlined in the *Examiner's Manual* (Adkins and Ballif, 1973).

Comments: Animal Crackers appears to be a promising measure of achievement motivation, with good psychometric properties and appealing item content. Its forerunner, Gumpgookies, has been well received and widely used by educational researchers. Animal Crackers, while benefitting from the comprehensive developmental work done on Gumpgookies, offers further item refinement and a correction for response sets. Though preliminary psychometric data on Animal Crackers are adequate, continuing developmental efforts should produce even more satisfactory validity, reliability, and normative information. Since this instrument is not considered valid for bilingual children, a Spanish language version is currently being designed (Adkins and Ballif, 1973).

References: Adkins, D. C., and B. L. Ballif, *Motivation to achieve in school.* Report to the United States Office of Economic Opportunity, Contract No. OEO B89-4576 and OEO 4121. Honolulu, Hawaii: Education Research and Development Center, University of Hawaii, 1970. (a)

Adkins, D. C., and B. L. Ballif, "Factors of motivation in young children: Theoretical and empirical." *Educational Perspectives,* 1970, **9**, 7–11. (b)

Adkins, D. C., and B. L. Ballif, *Preschool motivation curriculum.* United States Office of Economic Opportunity, Grant No. 9929. Honolulu, Hawaii: Education Research and Development Center, University of Hawaii, 1971.

Adkins, D. C., and B. L. Ballif, "A new approach to response sets in analysis of a test of motivation to achieve." *Educational and Psychological Measurement,* 1972, **32**, 559–577.

Adkins, D. C., and B. L. Ballif, *Animal Crackers: A test of motivation to achieve. Examiner's manual.* Monterey, California: CTB/McGraw-Hill, 1973.

Adkins, D. C., F. Payne, and B. L. Ballif, "Motivation factor scores and response set scores for ten ethnic-cultural groups of preschool children." *American Educational Research Journal,* 1972, **9**, 557–572.

Name: ART JUDGMENT TEST

Author: Norman C. Meier

Type of Measure: Rating scale

Availability: Meier, N. C. *The Meier art tests. I. Art judgment.* Iowa City, Iowa: Bureau of Educational Research and Service, State University of Iowa, 1940.

Description: The Art Judgment Test (AJT) is one of 3 instruments in a battery designed to measure aesthetic talent and sensitivity in secondary students and adults. The AJT specifically assesses judgment of artistic organization. Each of 100 items presents 2 black-and-white reproductions of a recognized work of art, one of which has been altered to violate a particular aesthetic convention. The respondent indicates which of the 2 reproductions he or she considers most pleasing.

　　The original version of the AJT, developed by Meier and Seashore in 1929, contained 125 items drawn from a pool of 300. Selection criteria were: (1) agreement of 25 art experts on each item's quality and exemplification of a particular aesthetic principle; and (2) preference for the item by at least 60% of a group ($N = 1,081$) ranging in age from 11 years to middle adulthood. The current (1940) version emerged after item analyses eliminated 25 items from the original form.

Sample Items: The way in which the paired pictures differ is specified for the subject, who then compares the 2 and indicates his or her preference. The pictures vary in respects similar to those listed here:

	Left	Right	
1.	O	O	Position of sun
2.	O	O	Size of ship
3.	O	O	Arrangement of objects on desk
4.	O	O	Presence or absence of trees
5.	O	O	Development of background

Reliability: The AJT manual (Meier, 1942) presents split-half reliability coefficients obtained on the following populations: 100 junior high school students (.71); 100 senior high school students (.81); 150 college undergraduates (.75); 70 students attending Pratt Institute (.70); and 100 students from the Rhode Island School of Design (.84).

Validity: Content validity of the AJT may be inferred from methods used in constructing the test. All reproductions included on the test are considered reputable works of art. Alterations are limited to areas of accepted art principles. Furthermore, items retained on the final form survived several item analyses as well as empirical testing with art experts and a large number of students.

Further evidence of validity is provided by studies of contrasted group performance. Art faculty, for example, were found to score higher than both non-art faculty and non-art adults of superior intelligence. Also, art students were found to score higher than non-art students of the same age (reported in Anastasi, 1968). Some junior high school students obtained scores as high as those of adults, college art students, and students in professional art schools. According to the author, this indicates that the test measures natural capacity rather than the degree of learning or maturation (Meier, 1942). The test has a negative or low positive correlation with intelligence.

Scores on the original form of the AJT have been correlated with art grades and ratings of artistic ability. Coefficients obtained ranged from .40 to .69 (Carroll, 1933; Kinter, 1933; Morrow, 1938).

Norms: Normative information in the form of percentiles is given for 3 populations: 1,445 junior high school students, 892 senior high school students, and 982 adults, including college and art school students.

Administration and Scoring: The test booklet contains 100 pairs of pictures and an answer sheet. Instructions and criteria for differentiating items within a pair are printed on the answer sheet. Average testing time is from 45 to 60 minutes. Stencils are provided for hand-scoring. The correct choices are summed to obtain the total score.

Comments: The Art Judgment Test is a well constructed instrument. Reliability, validity, and normative data are satisfactory. Although the AJT was last revised in 1940, the paintings and drawings it employs are relatively timeless and thus unlikely to appear dated. When used in conjunction with its companion instruments, this test provides a good measure of artistic ability and appreciation.

References: Anastasi, A., *Psychological testing* (3rd ed.). New York: Macmillan Co., 1968.

Carroll, H. A., "What do the Meier-Seashore and the McAdory art tests measure?" *Journal of Educational Research*, 1933, **26**, 661–665.

Kinter, M., *The measurement of artistic abilities.* New York: Psychological Corporation, 1933.

Meier, N. C., *The Meier art tests. I. Art judgment. Examiner's manual.* Iowa City, Iowa: Bureau of Educational Research and Service, State University of Iowa, 1942.

Morrow, R. S., "An analysis of the relations among tests of musical, artistic, and mechanical abilities." *Journal of Psychology*, 1938, **5**, 253–263.

Remmers, H. H., and N. L. Gage, *Educational measurement and evaluation.* New York: Harper & Brothers, 1955.

Name: CALIFORNIA STUDY METHODS SURVEY

Author: Harold D. Carter

Type of Measure: Self-report questionnaire

Availability: Carter, H. D., *California study methods survey.* Monterey, California: California Test Bureau/McGraw-Hill, 1958.

Description: The California Study Methods Survey (CSMS) assesses the study techniques and attitudes of students in grades 7 through 13. The 150 CSMS items cover 4 scales: (1) Attitude Toward School; (2) Mechanics of Study; (3) Planning and System; and (4) Verification. While items on the first 3 scales are grouped, those composing the Verification Scale are scattered throughout the test.

Originally intended as an aid in predicting academic success, the CSMS underwent 10 years of developmental effort and a series of revisions involving successive item analyses and discrimination studies. An early form, the 60-item California Mechanics of Study Test, was eventually supplemented by 90 additional items to produce the CSMS, a diagnostic measure which correlates with grade-point average and is thus considered an effective predictor of academic success.

Sample Items: The CSMS contains 150 items of the following type, to which the student responds " yes " or " no."

Subscale	*Item*
Attitude Toward School	Must you be in the proper mood in order to study well?
Mechanics of Study	Do you develop an outline before writing essays or reports?
Planning and System	When studying, do you find it important to talk over the lesson with someone else?

Reliability: Test/retest coefficients obtained on tenth-grade students ($N = 215$) over an unspecified interval, are reported for CSMS total and subscale scores (Carter, 1958). These are estimated at .86 for total scores, .78 for Attitudes Toward School, .80 for Mechanics of Study, and .76 for Planning and System.

Kuder-Richardson (formula 21) coefficients of internal consistency are provided for grades 8 ($N = 148$) and 13 ($N = 211$). The eighth-grade sample yielded composite coefficients of .85 for total scores, .74 for Attitudes Toward School, .64 for Mechanics of Study, and .64 for Planning and System. The corresponding figures for college freshmen were .86, .70, .72, and .71. In the high school sample, reliabilities were slightly higher for females than for males (Carter, 1958).

Validity: Content validity is assured through test development procedures, which included (1) item construction based on an extensive review of the literature, (2) item analyses to determine the discriminating power of CSMS questions, and (3) pilot testing selected items on 1,000 tenth-grade students in three high schools.

Evidence of construct validity for the CSMS Mechanics of Study variable is provided by data obtained during test development. An earlier form of the inventory, the California Mechanics of Study Test, differentiated high and low achieving ninth-graders and correlated .41 and .47 with grade-point average among high and low achieving tenth-graders, respectively. Coefficients of .53 and .47 were obtained between the final form of the CSMS and GPA for 174 high school sophomores (Carter, 1958).

Several other indices of academic achievement and ability have been compared to the CSMS. Total CSMS scores obtained from 800 students correlated .41 with the California Achievement Tests (CAT) and .33 with the California Test of Mental Maturity (CTMM). High achievers (based on CAT scores) obtained significantly higher ($p < .001$) CSMS scores than lower achieving students.

An intercorrelation matrix, based on 324 cases in grades 8 through 12, revealed some degree of commonality among the CSMS scales (e.g., $r = .56$ between Attitude Toward School and Planning and System). However, Carter (1958) suggests that these relationships do not affect the usefulness of the scales.

Norms: Norms presented in the manual are based on approximately 1,000 students in grades 8 through 13 from all sections of the country. Normative data include standard scores and percentile ranks for male and female groups.

Administration and Scoring: The CSMS may be administered individually or in groups. Answers may be marked in test booklets or on machine-scoreable answer sheets. Instructions, administration, and material collection generally require no more than one class period.

Responses may be hand- or machine-scored. "Correct" answers, tallied within each subscale, can be converted to normalized standard scores and percentile ranks. A score below 17 on the Verification Scale casts doubt on the validity of the other scale scores.

Comments: The California Study Methods Survey is a carefully developed test which demonstrates adequate reliability and validity. Though retest intervals should be specified, the CSMS manual is otherwise quite complete. Further research on the subscales is needed to clarify profile interpretation, which is presently clouded by high intercorrelations among 3 CSMS dimensions.

References: Carter, H. D., "Methods of learning as factors in the prediction of school success." *The Journal of Psychology*, 1948, **26**, 249–258.

Carter, H. D., *Manual for the California Study Methods Survey*. Monterey, California: California Test Bureau/McGraw-Hill, 1958.

Carter, H. D., "The mechanics of study procedure." *California Journal of Educational Research*, 1958, **9**, 8–13.

Williams, R. L., "Personality, ability, and achievement correlates of scholastic attitudes." *Journal of Educational Research*, 1970, **63**, 401–403.

Name: CHILDREN'S AUDIENCE SENSITIVITY INVENTORY

Author: Allan Paivio

Type of Measure: Self-report questionnaire

Availability: This instrument may be obtained from Allan Paivio, Department of Psychology, University of Western Ontario, London, Ontario, Canada. A copy may also be found in: Paivio, A., A. R. Baldwin, and S. M. Berger, "Measurement of children's sensitivity to audiences." *Child Development*, 1961, **32**, 721–730.

Description: The Children's Audience Sensitivity Inventory (CASI) measures a child's predisposition to be anxious in front of an audience. It is appropriate for children in the third through tenth grades. The original CASI was developed by rewording the Adult Audience Sensitivity Inventory in language appropriate for children and adding some new items. The resulting 31-item form was revised after factor analysis. Six new items were added to increase the reliability of an Exhibitionism factor. The final form contains 13 items measuring Exhibitionism, 6 measuring Self-Consciousness, and 16 measuring Audience Anxiety. The Audience Anxiety scale refers specifically to situations involving performance before an audience. Self-Consciousness items express a disinclination toward self-exposure. Exhibitionism, on the other hand, refers to the need for self-exposure.

Sample Items: The child responds "true" or "false" to each of the 35 CASI items, 4 of which are negatively worded. Items of the following type are included on the 3 subscales:

Subscale	*Item*
Exhibitionism	1. I love to recite in front of the class.
	2. I like to raise my hand to answer questions.
Audience Anxiety	3. I find it hard to talk in front of the class.
	4. I'm often afraid I will be called upon to give answers.
Self-Consciousness	5. Others can not easily hurt my feelings. $(-)$
	6. When I goof in front of others, I feel bad.

Reliability: Test/retest and split-half reliabilities have been computed for fourth-, fifth- and sixth-graders (Paivio, Baldwin, and Berger, 1961). On a sample of 209 students, over a 6-month interval, the following test/retest coefficients were obtained: .62 for Exhibitionism, .45 for Self-Consciousness, and .54 for Audience Anxiety. Split-half reliabilities, computed for a sample of 223 children and corrected by the Spearman-Brown formula, were: .67 for Exhibitionism, .66 for Self-Consciousness, and .80 for Audience Anxiety. For the earlier, 31-item

CASI, Paivio (1964) estimated total scale odd/even reliability, corrected by the Spearman-Brown formula, at .79 ($N = 192$).

Validity: Concurrent validity of the CASI has been determined (Paivio et al., 1961) by correlating the CASI with the Children's Manifest Anxiety Scale (CMAS) and the Test Anxiety Scale (TAS). On a sample of 421 third- through tenth-graders, Exhibitionism correlated $-.40$ and $-.27$ with TAS and CMAS scores. The corresponding figures for Audience Anxiety were .74 and .62.

The CASI subscales were also intercorrelated, producing coefficients of $-.21$ between Exhibitionism and Self-Consciousness, $-.55$ between Exhibitionism and Audience Anxiety, and .58 between Audience Anxiety and Self-Consciousness.

Paivio et al. (1961) also report biserial correlations between scale scores on the CASI and willingness to volunteer for "skit" night at a summer camp. For girls, a correlation of $-.45$ ($p < .01$) was obtained between willingness to participate and Audience Anxiety. Boys produced correlations of $-.35$ ($p < .05$), and .31 ($p < .05$) between willingness to participate and Audience Anxiety and Exhibitionism, respectively.

Norms: The CASI has been administered to several groups of students. Paivio (1961) and Paivio et al. (1964) report CASI administrations to samples of 56 boys and 54 girls at a summer camp, 192 Canadian students in the third and fourth grades, and 223 third-, fourth-, and fifth-grade students. Scores for the subjects, however, are not provided.

Administration and Scoring: The CASI is self-administering. Approximately 20 minutes are required for completion of the test. In scoring, the number of "true" responses are summed, and answers to negatively worded items are reversed and added to the total.

Comments: While the Children's Audience Sensitivity Inventory is a potentially useful measure, it requires further research. The absence of norms is a noticeable weakness, and high intercorrelations among the CASI factors cause one to question the validity of having 3 separate subscales. Though studies of concurrent validity are encouraging, at this point the CASI is most appropriate as a research tool.

References: Paivio, A., "Childrearing antecedents of audience sensitivity." *Child Development*, 1964, **35**, 397–416.

Paivio, A., A. L. Baldwin, and S. M. Berger, "Measurement of children's sensitivity to audiences." *Child Development*, 1961, **32**, 721–730.

Name: CHILDREN'S EMBEDDED FIGURES TEST

Authors: Stephen A. Karp and Norma L. Konstadt

Type of Measure: Perceptual performance test

Availability: Karp, S. A., and N. L. Konstadt, *Children's embedded figures test.* Palo Alto, California: Consulting Psychologists Press, 1971.

Description: The Children's Embedded Figures Test (CEFT) is a perceptual measure which assesses a dimension of individual difference initially labeled field-dependence/independence and more recently termed psychological differentiation (Witkin, Oltman, Raskin and Karp, 1971). Field-independence is a mode of perceiving in which objects are experienced as discrete from their backgrounds. Field-dependence, on the other hand, is a perceptual style characterized by a tendency to see the overall picture, in a relatively global manner, viewing the individual parts as "fused."

Because the most widely used measure of field-dependence/independence, the Embedded Figures Test (EFT) (reviewed in this volume), proved much too difficult for children, a less complex version of the EFT (the CHEF) was developed by Goodenough and Eagle (1963) for subjects between the ages of 5 and 9. However, the CHEF proved to be impractical for widespread use, necessitating the development of the current revision (CEFT). In designing this revised version, a large pool of potential items, many of which were drawn from the Goodenough-Eagle form, was collected. These items were administered to a sample of 100 children, which included 5- and 9-year-old boys and girls from 2 public elementary schools in Brooklyn. The pupils represented diverse ethnic, religious, and socioeconomic groups. The responses of these children were analyzed, and 25 items which differentiated the highest and lowest scorers at each age level were selected for inclusion on the final scale. As in the adult form, CEFT items require the subject to find a simple form embedded in a more complex figure. In the CEFT, however, the complex figures represent recognizable objects rather than geometric designs. This makes the child's task more attractive and insures that the complex figure is perceived as a whole.

Sample Items: The CEFT contains two series of items. The "tent" series includes 11 items in which a simple, tent-like figure is embedded in the stimulus figure. The "house" series presents 14 items in which a house-like form is hidden in a more complex picture.

Reliability: Reliability studies were performed on the standardization sample of 160 children ranging in age from 5 to 12 years. Internal consistency estimates from .83 to .90 were obtained for the 7- to 12-year-old age range. Estimates of internal consistency could not be determined for the 5- to 6-year-old group because a considerable number of children were not administered all of the CEFT items. (After a child fails a specified number of items, CEFT testing is stopped.) However, test/retest data for 5- to 6-year-olds are reported by Dreyer,

Nebelkopf, and Dreyer (1969). Retesting 46 middle-class children in this age range after a 6-month interval, they obtained a Pearson correlation of .87.

Validity: The manual for the Embedded Figures Test (Witkin et al., 1971) presents validity information on the CEFT. Construct validity was established by correlating the CEFT and EFT scores of older children. Coefficients obtained for the 11-year-olds in the standardization sample ranged from .83 to .86. Lower coefficients (.70 to .73) were found for 9-year-old subjects. However, when the latter coefficients were corrected for attenuation, they reached .80, becoming comparable to those obtained for the 11-year-olds. Other studies which have correlated these 2 tests indicate that the optimal age at which to shift from use of the CEFT to the EFT is somewhere between 10 and 12 years in normal populations.

The CEFT has also been related to variables known to be associated with EFT performance. For example, Corah (1965), comparing CEFT scores and articulation-of-body-concept ratings obtained from human figure drawings, found a significant correlation ($r = .40$, $N = 30$) for boys, but not for girls ($r = .02$, $N = 30$). The CEFT scores of boys also correlated significantly ($r = .38$) with articulation ratings of their mothers' figure drawings. These findings parallel the results of similar studies using the EFT.

The EFT manual also reports significant correlations between CEFT scores and a composite of 3 subtests of the WISC performance scale (Block Design, Object Assembly, and Picture Completion) which Goodenough and Karp (1961) found to load on the same factor as the EFT. As expected, no relation was found between CEFT scores and the WISC verbal comprehension subtests.

Norms: Means and standard deviations are published for 160 children, ranging in age from 5 to 12 years. These children were randomly selected from the public elementary schools in Brooklyn, New York. Figures are reported by sex and age group (5 to 6, 7 to 8, 9 to 10, and 11 to 12 years). The authors warn that these normative data are tentative because of the small sample used. Also, recent data suggest that CEFT performance may be related to social class. Therefore, caution should be exercised in applying these norms to children from different social backgrounds (Witkin et al., 1971).

Administration and Scoring: The manual provides instructions to be read verbatim by the examiner, who administers this test individually. The authors urge examiners to note the child's understanding of the task requirements and his or her readiness to perform, and, if necessary, to modify test administration according to these observations. Examiners are permitted to alter the amount of "warm-up" and pretest training given to a subject. In the standardization study, no specific time limit was imposed on the child's search for the embedded figure, since most subjects either pointed at the simple form rather quickly, or gave signs of wanting to discontinue their efforts.

CEFT responses are scored 1 or 0. A score of 1 is given when the first choice is correct and verified, or when an incorrect response is spontaneously corrected by the child. The total score equals the number of items passed, 25 being the maximum.

Comments: The Children's Embedded Figures Test offers a technique for assessing important cognitive and perceptual dimensions in children. The test materials are attractive to children, and the task is interesting and challenging. However, the authors recommend that the CEFT be used for research purposes only since validation data are still sparse and incomplete. It should be noted that criticisms directed at the EFT (questioning field-independence as a distinct factor and as a construct separate from the ability to resist distraction) also apply to the CEFT.

References: Corah, N. L., "Differentiation in children and their parents." *Journal of Personality*, 1965, **33**, 300–308.

Dreyer, A. S., F. Nebelkopf, and C. A. Dreyer, "Note concerning stability of cognitive style measures in young children." *Perceptual and Motor Skills*, 1969, **28**, 933–934.

Goodenough, D. R., and C. Eagle, "A modification of the Embedded Figures Test for use with young children." *Journal of Genetic Psychology*, 1963, **103**, 67–74.

Goodenough, D. R., and S. A. Karp, "Field dependence and intellectual functioning." *Journal of Abnormal and Social Psychology*, 1961, **63**, 241–246.

Karp, S. A., and N. L. Konstadt, *Children's embedded figures test*. Palo Alto, California: Consulting Psychologists Press, 1971.

Witkin, H. A., P. K. Oltman, E. Raskin, and S. A. Karp, *A manual for the Embedded Figures Test*. Palo Alto, California: Consulting Psychologists Press, 1971.

Name: CHILDREN'S MANIFEST ANXIETY SCALE

Authors: Alfred Castaneda, Boyd McCandless, and David Palermo

Type of Measure: Self-report questionnaire

Availability: Castaneda, A., B. R. McCandless, and D. C. Palermo, "The children's form of the Manifest Anxiety Scale." *Child Development*, 1956, **27**, 317–326.

Description: The Children's Manifest Anxiety Scale (CMAS) is an adaptation of the Taylor Manifest Anxiety Scale, designed for use with fourth-, fifth-, and sixth-grade children. It contains 53 items, 42 of which measure anxiety, and 11 of which provide an index of the examinee's tendency to falsify responses. These 11 items constitute the L Scale, which is similar to the L Scale on the MMPI.

As part of its development, the CMAS was administered on a group basis to approximately 400 students at 2 different points in time in order to test item comprehensibility. The 2 scales, as predicted, did not correlate significantly, and CMAS items were found to successfully measure anxiety and its effect on children's performance.

Although the CMAS is generally administered as a group test, it can be adapted to permit oral examination on an individual basis or testing of educable mentally retarded children.

Sample Items: The examinee responds to the CMAS by indicating agreement (yes) or disagreement (no) with 53 items of the following type.

Anxiety Scale:
 I would like to be far away from this place.
 I often have my feelings hurt.
 I often feel lonely when I am with people.

L Scale:
 I always tell the truth.
 I always use good manners.
 I never lose my temper.

Reliability: Retest reliability coefficients have been obtained for 2 different populations: (1) 386 white fourth-, fifth-, and sixth-grade students of both sexes; and (2) a group composed of 44 black males, 55 black females, 196 white males, and 175 white females in the fourth, fifth, and sixth grades at 7 public elementary schools in Illinois.

After an interval of 1 week, reliability estimates for the first population were .90 for the Anxiety Scale and .70 for the L Scale (Castaneda, McCandless, and Palermo, 1956). Reliability coefficients for the second group ranged from .59 to

.91 for the Anxiety Scale and from .77 to .80 for the L Scale, after a 1-month interval (Palermo, 1959).

Validity: Several investigations of the construct validity of the CMAS have been conducted. McCandless and Castaneda (1956) found both scales of the instrument related to school achievement for a group of fourth-, fifth-, and sixth-grade boys and girls, and to intelligence for the girls. Palermo (1959) found the mean CMAS scores of black children to be significantly higher than those of white children in grades 4, 5, and 6. The CMAS scores of retarded adolescents achieving at the fourth-grade level indicated significantly more anxiety than those of fourth-grade children of normal intelligence (Cochran and Cleland, 1963).

The CMAS was also found to correlate highly with Sarason's Score for Anxiety among children of both sexes in the fourth, fifth, and sixth grades. Coefficients ranged from .76 to .79. However, CMAS scores did not correlate significantly with teacher's ratings of anxiety (Grams, Hafner, and Wentworth, 1962).

Norms: Normative data, in the form of means and standard deviations, are provided for the following populations: 386 white students in grades four, five, and six; 61 black males and 75 black females in grades four through six; 37 13- to 18-year-old educable mental retardates achieving at a fourth-grade level; and 27 noninstitutionalized and 17 institutionalized educable mental retardates with a mean age of 12 years, 11 months.

Administration and Scoring: Instructions for group or individual administration are printed on each test form. The level of anxiety is determined by summing the number of items on the Anxiety Scale marked "yes." The index of an examinee's tendency to falsify responses is obtained by summing the number of items on the L scale (excluding items 10 and 49) which are marked "yes." Items 10 and 49 are added to the L Scale score if they are marked "no."

Comments: The Children's Manifest Anxiety Scale demonstrates adequate reliability and normative data and promising validity information. Yet caution should be exercised in interpreting CMAS scores since they may be affected by acquiescent response sets. The CMAS has value as a research, diagnostic, and predictive tool.

References: Castaneda, A., B. R. McCandless, and D. C. Palermo, "The children's form of the Manifest Anxiety Scale." *Child Development*, 1956, **27**, 317–326.

Cochran, I. J., and C. C. Cleland, "Manifest anxiety of retardates and normals matched as to academic achievement." *American Journal of Mental Deficiencies*, 1963, **67**, 539–542.

Grams, A., A. J. Hafner, and Q. Wentworth, *Children's anxiety as compared with parents' reports and teachers' ratings of adjustment.* Paper presented at the meeting of the American Psychological Association, St. Louis, August 1962.

McCandless, B. R., and A. Castaneda, "Anxiety in children, school achievement, and intelligence." *Child Development*, 1956, **27**, 379–382.

Palermo, D. S., "Racial comparisons and additional normative data on the Children's Manifest Anxiety Scale." *Child Development*, 1959, **30**, 53–57.

Name: CONCEPT ASSESSMENT KIT—CONSERVATION

Authors: Marcel L. Goldschmid and Peter M. Bentler

Type of Measure: Cognitive ability test

Availability: Goldschmid, M. L., and P. M. Bentler, *Conservation concept diagnostic kit, manual and keys.* San Diego, California: Educational and Industrial Testing Service, 1968.

Description: The Concept Assessment Kit—Conservation is designed to measure the 4- to 7-year-old child's attainment of the Piagetian concept of conservation (the ability to realize that properties such as weight and volume remain constant despite transformations in shape or position). Focusing both on the child's behavior in solving conservation tasks and on his or her explanation of these solutions, this instrument can provide evidence of cognitive change from the prelogical mode of thought to the concrete operational mode, which, according to Piaget, generally occurs at age 7 or 8. However, because it measures only conservation, this instrument cannot be used alone to establish the presence of concrete operational thought.

The test is available in 3 forms, A, B, and C, each of which contains 12 items. Forms A and B, which are parallel, consist of 6 conservation tasks, each involving objects that are identical with regard to amount of matter of a given type: particled material (discontinuous quantity); plastic material (substance); blocks of solid material (2-dimensional space); liquid (continuous quantity); pieces (number); and weight. Items on Form C present objects which are the same in length or area.

These 3 forms were developed primarily through multidimensional homogeneity scaling (Bentler, 1966) of an initial battery composed of 3 to 7 tasks representing 10 types of conservation. This battery contained 44 behavior items and 43 explanation items. Test results from 142 children in kindergarten, first, and second grades yielded 3 factors for explanation and a general dimension, Amount of Matter, which accounted for all 6 types of conservation on Forms A and B. Two minor factors, Area and Length, emerged for Form C.

Sample Items: The subject is presented with 2 objects or sets of objects that are identical with respect to amount of matter (Forms A and B), or length or area (Form C). One object or set of objects is changed in position or in shape, and the child is asked if there is now a difference between the two. A question of the following type is asked: "Is there as much cereal in this glass as in that one, or does one have more in it?" The subject is required to answer the question and then to explain his answer.

Reliability: Reliability studies reported by Goldschmid and Bentler (1968b) are based on a single sample of 36, 37, and 34 children in kindergarten, first, and second grades, respectively. Kuder-Richardson (formula 20) estimates of internal consistency are .96, .97, and .95 for the final versions of Forms A, B, and C.

Parallel form and test/retest reliabilities are also very high, typically .94 or .95.

KR$_{20}$ reliabilities, computed for the 10 conservation tasks administered to 142 children in the developmental and standardization studies, ranged from .58 to .96, with most at or above .80. Loevinger coefficients in the .60s, .70s and .80s were also obtained, indicating reasonable homogeneity within sets of items (Goldschmid and Bentler, 1968b).

Validity: Content validity, originally established through multidimensional homogeneity scaling of the initial battery, was confirmed in the standardization studies, which demonstrated good scale homogeneity. Correlations between Forms C and A, and C and B, ranged from .69 to .78 and were considerably lower than the correlation between the two parallel forms, supporting the authors' contention that A and B measure something different from C. While Forms A and B assess both conservation behavior and comprehension of conservation principles, Form C may serve as an index of the generalization of conservation (Goldschmid and Bentler, 1968b).

Scores on Forms A and B correlated significantly and positively with age, verbal ability (determined by WISC vocabulary scores) and popularity (assessed by sociometric peer ratings). Negative correlations were obtained between conservation and maternal dominance (assessed by the Parental Attitude Survey) and scores on the Lie Scale of the Children's Manifest Anxiety Scale (Goldschmid, 1967; Rardin and Moan, 1971).

Norms: Normative data in the manual are based on the scores of 560 children tested individually with Forms A and C, or B and C. These children attended 20 schools, day care centers, and Head Start projects in the Los Angeles area. Although the schools were intended to represent diverse socioeconomic and racial groups, the sample is slightly biased toward lower-middle-class children (reported in Buros, 1972). The norms are presented as percentile ranks for a variety of age ranges. Means and standard deviations are also reported.

Administration and Scoring: The test is individually administered by an examiner, according to detailed instructions provided in the manual (Goldschmid and Bentler, 1968a). The directions for each task are separated into 5 columns: pictorial illustration, specific procedures, verbal instructions and questions, recording of responses, and scoring. If the child correctly answers the question asked, he or she gets 1 point for behavior. An adequate explanation of the answer earns the subject another point.

Comments: The Concept Assessment Kit—Conservation is the first instrument measuring a single Piagetian concept among 4- to 7-year-olds. The authors have designed a clear, well organized manual containing considerable data on validity and reliability. Still, this test has been criticized on several counts. Ayers (reported in Buros, 1972) maintains that normative data, and general experience, indicate that the age range should be changed to $5\frac{1}{2}$ to $7\frac{1}{2}$ years since the test is difficult for children under $6\frac{1}{2}$. Also, most of the reliability and validity data reported in the manual are based on the initial battery rather than the final scales. Other criticisms involve the limitations of percentile ranks, the dangers of overinterpretation, and the suitability of the questioning technique used. Yet, in spite of these criticisms, the Concept Assessment Kit is a valuable tool in research regarding children's thinking and the Piagetian approach.

References: Bentler, P. M., *Multidimensional homogeneity scaling.* Paper presented at a special meeting of the Psychometric Society, Chicago, 1966.

Buros, O. K., *The seventh mental measurements yearbook.* Highland Park, New Jersey: The Gryphon Press, 1972.

Goldschmid, M. L., "Different types of conservation and nonconservation and their relation to age, sex, IQ, MA, and vocabulary." *Child Development,* 1967, **38**, 1229–1246.

Goldschmid, M. L., and P. M. Bentler, *Conservation concept diagnostic kit, manual and keys.* San Diego, California: Educational and Industrial Testing Service, 1968. (a)

Goldschmid, M. L., and P. M. Bentler, "The dimensions and measurement of conservation." *Child Development,* 1968, **39**, 787–802. (b)

Rardin, D. R., and C. E. Moan, "Peer interaction and cognitive development." *Child Development,* 1971, **42**, 1685–1699.

Name: CREATIVITY ATTITUDE SURVEY

Author: Charles E. Schaefer

Type of Measure: Questionnaire

Availability: Schaefer, C. E., *Manual for the Creativity Attitude Survey.* Jacksonville, Illinois: Psychologists and Educators, 1971.

Description: The Creativity Attitude Survey (CAS) assesses a child's creativity by requiring him or her to respond to 32 statements covering 5 dimensions normally associated with creativity: Confidence in Own Ideas; Appreciation of Fantasy; Theoretical and Aesthetic Orientation; Openness to Impulse Expression; and Desire for Novelty (Schaefer, 1971).

The CAS is based on the belief that attitude is an important correlate of creativity—or, specifically, on Hudson's (1966) contention that the roots of creativity lie in the attitude and motivation of the personality, and not in the convergent or divergent thinking of the individual. Since the CAS was developed to measure progress in upper level elementary school creativity training programs, it is appropriate for children in grades 4 through 6.

Sample Items: The subject answers "yes" or "no" to each of 32 statements, 2 of which are filler items designed to reduce the visibility of the instrument. The remaining 30 questions are of the following type:

1. Yes No   I would rather buy a paint-by-number kit than paint a picture by myself.
2. Yes No   Artists are sissies.
3. Yes No   I have fun daydreaming.

Reliability: Schaefer (1971) and Schaefer and Bridges (1970) provide several reliability estimates. Internal consistency coefficients of .81 and .75 were obtained for 2 samples of fifth-grade students ($N = 30$ each). A test/retest reliability study on another fifth-grade sample ($N = 50$) yielded a coefficient of .61 over a 5-week period.

Validity: Schaefer (1970b) investigated the validity of the CAS in 2 creativity training studies. In both studies, pre- to posttest gain scores on the CAS were significantly higher for the experimental group than the control groups. Also, increased creativity training generally led to higher CAS scores. In a 20-month follow-up study of Schaefer's (1970b) research, Locurto (1970) found that the significant gains previously recorded on the CAS were maintained by the experimental groups. The CAS was the only test in a battery of 5 creativity measures which recorded this stability.

A study by Schaefer and Bridges (1970) gives evidence of concurrent, criterion-related validity. A fifth-grade language arts teacher selected 2 groups of bright students, one creative and the other noncreative, and the CAS was administered to both. The mean score for the creative group ($N = 17$) was significantly higher ($p < .05$) than that for the control group ($N = 16$).

Norms: Normative data for the CAS are based on 21 groups of elementary students, including both sexes and various socioeconomic and ability levels. Means and standard deviations for a group of emotionally disturbed boys are also available in the manual.

Administration and Scoring: The CAS can be self-administered, since the child is merely required to circle "yes" or "no" to indicate his agreement or disagreement with each statement. If the response is considered conducive to creativity, it is scored 1; if not, it is scored 0. Thus, higher scores indicate more favorable attitudes toward creativity.

Comments: The CAS is the first test designed to measure attitudes toward creativity. It is easily administered and scored, but the population for which it is appropriate is rather limited. Since the CAS was constructed to measure the attitudes of subjects in creativity training programs, its most valid use is for that purpose.

References: Hudson, L., *Contrary imagination: A psychological study of the young student.* New York: Shocken Books, 1966.

Locurto, C., *Follow-up study on the effects of a creativity training program on middle-class children.* New York: Creativity Center, Fordham University, 1970.

Schaefer, C. E., *The effect of creativity training on test performance of fifth grade children from two socio-economic levels.* New York: Creativity Center, Fordham University, 1970 (a).

Schaefer, C. E., *Evaluation of a program for developing creative thinking in teachers and children at the fourth and fifth grade levels.* New York: Creativity Center, Fordham University, 1970 (b).

Schaefer, C. E., *Manual for the Creativity Attitude Survey.* Jacksonville, Illinois: Psychologists and Educators, 1971.

Schaefer, C. E., and C. I. Bridges, "Development of a creativity attitude survey for children." *Perceptual and Motor Skills,* 1970, **31**, 861–862.

Name: DEPENDENCE PRONENESS SCALE

Authors: Ned A. Flanders, J. Paul Anderson, and Edmund J. Amidon

Type of Measure: Self-report questionnaire

Availability: Flanders, N. A., J. P. Anderson, and E. J. Amidon, "Measuring dependence proneness in the classroom." *Educational and Psychological Measurement*, 1961, **21**, 575–587.

Description: The Dependence Proneness Scale (DPS) is a 45-item rating scale designed to determine how prone students are toward dependency upon the teacher. Dependency proneness is defined as student behavior which tends to comply with authority and conform to peer group pressure. This characteristic is of research interest since the more sensitive, dependent pupil may be disposed to learn only after approval and support are offered.

In developing the DPS, psychologists wrote 150 items concerning peer or adult affiliation, compliance, and approval. These items were administered to 1,243 eighth-grade students, whose responses were subjected to four item analyses. The final 45-item scale which emerged from these analyses may be administered to students in grades 3 through 6 or grade 8.

Sample Items: The DPS includes items of the following type, with which the pupil agrees or disagrees. Each item is keyed according to the response indicative of dependence proneness (D for disagree, A for agree).

1. I dislike asking for assistance from others.   (D)
2. I always ask permission before doing things at home.   (A)
3. I try to agree with other kids.   (A)
4. School grades don't matter much to me.   (D)

Reliability: The reliability of the DPS was estimated at .68, using Hoyt's (1941) analysis of variance technique. The standard error of measurement was estimated at 2.93.

Validity: The validity of the DPS may be determined from the following studies. Amidon (1959) found that high scoring (dependence prone) students were less likely than low scoring students to take an extreme position on an opinionnaire. Anderson (1960) found that high dependence prone students preferred "less directive" teachers than low scoring students. This difference was significant at the .05 level. Group differences were also found by Flanders, Anderson, and Amidon (1961), who report that high and low scorers exhibited expected differences on other measures of dependence in the classroom.

The 4 separate item analyses performed on the DPS during its development provide further evidence of validity. From the original pool of 150 items, only those which discriminated between extreme groups (the top 100 scorers and the bottom 100 scorers out of a sample of over 1,200 students) were retained.

Norms: The DPS was initially administered to 1,290 eighth-grade students, 646 males and 644 females from 44 classes in the Minneapolis-St. Paul area. The mean for the male students was 27.30, with a standard deviation of 5.77, and the mean for females was 30.68, with a standard deviation of 4.98. Since these figures differ significantly, the authors suggest that separate norms be used for interpreting the scores of boys and girls (Flanders et al., 1961).

Administration and Scoring: The DPS is easily administered. After brief directions are read by the examiner, the child responds to each item by indicating whether he agrees or disagrees. The test can be completed in 15 to 20 minutes. In scoring the DPS, responses indicating dependence proneness are totalled.

Comments: Although the Dependence Proneness Scale may be useful in research and school settings, its authors suggest the need for more elaborate scaling procedures and more extensive normative data. This suggestion is appropriate considering the limited reliability and normative data now available.

References: Amidon, E. J., *Dependent-prone students in experimental learning situations.* Unpublished doctoral dissertation, University of Minnesota, 1959.

Anderson, J. P., *Student perceptions of teacher influence.* Unpublished doctoral dissertation, University of Minnesota, 1960.

Flanders, N. A., J. P. Anderson, and E. J. Amidon, "Measuring dependence proneness in the classroom." *Educational and Psychological Measurement*, 1961, **21**, 575–587.

Hoyt, C., "Test reliability estimated by analysis of variance." *Psychometrika*, 1941, **6**, 153–160.

Name: FAMILY RELATIONS TEST

Authors: Eva Bene and James Anthony

Type of Measure: Projective test

Availability: Obtainable from the National Foundation of Educational Research in England and Wales, The Mere, Slough, Bucks, England.

Description: The Family Relations Test measures a child's emotional attitudes by examining the probable structure of relationships within his family. The subject is initially shown 20 cardboard figures representing people of various ages, including a "Mr. Nobody." From these he selects a figure to represent himself and each member of his family. Each figure is attached to a red cardboard box with a slot in the top. The child is then given cards on which various statements are printed. These statements express attitudes related to love and hate, maternal overprotection, and parental overindulgence. The child deposits the card in the box attached to the family member to which the statement applies. If the statement applies to no one, the card is placed in "Mr. Nobody's" box. Since cards disappear into the boxes, the accumulation is not obvious, and the child is assumed to be protected from excessive guilt and remorse. Children of 8 or more years are given 86 cards while younger children receive only 40.

Sample Items: Items for older children are divided into several groups, the first two of which represent feelings coming from the child and feelings directed toward the child. Items in these groups are subdivided into the following categories: (1) mild positive (affectionate) feelings; (2) strong positive (sexualized) feelings; (3) mild negative feelings; and (4) strong negative (hostile) feelings. Three additional item groups represent maternal overprotection, paternal overindulgence, and maternal overindulgence. Items for older children are of the type below:

This person is sometimes too picky.

Items for young children cover 5 classes: (1) positive and (2) negative feelings coming from the child; (3) positive and (4) negative feelings directed toward the child; and (5) dependence. These items are of the following type.

I would like this person to sleep in the same room with me.

Reliability: Split-half reliabilities for combinations of affect categories vary from .68 to .90 (reported in Buros, 1959).

Validity: No validation studies are reported for preschool or kindergarten children. Bene and Anthony (1959) report evidence of validity for the older children's forms based on comparisons of test results with case history material, congruence between feelings reported by sets of siblings, and relationships between test data and independent psychiatric diagnoses. Agreement between test results and case history data involving sibling conflict, for example, is reported at 64% ($p < .05$).

The predictive validity of the Family Relations Test is supported by several independent studies. Frost (1969) found that test scores showed significant differences among normal, clinic, delinquent, and nonreading groups. Van Slyke and Leton (1965) reported consistent but nonsignificant differences in the test results of well adjusted and poorly adjusted school children. Swanson and Parker (1971) found that test scores differentiated among normal, learning disabled, and emotionally disturbed boys, aged 6 to 12 years.

The Family Relations Test has also been compared to other instruments measuring parent-child relationships. Van Slyke and Leton (1965) correlated the scores of 18 fourth-grade children with results on the Swanson Child-Parent Relationship Rating Scale and the Forer Structured Sentence Completion Test. In general, items expressing negative feelings correlated most highly ($p < .01$). A coefficient of $-.49$ was obtained between the negative items on the Family Relations Test and the positive items on the Swanson Test.

Norms: Norms published in the test manual, based on a small clinic group, are sketchy and incomplete. Frost (1969) provides means and standard deviations for several item categories derived from the scores of 190 sixth-graders, 86 boys and 104 girls. No normative data are available for younger children.

Administration and Scoring: Testing time is 20 to 25 minutes. If an item applies to several family members, the examiner makes a note of this. When the child has completed the test, cards are collected from the boxes and tabulated on a special scoring form. The number of items expressing each type of feeling is tallied for each family member. These totals are used to estimate the child's degree of involvement with each person in the family.

The manual provides profiles exemplifying the following personality patterns: paranoid tendency; idealizing tendency; and egocentric states. The authors assign great importance to certain test results, such as the balance between self-love and self-hate items, the selection and treatment of significant figures, and deviation from a theoretical frequency of items expected for certain family members.

Comments: The Family Relations Test assesses important aspects of the child's personality, offers item content which is appealing to children, and employs completely objective scoring techniques. However, the validity of this test needs further clarification. The statistical procedures and computations used in validity studies reported in the manual have been criticized as incorrect or inappropriate (Kauffman, 1970). Furthermore, the practice of validating the child's perceptions against independent, objective behavioral criteria or the reports of other individuals has been questioned (Ausubel, Balthazar, Rosenthal, Blackman, Schpoont, and Welkowitz, 1954; Rabkin, 1963). Although further research is needed to answer these criticisms, the Family Relations Test does have merit for rapid assessment of the child's attitudes toward his family, as long as results are interpreted cautiously.

References: Ausubel, D. P., E. E. Balthazar, I. Rosenthal, C. S. Blackman, S. H.

Schpoont, and J. Welkowitz, "Perceived parent attitudes as determinants of children's ego structure." *Child Development*, 1954, **25**, 173–183.

Bene, E., and J. Anthony, *Manual for the Family Relations Test*. London: National Foundation for Educational Research, 1957.

Buros, O. K., *The fifth mental measurements yearbook*. Highland Park, New Jersey: The Gryphon Press, 1959.

Frost, B. P., "Family Relations Test: A normative study." *Journal of Projective Techniques and Personality Assessment*, 1969, **33**, 409–413.

Kauffman, J. M., "Validity of the Family Relations Test: A review of research." *Journal of Projective Techniques and Personality Assessment*, 1970, **34**, 186–189.

Rabkin, L. Y., *The disturbed child's perception of parental attributes*. Unpublished doctoral dissertation, University of Rochester, 1963.

Van Slyke, V., and D. A. Leton, "Children's perception of family relationships and their school adjustment." *Journal of School Psychology*, 1965, **4**(1), 19–28.

Name: GEIST PICTURE INTEREST INVENTORY

Author: Harold Geist

Type of Measure: Self-report questionnaire and checklist

Availability: Geist, H., *The Geist picture interest inventory*. Missoula, Montana: Psychological Test Specialists, 1959.

Description: The Geist Picture Interest Inventory (GPII) assesses interest in 11 general occupational areas (Persuasive, Clerical, Mechanical, Dramatic, Musical, Scientific, Outdoor, Literary, Computational, Artistic, and Social Service), as well as possible reasons for the interests expressed. Available in English or Spanish, it is designed primarily for males, though local norms can be developed for females.

The inventory consists of 44 sets of 3 pictures depicting various types of work. The student must indicate his preference within each set. Having done so, he then selects from several alternatives the reason for his choice. The information obtained on the GPII can aid psychologists, teachers, and counselors working in vocational guidance, as well as researchers studying personality determinants of occupational choice.

This inventory was developed on the assumption that the use of pictures to assess interests would remove some of the semantic difficulties associated with more verbal measures. Pictures were selected over a 10-year period (1949–1959), during which time photographs and drawings corresponding to the occupational areas represented on the Kuder Preference Record were carefully analyzed.

Sample Items: Pictures included in each triad typically depict men engaged in 3 different vocational activities. For example, an item might present the following pictures:

1. A man standing at a blackboard, behind a table of beakers (chemist);
2. A man with a tool box, examining the inside of a tree (tree surgeon);
3. A man reading from a paper into a microphone (radio announcer).

After the subject has indicated which of these activities he prefers, he may select the reason for his choice from a list of statements similar to those below.

1. My father is engaged in this type of work.
2. This occupation offers a chance for advancement.
3. I like working with numbers.
4. This job will give me independence.

This latter task—indicating the motivating factor behind one's choice—is optional. The examiner may or may not decide to have the students complete this part of the test.

Reliability: Test/retest reliability was assessed over an interval of 6 months on 15 samples of remedial readers, trade school, high school, and college students, representing various cultural backgrounds, including Hawaiian and Puerto Rican. These samples each contained from 48 to 170 individuals. Coefficients for each of the 11 interest areas and 15 subject groups are presented by Geist (1959). For unselected groups of normal high school seniors and college students, coefficients range from .37 to .94 for the various scales (median .77), with 10 of the 22 estimates over .85. Percentages of same responses on retesting showed that 126 of the 132 items were reselected 40% or more of the time, indicating agreement well beyond chance.

Validity: GPII drawings were carefully revised and selected during test construction to ensure content validity of the scale. Photographs of representative occupations and hobbies were administered to more than 1,500 boys in grades 4 through 12 in 4 California communities (Geist and McDaniel, 1952). Those which were not recognized by 90% of the subjects were eliminated. This procedure was followed with subsequent forms of the test.

Concurrent validity coefficients based on correlations between 10 GPII and 10 comparable Kuder scales are presented for 5 U.S. mainland and 7 Hawaiian samples (Geist, 1959). Excluding the responses of retarded readers, only 1 out of 40 correlations for U.S. mainland groups is negative. Median scale correlations for these groups range from .16 to .62. All 50 correlations for the Hawaiian samples are positive, median scale coefficients ranging from .26 to .69.

Norms: T-score norms are provided for over 1,200 U.S. mainland, Hawaiian and Puerto Rican high school, trade school, and college students. These norms apply only to the selection of interest areas and not to the reasons indicated for the selections.

Administration and Scoring: The GPII may be self-administered to groups or individuals. High school and college students should be able to finish the inventory in 10 to 25 minutes and the optional checklist of reasons for their choices in an additional 25 to 40 minutes.

The inventory may be either hand- or machine-scored. In either case, 11 stencils are used for obtaining the raw scores for each interest area. With the use of tables, raw scores may be converted to T-scores, which are plotted and interpreted on an interest profile sheet. A T-score over 70 indicates relatively high interest in an area, while one below 30 suggests lack of interest. The manual provides interpretations for high T-scores and explains procedures for examining scores.

Reponses on the optional checklist of reasons are added horizontally and then totalled. Area totals and percentages can be computed. These are transferred to the profile for interpretation.

Comments: The Geist Picture Interest Inventory has good psychometric properties. The product of extensive pretesting, this measure correlates significantly with Kuder scores. It also offers the advantages of quick, easy administration, minimal reading requirements, and a Spanish edition. Its weaknesses involve the use of somewhat dated pictures (featuring males only) and an absence of reliability and validity data for the optional check list of reasons. Although the authors maintain that local norms can easily be developed for females, there is no evidence that this test is valid for females since psychometric data were obtained on male populations.

References: Abdel-Meguid, S. G. M., *The reliability of an experimental picture inventory of vocational interests.* Unpublished master's thesis, Stanford University, 1951.

Clarke, C., *A correlation of the scales of a picture interest inventory with the comparable scales of the Kuder.* Unpublished master's thesis, University of Hawaii, 1958.

Geist, H., "The Geist Picture Interest Inventory: General Form: Male." *Psychological Reports*, 1959, **5**, 413–438.

Geist, H., and H. B. McDaniel, "Construction and validation of a picture vocational interest inventory." *American Psychologist*, 1952, **7**, 383–384.

Name: GUESS WHO

Authors: Judith A. Agard and Sandra M. Harrison

Type of Measure: Sociometric questionnaire

Availability: Agard, J. A., and S. M. Harrison, *Guess Who* (*developmental stage*). *Test administrator's instructions.* Austin, Texas: Project PRIME, undated.

Description: Guess Who is a sociometric instrument which requires the child to name a classmate for each of 31 descriptions. Although originally developed for Project PRIME (Programmed Re-Entry Into Mainstream Education) and used to compare student perceptions of normal, mentally retarded, and learning disabled children, this scale may be applied in any elementary classroom.

    Factor analyses of the Guess Who yielded four scales—Disruptive, Quiet, Dull, and Bright—which suggested 2 bipolar dimensions: Academic Achievement and Misbehavior. Because interpretation of scale scores was complicated by class size (a score of 15 in a class of 15 is very different from a score of 15 in a class of 30), 5 scoring methods (raw frequency of nomination, proportion scores, fixed-size panel, binary truncation, and standardization within classes) were developed in an attempt to discover the optimum procedure (Veldman and Sheffield, 1974).

Sample Items: The Guess Who contains 31 questions of the following type. In response to each, the child writes the name of one classmate.

Scale	*Item*
Disruptive	1. Who fights a lot with the other children?
Bright	2. Who is the best reader?
Dull	3. Who always gets the wrong answers in math?
Quiet	4. Who never talks in class?

Reliability: Alpha coefficients of internal consistency were computed on raw frequency data (uncorrected for class size) obtained from a sample of 13,045 children. These ranged from .86 to .93 for Factor I (Disruptive), .90 to .93 for Factor II (Bright), .84 to .88 for Factor III (Dull), and .72 to .83 for Factor IV (Quiet). Recomputed using binary-truncated item data (corrected for class size), alpha coefficients ranged from .56 to .82 for Factor I, .61 to .77 for Factor II, .56 to .70 for Factor III, and .46 to .61 for Factor IV. This second reliability analysis suggests that coefficients obtained using raw frequency data were inflated due to failure to meet the assumption of normal item distribution (Veldman and Sheffield, 1974).

    Split-half reliabilities were also computed for each scale, using a sample of 11,215 children in 422 classes. These were: .74, .72, .67, and .56 (Veldman and Sheffield, 1974).

Validity: Evidence of construct validity is provided by scale intercorrelations and typal analysis. The former indicated stronger relationships *across* than within logical factors—a finding which might be expected since, on these scales, a high score on one trait does not suggest a low score on its logical opposite. Failure to be nominated as "bright" does not imply that a pupil is "dull." Thus, the correlation between the Disruptive and Dull scales (.44) was stronger than that between Disruptive and Quiet (−.26). Similarly, Bright correlated .39 with Quiet, but only −.30 with its opposite, Dull.

Typal analysis was undertaken to empirically determine whether or not the 4 Guess Who factors could be interpreted as *types* of people rather than traits possessed by people. A procedure known as hierarchical grouping analysis was employed on a sample of 1,586 subjects, yielding 7 types: Disruptive; Bright; Dull; Quiet; Disruptive and Dull; Bright and Quiet; and Ignored. A type emerged for each factor, for the 2 factor combinations suggested by the scale intercorrelations, and for a group of children who simply weren't nominated on any dimension.

Correlations between Guess Who scores and scores obtained on 2 other Project PRIME measures provide evidence of validity against external criteria. Five sets of Guess Who scores (derived using the 5 different scoring procedures) were correlated with 8 variables from About You and Your Friends (AYYF) and the Teacher Rating Scale (TRS). For all 5 scoring systems, the Guess Who Disruptive factor correlated .18 to .27 with the AYYF Misbehavior scale, and .47 to .59 with the TRS Misbehavior scale. The Bright factor correlated .22 to .23 with the AYYF Does Well in School scale, and .43 to .51 with the TRS Concentration scale. Similarly, the Dull factor showed a positive relationship (.22 to .26) with Loneliness-Rejection on the AYYF, and a negative relationship (−.44 to −.57) with Concentration on the TRS. Finally, the Quiet factor related negatively to Misbehavior on both the AYYF and the TRS (−.18 to −.21 and −.31 to −.38, respectively). When Guess Who factors were converted to bipolar composite scales (Quiet subtracted from Misbehavior to form Composite I, and Dull from Bright to form Composite II), correlations with corresponding TRS and AYYF variables were even stronger (Veldman and Sheffield, 1974).

Norms: Because this instrument is a sociometric scale, normative data are not provided.

Administration and Scoring: In administering the Guess Who, the examiner first writes the name of each child in the class on the blackboard. After passing out answer sheets, he or she reads the questions aloud to the pupils, using the first 2 as instructive examples.

Any one of the 5 scoring systems previously mentioned may be used, although in preliminary analyses, the binary-truncated procedure has produced the most valid scores.

Comments: The Guess Who is an effective device for obtaining students' perceptions of their peers. It is well designed and demonstrates adequate construct and criterion related validity. Coefficients of internal consistency indicate that

Factor IV (Quiet) is the least reliable of the instrument's 4 scales. Test/retest reliabilities, not currently available, would be of interest. More information about this instrument should become available as Project PRIME reports are published.

References: Agard, J. A., and S. M. Harrison, *Guess Who* (*developmental stage*). *Test administrator's instructions.* Austin, Texas: Project PRIME, undated.

Veldman, D. J., and J. R. Sheffield, *Guess Who: The scaling of sociometric nominations.* Austin, Texas: Project PRIME Data Analysis Center, University of Texas, 1974.

Name: THE INDEX OF ADJUSTMENT AND VALUES

Authors: Robert E. Bills, Edgar L. Vance, and Orison S. McLean

Type of Measure: Rating scale

Availability: Bills, R. E., E. L. Vance, and O. S. McLean, "An index of adjustment and values." *Journal of Consulting Psychology*, 1959, **15**, 257–261. A copy of this instrument may also be found in: Robinson, J. R., and P. R. Shaver, *Measures of social psychological attitudes*. Ann Arbor, Michigan: Institute for Social Research, University of Michigan, 1969.

Description: The Index of Adjustment and Values (IAV) is designed to reveal changes in an individual's values, which in this context refer to personal traits he or she considers desirable. In constructing the instrument, 124 items representing clear definitions of self-concept were selected from Allport's list of 17,953 traits (Allport and Odbert, 1936). Forty-nine of these items which demonstrated adequate reliability in a 3-week test/retest study were selected to form the final version of the IAV.

   To assess change in a value system, the IAV measures self-concept, ideal self-concept, and the individual's present attitude toward himself. The measure of adjustment is the total discrepancy between the real and the ideal selves. The IAV has 4 forms: Elementary School, grades 3–5; Junior High School, grades 6–8; High School, grades 9–12; and Adult.

Sample Items: When taking the IAV, the subject inserts each of the 49 traits in the following sentence: "I am a (an) _____ person." The subject then rates this sentence on a 5-point scale (from "seldom" to "most of the time"), according to how frequently it describes him or her. This rating is marked in column I. In column II, the subject indicates his or her feeling about this self-evaluation, using a 5-point scale, from "I very much dislike being as I am in this respect" to "I very much like being as I am in this respect." Column III measures ideal self-concept by requiring the subject to place each of the 49 words in the following sentence: "I would like to be a (an) _____ person." Responses are recorded on the 5-point scale used for column I answers. The instrument contains items of the following type:

	I	II	III
1. Trustworthy	_____	_____	_____
2. Reliable	_____	_____	_____

Reliability: Bills, Vance, and McLean (1951) computed the split-half reliability for the self-acceptance scale (column II) after administering it to 237 students at the University of Kentucky. The corrected r was .91 ($p < .001$). A coefficient of .88 ($p < .001$) was obtained for discrepancy scores (the difference between column I and III). Test/retest reliability, after a 6-week interval, was .83 ($p < .001$) for self-acceptance, and .87 ($p < .001$) for discrepancy. A coefficient of $-.77$ ($p < .001$) was obtained when self-acceptance and discrepancy scores were correlated. These data indicate that subjects scoring high on self-acceptance score low on discrepancy, and that subjects scoring low on self-acceptance score high on discrepancy.

Validity: Three investigations to establish validity are reported by Bills, Vance, and McLean (1951). First, 20 female college students were administered both the IAV and the Rorshach. The results were compared by independent judges, and a *rho* of .60 ($p < .05$) was obtained.

Second, 3 classes of mental hygiene students ($N = 38$) were given pre- and postsemester administrations of the IAV. In this test/retest study, 14 students showed progress toward greater acceptance. This is 7 times the number of students whose scores would be expected by chance to increase more than 1.97 times the standard error of measurement.

Third, 142 college students were given the IAV 1 week prior to completing a questionnaire concerning personal unhappiness. The data were compared by independent judges, and the resulting *chi* square was 24.6 ($p < .001$).

Norms: The IAV has been administered to 482 college students, for whom both self-acceptance and discrepancy scores were computed. These norms are provided in the 1975 revised manual. The inventory has also been administered in several independent studies to thousands of high school students and to various nonstudent groups.

Administration and Scoring: The IAV is self-administering. To obtain an acceptance score, column II ratings are summed for all 49 words. Discrepancy scores equal the difference between column I and column III sums (ignoring sign).

Comments: The Index of Adjustment and Values effectively measures 3 dimensions of self-concept. Available data indicate good reliability and validity, though it should be noted that validity figures are based on relatively small populations. This scale can be used for both research and therapy.

References: Allport, G. W., and H. S. Odbert, "Trait names: A psycho-lexical study." *Psychological Monographs*, 1936, (211).

Bills, R. E., *Index of Adjustment and Values: Manual for adult and high school senior version.* Birmingham, Alabama: University of Alabama, undated.

Bills, R. E., E. L. Vance, and O. S. McLean, "An index of adjustment and values." *Journal of Counseling Psychology*, 1951, **15**, 257–261.

Robinson, J. R., and P. R. Shaver, *Measures of social psychological attitudes.* Ann Arbor, Michigan: Institute for Social Research, University of Michigan, 1969.

Name: INTELLECTUAL ACHIEVEMENT RESPONSIBILITY QUESTIONNAIRE

Authors: Virginia C. Crandall, Walter Katkovsky, and Vaughn J. Crandall

Type of Measure: Forced-choice questionnaire

Availability: Crandall, V. C., W. Katkovsky, and V. J. Crandall, "Children's belief in their own control of reinforcements in intellectual-academic achievement situations." *Child Development*, 1965, **36**, 91–109.

Description: The Intellectual Achievement Responsibility (IAR) Questionnaire was designed to determine whether the child in elementary or secondary school believes the responsibility for his or her progress is internally or externally controlled. The 34 forced-choice items on the IAR deal exclusively with situations involving intellectual/academic achievement. Each is composed of a stem followed by 2 statements. The stem describes an achievement situation in which the child is successful or unsuccessful. One of the accompanying statements places responsibility for the situation on the child, while the other places responsibility on other people in the child's environment. The total of all positive items for which the child takes credit is referred to as a I+ score, while the total of all negative statements for which he or she accepts blame is a I− score.

Sample Items: Half of the IAR items describe negative experiences and the other half positive experiences. The respondent selects the statement which best describes the feelings the item stem has provoked. Stems and completion statements are of the following type.

− 1. If you do poorly on a multiple choice test, it is because
    A. the test was too hard, or
    B. you did not study enough.
+ 2. When the principal tells you that you are doing very well in school, it is
    A. because you have studied hard, or
    B. because he is in a good mood.

Reliability: Crandall, Katkovsky, and Crandall (1965) report test/retest reliabilities obtained for 47 children in grades 3, 4, and 5 over an interval of 2 months. Correlation coefficients were .69 for total scores, .66 for I+ scores, and .74 for the I− scores. All these correlations were significant at the .001 level. Split-half reliabilities for a random sample of 130 younger children are reported at .54 for I+ and .57 for I− (corrected by the Spearman-Brown formula). Correlations between I+ and I− scores are variable (.11 to .43) but generally low.

Validity: Crandall, et al. (1965) report correlations between IAR total scores and 2 measures of academic achievement: report-card grade averages and scores on the Iowa Test of Basic Skills. These were positive and significant for children in grades 3, 4, and 5. For grades 6, 8, 10, and 12, report-card grade averages correlated significantly (in the .20s and .30s) with total IAR scores, but achievement test scores were consistently related to IAR results only among younger girls and older boys.

The IAR has also shown a moderate relationship to intelligence (.16 to .26), and has discriminated between first-born and later-born children in the upper grade levels ($t = 2.15$, $p < .05$).

Norms: Means, standard deviations and score ranges are provided for total, I+, and I− scores on the IAR. These data are based on the responses of 923 subjects in grades 3 through 12 and are separated by grade and sex (Crandall et al., 1965).

Administration and Scoring: The IAR is self-administering for children in grades 6 and above. The respondent need only select the answer which best describes his or her feelings. For subjects below the sixth-grade level, however, it is recommended that the IAR be individually and orally administered. In the past, stimulus questions have been recorded on tape, for purposes of standardization, and an examiner has recorded the child's verbal responses (Crandall et al., 1965).

The IAR is scored by summing the subject's "internal control" responses separately for items keyed with a " + " or a " − ". The I+ total indicates how much credit the child takes for positive situations, while the I− total suggests how much blame he or she accepts for negative situations. I+ and I− totals may be summed to obtain an overall score.

Comments: The Intellectual Achievement Responsibility Questionnaire appears to be a well constructed instrument with moderate validity and widely applicable norms. Both retest and split-half reliabilities, however, are somewhat low. The IAR predicts achievement test scores differentially, according to sex and age level, but consistently predicts report-card grades.

References: Crandall, V. C., W. Katkovsky, and V. J. Crandall, "Children's belief in their own control of reinforcements in intellectual-academic achievement situations." *Child Development*, 1965, **36**, 91–109.

Crandall, V. C., and B. W. Lacey, "Children's perceptions of internal-external control in intellectual-academic situations and their Embedded Figures Test performance." *Child Development*, 1972, **43**, 1123–1134.

Godfrey, E. (ed.), *Intelligence, achievement, self-concepts, and attitudes among 1,216 typical sixth- and seventh-grade students in fourteen North Carolina public schools: Preliminary results of a study conducted January, 1970.* Winston-Salem, North Carolina: North Carolina Advancement School, 1970.

Katkovsky, W., V. C. Crandall, and S. Good, "Parental antecedents of children's belief in internal-external control of reinforcements in intellectual a-chievement situations." *Child Development*, 1967, **38**, 765–776.

Name: IPAT CHILDREN'S PERSONALITY QUESTIONNAIRE

Authors: R. B. Porter and R. B. Cattell

Type of Measure: Self-report questionnaire

Availability: Porter, R. B., and R. B. Cattell, *The IPAT children's personality questionnaire. Forms A and B (what you do and what you think).* Champaign, Illinois: The Institute for Personality and Ability Testing, 1959–1963.

Description: The IPAT Children's Personality Questionnaire (CPQ), developed for 8- to 12-year-old subjects, is one in a series of inventories designed to measure a number of personality variables. The CPQ is a downward extension of the IPAT High School Personality Questionnaire (HSPQ) and the Sixteen Personality Factor Questionnaire (16PF). Accordingly, the 14 traits measured by the IPAT correspond to many of those represented on the HSPQ and the 16PF. These variables are listed below:

1. Stiff, Aloof vs. Warm, Sociable

2. Dull vs. Bright

3. Emotional, Immature, Unstable vs. Mature, Calm

4. Stodgy vs. Unrestrained

5. Mild vs. Aggressive

6. Sober, Serious vs. Enthusiastic, Happy-go-lucky

7. Casual, Undependable vs. Conscientious, Persistent

8. Shy, Sensitive vs. Adventurous, "Thick-skinned"

9. Tough, Realistic vs. Esthetically Sensitive

10. Liking Group Action vs. Fastidiously Individualistic

11. Simple, Awkward vs. Sophisticated, Polished

12. Confident vs. Insecure

13. Uncontrolled, Lax vs. Controlled, Showing Willpower

14. Relaxed Composure vs. Tense, Excitable

The 1959 edition of the CPQ is available in 2 forms (A and B), each of which contains 70 items, 5 per factor. The authors suggest that both forms be administered in order to provide 10 items for each factor. A more recent edition (1963), also published in 2 forms, contains twice as many items as the earlier version. However, limited psychometric data are available for this edition.

Sample Items: Each item on the CPQ presents 2 or 3 statements similar to those below. The subject is asked to check the statement in each item which best describes him or her.

1. You like to participate in team sports.
   You like to play games by yourself.
2. Dark places frighten you.
   You don't mind dark places.
3. You get angry at people who play jokes on you.
   You just laugh even when the joke is on you.
4. In groups, you like to be the leader.
   You don't like to be the leader.

Reliability: The manual (Porter and Cattell, 1959) presents considerable reliability data based on 260 9-year-old children. When forms A and B were combined, test/retest coefficients, obtained over an 18-day interval, ranged from .52 to .83 for CPQ factor scores. Alternate form reliabilities ranged from .32 to .67, and split-half coefficients fell between .30 to .64 for single trait scores.

Validity: The CPQ manual is concerned primarily with the test's construct validity—the extent to which individual scale scores correlate with the pure factors they purport to measure. Thus validation has been approached by 3 methods: (1) multiple correlation of the pure factor with the 10 CPQ items measuring it; (2) the square root of the equivalency coefficient; and (3) circumstantial or indirect evidence of validity. The multiple r yielded estimates of validity ranging from .53 to .84 for combined form factor scores. Coefficients of equivalence ranged from .56 to .82, and estimates of circumstantial validity fell between .43 to .82. These coefficients were obtained on samples of 200 to 260 children.

Intercorrelations among the 14 trait scores indicated considerable factorial independence. None of these correlations exceeded .50, and half fell below .20.

Werner (1966), estimating the concurrent validity of the CPQ, found that test scores discriminated significantly between talented and underachieving children. Data from 87 subjects, ranging in age from 8 to 12, showed that the CPQ score profiles of talented children resembled those of creative adults on the 16PF, while the score profiles of underachievers resembled those of older delinquents on the 16PF and HSPQ. Although CPQ factor scores discriminated well between underachieving and talented groups, differentiation was clearest among boys. A similar study by Lessing and Smouse (1967) showed significant differences in factor scores between clinic and school children and between boys and girls.

Norms: The manual for the 1959 edition presents standard scores obtained on 735 boys and 741 girls, from 8 to 12 years old. Lessing and Smouse (1967) present mean factor scores for a sample of 227 normal and emotionally disturbed children in the fifth and sixth grades.

Administration and Scoring: The CPQ may be administered individually or in groups. The 1959 edition requires about 50 minutes to complete, the 1963 edition, between 60 and 120 minutes. Scoring involves the use of a stencil to tally responses on each factor. Scoring time for each form is about 2 minutes.

Comments: The Children's Personality Questionnaire is a well designed instrument measuring 14 apparently independent traits. However, since the reliabilities of factor scores are too low for individual clinical use, and evidence of validity is incomplete, the CPQ should be considered a research tool at present.

References: Lessing, E. E., and A. D. Smouse, "Use of Children's Personality Questionnaire in differentiating between normal and disturbed children." *Educational and Psychological Measurement*, 1967, **27**, 657–669.

Porter, R. B., and R. B. Cattell, *Handbook for the IPAT Children's Personality Questionnaire*. Champaign, Illinois: Institute for Personality and Ability Testing, 1960.

Werner, E. E., "CPQ personality factors of talented and underachieving boys and girls in elementary school." *Journal of Clinical Psychology*, 1966, **22**, 461–464.

Name: JUDGMENT: DEDUCTIVE LOGIC AND ASSUMPTION
RECOGNITION, GRADES 7–12

Author: Instructional Objectives Exchange

Type of Measure: Battery of cognitive ability tests

Availability: Instructional Objectives Exchange. *Judgment: Deductive logic and
assumption recognition, grades 7–12.* Los Angeles: Author, 1971. This battery
may be obtained from the Instructional Objectives Exchange, Distribution
Center, P.O. Box 24095, Los Angeles, California 90024.

Description: The Instructional Objectives Exchange (1971) describes this
criterion-referenced test battery as a "collection of objectives and related measures" dealing with 2 aspects of judgment: deductive logic and assumption
recognition. These objectives, focusing on ability to make judgments based on
logical analysis in emotional and nonemotional situations, are the criteria by
which the student's test performance is evaluated. Each of the measures in this
battery, along with its associated objectives (taken verbatim from the manual) is
briefly described below.

1. *Conditional Reasoning Index*

   Objective 1: Given a series of statements which are expressed in various
   conditional logic formats, the students will discriminate which of the conclusions are logically valid and which are logically invalid.

   Objective 2: Given a series of "emotionally-laden" statements expressed in
   various conditional logic formats, the students will discriminate which of the
   conclusions are logically valid and which are logically invalid, regardless of
   the "emotionally-laden" character of the statements.

   This instrument contains 48 items requiring the respondent to judge the
   validity of conclusions. Each item expresses one of Ennis' (Ennis and Paulus,
   1965) 12 principles of conditional logic, a type of deductive reasoning concerned with "if/then" statements. The presence of both emotionally-laden
   and emotionally-neutral items allows inferences about the student's functioning in 2 kinds of situations.

2. *Class Reasoning Index*

   Objective 3: Given a series of statements which are expressed in various class
   logic formats, the students will discriminate which of the conclusions are
   logically valid and which are logically invalid.

   Objective 4: Given a series of "emotionally-laden" statements expressed in
   various class logic formats, the students will discriminate which of the conclusions are logically valid and which are logically invalid, regardless of the
   "emotionally-laden" character of the statements.

   This 32-item measure also requires the respondent to judge the validity
   of conclusions. In this case, however, each item expresses one of Ennis'

(Ennis and Paulus, 1965) 8 principles of class logic, a type of deductive reasoning involving the arrangement of subjects and predicates within "all," "none," or "some" statements. Again, both emotionally-laden and emotionally-neutral items are included.

3. *Assumption Recognition Index I*

Objective 5: Given a series of statements, each of which is followed by several proposed assumptions, the students will determine whether, within each question set, each of the assumptions listed is necessary to the particular statement.

This test is composed of 5 statements, each accompanied by several proposed assumptions. The student's task is to decide whether or not each proposed assumption is implied in the associated statement. He does this by marking "assumption made" or "assumption not made" on his answer sheet.

4. *Assumption Recognition Index II*

Objective 6: Given an argument and a set of proposed assumptions, the student will identify those assumptions necessary to the argument.

This instrument presents 5 arguments, each followed by 4 proposed assumptions. For each item, the student decides which assumptions must be made if the argument is to be reasonable and consistent.

5. *Recognizing Reliable Observations*

Objective 7: Given sets of descriptions of observations, the student will choose the observation with the highest reliability.

Based on Ennis' (1962) criteria for assessing the reliability of observations, this measure contains 30 observation statements grouped into sets of 3. Within each set, the student selects the observation in which he would place most confidence.

Sample Items: The instruments in this battery include items and response alternatives of the following types:

Test	*Item*	*Response Alternatives*
1. *Conditional Reasoning Index*	Given: If school busing for integration is the right thing to do, it will eventually come to pass.	Valid Invalid
(emotionally laden)	Then, would this conclusion be valid? If school busing does not come to pass, it is not the right policy.	
2. *Class Reasoning Index*	Given: All the blue books are thick. All the thick books have large print.	Valid Invalid
(emotionally neutral)	Then, would this conclusion be valid? All the blue books have large print.	

Test	*Item*	*Response Alternatives*	

		Assumption Made	Assumption not Made
3. *Assumption Recognition Index I*	Statement: Buy a home in Marble Glen—the hurricane-proof subdivision.		
	Proposed Assumptions:		
	a) It is possible to build a hurricane-proof structure.	a) ____	____
	b) Most people want to own their own home.	b) ____	____
	c) Marble Glen is located in an area where hurricanes occur.	c) ____	____
	d) It costs a lot to live in Marble Glen.	d) ____	____
4. *Assumption Recognition Index II*	Statement: Extreme action should be taken to guarantee that no individual bring more than 2 children into the world. If people will not voluntarily agree to this limit, they should be forced to comply. Otherwise we will all be crowded, starved, or polluted off the earth. We can solve our problem only when we stabilize our population growth at zero.		
		Assumption Made	Assumption not Made
	Proposed Assumptions:		
	a) Continued population growth is more dangerous than government control of family planning.	a) ____	____
	b) Great problems are caused by population growth.	b) ____	____
	c) When the population growth rate is at zero, the world will be at peace.	c) ____	____
	d) It is unrealistic to expect that population growth will be controlled by natural forces.	d) ____	____
5. *Recognizing Reliable Observations*	a) At the tennis match, John's mother said his shot was in-bounds.	Mark the most accurate observation.	
	b) At the tennis match, John's opponent said John's shot was out-of-bounds.	(a) (b) (c) ____ ____ ____	
	c) At the tennis match, the line judge said John's shot was in-bounds.		

Reliability: No reliability data are reported in the Instructional Objectives Exchange (1971) publication which includes this battery, its description and rationale, and administration and scoring procedures.

Validity: Although an examination of the tests in this battery indicates that they correspond very closely to the objectives they are designed to measure, no formal evidence of validity is reported by the Instructional Objectives Exchange (1971).

Norms: Because the tests in this battery are criterion- rather than norm-referenced, normative data are inapplicable to them.

Administration and Scoring: Although directions for administration and scoring vary from test to test, they are in every case clearly specified and easy to follow. Before each test is given, any relevant terms with which the student may be unfamiliar (such as " valid " or " assumption ") are carefully explained according to standard definitions. In general, the tests require 10 to 40 minutes to complete.

All of the measures in this battery are distributed as preprinted spirit masters, from each of which 200 to 300 copies can be duplicated. Alternate forms are available for every test.

When a small group of children is tested, hand scoring is feasible. However, machine scoring is recommended for larger groups. Several scoring options, explained in the manual, are available.

Comments: This battery, when used in its entirety, offers good coverage of the student's skill in deductive logic and assumption recognition. The provision of 5 tests, a number of emotionally laden items, and a variety of scoring procedures yields data which may be used for individualized instruction, needs assessment, classroom pre- and posttest evaluation, school- or district-wide evaluation, or teaching assessment. Because the measures in this battery are criterion- rather than norm-referenced, they focus on degree of proficiency, not comparative status. While these tests appear to be well constructed, especially in regard to face validity, they could be used with greater confidence if their reliability and validity were documented.

References: Ennis, R., "A concept of critical thinking." *Harvard Educational Review*, 1962, **32**, 90.

Ennis, R., and D. Paulus, *Critical thinking readiness in grades 1–12* (Phase I, Deductive Reasoning in Adolescence). Cooperative Research Project No. OE 1680. Ithaca, New York: New York State College of Agriculture and the School of Education, Cornell University, 1965.

Instructional Objectives Exchange. *Judgment: Deductive logic and assumption recognition, grades 7–12*. Los Angeles: Author, 1971.

Name: JUNIOR EYSENCK PERSONALITY INVENTORY

Author: Sybil B. G. Eysenck

Type of Measure: Self-report questionnaire

Availability: Eysenck, S. *The junior Eysenck personality inventory.* San Diego, California: Educational and Industrial Testing Service, 1965. A British edition of this test is published by the University of London Press.

Description: The Junior Eysenck Personality Inventory (JEPI) is a 60-item questionnaire designed to measure neuroticism and extroversion in children. The choice of these 2 variables is based on Eysenck and Eysenck's (1964) factor analytic study of personality, which indicated that these 2 higher-order, uncorrelated factors are the basis of all human personality traits. The Eysenck Personality Inventory (EPI) was developed to measure these variables among adults.

The JEPI is a downward extension of the EPI. From an original list of 124 items, many derived from the EPI, 60 were retained after factor analysis of scores obtained from testing 2 large samples of English children. These 60 items include 24 relating to neuroticism, 24 relating to extroversion, and 12 composing a Lie Scale. The JEPI is appropriate for children between the ages of 7 and 16. Two forms are available: the American Edition (including a Spanish translation) and the British Edition. These 2 editions are identical except for instructions and several words used in the items.

Sample Items: The subject responds to JEPI items by answering either " yes " or " no." The following items are similar to those which appear on the test, the last 3 being representative of the Lie Scale:

1. Do you like to have company when you do things?
2. Do you often worry about getting sick?
3. Are you seldom happy?
4. Do you enjoy playing pranks?
5. Do you find yourself getting angry at others at times?
6. Do you ever talk back to your parents?
7. Do you ever leave things on your plate at meals?

Reliability: Since the JEPI was developed in Great Britain, reliability and validity data have been obtained primarily for the British Edition on samples of English children. Eysenck (1965) reports split-half reliabilities for neuroticism ranging from .80 to .90, with no changes occurring with age. Reliabilities for extroversion range from .65 to .90 and increase with age. Coefficients for the Lie Scale range from .41 to .78 and also increase with age. Waters (1968), testing 14- and 15-year old subjects, obtained a split-half coefficient of .55.

Test/retest reliabilities were also computed by Eysenck (1965) for 1,056

English boys and 1,074 English girls. Though these figures rise slightly with age, with the exception of those obtained for the Lie Scale, they typically fall between .70 and .80.

Validity: Eysenck (1965) reports that little is known about the validity of the JEPI. She does note, however, significant group differences in the JEPI scores of normal and neurotic subjects, the latter group being composed of 229 children receiving treatment at a child guidance clinic. Waters (1968) investigated the validity of the JEPI by administering the test to several groups. He told the experimental group that scores would be used to make administrative decisions concerning the respondents. The control group, on the other hand, was simply asked to complete the questionnaire. Results indicated that the experimental group scored significantly lower on neuroticism and significantly higher on the Lie Scale than did the control group.

Norms: Preliminary norms derived from the scores of 199 children are available for the American Edition. Waters (1968) also reports the scores of 122 American high school students. For the British Edition, normative data based on large and diverse samples of English children are provided. Though the English norms are far more complete than the American, differences between the 2 populations on the Lie and Neuroticism Scales preclude the application of English norms to American children.

Administration and Scoring: The JEPI is self-administering, although children younger than 10 years of age may have difficulty with some of the words. Approximately 15 to 20 minutes are required to complete the test. Scoring stencils and a scoring service are available.

Comments: While the JEPI is based upon a well documented theory, users of the test should heed the author's recommendation that the test be used only for research. The absence of validation data and the inadequacy of the American norms limit this scale somewhat. Although the JEPI is not yet ready for general use, it has potential as a research instrument.

References: Eysenck, H. J., and S. B. G. Eysenck, *Manual for the Eysenck Personality Inventory.* San Diego, California: Educational and Industrial Testing Service, 1963.

Eysenck, S. B. G., "A new scale for personality measurements in children." *British Journal of Educational Psychology*, 1965, **35**, 362–367.

Waters, T. J., "The validity of the Junior Eysenck Personality Inventory Lie Scale." *Educational and Psychological Measurement*, 1968, **28**, 1197–1206.

Name: JUNIOR INDEX OF MOTIVATION

Author: Jack R. Frymier

Type of Measure: Rating scale

Availability: Frymier, J. R., "Development and validation of a motivation index." *Theory into Practice*, 1970, **9**, 56–88.

Description: The Junior Index of Motivation (JIM) assesses the adolescent's motivation toward school. In developing this instrument, school-related motivation was assumed to represent an internalized state of being which manifests itself through particular behaviors (i.e., actions, attitudes, and values). It was further assumed that motivation can be measured. Working from these assumptions, 50 items which discriminated between highly motivated and poorly motivated students were identified on the basis of teacher ratings of pupil motivation. These items, along with 30 "filler" items, comprise the JIM scale.

The author emphasizes that this test should be used as a total scale, since individual items, considered alone, are not significant or meaningful. He also cautions that the JIM scale should not be used in making decisions about individual students, but should instead be used in studying academic motivation among groups of students in grades 7 through 12.

Sample Items: Items of the following type appear on the JIM scale:

1. Asking questions often gets you into trouble.
2. A lot of young people do not want to go to school.
3. I would like school better if teachers did not give grades.
4. Very few people in this world are really kind.

The student responds to these items by indicating the extent of his or her agreement according to the following scale.

$+1 =$ slight support, agreement

$+2 =$ strong support, agreement

$-1 =$ slight opposition, disagreement

$-2 =$ strong opposition, disagreement

A student may choose to leave the answer space blank if the question has no impact on him or her, in which case the item is scored 0.

Reliability: Initial studies yielded split-half reliabilities ranging from .63 to .74 for total scores. Later analyses produced very similar split-half coefficients, falling between .63 and .72. A more recent study of 181 high school students yielded a split-half estimate of .83, and scores from a random sample of 1,200 students included in a national norming study produced coefficients ranging from .70 to .86. Test/retest reliabilities, obtained over a 10-month interval, ranged from .63 to .72 (Frymier, 1970).

Validity: Frymier (1970) presents several validity studies which were conducted during development of the JIM scale. The first series of studies correlated JIM scale scores with academic achievement, experts' opinions, and teacher estimates of motivational level. Data from 4 comparable groups of 30 students each (60 boys and 60 girls) indicate that pupils who scored high on the JIM scale also made higher achievement scores on the Sequential Test of Educational Progress (STEP), when ability (estimated by Kuhlmann-Anderson IQ's) was controlled. Group differences were significant at the .01 level. Although the figures demonstrate conclusively that, among girls, high JIM scale scores were associated with significantly higher levels of achievement, the results for boys were less convincing. A comparison of the STEP scores of boys with high and low JIM scale scores indicated that differences in achievement, though in the expected direction, were not statistically significant.

Other validity analyses required experts (teachers and professors) to respond to the JIM scale as they thought highly or poorly motivated students would respond. Those who completed the questionnaire as highly motivated students produced significantly higher scores (F ratio = 181.84) than those experts answering as poorly motivated students.

Similarly, correlations between JIM scale scores and teachers' rankings of students produced rank-order coefficients ranging from .21 to .65, indicating a strong positive relationship between the 2 indices of motivation.

Another validity study by Frymier (1970) yielded statistically significant correlations of .44 and .57 between the JIM scale scores and Farquhar M-scale scores of 9th- and 11th-graders, respectively. Frymier also compared the achievement scores (Iowa Tests of Educational Development) of these 9th- and 11th-graders with their JIM scale scores and obtained statistically significant coefficients of .44 and .50.

Rodgers (1974) compared the JIM scale scores of 296 high school freshmen to the following variables: grade-point averages (GPA); total reading scores from the Iowa Test of Educational Development; scores on the Short Test of Educational Ability (STEA); and school attendance. The data showed predicted relationships between the JIM scale and GPA, STEA scores, and ITED total reading scores. However, the relationship between JIM scale scores and number of days absent was irregular and unclear.

Norms: Standard deviations and standard error of measurement values are presented for 3,189 students from the norming sample, according to sex and grade level (Frymier, 1970).

Administration and Scoring: The JIM scale is easily administered and scored. The questionnaire is not timed, though it usually requires less than 30 minutes to complete. In scoring the scale, the values of selected responses are added, the sign of this total is reversed, and 100 is added algebraically to this raw sum to produce the student's converted motivation score. Students who consistently disagree with JIM scale items achieve high scores; students who agree with most items achieve low scores.

Comments: The Junior Index of Motivation provides a technique for assessing the academic motivation of junior high and high school students. Preliminary reliability and validity data are moderate, but encouraging. Further research on this instrument should confirm its value as a measure of student motivation.

References: Frymier, J. R., "Development and validation of a motivation index." *Theory into Practice*, 1970, **9**, 56–88.

Rodgers, R., *Item and total score characteristics and correlates of the JIM scale.* Paper presented at the annual meeting of the National Council on Measurement in Education, Chicago, April, 1974.

Name: THE KIDDIE MACH

Authors: Richard Christie and Susan Nachamie

Type of Measure: Rating scale

Availability: Christie, R., and F. L. Geis, *Studies in Machiavellianism*. New York: Academic Press, 1970. A copy of this instrument also appears in: Robinson, J. P., and P. R. Shaver, *Measures of social psychological attitudes*. Ann Arbor, Michigan: Institute for Social Research, University of Michigan, 1969.

Description: The Kiddie Mach is the children's form of the Machiavellian Scales developed by Christie (Christie and Geis, 1970) to measure interpersonal style, particularly one's inclination to view others impersonally and amorally in terms of their usefulness for his or her own purposes. The adult versions of the test (the Mach II, Mach IV, and Mach V) were originally designed to assess the psychological characteristics of political and religious leaders who were adept at manipulating people. Christie and others wrote 71 items, based on statements from Machiavelli's writings (*The Prince* and *The Discourses*), covering 3 areas: interpersonal tactics; views of human nature; and moral philosophy. These items were administered to several college populations, analyzed for discriminating power, and reduced in number to 20. The final adult forms, the Mach IV and the Mach V, are similar, except that the latter employs a forced-choice response format to control for the effects of social desirability.

Because evidence suggests that Machiavellian tendencies develop before adulthood (Christie and Geis, 1970), Nachamie (1969) administered the Mach IV to fifth- and sixth-grade students. An analysis of their responses revealed an agreement response set as well as inadequate discriminatory power for a number of items. Assuming that the vocabulary and wording of the Mach IV statements were too sophisticated for younger children, Nachamie edited and simplified the items, especially those with the poorest discriminating power, employing a vocabulary and grammatical style comparable to that of a fourth-grade reader used in the New York City public schools. She then submitted these edited items to individuals familiar with the Mach IV, who judged them for congruence with the original items. Finally, a school guidance counselor, a reading coordinator, and a school principal reviewed the items for comprehensibility and appropriateness for the age level of potential respondents. The final scale, labelled the Kiddie Mach, includes both positively and negatively worded items.

Sample Items: The Kiddie Mach contains 20 items of the following type, to which the child responds by indicating degree of agreement on a 4-point scale:

1. You should always tell the truth, no matter what.
2. It's a good idea to be nice to important people, even if they aren't nice to you.
3. It's possible to be good all the time, if you try.
4. Sometimes you have to lie to get the things you want.

Reliability: Nachamie (1969) administered both the Kiddie Mach and the Mach IV to 4 sixth-grade classes ($N = 91$). In 1 class, nonsignificant (and unexplained) split-half reliabilities were obtained for both scales. The other 3 classes, however, yielded reliabilities in the .50s for both scales, with the Kiddie Mach coefficients being slightly higher than those for the Mach IV.

Administering a 16-item, independently developed Kiddie Mach to a sample of fifth-graders, Braginsky (1966) found a split-half reliability of .43 and a test/retest coefficient, over a 2-week interval, of .87.

These reliabilities fall short of those obtained using the adult forms on college samples.

Validity: Although evidence of validity is somewhat limited, 2 studies have indicated that children high in Machiavellianism (high Machs) are more successful manipulators than those low in Machiavellianism (low Machs). In an investigation of children's game playing strategies (Christie and Geis, 1970), a payoff matrix was designed to reward successful bluffing and challenging. The child who successfully deceived or challenged his or her opponent in a dice-throwing game was rewarded with more M & M candies. Subjects were matched for sex and ethnicity, and each pair consisted of one child who scored high on the Kiddie Mach and another who scored low. It was hypothesized that high Machs, being more successful manipulators, would win more M & M's. This prediction was confirmed at the .002 level of significance: in the 36 pairs run, high Machs won in 26 cases, lost in 8, and tied in 2.

Using an independently developed Kiddie Mach, Braginsky (1966) classified fifth-graders as high, average, or low in Machiavellianism. Controlling for sex, age, IQ, friendship, and parental socioeconomic status, she paired each middle Mach with a high or a low Mach. Then, posing as a home economist from a cracker company, Braginsky directed the high- and low-Mach children to persuade their middle-Mach partners to eat as many quinine flavored crackers as possible. Each subject was promised a nickel for every cracker consumed by his partner. The high Machs persuaded the target children to eat an average of 6.46 crackers, while the low Machs persuaded their partners to eat an average of only 2.79 (a difference significant at the .003 level). Furthermore, an analysis of the persuasive techniques used indicated that, although high-Mach children did not tell significantly more lies overall, high-Mach boys distorted information more often than low-Mach boys, and high-Mach girls withheld information more frequently than low-Mach girls.

Norms: Christie and Geis (1970) report no normative data for the Kiddie Mach. The sample used by Nachamie (1969) was composed of 4 sixth-grade classes ($N = 91$) in a school located in a low-income area of a large city. The population used by Braginsky (1966) consisted of white fifth-graders attending public schools in 2 small cities in eastern Connecticut.

Administration and Scoring: In the Nachamie study (1966), items were read aloud by the administrator while subjects followed along silently and then circled the response which best described their feeling about each statement. If the subjects have a fourth-grade reading level, however, it is not necessary that the examiner read each item.

After reversing the values of negatively worded items, scores are obtained by simple summing.

Comments: Preliminary work with the Kiddie Mach suggests that this scale is sensitive to differences in interpersonal style. There is some question, however, about whether it distinguishes successful manipulators from individuals who are *unwilling* to manipulate others or from those who are *unable* to do so. In experimental situations, the average low scorer, according to Christie and Geis (1970), is characterized more by ineptness in deception than by refusal to engage in deception. This distinction, along with the possibility of social desirability response sets and scale unreliability, should be kept in mind by users of the Kiddie Mach. Although Christie and Geis (1970) maintain that low reliabilities may be a product of response sets or the counterbalancing of the scale, these reliabilities discourage use of the Kiddie Mach for prediction or interpretation of individual behavior.

References: Braginsky, D. D., *Machiavellianism and manipulative interpersonal behavior in children: Two exploratory studies.* Unpublished doctoral dissertation, University of Connecticut, 1966.

Christie, R., and F. L. Geis, *Studies in Machiavellianism.* New York: Academic Press, 1970.

Nachamie, S. S., *Machiavellianism in children: The children's Mach scale and the bluffing game.* Unpublished doctoral dissertation, Columbia University, 1969.

Name: LET'S LOOK AT FIRST GRADERS

Authors: This test was developed jointly by the New York City Board of Education and the Educational Testing Service. The project was initiated and directed by Joseph O. Loretan and Henry Chauncey.

Type of Measure: Cognitive ability test

Availability: *Let's look at first graders.* New York: Board of Education of the City of New York, 1965. This instrument is distributed by the Educational Testing Service, Cooperative Tests and Services, Box 999, Princeton, New Jersey 08540.

Description: Let's Look at First Graders is designed to help first-grade teachers understand, recognize, and foster the intellectual development of their students. Based on the view that intelligence comprises a number of intellectual abilities used by the child to process, organize, and manipulate information from the environment, this test allows the teacher to systematically observe and assess the child's interaction with his or her surroundings and to combine this assessment with daily classroom instruction.

The instrument consists of a *Guide*, a set of instructional and assessment materials, and a series of written exercises. The *Guide* describes 6 major areas of intellectual development, each of which is associated with certain behaviors. These 6 areas and the developmental concepts they incorporate are listed below.

1. Basic Language Skills—Auditory Discrimination and Attention, Listening Comprehension, Learning to Communicate, and Language for Thinking.
2. Concepts of Space and Time—Learning Shapes and Forms, Spatial Perspective, and the Notion of Time.
3. Beginning Logical Concepts—Logical Classification, Concepts of Relationship.
4. Beginning Mathematical Concepts—Conservation of Quantity, One-to-one Correspondence, and Number Relations.
5. The Growth of Reasoning Skills—Understanding Cause and Effect, Reasoning by Association, and Reasoning by Inference.
6. General Signs of Development—Growing Awareness and Responsiveness, Directed Activity, General Knowledge, and Developing Imagination.

The instructional and assessment materials provide tasks designed to elicit behavior associated with each of the 6 areas of intellectual development. These tasks allow the student to demonstrate acquisition of the concepts listed above, thus giving the teacher an opportunity to assess his or her progress. Yet these materials have instructional as well as assessment value since they provide the kind of experiences needed to develop the student's intellect in each of the 6 areas.

The 30 written exercises are the most "test-like" of all the materials.

Related to various concepts in the *Guide*, they help measure the child's under-standing of and ability to deal with: Shapes and Forms, Spatial Relations, Time Concepts, Mathematics, Communication Skills, and Logical Reasoning. One of the most unique and important aspects of these exercises is their instructional nature. For each area, there are 5 exercises, the first 3 of which function as practice problems and the last 2 of which are graded for assessment purposes. This arrangement allows the student to become acquainted with the skills required in each area before being evaluated.

Let's Look at First Graders was pilot tested in 25 New York City elemen-tary schools during the 1964–65 school year. The information obtained during this trial year was used in developing the final, published forms of the project materials. The authors point out that, in a very real sense, the materials were written and produced in the classroom.

Sample Items: The Guide provides behavior samples for each theoretical concept included in the 6 areas of intellectual development. For example, under Basic Language Skills, Listening Comprehension is manifested when a child laughs at appropriate points as the teacher reads a story aloud. This behavior demon-strates that the child understands what he or she is hearing.

A typical task included among the instructional and assessment materials is the "conservation problem." A given number of beads are dropped first into a tall, narrow jar and then into a short, wide jar. The child's task is to demon-strate whether he understands the principle that a physical quantity remains the same despite transformations in shape or position.

The written exercises are composed of items of the following type. Under Time Concepts, 3 faces are shown to the child, who must then choose the youngest face. Under Spatial Relations, the child, presented with a picture of a boy and several balls, is asked to point to the ball which is farthest away from the boy.

Reliability, Validity, and Norms: Because Let's Look at First Graders is intended to yield only qualitative information about the child's intellectual growth in several areas, no psychometric data are provided. The test is designed primarily to systematize teachers' observations and to incorporate assessment into instruction. Therefore, usual standardization procedures have not been undertaken.

Administration and Scoring: The manual provides very clear and thorough in-structions for using this instrument. Some of the instructional and assessment materials can be given to the whole class, while others are more appropriate for small-group or individual administration. Many of these materials were designed and constructed specifically for this test. Others, however, are nor-mally found in the classroom.

Comments: Let's Look at First Graders is a well designed instrument which provides an interesting alternative to standard intelligence testing. By placing assessment in a natural context, this battery samples behaviors which are very similar to those exhibited daily in the classroom. It is therefore relatively non-threatening to children. Furthermore, this instrument encourages the teacher to include evaluation as an integral and continuing part of instruction, and at the same time sharpens and systematizes his observational skills. The *Guide* which accompanies the instructional and assessment materials is well organized, explicit, and easy to use.

References: Anastasi, A., *Psychological testing* (third ed.). London: The Macmillan Co., 1968.

Let's look at first graders. New York: Board of Education of the City of New York, 1965.

Loretan, J. O., "Alternatives to intelligence testing." *Proceedings of the 1965 Invitational Conference on Testing Problems.* Princeton, New Jersey: Educational Testing Service, 1966, 19–30.

Name: A LOOK AT LITERATURE: THE NCTE COOPERATIVE TEST OF CRITICAL READING AND APPRECIATION.

Authors: Developed and sponsored jointly by the Research Foundation of the National Council of Teachers of English and the Educational Testing Service.

Type of Measure: Questionnaire

Availability: The Research Foundation of the National Council of Teachers of English and the Educational Testing Service. *A look at literature: The NCTE cooperative test of critical reading and appreciation.* Princeton, New Jersey: Educational Testing Service, 1969.

Description: A Look at Literature is a research instrument designed to measure the ability of fourth-, fifth-, and sixth-grade children to respond critically to imaginative prose and poetry. The manual reports that, while some items deal with comprehension of meaning, a large number of questions test "the creative-extension of meaning and the awareness of literary qualities (The Research Foundation of the National Council of Teachers of English and the Educational Testing Service, 1969a, p. 1)." In responding to these questions the student is required to perform mental operations such as interpreting, valuing, comparing, inferring, appreciating, restating, attending to, relating, identifying with, and understanding.

Two parallel forms of this instrument (A and B) each contain 50 multiple choice items, based on 14 brief literary selections. These selections represent diverse modes of literary expression drawn from poetry and prose suitable for children. Both forms A and B are divided into 2 sections of 25 questions each. While questions in the first section are read orally by the examiner, those in the second section are read silently by the subject. This procedure is intended to emphasize the fact that one can listen to as well as read literature. This partially oral presentation also decreases the effect of the student's reading ability.

Questions included on A Look at Literature were designed to produce 1 of 3 response modes defined prior to the development of the test: translation, extension, and awareness. Translation requires the student to make low-level inferences, to define, restate, comprehend meanings, and recognize elements. Extension involves interpretation, prediction, comparison, and higher-level inferences, while awareness demands perception of literary style, point of view, and the author's craft.

This instrument was developed in part to encourage the inclusion of literature in the elementary curriculum. The authors hoped to provide some insight and information regarding students' reactions to literature and to enhance interest on the part of curriculum planners and teachers in making more literature courses available to upper elementary students. In addition to being used for assessment purposes, this test may also be employed informally as an aid in classroom instruction.

Sample Items: Each literary selection is followed by questions and response alternatives of the following type:

1. Why doesn't the writer tell where and when the story takes place?
   a. Those details wouldn't be of interest.
   b. The reader is supposed to figure out where and when it happened.
   c. It doesn't matter because it clearly happened a long time ago.
   d. It could have happened any place, at any time.

2. The author wants you to
   a. laugh at the man in the story.
   b. feel sorry for the man in the story.
   c. learn about loneliness.
   d. think the man in the story is crazy

3. The author writes about lightening bugs as if they were people. Which lines in the story show this best?
   a. 1 and 2
   b. 4 and 5
   c. 7 and 8
   d. 10 and 11

Reliability: Reliability studies were conducted by the authors on samples of approximately 500 students each, selected from several different schools. The manual reports reliability coefficients (computed using the Kuder-Richardson formula 20) and their associated standard errors of measurement. Coefficients range from .68 to .76 for part scores on Forms A and B. Total score coefficients fall at .83 for both forms. The average standard error of measurement for total test scores is 3.15 raw or 4.11 standard score points.

Validity: The authors cite the NCTE committee's expertise as evidence for content validity. They admit, however, an absence of data supporting statistical or criterion-related validity of the test, suggesting that further research will correct this situation.

A Look at Literature has been correlated with STEP reading scores, yielding coefficients of .78 and .79, which, according to the authors, indicate that what is being measured by this test is not distinct from reading in general.

Norms: Normative data are not available. Test results reported in the manual were obtained from a select group composed largely of middle-class, urban and suburban pupils of average or above-average academic ability, who were also above-average readers.

Administration and Scoring: A Look at Literature is easily administered and scored. The first half is presented orally and the second read silently by the respondent. The entire test takes no longer than 70 minutes. The students can mark their answers either in the test booklet or on separate answer sheets. The total number of correct responses for each part is computed and then summed to yield the total raw score. The manual includes a table for converting raw scores into standard scores. The authors indicate that converting scores is necessary if data from both forms are to be compared or summarized.

Comments: A Look at Literature is the only test of its kind. Its use, however, is restricted until standardization or normative data are available. Also, further research is needed to establish statistical validity. On the positive side, the literary selections included in the test are appealing, diverse, and up-to-date, and the vocabulary level is appropriate for the intended population. The manual is well written and includes an outline of possible uses for this instrument as well as a frank report of its limitations.

References: Buros, O. K., *The seventh mental measurements yearbook.* Highland Park, New Jersey: The Gryphon Press, 1972.

The Research Foundation of the National Council of Teachers of English and the Educational Testing Service. *Handbook. A Look at Literature.* Princeton, New Jersey: Educational Testing Service, 1969. (a)

The Research Foundation of the National Council of Teachers of English and the Educational Testing Service. *A look at literature: The NCTE comparative test of critical reading and appreciation.* Princeton, New Jersey: Educational Testing Service, 1969. (b)

Name: MANIFOLD INTEREST SCHEDULE

Authors: L. M. Heil, G. V. Sheviakov, and Solomon Stone

Type of Measure: Rating scale

Availability: A copy of this instrument may be found in: Heil, L. M., M. Powell, and I. Feifer, *Characteristics of teacher behavior and competency related to the achievement of different kinds of children in several elementary grades* (Contract No. SAE 7285). Washington, D.C.: Office of Education, U.S. Department of Health, Education, and Welfare, 1960.

Description: Based on the assumption that interests, particularly those related to psychoanalytic variables, can reflect personality, the Manifold Interest Schedule (MIS) assesses the preferences of high school and college students as an indirect estimate of personality. The MIS consists of 420 items describing various activities. These are divided into 30 14-item categories, 12 of which are related to academics and 18 of which are associated with personality. Twenty-eight of the academic interest items are cross-coded, producing 2 additional classifications, Reading and Manipulative. All of the MIS categories are listed below.

Academic Categories

Social science	Mathematics	Music
Physical science	Industrial arts	Sports
Biological science	Home economics	Reading
English	Business	Manipulative
Foreign language	Fine arts	

Nonacademic Categories

Human Relations	*Fantasy Life*	*Organization of Drives and Impulses*
Authority	Magic	Preoccupation with
Opposite sex	Mystery	cleanliness
Leadership	Humor	Self-severity
Family	Dramatics	Methodical
Same sex	Fantasy	Acceptance of impulses
Identification with	Life/death/	Aggression
others	universe	
Solitary		

As these categories indicate, the Manifold Interest Schedule measures the student's (1) interest in various academic areas, (2) preference for social interaction, (3) preoccupation with "escape mechanisms," and (4) manner of coping with impulses.

Sample Items: The MIS contains items of the following type, which the student rates by marking "Like," "Indifferent" or "Dislike" on an answer sheet:

Category	*Item*
Fantasy	1. Wondering what it would be like to be loved by a famous person.
Family	2. Spending an evening with my family.
Methodical	3. Making a list of the things I must accomplish.
Opposite Sex	4. Planning how to attract members of the opposite sex.

Reliability: Estimates of internal consistency computed according to Dressel's formula (1940) are reported for raw "Like minus Dislike" category scores (Heil, Powell, and Feiffer, 1960). These values are quite variable, ranging from .44 (Home Economics) to .90 (Mathematics) for the Academic categories, and from .33 (Mystery) to .83 (Opposite Sex) for the Nonacademic categories.

Validity: Evidence of concurrent validity is provided in several studies reported by Heil, Powell, and Feifer (1960). The scores of 139 Brooklyn College seniors on the Academic categories of the MIS were compared with their major fields of study. Results indicated that interests corresponded with field of study in almost all cases. For example, economics majors were highest and English majors lowest in Business interest. Similarly, significant differences were found among groups in relation to Industrial Arts, with physical science majors showing greatest interest and political science majors showing least.

In a second study, complete MIS profiles were used to derive sets of behavioral characteristics which might appear among students requesting counseling. These inferred characteristics were given to 6 counselors at the Brooklyn College Department of Personnel Services, who were asked to judge the following: (1) whether each inferred characteristic appeared; (2) whether they were certain about its appearance; (3) whether they had enough data to make a valid judgment; and (4) whether the inferred characteristic was incorrect. Results of the counselors' observations are summarized below.

Number of agreements	50 (48.5%)
Number of disagreements	15 (14.5%)
Number of uncertainties	23 (22.3%)
Number of cases of no data	15 (14.5%)

These findings suggest that predictions of student behavior inferred from MIS scores are more likely to be correct than incorrect.

Other investigations conducted at Brooklyn College related MIS profiles to academic achievement and proficiency. Students classified as "fearful" or "feeling" according to their MIS scores had the lowest first-year college achievement of the 6 standard profile groups. "Self-confident, assertive" students, on the other hand, obtained the highest first-year college grades. These findings, and those from similar studies described in detail in the MIS manual (Heil, Sheviakov, and Stone, 1959), support the validity of this instrument.

Norms: Norms, based on 1,475 freshmen (690 males and 785 females) entering Brooklyn College in the fall of 1957, are reported as stanines for each MIS category.

Administration and Scoring: The MIS requires no special administration procedures. Students simply read the directions and respond to the 420 items.

Each interest category is scored by subtracting "Dislikes" from "Likes." ("Indifferents" are ignored.) Theoretically, then, the range of scores within a category should be from $+14$ to -14. This is not the case, however, since scores are modified to compensate for varying overall "Like" levels expressed by students. The scores of students with a low number of "Like" responses, for example, are modified upward. Those of students with a high number of "Like" responses are modified downward. These modified category scores are converted to stanines and reported on 2 sheets, one outlining "Academic Interests" and the other, "Nonacademic Interests." In all MIS categories except Authority, a high score reflects high interest in or liking for the variable in question.

Six standard profiles have been empirically generated according to a method suggested by Cronbach and Gleser (1953). Each of these profiles, representing a particular configuration of the 18 Nonacademic categories, is described and interpreted by Heil, Powell, and Feifer (1960).

Comments: The Manifold Interest Schedule, designed for use in counseling and research, is intended to yield an estimate rather than a precise measure of personality. The validity of inferences derived from MIS scores depends on the user's perception and understanding of personality theory. Similarly, the weight placed on MIS profile interpretations may depend on the degree to which the user accepts the psychoanalytic concepts on which they are based. The usefulness of this instrument is somewhat limited by restricted normative data and low reliabilities in several of the Nonacademic categories.

References: Cronbach, L. J., and G. C. Gleser, "Assessing similarity between profiles." *Psychological Bulletin*, 1953, **50**, 456.

Dressel, P., "A note on the Kuder-Richardson formula." *Psychometrika*, 1940, **5**, 305.

Heil, L. M., M. Powell, and I. Feifer, *Characteristics of teacher behavior and competency related to the achievement of different kinds of children in several elementary grades* (Contract No. SAE 7285). Washington, D.C.: Office of Education, U.S. Department of Health, Education, and Welfare, 1960.

Heil, L. M., G. V. Sheviakov, and S. Stone, *A manual on the Manifold Interest Schedule*. 1959.

Name: MARIANNE FROSTIG DEVELOPMENTAL TEST OF VISUAL PERCEPTION, THIRD EDITION.

Authors: Marianne Frostig, D. Welty Lefever, and John Whittlesey

Type of Measure: Perceptual performance test

Availability: Frostig, M., D. W. Lefever and J. R. B. Whittlesey, *Marianne Frostig development test of visual perception, third edition.* Palo Alto, California: Consulting Psychologists Press, 1964.

Description: The Marianne Frostig Developmental Test of Visual Perception (DTVP) is composed of 5 subtests, each of which measures an operationally defined perceptual skill. The abilities assessed were selected by the authors on the basis of (1) clinical observation and (2) relationship to preschool and early elementary school academic performance. The subtests measuring these abilities are: Eye-hand Coordination; Figure-Ground; Constancy of Shapes; Position in Space; and Spatial Relationships. These subtests, which are assumed to be relatively independent, serve as diagnostic tools for identifying 3- to 8-year-old children who need training in specific areas of visual perception. Each one requires the subject to perform various paper-and-pencil perceptual tasks. Raw scores from the subtests are converted into scale scores, which are then summed to obtain a "perceptual quotient."

Preliminary construction of the DTVP began in 1958. A second version appeared in 1960, and the present form, referred to as the "Third Edition," was first published in 1961. Items included on the latest revision were required to demonstrate good age progression and a low degree of contamination with other abilities. The manual was revised in 1966, primarily to incorporate new normative data and to clarify directions which were previously somewhat ambiguous. Since this instrument is concerned exclusively with visual perception, the authors caution that it should be supplemented with auditory and haptic measures. When used as intended, it can provide valuable information regarding the child's methods of processing information and his level of functioning in several areas related to academic achievement. If a child scores low, it is likely that he will have difficulty in school. The converse is not always true, however, since a high scorer may suffer from developmental deficits not measured by this test.

Sample Items: DTVP items consist of line segments and angles which the subject is asked to copy, employing dots as guide points. The following is a brief description of the task involved in each subtest.

Test I   Eye/Hand Coordination requires the child to draw continuous straight, curved, or angled lines between boundaries, from point to point.

Test II   Figure/Ground involves the ability to perceptually shift geometric figures against increasingly complex grounds.

Test III   Constancy of Shapes (Perceptual Constancy) tests the subject's ability to perceive that an object possesses unchanging properties, such as a specific shape or size.

Test IV   Position in Space involves discrimination perception of reversals and rotation of common object figures and their relationship to the observer.

Test V   Spatial Relationships tests the child's ability to perceive the position of 2 or more objects in relation to himself and in relation to each other.

Reliability: The authors report a test/retest coefficient of .80 for the perceptual quotient. This was obtained on a sample of 72 first- and second-graders who were retested as a group after an interval of 2 weeks. Subtest reliabilities ranged from .42 to .80. However, when administered individually to a sample of learning disabled children, the DTVP produced a retest coefficient of .98 for total scores, over a 3-week period. Another reliability study (reported in Buros, 1972), in which trained nonpsychologists administered the test to kindergarten and first-grade pupils over an unspecified interval, yielded a coefficient of .69 for the perceptual quotient.

Split-half reliabilities have also been computed, producing total score coefficients ranging from .78 to .89. Subtest II and Subtest V show greater internal consistency than the other subtests, with coefficients in the .90s for Subtest II and in the .60s, .70s, and .80s for Subtest V. Coefficients for Subtest I are at or below .60, for Subtest III, at or below .77. Those for Subtest IV range from .35 to .70.

Validity: Several validity studies have been performed on the DTVP. The authors report that scores discriminate poor from good readers at the first-grade level, with correlations of .40 to .50 between the DTVP and reading measures. Chissom (reported in Buros, 1972) also cites significant relationships between the DTVP and indices of reading achievement and reading readiness. There is no evidence, however, that the DTVP predicts specific reading difficulties.

Culbertson and Gunn (1966), working with abnormal children in clinical settings, compared DTVP scores to Bender Gestalt scores and to IQ (WISC or Stanford Binet, LM). The DTVP correlated .41 ($p < .01$) with IQ and .52 ($p < .01$) with the Bender Gestalt. These results indicate that intellectual functioning is an important factor in visual perceptual performance, and that the 2 tests of visual perception are closely related, probably tapping many of the same variables.

Factor analyses performed on this instrument suggest that the DTVP is a single factor test at least up to grade 2 (Sprague, 1963; Trussell, 1969; Ward, 1970). These studies reveal a degree of overlap among the DTVP subtests, thus failing to support the authors' claim of subtest independence.

Norms: The standardization sample, upon which all of the score conversions are based, consists of 2,116 subjects from schools in southern California. The authors state that the subjects are "overwhelmingly middle class in nature." No black children, and few other minority group members, are included.

Administration and Scoring: This test may be administered to individuals or to small groups in 30 to 45 minutes. The manual presents clear instructions for administration and scoring, but warns that only experienced persons should administer the DTVP. In addition, the Frostig program recommends a daily gross motor program along with specific remediation exercises before the actual paper-and-pencil test is administered.

The DTVP yields three types of scores: (1) Perceptual Age (PA) for each of the 5 subtests, defined in relation to the performance of the average child in the appropriate age group; (2) Scale Score, which is the subject's PA divided by his Chronological Age and multiplied by 10; and (3) Perceptual Quotient (PQ), which is a normalized deviation score obtained by totalling the subtest Scale Scores after a correction for age variation.

Comments: Although normative data are inadequate and scale independence is questionable, this test is among the best measures of visual perception available. It has been used extensively by independent investigators, and although their findings are not summarized in the manual, they are available elsewhere for the interested prospective user of the DTVP. When employed as a part of a larger evaluation of a child's performance, this test can contribute valuable information for both diagnosis and instruction.

References: Buros, O. K., *The seventh mental measurements yearbook.* Highland Park, New Jersey: The Gryphon Press, 1972.

Culbertson, F. M., and R. C. Gunn, "Comparison of the Bender Gestalt Test and Frostig Test in several clinical groups of children." *Journal of Clinical Psychology*, 1966, **22**, 439.

Frostig, M., D. W. Lefever, and J. R. B. Whittlesey, *Marianne Frostig developmental test of visual perception, third edition.* Palo Alto, California: Consulting Psychologists Press, Inc., 1964.

Maslow, P., M. Frostig, D. W. Lefever, and J. R. B. Whittlesey, "The Marianne Frostig Developmental Test of Visual Perception, 1963 standardization." *Perceptual and Motor Skills*, 1964, **19**, 463–499.

Sprague, R., *Learning difficulties of first-grade children diagnosed by the Frostig visual perceptual tests: A factor-analytic study.* Unpublished doctoral dissertation, Wayne State University, 1963.

Trussel, E. M., "Relation of performance of selected physical skills to perceptual aspects of reading readiness in elementary school children." *Research Quarterly*, 1969, **40**(2), 383–390.

Ward, J., "The factor structure of the Frostig Developmental Test of Visual Perception." *British Journal of Educational Psychology*, 1970, **40**(1), 83–87.

Name: MATCHING FAMILIAR FIGURES TEST

Authors: Jerome Kagan, Bernice L. Rosman, Deborah Day, Joseph Albert, and William Phillips.

Type of Measure: Individual picture performance test

Availability: This instrument may be obtained from: Jerome Kagan, Harvard University, William James Hall, Cambridge, Massachusetts, 02138.

Description: The Matching Familiar Figures Test (MFFT) was designed to measure reflection/impulsivity in preschool and elementary school children. The MFFT presents the child with a picture of a familiar figure (the standard) and then asks him to choose, from a set of 4 to 6 facsimilies, the figure which is identical to it. In performing this task, the child must use various problem solving strategies and hypotheses. It is theorized that the impulsive child will respond quickly and make more errors, while the reflective child will be slow to respond and make fewer errors.

Three scores may be obtained on the MFFT: (1) mean response time; (2) the total number of errors made; and (3) the number of correct first choices.

Sample Items: The 14 MFFT items present pictures of objects which are familiar to the child, such as a telephone, a tree, a house, or a lamp. All the facsimilies, except the one which is identical to the standard, differ in one or more details. The position of the correct response figure changes with each item set.

Reliability: Yando and Kagan (1968) report that the stability of mean response time was .70 for girls and .13 for boys taking the MFFT in the fall and again in the spring. The test/retest coefficient for error scores was .23 for girls and .24 for boys. Egeland (1974), using three alternate forms of the MFFT, obtained retest correlations for response time and errors ranging from .92 to .98.

Block, Block, and Harrington (1974) report the following internal consistency reliabilities for the preschool form of the MFFT: .89 for response time and .62 for errors.

Validity: Efforts to validate the MFFT have focused primarily on convergent validity. Kagan, Pearson, and Welch (1966) report that MFFT response times were highly correlated (.51 for boys and .76 for girls) with those on the Haptic Visual Matching Test. Studies by Mann (1973), Kagan et al. (1966), and Ault (1973), have revealed a relationship between the MFFT response times and time required to make other decisions.

Yando and Kagan (1970) found that response time and number of errors for 7-year olds were stable over 10 separately constructed forms of the MFFT. In fact, most children retained their relative rank on both scoring dimensions. As would be expected from theory, Kagan et al. (1966) found strong negative correlations between response time and number of errors. Ault (1973), however, found no significant correlations between MFFT response times and MFFT errors.

Norms: The MFFT has been administered to 79 boys and 76 girls in the first grade (Kagan, et al., 1966), 62 Caucasion middle-class boys in the first and second grades (Kagan et al., 1963), 35 6-year-olds, and 28 8-year-olds (Mann, 1973), and 182 first-, third-, and fifth-grade students (Ault, 1973). McCluskey and Wright (1973) give normative data for larger, more diverse groups.

Administration and Scoring: Administration procedures vary according to the user's purpose, though the test is always given individually. Often the child is directed to find the matching figure and allowed to make as many as 3 errors before the correct response is indicated by the examiner. As previously noted, 3 scores are obtained: (1) the number of errors made; (2) the response time; and (3) number of correct first choices.

Comments: The Matching Familiar Figures Test is a research instrument which has received considerable acceptance as a measure of reflection/impulsivity. Weaknesses of the MFFT include inconsistent retest reliability data, a lack of national norms, and an absence of item-analysis data from which to determine the test's optimum length. In spite of these weaknesses, the MFFT has aroused the interest of researchers, and, therefore, a number of studies employing this test are available for potential users interested in further evaluating the MFFT.

References: Ault, R., "Problem-solving strategies of reflective, impulsive, fast-accurate, and slow-inaccurate children." *Child Development*, 1973, **44**, 259–266.

Block, J., J. H. Block, and D. M. Harrington, "Some misgivings about the Matching Familiar Figures test as a measure of reflection-impulsivity." *Developmental Psychology*, 1974, **10**, 611–632.

Egeland, B., "Training impulsive children in the use of more efficient scanning techniques." *Child Development*, 1974, **45**, 165–171.

Kagan, J., "Reflection-impulsivity: The generality and dynamics of conceptual tempo." *Journal of Abnormal Psychology*, 1966, **71**(1), 17–24.

Kagan, J., L. Pearson, and L. Welch, "Conceptual impulsivity and inductive reasoning." *Child Development*, 1966, **37**, 583–594.

Kagan, J., B. L. Rosman, D. Day, J. Albert, and W. Phillips, "Information processing in the child. Significance of analytic and reflective attitudes." *Psychological Monographs*, 1963, **78**(1, Whole No. 578).

McCluskey, K. A., and D. C. Wright, *Age and reflection-impulsivity as determinants of selective and relevant observing behavior.* Paper presented at the meeting of the Society for Research in Child Development, Philadelphia, March, 1973.

Mann, L., "Differences between reflective and impulsive children in tempo and quality of decision-making." *Child Development*, 1973, **44**, 274–279.

Yando, R. M., and J. Kagan, "The effect of teacher tempo on the child." *Child Development*, 1968, **39**, 27–34.

Name: MINNESOTA COUNSELING INVENTORY

Authors: Ralph F. Berdie and Wilbur L. Layton

Type of Measure: Self-report questionnaire

Availability: Berdie, R. F., and W. L. Layton, *Minnesota counseling inventory.* New York: The Psychological Corporation, 1953.

Description: The Minnesota Counseling Inventory (MCI) is a self-report instrument designed to measure the structure and functioning of personality in high school students. It contains 7 diagnostic scales, a validity scale, and a number-of-omissions scale. Three of the diagnostic scales—Family Relations (FR), Social Relations (SR), and Emotional Stability (ES)—were developed directly from the Minnesota Personality Scale. The remaining diagnostic scales— Conformity (C), Adjustment to Reality (R), Mood (M) and Leadership (L)—and the Validity (V) scale were derived from corresponding scales of the Minnesota Multiphasic Personality Inventory: Psychopathic Deviate; Schizophrenia; Depression; Social Introversion; and the Lie Scale. Some items from the scales of the MMPI and MPS were rewritten for clarity, and others were omitted due to objections of parents, teachers, and clergymen. Initial testing also eliminated several items, and subsequent experimentation further refined the scales, producing a final form containing 355 statements.

Though the MCI was developed for use with high school students, it has been administered to college freshmen to distinguish between dropouts and graduates of an engineering program (Watley, 1965).

Sample Items: The subject responds to MCI items by marking them true or false. Items on all scales are of the following type:

1. It is hard for me to keep my mind on a task.
2. I used to steal things when I was younger.
3. I have a lot of fun at parties.
4. I do not have very many headaches.

Reliability: Reliability studies on the MCI are reported in the manual (Berdie and Layton, 1957). For each of the diagnostic scales, split-half and test/retest reliabilities are provided.

Four sample groups of 200 cases each, separated by grade level, were used in obtaining split-half reliabilities. Coefficients were highest for the FR, SR, ES, and R scales, all being greater than .81, with several over .90. The other scales (C, M, and L) produced odd/even reliabilities between .56 and .80.

Sex-differentiated test/retest reliabilities are reported only for students in grade 12. Two studies were conducted over 1-month and 3-month intervals. The FR, SR, ES, and R scales were most stable, with 12 of 16 coefficients greater than .80. Only 1 of 12 coefficients for scales C, M, and L was over .78.

Validity: The few major studies which have been conducted to determine the validity of the MCI are reported in the manual (Berdie and Layton, 1957). The authors used a group comparison approach to establish validity. Fourteen behavioral descriptions characteristic of high or low scores on each of the 7 scales were prepared. These descriptions were given to teachers who then nominated students whose behavior corresponded closely to the descriptions. Principals, counselors, and school nurses helped to identify student leaders, delinquents, and students with serious family problems in 2 populations, 1 composed of students from Phoenix, Arizona, and 1 composed of students from 9 other states. A random sample of 200 was selected from each population for comparison with the nominated groups.

Using differences between group means and the standard error of the difference, critical ratios were computed for each comparison. Critical ratios which reached the .01 level of probability indicated statistical significance. The FR, SR, C, and L scales showed substantial validity, with virtually all comparisons reaching significance for each scale. (There were at least 16 comparisons for each scale.) The R scale was least valid, with only one of 8 comparisons reaching significance. The other scales, ES and M, showed moderate validity.

No validity studies have been conducted on combinations of scales or profiles. Profile interpretation is presently intuitive at best.

Factor analysis (Bierman, Carkhuff, and Lependorf, 1964) suggests that score differences are due to broader factors. One general factor loads substantially on the ES, R, and M scales. It also correlates with 2 other mutually independent factors which load heavily on the remaining scales. Factor I is termed Emotional Adjustment, Factor II, Extra-Familial Sociability, and Factor III, Acceptance of Adult Values and Authority.

Norms: Norms are based on samples of students from several high schools in Iowa and Minnesota. There are 4 norm groups: boys, grades 9 and 10 ($N = 1,378$); girls, grades 9 and 10 ($N = 1,562$); boys, grades 11 and 12 ($N = 1,247$); and girls, grades 11 and 12 ($N = 1,256$). Raw scores are converted to standard scores with a mean of 50 and a standard deviation of 10.

Comparisons were made between the norm group and samples drawn from 10 other states. Differences were negligible, and the authors concluded that the norms are applicable to students in other geographical areas.

Administration and Scoring: The MCI can be administered to a large group of students at one time. The manual suggests using an additional proctor for every group of 25 students in excess of 35 (which a single proctor can monitor). The test takes approximately 50 minutes, but there is no time limit. It may be scored by either machine or stencil. Omitted items are tallied before scoring. (If more than 25 items are omitted, the answer sheet is not scored.) Raw scores are plotted on a profile sheet which allows easy conversion to standard scores.

Comments: Validity studies on the MCI are needed, especially for profile and score pattern interpretation. Reliabilities for 4 of the scales (FR, SR, ES, and R) are adequate but others are somewhat low. Further refinement of the scales should increase reliability. High intercorrelations among the scales indicates that fewer might provide the same information.

The MCI may be used as a measure of general emotional adjustment and as an indicator of broad problem areas in individual students.

References: Berdie, R. F., and W. L. Layton, *Manual, Minnesota Counseling Inventory.* New York: The Psychological Corporation, 1957.

Berdie, R. F., and W. L. Layton, *Minnesota counseling inventory.* New York: The Psychological Corporation, 1953.

Bierman, R., R. Carkhuff, and S. Lependorf, "A factor analysis of the Minnesota Counseling Inventory for adolescents." *The Journal of Educational Research,* 1964, **58**, 186–187.

Watley, D. T., "The Minnesota Counseling Inventory and persistence in an institute of technology." *Journal of Counseling Psychology,* 1965, **12**, 94–97.

Name: MOOD ADJECTIVE CHECK LIST

Author: Vincent Nowlis

Type of Measure: Rating scale

Availability: Vincent Nowlis, Department of Psychology, University of Rochester, Rochester, New York. A short form of the instrument appears in: Arnold, M. (ed.), *Feelings and emotions.* New York: Academic Press, 1970; and Nowlis, V., "Research with the Mood Adjective Check List." In S. Tomkins and C. Izard (eds.), *Affect, cognition, and personality.* New York: Springer, 1965.

Description: The Mood Adjective Check List (MACL) monitors the current affective status of an individual. It is based on the tendency of persons in our culture to describe mood by using adjectives to complete the sentence "I feel _____." The MACL attempts to elicit within a short period of time the verbal responses associated with variations in mood. An evaluation of the subject's immediate feelings, rather than his typical mood, is requested in order to reduce the effect of a social desirability set.

The initial version of the MACL required the subject to respond to 140 adjectives by indicating the degree to which each adjective described his feelings. Originally, 120 of these adjectives were selected to represent 4 hypothesized dimensions (Activation vs. Deactivation; Pleasantness vs. Unpleasantness; Positive vs. Negative Social Orientation; and Control vs. Lack of Control); 4 were included to monitor the subject's attitude toward the test; 6 were added to assess recurring states which might influence responses; and 10 were repeated to estimate the test's reliability. Administering the original version to 450 college men at the beginning and end of 6 weekly, 1-hour experimental sessions, Nowlis induced different moods using various films, a frustrating hoax, and a contest for cash prizes. Results from these administrations produced 5 separate data sets containing 96 items. (Thirty-four items were eliminated because of skewed response distributions, low reliabilities, susceptibility to order effects, and patterns of correlation with other items.) Factor analyses of these items revealed 4 factors occurring in all 5 sets: Aggression, Anxiety, Surgency, and Concentration. In 4 of the sets, 4 additional factors emerged: Fatigue, Social Affection, Sadness, and Skepticism. Egotism was found in 3 sets, and Elation and Nonchalance in 2. A final factor, Vigor, emerged in 1 data set. These analyses failed to confirm the bipolarity indicated in the 4 originally hypothesized dimensions, suggesting that these 4 may in fact be viewed as 8.

Comparing the hypothesized and empirical factors, Nowlis found the following combinations to be associated: Activation with Vigor; Deactivation with Fatigue; Pleasantness with Surgency and Elation; Unpleasantness with Sadness; Positive Social Orientation with Social Affection; Negative Social Orientation with Aggression, Skepticism, and Egotism; and Lack of Control with Anxiety. The hypothesized dimensions, then, are fairly well supported by the empirical findings.

These 8 dimensions are represented on the long form of the MACL and also on an abbreviated, 24-item version.

Sample Items: The subject responds to each adjective according to a 4-point scale ("definitely," "slightly," "undecided," "definitely not"). Adjectives of the following type are used:

Right now I feel: clever
                     depressed
                     sleepy

Reliability: The 10 repeated adjectives were used to obtain both contingency and Pearson product-moment coefficients. Six tests of reliability produced 60 contingency coefficients ranging from .57 to .80, the mean of the range for a single adjective being .10. The Pearson rs for the 10 adjectives fell between .45 and .89 with a mean range of .14 for a single adjective.

Test/retest studies have been performed on the MACL, although Nowlis warns that mood changes within brief periods preclude perfect test/retest reliabilities. Reimanis (1965) tested 76 residents (mean age = 67) of a Veterans Administration home, using a 30-item form of the MACL. Coefficients obtained after intervals of 2 to 5 years fell between .50 and .66 for 7 factors, and at .38 for an eighth (Aggression). Borgatta (1961) found test/retest rs ranging from .40 (Fatigue) to .71 (Social Affection) for college men, and from .07 (Fatigue) to .78 (Social Affection) for college women. Green (1964), testing 51 college men daily for 25 to 60 days, obtained higher correlations (.50 to .75). His findings, however, indicated that either stereotyping of answers or increased accuracy occurred with practice in responding.

Validity: Various forms of the MACL have been used in a great number of research studies. Scores have been correlated with many personality, situational, physiological, and response variables, and results of these correlations have generally supported the validity of the test, particularly when subjects were instructed to evaluate immediate, rather than typical or past feelings.

Norms: Score profiles are provided for 140 Navy enlisted men who were administered a shortened, 40-word form of the MACL (Nowlis and Green, 1965). Response distributions are also available for college males and females who completed the 40-word form after a final examination. Nowlis (1965) presents difference scores along 12 factors for mood changes in 6 experimental sessions with college males.

Administration and Scoring: The MACL may be self-administered, preferably in a quiet setting. Scoring can be done by machine or by hand, using a 3 to 0 scale for the 4 alternative responses.

Comments: The Mood Adjective Check List offers an uncomplicated and economical technique for monitoring the current affective status of an individual. It is easy to administer and covers a broad range of mood states. Content and administration and scoring are flexible and can be easily adapted to accomodate a number of research purposes. The author suggests that the MACL is a valuable exploratory tool but does not recommend its use as the primary or sole index of the dependent variable in a study.

References: Borgatta, E. F., "Mood, personality, and interaction." *Journal of General Psychology*, 1961, **64**, 105–137.

Green, R. F., *The measurement of mood*. Technical Report No. 16. Office of Naval Research: Contract Nonr-668 (12), 1965.

Nowlis, V., "Research with the Mood Adjective Check List." In S. Tomkins and C. Izard (eds.), *Affect, cognition and personality*. New York: Springer, 1965.

Nowlis, V., and R. F. Green, *Factor analytic studies of the Mood Adjective Check List*. Technical Report No. 11. Office of Naval Research: Contract Nonr-667 (12), 1965.

Reimanis, G., "Mood Adjective Check List in a VA domiciliary population." *Newsletter for Research in Psychology*, 1965.

Name: MOONEY PROBLEM CHECK LIST, 1950 REVISION

Authors: Ross L. Mooney and Leonard V. Gordon

Type of Measure: Checklist

Availability: Mooney, R. L., and L. V. Gordon, *Mooney problem check list, 1950 revision.* New York: Psychological Corporation, 1950.

Description: The Mooney Problem Check List is designed to identify problems for purposes of group discussion and individual counseling. Since it requires the subject to select from a list of common problems those which apply to him, this instrument is sometimes used by professional counselors during preliminary interviews to obtain an indication of the client's salient concerns.

Forms of the Check List are available for junior high school, high school, and college students, as well as adults. A special form for rural youth, ages 16 to 30, is also available. The college and high school versions each contain 330 short items, which are classified into 11 areas: Health and Physical Development; Finances, Living Conditions, and Employment; Social and Recreational Activities; Social-Psychological Relations; Personal-Psychological Relations; Courtship, Sex, and Marriage; Home and Family; Morals and Religion; Adjustment to School Work; the Future, Vocational and Educational; and Curriculum and Teaching Procedures. Seven of these areas are represented on the junior high school Check List and 9 on the adult version. Items on all student forms of the test were drawn from case records, counseling interviews, and written statements of problems submitted by about 4,000 high school students.

This test does not measure personality traits or degree of adjustment, but instead indicates self-perceived and self-reported problems or sources of difficulty. Thus, the Check List relies on the subject's willingness to cooperate. Evidence suggests that such reliance is justified: more than 60% of a group of 1,000 college students and 70% of a sample of 1,025 high school students who had taken the test requested a chance to discuss their problems with someone. Over 90% of the subjects in these two groups reported that they enjoyed filling out the Check List. Examinees felt that the test helped them review their problems and place their difficulties in perspective (Greene, 1952).

Sample Items: The high school and college forms of the test contain items of the following type. The subject checks those which concern him or her.

Category	Item
1. Health and Physical Development	Frequent fatigue
2. Finances, Living Conditions, and Employment	Lack of privacy
3. Social and Recreational Activities	Shyness
4. Courtship, Sex, and Marriage	Rejection by opposite sex
5. Social-Psychological Relations	Lack of popularity
6. Personal-Psychological Relations	Discouragement
7. Morals and Religion	Alcohol

8. Home and Family	Arguments with parents
9. The Future, Vocational and Educational	Indecision
10. Adjustment to School Work	Failing grades
11. Curriculum and Teaching Procedures	Irrelevant subject material

On the last page of the test, the subject is asked to respond to questions similar to the following:

1. Did you like filling out this check list of problems?
2. Which of the problems you've marked disturb you the most?
3. Do you want to talk to someone about your problems?

Reliability: The test authors, maintaining that internal consistency estimates do not apply to the Check List and that retest figures are subject to error due to changes in the subject's perception of his problems, provide no reliability information. They do, however, report data indicating considerable stability of pooled results for groups (Mooney and Gordon, 1950).

Validity: Published research on the Mooney Problem Check List provides evidence of both content and concurrent validity. The former is indicated by the fact that students, on the average, check 20 to 30 problems, which suggests that the Check List provides good coverage of the concerns that students are willing to report (Remmers and Gage, 1955).

The authors present data on cucurrent validity in the manual (Mooney and Gordon, 1950). Research contrasting the responses of a remedial study skills class and a mental hygiene class revealed differences appropriate to the 2 classes. Other studies reported in the literature indicate that problem frequencies differ in the expected direction from group to group. For example, academically successful students check fewer problems under Adjustment to School Work than do students on probation (reported in Buros, 1965).

Norms: Normative data are not provided: the authors recommend the use of local norms.

Administration and Scoring: This test requires 20 to 50 minutes to complete and is essentially self-administering. Forms are available for both machine and hand scoring.

Comments: Designed specifically for counselors, but also useful to students, teachers, and researchers, the Mooney Problem Check List is a very popular and widely used instrument. The authors warn, however, that it should be interpreted cautiously and used only as recommended (primarily for individual counseling). Although evidence of validity is adequate, reliability data and norms (or at least figures on the relative frequency of various problems among different groups) are needed.

References: Bernofsky, S., *Problems of junior high school students as expressed through the Mooney Problem Check List*. Master's thesis, University of Kansas, 1963.

Buros, O. K., *The sixth mental measurements yearbook.* Highland Park, New Jersey: The Gryphon Press, 1965.

Greene, E. B., *Measurements of human behavior* (rev. ed.). New York: The Odyssey Press, 1952.

Mooney, R. L., and L. V. Gordon, *Manual for the Mooney Problem Check List, 1950 Revision.* New York: Psychological Corporation, 1950.

Remmers, H. H., and N. L. Gage, *Educational measurement and evaluation.* New York: Harper & Brothers, 1955.

Name: PICTORIAL TEST OF INTELLIGENCE

Author: Joseph L. French

Type of Measure: Cognitive ability test

Availability: French, J. L., *Pictorial test of intelligence*. Boston: Houghton Mifflin Company, 1964.

Description: The Pictorial Test of Intelligence (PTI) provides an objectively scored, easily administered individual test for the assessment of children's intelligence. The PTI is a nonverbal measure standardized for children 3 to 8 years of age. It consists of 6 subtests of a visual type: Picture Vocabulary; Form Discrimination; Information and Comprehension; Similarities; Size and Number; and Immediate Recall. These subtests are arranged in order of difficulty, and all items are administered regardless of the subject's failures or successes.

The subject responds to each PTI question by pointing to 1 of 4 pictures printed on a test card. Only a limited knowledge of English is necessary in order to understand the instructions and respond properly. The PTI can be successfully administered to verbally constricted (or excessively impaired) children since they can indicate the desired response by pointing. Children with motor impairment of the arms or hands need only look at the desired response since the examiner can perceive the object of their observation.

Since its development, the PTI has been used primarily as part of a psychological evaluation of children for placement in educational programs (French, 1964).

Sample Items: The PTI contains items of the following type to which the subject responds by pointing to 1 of 4 alternative pictures:

Which of the following do we use to tell the time?

Reliability: According to the manual (French, 1964), test/retest reliability coefficients range from .90 to .96 for a 2- to 6-week interval. However, after intervals of 45 and 53 days, Sawyer (1968) obtained coefficients of .77 for a sample of 52 kindergarten children and .88 for 38 second-graders.

Split-half reliabilities reported in the manual range from .87 to .93, while those obtained by Sawyer (1968) range from .95 to .98. Sawyer also found intercorrelations between subtests which were higher than those reported in the manual.

Validity: The validity studies presented by the author (French, 1964) are based on rather small samples (9 to 32 subjects). He reports rank-order correlations from .74 to .82 between a preliminary edition of the PTI (the North Central Individual Test of Mental Ability) and mean scores obtained 4 years later on 3 achievement tests. Rank correlations of .68 and .77 are also reported between the PTI and two group intelligence tests administered 3 to 5 years later.

Evidence of concurrent validity is provided by correlations between the PTI and the Stanford-Binet (.72), the WISC (.65) and the Columbia Mental Maturity Scale (.53).

Pasewark, Sawyer, Smith, Wasserberger, Dell, Brito, and Lee (1967) found that PYI scores and WISC IQs correlated .75 for a kindergarten sample and .71 for second-grade children. When the PTI was compared with the Lorge Thorndike Intelligence Test, correlations of .51 (at the kindergarten level) and .42 (at the second-grade level) were obtained. Patterson (1968) compared the PTI and Stanford-Binet and reported correlations of .78 for randomly selected children, .38 for superior children, and .65 for retarded children. Mueller (1968) obtained a correlation of .72 between the PTI and the Stanford-Binet. In a study comparing the PTI with the Peabody Picture Vocabulary Test and the Wide Range Achievement Test, Elliott (1969) found the PTI more effective than the other 2 measures in the class placement of institutionalized educably retarded students.

Norms: Standardization of the PTI was based on 1,830 randomly selected children from various regions, communities, and socioeconomic backgrounds.

Administration and Scoring: The PTI is administered individually by an examiner. The full test takes 45 minutes, but a shorter form for 3- and 4-year-old children is available.

The examiner's kit includes 137 response cards and 54 stimulus cards. He records the subject's choice by indicating its position on an answer sheet. The number of correct items is then summed and converted via a table to mental age units and deviation IQ's.

Comments: The PTI has been criticized for its limited age range and questionable validity at the 8-year-old level (Pasewark et al., 1967). There is also some question about the difficulty of each of the subtests; more research is needed to determine if all questions are truly arranged in order of ascending difficulty. Nevertheless, validity studies suggest that the PTI correlates about as well with the Stanford-Binet as the WISC does, and better than the PPVT does. Furthermore, subjects maintain a high interest level while taking the PTI, and administration time is fairly short. This instrument's special advantage, of course, is its suitability for children with motor or speech handicaps.

References: Buros, O. K., *The seventh mental measurements yearbook.* Highland Park, New Jersey: The Gryphon Press, 1972.

Elliott, R. N., Jr., "Comparative study of the Pictorial Test of Intelligence and the Peabody Picture Vocabulary Test." *Psychological Reports,* 1969, **25,** 528–530.

French, J. L., *Manual, Pictorial Test of Intelligence.* Boston: Houghton Mifflin, 1964.

Mueller, M. W., "Validity of six tests of ability with educable mental retardates." *Journal of School Psychology,* 1968, **6**(2), 136–145.

Pasewark, R. A., R. N. Sawyer, E. Smith, M. Wasserberger, D. Dell, H. Brito, and R. Lee, "Concurrent validity of the French Pictorial Test of Intelligence." *The Journal of Educational Research*, 1967, **61**(4), 179–183.

Patterson, H. J., *A validation and comparison of the Pictorial Test of Intelligence with the Stanford-Binet (L-M)*. Unpublished doctoral dissertation, University of Arizona, 1968.

Sawyer, R. N., "An investigation of the reliability of the French Pictorial Test of Intelligence." *The Journal of Educational Research*, 1968, **61**(5), 211–214.

Name: THE PIERS-HARRIS CHILDREN'S SELF CONCEPT SCALE

Authors: Ellen V. Piers and Dale B. Harris

Type of Measure: Self-report questionnaire

Availability: Piers, E. V., and D. B. Harris, *The Piers-Harris children's self concept scale.* Nashville, Tennessee: Counselor Recordings and Tests, 1969.

Description: The Piers-Harris Children's Self Concept Scale (P-HCSCS) is an 80-item questionnaire designed to measure children's concerns and feelings about themselves. It is most appropriate for use with children in grades 3 through 12, though it may be administered individually to bright children below grade 3.

   The original item pool consisted of 164 selections from Jersild's (1952) collection of children's statements describing what they liked and disliked about themselves. Twenty-four items were eliminated from the original pool because they were answered in the same direction by more than 90% of the subjects. A second study further reduced the instrument by eliminating repetitious items and dropping the entire Lie Scale. The 100 items remaining were then judged by 3 persons as reflecting high or low self-concept. The final 80 items selected were required to discriminate between high and low self-concept groups at the .05 level of significance and to yield responses in the expected direction from over half of the high self-concept group.

Sample Items: The P-HCSCS consists of 80 simple, declarative statements to each of which the child responds "yes" if the statement is true of him or her, and "no" if it is not. The instrument contains items of the following type:

1. I get sick a lot . . . . .yes   no
2. I have ugly hair . . . . .yes   no
3. I am fast at finishing my work . . . . .yes   no
4. I have lots of energy . . . . .yes   no

Reliability: Piers and Harris (1964) report reliability data gathered on boys and girls in the third, sixth, and tenth grades in several public schools in Pennsylvania, who were administered an early 95-item form of the test. Internal consistency was assessed by the Kuder-Richardson formula 21. Reliability coefficients ranged from .88 to .93 for boys, and from .78 to .90 for girls. To further check internal consistency, split-half reliability was computed for half of the sixth-grade and tenth-grade samples. Coefficients were .90 and .87, respectively. Test retest reliability over a 4-month interval was computed for half of each of the 3 grade levels, producing coefficients of .72 for grade 3, .71 for grade 6, and .72 for grade 10.

   Wing (1966) reports retest reliability for the current 80-item form of the P-HCSCS derived from a sample of 244 fifth graders of both sexes in the Oregon public schools. Using 2- and 4-month intervals, Wing obtained a reliability coefficient of .77.

Validity: Validity has been approached through several methods. Mayer (1965) compared scores of 98 children from 12 to 16 years of age on the P-HCSCS and the Lipsitt Children's Self-Concept Scale, and obtained a correlation of .68. Similarly, Cox (1966), using a sample of 97 children in grades 6 to 9, related P-HCSCS scores to "health" and "big" problems checked on the SRA Junior Inventory. Resulting correlations were −.48 and −.64, respectively. (A high P-HCSCS score reflects high self-concept.) Cox also compared P-HCSCS scores with teacher and peer ratings of socially effective behavior and superego strength and obtained correlations ranging from .31 to .43.

Piers (1965) used samples of fourth- and sixth-grade boys and girls to relate P-HCSCS scores to teacher and peer ratings. Correlations ranged from .06 to .49 for boys, and from .17 to .41 for girls. Peer ratings correlated better than teacher ratings (.26 to .49 as compared with .06 to .41).

Norms: Norms for the P-HCSCS are based on a sample of 1,183 students in grades 4 through 12 from a single school district in Pennsylvania. The authors of the test emphasize that these norms have very limited application. They present data from several different samples in order to indicate the variance in means and standard deviations from group to group. Users of the test are encouraged to develop and use local norms.

Administration and Scoring: The P-HCSCS can be administered in 15 to 20 minutes to groups or individuals in grades 3 through 12. It is recommended that items be read aloud for children below grade 6 to eliminate the effect of possible reading difficulties. It is also recommended that the administrator first discuss with the children the value of finding out how they feel about themselves and the importance of honest responses. Next, the children should be helped to fill out the identifying information on the test booklet. Omissions and double answers (circling both "yes" and "no") should be strongly discouraged. Children may then complete the questionnaire. The administrator may define words for younger children if necessary.

Items are scored in the direction of a positive self-concept using a key included in the manual (Piers, 1969). The total score equals the number of items marked in a positive direction.

Comments: The authors of the P-HCSCS emphasize the research rather than the clinical applications of this instrument. There are as yet no validity studies supporting the predictive power of the P-HCSCS. Therefore, clinical use with individual children should be limited to the identification of low scorers.

Reliability of the P-HCSCS is adequate, and validity studies are encouraging. There is some question about the scale's dimensionality, however. Factor analysis suggests the presence of 6 factors; yet the instrument yields only one score.

References: Cox, S. H., *Family background effects on personality development and* *social acceptance.* Unpublished doctoral dissertation, Texas Christian University, 1966.

Jersild, A. T., *In search of self.* New York: Teachers College, Columbia University, Bureau of Publications, 1952.

Mayer, C. L., *A study of the relationship of early special class placement and the self-concepts of mentally handicapped children.* Unpublished doctoral dissertation, Syracuse University, 1965.

Miller, L., *The relationship between self-concept, social desirability and anxiety in children.* Unpublished master's thesis, Pennsylvania State University, 1966.

Piers, E. V., *Children's self-ratings and ratings by others.* Unpublished paper, 1965.

Piers, E. V., *Manual for the Piers-Harris Children's Self Concept Scale.* Nashville, Tennessee: Counselor Recordings and Tests, 1969.

Piers, E. V., and D. B. Harris, "Age and other correlates of self-concept in children." *Journal of Educational Psychology,* 1964, **55**, 91–95.

Wing, S. W., *A study of children whose reported self-concept differs from classmates' evaluations of them.* Unpublished doctoral dissertation, University of Oregon, 1966.

Name: PREFERRED INSTRUCTOR CHARACTERISTICS SCALE

Authors: John D. Krumboltz and William W. Farquhar

Type of Measure: Forced-choice questionnaire

Availability: Krumboltz, J. D., and W. W. Farquhar, "The effect of three teaching methods on achievement and motivational outcomes in a how-to-study course." *Psychological Monographs*, 1957, **71**(14), 1–26.

Description: The Preferred Instructor Characteristics Scale (PICS) measures student preferences in regard to teachers. The PICS is a paired-comparison forced-choice test, which utilizes a "cognitive-affective" continuum of instructor characteristics. The subject responds to 36 items, each of which is composed of 2 statements about instructors. One of these statements describes a cognitive instructor (one who is concerned with the intellectual, abstract, subject-matter goals of teaching), while the other describes an affective instructor (one concerned with students' emotional adjustment and social interaction in the classroom). If the respondent selects more statements describing affective rather than cognitive instructors, he or she is said to have an affective orientation, which is reflected by a low PICS score.

Originally administered to 692 eighth-grade pupils in a study of teaching methods and student outcomes, the PICS was developed in an attempt to identify student preferences for various teaching styles and to gauge the effect of such preferences. This test was patterned after an earlier measure designed by Gage, Leonard, and Stone (1955).

An extension of the PICS, called the Preferred Student Characteristics Scale, has been developed by Nelson (1964) and administered to 61 junior high teachers. It measures instructor attitudes toward pupils, and when used in conjunction with the PICS, permits a direct comparison of teacher and pupil attitudes toward each other.

Sample Items: Each item reflects 2 instructor characteristics. The student selects the statement which describes the kind of instructor who appeals to him or her. Items of the following type appear on the scale:

I prefer an instructor who:
    a. is famous in his field.
    b. is friendly toward the students.

    a. is dedicated to his field.
    b. creates a pleasant classroom situation.

    a. regards students as mature people.
    b. covers all the relevant material.

Reliability: The authors report several reliability studies (Krumboltz and Farquhar, 1957). The PICS was administered to 2 different sections of a how-to-study class in the fall of 1954. A *phi* coefficient of at least .20 was obtained for 34 of the

36 items, indicating that the majority successfully discriminated between the upper and lower 27% of the distribution. Test/retest reliability, computed over a 4-week interval on a sample of 21 night school students, was .88. An investigation of internal consistency, using Hoyt's analysis of variance technique (1941) on the responses of 50 eighth-grade students, produced a reliability coefficient of .90.

Validity: The PICS was was originally used in an evaluation of a how-to-study course. Differences on the criterion instruments were related to preferences for different teaching methods, as expressed on the PICS. The Survey of Study Habits and Attitudes (SSHA), used to measure changes in students' study practices, was administered before and after the course. The PICS correlated .47 with posttest SSHA scores, but only .12 with pretest SSHA scores. Since PICS scores also correlated significantly with both pre- and posttest administrations of the Opinion, Attitude, and Interest Survey (a measure of personality factors related to academic success), the authors hypothesized that the PICS measures motivation toward academic success. However, they admitted the need for further research to substantiate this theory (Krumboltz and Farquhar, 1957).

Other studies showed that the SSHA scores of students preferring affective instructors tended to decrease, while those of students preferring cognitive instructors increased over the how-to-study course. Students who showed no preference for one type of instructor over another showed no change in SSHA scores.

Norms: No normative data are reported by Krumboltz and Farquhar (1957).

Administration and Scoring: This instrument can be easily administered in a relatively short period of time. The scoring procedures are also uncomplicated. A high score indicates a preference for a cognitive teaching approach, while a low score reflects a preference for affective style. Thus, selecting every cognitive statement produces a score of 36, every affective statement, a score of 0.

Comments: The Preferred Instructor Characteristics Scale is useful in measuring the overall balance of affective-cognitive attitudes in the classroom. According to Nelson (1964), effective group action can occur as a result of the teacher's recognition of the affective or cognitive orientation of students. If their affective needs are met, pupils will be more likely to respond cognitively. The PICS can serve as a measure of these needs, although results should be interpreted with some caution until more extensive evidence of validity is available.

References: Krumboltz, J. D., and W. W. Farquhar, "The effect of three teaching methods on achievement and motivational outcomes in a how-to-study course." *Psychological Monographs*, 1957, **71**(14), 1–26.

Hoyt, C. J., "Test reliability estimated by analysis of variance." *Psychometrika*, 1941, **6**, 153–160.

Nelson, C. C., "Affective and cognitive attitudes of junior high school teachers and pupils." *The Journal of Educational Research*, 1964, **58**(2), 81–83.

Name: PRESCHOOL INVENTORY

Author: Bettye M. Caldwell

Type of Measure: Performance test

Availability: Caldwell, B. M., *Preschool inventory* (rev. ed.). Princeton, New Jersey: Cooperative Tests and Services, Educational Testing Service, 1970.

Description: The 64-item Preschool Inventory (PSI) measures a child's achievement in areas related to success in school. The child is asked to provide information and perform simple tasks which assess his knowledge of time sequences, locational associations, and social roles, such as those of mother and father, and his or her sensory perception as indicated by objective comparisons, associations, and the construction of simple geometric figures. The instrument is appropriate for children from 3 to 6 years of age.

The PSI was developed in response to the need for an instrument to measure the prior achievement of children from culturally different or disadvantaged backgrounds entering the Head Start program. An original 161-item version was assembled by the author and chosen for use in evaluating the effectiveness of Project Head Start. Several items were subsequently removed because of ambiguity and other problems. Statistical studies resulted in further reduction of the test, producing the current 64-item revised edition.

The PSI has been used primarily in evaluating Head Start programs (Nimnicht, Rayder, and Tuck, 1970).

Sample Items: In giving the PSI, the administrator either requests information from the child or instructs him to perform a task. The revised edition contains items of the following type.

1. Administrator: "Tell me your name."
2. Administrator: "Show me your foot."
3. Administrator: "Put the blue marble in the small bowl."
4. Administrator: "What do fathers do?"
5. Administrator: "Which is brighter, the sun or the moon?"

The child is also asked to reproduce four standard drawings and to color several figures according to specifications.

Reliability: The *Handbook* for the PSI (Cooperative Tests and Services, 1970) reports 2 measures of internal consistency: Kuder-Richardson formula 20 and split-half reliabilities. These are provided for 5 age ranges: 3 years-0 months to 3 years-11 months; 4-0 to 4-5; 4-6 to 4-11; 5-0 to 5-5; and 5-6 to 6-5. Kuder-Richardson coefficients ranged from .86 to .92, with a total estimate of .91. Corrected split-half reliabilities ranged from .84 to .93, with a total sample coefficient of .92.

Walker, Bane, and Bryk (1973) report Kuder-Richardson reliabilities for total samples and subsamples used in the Fall, 1969 and Fall, 1970 Head Start Planned Variation studies. Reliability of the total 1969 sample was estimated at .925. Subsample coefficients ranged from .825 to .938. For the total 1970 sample, the coefficient was .924, and the subsample range was from .832 to .947.

Shipman (1972) reports alpha coefficients for the total sample in a longitudinal study conducted by the Educational Testing Service. For year 1, the coefficient was .92, and for year 2, .93. A retest reliability of .66 was also reported for the interval between years 1 and 2.

Validity: Evidence for validity consists primarily of correlations between the PSI and other tests. The PSI *Handbook* (Cooperative Tests and Services, 1970) reports correlations between PSI scores and Stanford-Binet IQs, which range from .39 to .65, and which tend to be greater at higher age levels.

Walker, Bane, and Bryk (1973) report correlations between PSI scores and scores obtained on the NYU Booklets 3D and 4A, the CPSCS, the Motor Inhibition Subtests, and the Eight-Block Sort, as well as Stanford-Binet IQ's and MA's. Correlations were highest with Stanford-Binet MA's (.76) and NYU Booklet 3D (.70). Since the NYU Booklet 3D is an achievement test designed to measure relational concepts similar to those measured by the PSI, the fairly high correlation between the 2 provides some evidence of concurrent validity.

Shipman (1972) reports that cognitive/perceptual tests correlate highly with PSI scores.

Norms: National norms are available for the PSI, based on a 1,531-subject sample, which includes a number of age and ethnic groups. The 5 age groups represented are: 3-0 to 3-11; 4-0 to 4-5; 4-6 to 4-11; 5-0 to 5-5; and 5-6 to 6-5. The ethnic proportions are: 68.2% black, 16.5% white, 5.9% Mexican-American, 5.1% Polynesian, and 4.2% other.

In addition to national norms, regional scores are available for particular age groups. New England norms are supplied for the age groups 4-0 to 4-5 and 4-6 to 4-11. Norms for the Southeastern United States are provided for the age group 5-0 to 5-5, and for the Plains region for the 4-0 to 4-5 age range. Far West norms are available for ages 4-0 to 4-5 and 4-6 to 4-11.

Walker, Bane, and Bryk (1973) cite other normative data from the Research Triangle Institute, the Educational Testing Service Longitudinal Study and the Head Start Planned Variation project.

Administration and Scoring: The booklet, *Preschool Inventory, Revised Edition— 1970: Directions for Administering and Scoring,* discusses in detail the procedures for administering and scoring the PSI. The test must be given individually by an administrator, who reads each item to the child. The child's response is scored either "right," "wrong," or "don't know" (when he or she specifically says "I don't know"). A correct answer increases the score by one point; an incorrect answer or no answer does not affect the score. Maximum score is 64.

Comments: The PSI is a very sound instrument, both practically and psychometrically. It has a great deal of face validity and correlates fairly well with similar measures. Reliabilities are adequate as well. Furthermore, the PSI is relatively easy to administer and score. This instrument was originally used as a pre/post measure in evaluating Head Start projects, and it remains a valuable tool for assessing the effectiveness of preschool programs. However, it also provides useful data on individual children.

References: Cooperative Tests and Services, *Preschool Inventory, revised edition—1970: Directions for administering and scoring.* Princeton, New Jersey: Educational Testing Service, 1970.

Cooperative Tests and Services, *Preschool Inventory, revised edition—1970: Handbook.* Princeton, New Jersey: Educational Testing Service, 1970.

Nimnicht, G., N. Rayder, and B. Tuck, *Preliminary analysis of 1968–69 Head Start data.* Berkeley, California: Far West Laboratory for Educational Research and Development, 1970. (ERIC Document Reproduction Service No. ED 045 203).

Shipman, N. C. (ed.), *Disadvantaged children and their first school experience: Technical report series.* Prepared for the Office of Child Development, Department of Health, Education, and Welfare, under grant No. H-8526. Princeton, New Jersey: Educational Testing Service, 1972.

Walker, D. K., M. J. Bane, and A. Bryk, *The quality of the Head Start Planned Variation data* (Vol. II). Prepared for the Office of Child Development, Department of Health, Education, and Welfare, under grant No. H-1926. Cambridge, Massachusetts: Huron Institute, 1973.

Name: PRESCHOOL PREPOSITION TEST

Authors: May Aaronson and Earl S. Schaefer

Type of Measure: Performance test

Availability: Aaronson, M., and Schaefer, E. S. *Preschool Preposition Test: Manual of instructions.* Unpublished, 1968. This instrument is available for research use from the authors, at the Center for Studies of Child and Family Mental Health, National Institute of Mental Health, 5454 Wisconsin Ave., Chevy Chase, Maryland.

Description: The Preschool Preposition Test (PPT) measures a child's knowledge of prepositions, which, according to preliminary evidence, is related to verbal comprehension in the early years. Developed as part of the Infant Education Research Project, the PPT is intended for use with 3- and 4-year-old children (or, in disadvantaged populations, 5-year-old children).

Test materials include a yellow board, and two 3-dimensional figures—a green automobile and red boy. Most test items require the child to place a ball in the position indicated by the examiner's command, the key word of which is a preposition. The examiner issues a total of 33 commands, in a random order of difficulty.

Although still in research status, the PPT has been administered to rural, suburban, and urban, black and Caucasian, lower- and middle-class subjects in a variety of settings. It has proved effective, particularly in nonverbal or nearly nonverbal populations, in measuring children's understanding of both prepositions and instructions. According to its authors, the PPT can be used to identify children who need an intensive language development program or a meaningful, one-to-one relationship with a warm adult.

Sample Items: The PPT is divided into two parts, the first of which contains items designed to determine the subject's understanding of the vocabulary used in the test. The examiner issues instructions of the following type.

Point to the car.

Point to the board that the car and boy are on.

Part II contains 23 items similar to these:

Place the ball between the car's wheels (pause),
    between the car's wheels.
Place the ball down as low on the board as you can (pause),
    down as low on the board as you can.

Reliability: No reliability data are available.

Validity: As part of the Infant Education Research Project, the PPT was administered, along with the Stanford-Binet, the Johns Hopkins Perceptual Test, and the Peabody Picture Vocabulary Test, to 60 black, inner-city 3-year-olds. PPT scores correlated as highly with the other test scores as the latter did with each other—about .57. Although the other tests differentiated between the experimental and control groups, The PPT did not. However, the PPT did identify those children who were typically hostile and negative (according to ratings on the Infant Behavior Inventory), and who had mothers who were ignoring, uninvolved and relatively nonverbal (as determined by ratings on the Mother's Behavior with Tutor and Child Inventory).

The PPT was also administered to 114 Head Start children in Maryland. Scores correlated positively and significantly ($p < .01$) with teachers' ratings of children's ability and school adjustment. Forty Head Start children were also administered the Peabody Picture Vocabulary Test, raw scores and IQ scores from which correlated at .70 and .66, respectively, with raw PPT scores.

The PPT manual cites preliminary data on children aged 2 to 8 years, indicating a regular progression of scores with age up to $5\frac{1}{2}$ or 6 years, at which time most subjects reach the test ceiling (Aaronson and Schaefer, 1960).

Norms: The manual presents mean scores by age for normal and disturbed children from various socioeconomic levels and ethnic backgrounds. Scores are also available for 114 Head Start children in six public schools in one Maryland county. This population included white, Spanish-speaking and black children from suburban and rural communities.

Administration and Scoring: Almost anyone can be trained in a relatively short time to administer the PPT. Testing time usually ranges from 7 to 15 minutes, depending on the setting, though emotionally disturbed children generally require 15 to 20 minutes. The examiner may score the child's responses immediately on an Individual Test Record, or may record the answers on Picture Score Sheets and score them later. When Part I is completed, the examiner reviews with the subject the words and objects used in failed items in order to familiarize the child with test materials and vocabulary. Part II is then administered and scored according to detailed instructions provided in the manual. The entire test should be used since items are randomly ordered.

Comments: The Preschool Preposition Test has several obvious advantages. It is short, easy and inexpensive to administer, and very appealing to children. Also, preliminary results indicate that this instrument is relatively culture free. Although the PPT is still in an experimental stage, it can be used to identify learning difficulties in preschool or primary-grade children.

References: Aaronson, M., and E. S. Schaefer, *Preschool Preposition Test: Manual of instructions*. Unpublished, 1968.

It works: Infant Education Research Project. Washington, D.C.: Office of Education, U.S. Department of Health, Education, and Welfare, 1969.

Schaefer, E., and M. Aaronson, "Infant Education Research Project: Implementation and implications of a home tutoring program." In R. K. Parker (ed.), *The preschool in action. Exploring early childhood programs* (rev. ed.). Boston: Allyn & Bacon, 1973.

Name: PSYCHOSOCIAL MATURITY SCALE

Authors: Ellen Greenberger, Paul Campbell, Aage B. Sørensen, and Jeanne O'Connor

Type of Measure: Self-report questionnaire

Availability: Greenberger, E., P. Campbell, A. B. Sørensen, and J. O'Connor, *Toward the measurement of psychosocial maturity.* Report No. 110. Baltimore, Maryland: Center for Social Organization of Schools, the Johns Hopkins University, 1971.

Description: The Psychosocial Maturity Scale (PMS) is based on the belief that schools should seek to develop in students aspects of maturity other than academic competence. Because the school provides a common experience for children from diverse backgrounds, it is viewed by the authors of this measure as a powerful socializing agent, capable of encouraging psychosocial maturity among students. The PMS was constructed to help schools fulfill this potential. Based on a concept of psychosocial maturity involving man's capacity to function effectively, individually and socially, and to invest in the survival of society (Greenberger, Campbell, Sørensen, and O'Connor, 1971), the PMS allows schools to measure attitudes among students as a first step toward developing procedures to engender maturity.

PMS items were originally drawn from attitude data collected from 6,000 Pennsylvania school children in grades 5 and 11. From 199 items, 101 were chosen for their theoretical relevance to psychosocial maturity. These items were then required to meet an empirical criterion: differentiation of 7.5% or better between fifth- and eleventh-grade students. Fifty-four items which satisfied both the theoretical and the empirical criteria were included on the final form of the PMS. These items were intuitively arranged into subscales, which were then validated through factor analysis. The 5 factor scales comprising the PMS are: Self-Esteem; Openness to Change; Independence; Identity; and Social Tolerance. Because these subscales do not measure independent traits, an overall maturity score is computed.

Sample Items: The PMS includes items of the following type. Response format varies from subscale to subscale.

Scale	Item
Self-Esteem	If I keep trying at a thing long enough, I'll succeed.
Openness to Change	Students will eventually use computers to solve arithmetic and other problems.
Independence	I don't need to worry about selecting a career until I'm finished with school.
Identity	I don't know what school subjects I should take.
Social Tolerance	How would you feel about having a close friend whose parents were poorer than yours?

Reliability: Factor analytic and reliability studies involved 850 5th-graders and 850 11th-graders. Eigenvalues computed in the factor analytic studies indicated adequate scale homogeneity. Analyses for 5th-graders yielded 19 eigenvalues greater than one and for 11th-graders 10 eigenvalues of this magnitude.

Internal consistency of the 54-item scale and of the individual subscales was also determined by means of the Kuder-Richardson formula 20. The manual (Greenberger et al., 1971) reports subscale coefficients ranging from .69 to .94 for the 11th-grade sample and from .41 to .77 for the 5th-grade sample. Total scale reliabilities were .96 for the older group and .81 for the younger.

Validity: The authors established validity by relating PMS scores to variables expected to be associated with psychosocial maturity. For example, PMS total and subscale scores were correlated with responses to items theoretically but not empirically relevant to maturity. At grade 11, nearly all of these items showed sizeable correlations with total scores, but lower correlations with subscale scores. At grade 5, the lower degree of scale homogeneity produced somewhat smaller correlations, but the validity of the Independence and Self-Esteem subscales was nevertheless supported.

Further evidence of validity is provided by comparisons between psychosocial maturity scores and sex, race, socioeconomic status, and academic achievement. As predicted, females, whites, and high SES children obtained higher PMS scores, respectively, than males, blacks, and low SES children. Psychosocial maturity accounted for about 16% of the variance in academic achievement at grade 5, but only 6% at grade 11, indicating that academic achievement is increasingly independent of the culturally desirable attitudes and values represented in the PMS (Greenberger et al., 1971).

The validity of the scale is also supported by its ability to discriminate younger from older children. The mean difference in total maturity scores between 5th- and 11th-grade levels was highly significant. The Social Tolerance and Independence subscales also significantly differentiated these groups.

The effect of social desirability response sets on PMS scores was investigated (Greenberger, 1972), using a sample of 4,739 white and 2,470 black 5th- and 11th-graders. PMS scores were related to 2 social desirability scales, yielding very modest correlations. Mean scores on the social desirability scales decreased with age, while those on the PMS increased with age. This finding indicates that the PMS measures a set of attitudes which are distinct from the disposition to "fake good."

Norms: The PMS was standardized on a random sample of 3,000 fifth-grade and 3,000 eleventh-grade students, as well as 1,500 black subjects at each of these grade levels. Group means and standard deviations are presented for 850 fifth-graders and 850 eleventh-graders for total and subscale scores. These figures are broken down by sex, race, and socioeconomic level (Greenberger et al., 1971).

Administration and Scoring: The PMS is easily administered and scored. Each subscale is preceded by specific, clearly written directions, including an explanation of the response format to be used. Subscales are individually scored and then summed to yield a total score.

Comments: Though the Psychosocial Maturity Scale is still in a developmental stage, it provides a good basis for further research on either student characteristics or the psychological and sociological aspects of the classroom environment. Subscale reliability coefficients indicate that analyses using total maturity scores are appropriate at higher and lower grade levels, but analysis using subscale scores should be confined to older age groups. While test/retest data are needed, this instrument can nonetheless serve as a valuable research tool for educators.

References: Greenberger, E., P. Campbell, A. B. Sørensen, and J. O'Connor, *Toward the measurement of psychosocial maturity.* Report No. 110. Baltimore, Maryland: Center for Social Organization of Schools, The Johns Hopkins University, 1971.

Greenberger, E., and M. M. Marini, *Black-white differences in psychosocial maturity: A further analysis.* Report No. 136. Baltimore, Maryland: Center for Social Organization of Schools, The Johns Hopkins University, 1972.

Starr, B. J. *Psychosocial maturity: A preliminary examination of validation techniques.* Report No. 157. Baltimore, Maryland: Center for Social Organization of Schools, The Johns Hopkins University, 1973.

Name: RAVEN PROGRESSIVE MATRICES (PM)

Author: J. C. Raven

Type of Measure: Perceptual cognitive ability test

Availability: Raven, J. C. *Progressive matrices.* New York: The Psychological Corporation, 1938–1965.

Description: The Progressive Matrices were designed in Great Britain to provide a nonverbal measure of intellectual functioning based on perceptual reasoning. Three forms of the instrument—the Standard Progressive, the Coloured Progressive, and the Advanced Progressive—are available. The Standard Progressive Matrices are the original version, constructed in 1938 for ages 6 and above. This form was revised in 1956 and in 1960. The Coloured Progressive Matrices are identical to the Standard Matrices, except that they are colored, a change which makes them suitable for the 5 to 11 age range only. The Advanced Progressive Matrices, first designed as a practice test for the Coloured Progressive Matrices or as a screening test, are referred to as "a test of intellectual capacity" when used without a time limit, or as "a test of intellectual efficiency" when used with a time limit.

Items on all forms of the test consist of incomplete designs which require the subject to perform some sort of logical reasoning. The subject may be asked to: (1) complete a pattern; (2) complete an analogy; (3) systematically alter a pattern; (4) introduce systematic permutations; or (5) systematically resolve figures into parts. Easier problems appear at the beginning of the test to provide the subject with training needed to solve the more difficult problems which come later.

The Matrices, regarded by most British psychologists as the best available measure of Spearman's *g*, have been widely used in Great Britain to compare the intellectual functioning of members of various psychiatric, socioeconomic, and ethnic groups. The author suggests that the Standard Progressive Matrices be used in conjunction with the Mill Hill Vocabulary Scale and that the Coloured Matrices be used along with the Crichton Vocabulary Scale in order to provide a measure of acquired information as a supplement to the Matrices' measure of "capacity" (reported in Buros, 1965).

Sample Items: This test presents 60 matrices, or designs, from each of which a part is missing. The subject chooses from among 6 to 8 multiple-choice options the missing part which best completes the design. Items are grouped in 5 series, A through E, each containing 12 matrices of increasing difficulty. The earlier series require ability to discriminate while the later, more difficult sets involve relationships, analogies, and pattern alterations.

For children from 3 to 8 years of age and for the mentally retarded there is a form of the test in which Series A and B are composed of colored patterns on cardboard. The subject inserts the missing piece in the board.

Reliability: The various editions of the Progressive Matrices manual supply little reliability information. The only mention of reliability is in relation to the Advanced Progressive Matrices for which coefficients of .76 to .91 are reported. Independent studies have reported test/retest reliability coefficients, obtained on normal adults in their late teens or early 20s, ranging from .79 to .93 (reported in Burke, 1958). Reliability estimates obtained in studies of children range from .71 (Keir, 1949) to .88 (Sinha, 1951). For all age groups, the lower score ranges are considerably less reliable. For a thorough evaluation of the reliability of the Progressive Matrices, see Burke (1958).

Validity: A great number of validity studies have been conducted on the Progressive Matrices. Those occurring prior to 1958 are summarized by Burke (1958). Content validity has been demonstrated by correlational data, comparing the Progressive Matrices with other tests of mental ability. Raven (1948) reported a correlation of .86 with the Terman-Merrill. High correlations (.74 and .75) were obtained between the Matrices and verbal and performance scores on the Wechsler tests. Other correlational studies indicate that the Matrices are more closely related to performance than verbal tests of mental ability.

Research studies have produced conflicting evidence regarding the predictive validity of this instrument. Nevertheless, correlations between the Matrices and indices of achievement vary in expected ways with (1) the nature of the achievement measure, (2) the sex of the subject, (3) the reliability of Matrices at different score levels, and (4) the age at which achievement is measured. Studies using the 1938 form have shown that mean scores discriminate children according to educational level and parental occupation. Cross-validation studies, however, indicate that the test's validity is lower with children than adults. Burke (1958), summarizing extensive evidence of the concurrent validity of Matrices, concludes that the test does discriminate among groups known by other criteria to differ in intellectual capacity.

Norms: Percentile norms are based on British samples of 1,407 children, 3,665 men in military service tested during World War II, and 2,192 civilian adults. Data are provided for each 6-month age interval between 8 and 14 years, and for each 5-year interval between 20 and 65 years. Estimated percentile norms are also available for the 1947 form of the Advanced Progressive Matrices.

Administration and Scoring: The Progressive Matrices are fairly easy to administer, with little verbal instruction. The subject acquires skill in responding by working on the first, relatively easy problems. Therefore, repeated verbal instructions are not necessary. The Matrices should be administered individually to children aged 5 and 6. Older subjects, however, can be given the test in groups. The number of correctly solved items constitutes the total score, which is converted into a percentile rank.

Comments: All 3 forms of the Progressive Matrices are particularly useful in measuring the intellectual capacity of nonverbal, mentally ill, deaf, or cerebral palsied subjects. The test has also proven valuable in studies of the growth and deterioration of mental efficiency. The Matrices have been widely criticized, however, on the grounds that the relevance of perceptual items to intelligence has not been documented. Bortner (in Buros, 1965) suggests that the aspects of perceptual adequacy measured by this test might better serve perceptual research studies than psychometric testing. Studies conducted in non-European cultures question the suitability of this test for subjects from very dissimilar backgrounds. These studies indicate that the Matrices are influenced by the educational level of the subject and are susceptible to the practice effect.

Reliability and validity studies of the Matrices are flawed and should be improved before this instrument is used in making important diagnostic decisions. Nevertheless, this measure, which has withstood the test of time, is an extremely useful supplement to other indices of mental ability.

References: Burke, H. R., "Raven's Progressive Matrices: A review and critical evaluation." *The Journal of Genetic Psychology*, 1958, **93**, 199–228.

Buros, O. K., *The sixth mental measurements yearbook.* Highland Park, New Jersey: The Gryphon Press, 1965.

Keir, G., "The Progressive Matrices as applied to school children." *British Journal of Psychology, Statistical Section*, 1949, **2**, 140–150.

Raven, J. C., "The comparative assessment of intellectual ability." *British Journal of Psychology*, 1948, **39**, 12–19.

Name: THE REVISED MINNESOTA PAPER FORM BOARD

Authors: Rensis Likert and William H. Quasha

Type of Measure: Perceptual test

Availability: Likert, R., and W. H. Quasha, *Revised Minnesota paper form board test.* New York: The Psychological Corporation, 1941.

Description: The Revised Minnesota Paper Form Board (PFB) measures spatial aptitude. Originally developed by Paterson, Elliott, Anderson, Toops, and Heidbreder (1930) and revised by Likert and Quasha (1941), this paper-and-pencil test is available in 2 equivalent forms, Series AA and Series BB, both containing 64 problems. Each of these problems presents the subject with a 2-dimensional figure, cut into parts. The subject's task is to choose from a number of whole figures the one which is composed of the exact parts shown in the stimulus diagram.

PFB scores have been used to predict achievement in artistic and mechanical fields and in shopwork, especially design and drafting. Though the test employs nonverbal and non-numerical items to assess ability to perceive spatial relations, scores are not entirely independent of general intelligence.

Sample Items: PFB items present broken geometric figures similar to that pictured below. The subject selects, from 5 alternatives, the diagram which is made up of the exact pieces shown in the item.

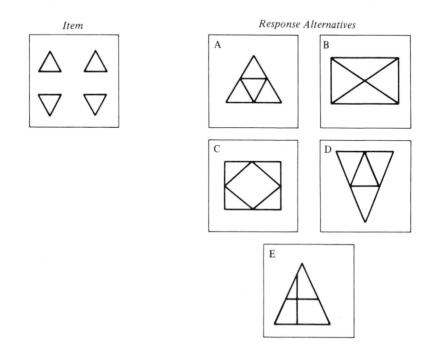

Item   *Response Alternatives*

Reliability: The authors (Likert and Quasha, 1948) report test/retest figures based on the scores of 290 high school seniors applying for admission to New York University. When alternate forms were administered, a coefficient of .92 was obtained (over an unspecified interval). When the same form was administered twice, reliability was found to be .85. Stephens (1942), testing New England students with a machine-scoreable edition of the PFB (Series MA and MB), obtained a retest coefficient of .85.

Validity: An unusually large number of validity studies have been conducted on the revised PFB, which correlates with the original form at .94 or better. The studies reported in the manual fall into 3 categories: (1) correlations between the PFB and educational achievement in high school and college; (2) use of the test in actual employment situations; and (3) miscellaneous applications of the PFB, especially in the field of art.

Studies of the following type are summarized in the first category. Moore (1941) reports that mechanical draftsmen and enrollees in engineering drafting courses obtained higher scores on PFB than did average adult men. Harrell (reported in Likert and Quasha, 1948), correlating course grades in a Basic Instruction Course for Aviation Mechanics with a number of measures, found that the PFB produced some of the highest correlations with Mechanical Drafting and Blueprint Reading, and Elements of Metalwork. At the University of Minnesota, correlations of .27, .33, and .60 were obtained between revised PFB scores and first-year grades in engineering, ability in engineering drawing, and quality of shopwork, respectively. Hunter (1945) reported a high relationship between the PFB and "pupil efficiency" (based on students' worksamples which were graded on accuracy, quality of finish, and speed) among 75 high school juniors and seniors.

Other studies reported in the manual summarize use of the PFB in actual employment situations. Anderson (1947), in a study of 174 machinists, notes that the PFB was included in several of the test batteries found to be most satisfactory in predicting job success, as measured by supervisors' ratings. Similarly, a multiple correlation of .57 was obtained between a composite score on a battery of tests, including the PFB, and the quality of work produced by power sewing machine operators. Reports are conflicting, however, in regard to the value of this test in predicting supervisory success.

The manual also reports relationships between PFB scores and success in various academic fields, particularly art. Typical of these relationships is that found by Barrett (1945), who reported that extreme scores on the PFB significantly differentiated art majors from control subjects. The scores were sufficiently diagnostic to warrant including the PFB in a final battery of tests intended to measure artistic ability.

Norms: Normative data are available for a considerable number and variety of educational and industrial groups. The manual presents norm tables for large, well defined samples tested according to prescribed timing and scoring formulae. In each table, norms for men and women are presented separately. The authors warn, however, that sex differences cannot be inferred for industrial groups since the men and women tested were not in the same kind of work. They also suggest that individuals planning to use the PFB on a large scale develop local norms relevant to their own subject populations.

Administration and Scoring: The PFB is easy to administer, even to large groups. Testing time is exactly 20 minutes. Forms AA and BB are hand scored, while Forms MA and MB employ IBM answer sheets and can be machine scored. The subject's score is the total number of correct responses.

Comments: The Revised Minnesota Paper Form Board has proven to be a very useful instrument in measuring the ability to visualize and manipulate objects in space. In addition, extensive research studies have consistently shown that this test is one of the most valid measures of mechanical ability. The revised edition is very similar to the original form in content, though administration and scoring procedures have been clarified. Test content, being perceptual, is not at all dated. The provision of interchangeable alternate forms facilitates retesting and minimizes the possibility of cheating in group administrations.

References: Anderson, R.G., "Test scores and efficiency ratings of machinists." *Journal of Applied Psychology*, 1947, **31**, 377–388.

Barrett, D. M., "Aptitude and interest patterns of art majors in a liberal arts college." *Journal of Applied Psychology*, 1945, **29**, 483–492.

Hunter, R. S., "Aptitude tests for the machine shop." *Industrial Arts and Vocational Education*, 1945, 58–64.

Likert, R. and W. H. Quasha, *Revised Minnesota paper form board test.* New York: The Psychological Corporation, 1941.

Likert, R., and W. H. Quasha, *Manual. The Revised Minnesota Paper Form Board Test.* New York: The Psychological Corporation, 1948.

Moore, B. V., "Analysis of results of tests administered to men in engineering defense training courses." *Journal of Applied Psychology*, 1941, **25**, 619–635.

Paterson, D. G., R. M. Elliott, L. D. Anderson, H. A. Toops, and E. Heidbreder, *Minnesota Mechanical Ability Tests.* Minneapolis, Minnesota: University of Minnesota Press, 1930.

Stephens, E. W., "A comparison of New England norms with national norms on the Revised Minnesota Paper Form Board Test—Series AA." *Occupations*, 1945, **24**, 101–104.

Name: SCIENCE RESEARCH ASSOCIATES YOUTH INVENTORY

Authors: H. H. Remmers, Benjamin Shimberg, and Arthur J. Drucker

Type of Measure: Checklist

Availability: Remmers, H. H., and B. Shimberg, *Manual: SRA Youth Inventory, Form S.* Chicago: Science Research Associates, 1960. Also: Remmers, H. H., B. Shimberg, and A. J. Drucker, *Manual: SRA Youth Inventory, Form A.* Chicago: Science Research Associates, 1953.

Description: The Science Research Associates (SRA) Youth Inventory consists of 296 statements representing problems with which students presumably can identify. The statements are classified into 8 problem areas: My School; After High School; About Myself; Getting Along with Others; My Home and Family; Boy Meets Girl; Health; and Things in General. Items in each area were derived from essays written by hundreds of teenagers describing problems that bothered them most. The final 296 statements were selected after review and editing by educators and psychologists.

Certain items in the 8 problem areas also form a Basic Difficulty Scale. This scale was derived by judges, who selected 101 of the inventory's 296 items which they felt were more likely to indicate a basic personality disturbance. Thus the instrument provides 8 scale scores and a Basic Difficulty Score.

The SRA Youth Inventory was designed to assist school personnel in identifying problems about which students worry. Form A, constructed in 1949, is appropriate for students in grades 7 through 12, while Form S, an extensive revision of Form A developed in 1955, is suitable for students in grades 9 through 12.

Sample Items: One of the major differences between Forms A and S involves response alternatives. On Form A, the student simply checks those problems which apply to him and leaves blank those which do not. On Form S, however, the student can indicate the intensity of any problem that applies to him by responding on a 4-point scale. The inventory contains items of the following type.

Scale	*Item*
My School	1. I often daydream in class.
After High School	2. I don't know what to do after high school.
Health	3. I get sick a lot.

Reliability: Split-half reliability of the eight area scores was estimated by the Kuder-Richardson method. Coefficients ranged from .75 to .94, with a median of .88. Only the Health scale produced a coefficient below .84. Jacobs (1951) computed test/retest reliabilities for Form A on a sample of 48 students over an interval of 1 month. He obtained coefficients ranging from .72 (Health) to .88 (My Home and Family), with a median of .82.

Validity: The authors maintain that the inventory has a high degree of face validity since items were initially derived from problems reported by students. Some construct validity may be inferred from correlations between scale and total scores, which yielded median coefficients ranging from .39 to .51. In addition, biserial correlations were determined between each item and the appropriate scale score, producing median coefficients from .50 to .70. Some evidence of concurrent validity is provided by a study reported in the manual, in which 22 of 35 students independently rated as "well adjusted" scored above the median on the Basic Difficulty Scale, while 36 of 57 "poorly adjusted" students scored below the median.

Norms: Remmers and Gage (1955) report that the preliminary form of the SRA Youth Inventory was administered to about 15,000 high school students and about 4,000 students in the seventh and eighth grades. Smith and Hudgins (1958) administered the inventory to 29 girls, whose ages ranged from 12 to 18. The norms in the manual, based on a large, diverse sample, include total score and scale score percentiles for boys and girls and for 16 subgroups (differentiated by sex, religion, socioeconomic status, etc.).

Administration and Scoring: The SRA Youth Inventory can be easily administered in about 45 minutes, using test booklets and IBM answer sheets. It may be scored either by hand or machine. The manual suggests using only high points on the profile in helping students to solve their problems since the scale scores themselves do not indicate maladjustment.

Comments: The SRA Youth Inventory is well organized, carefully constructed, and adequately normed. However, reliability data, though encouraging, are meager, and the usefulness of the Basic Difficulty Scale is questionable. The scarcity of validity data is not a serious shortcoming if the inventory is used only to provide an indication of what a student perceives his problems to be.

References: Jacobs, R., A report on experimental use of the SRA Youth Inventory in the fall testing program of the Educational Records Bureau. *Educational Records Bulletin* (No. 56). New York: Educational Records Bureau, 1951.

Remmers, H. H., and N. L. Gage, *Educational measurement and evaluation.* New York: Harper & Brothers, 1955.

Remmers, H. H., and B. Shimberg, *Manual: SRA Youth Inventory, Form S.* Chicago: Science Research Associates, 1960.

Remmers, H. H., B. Shimberg, and A. J. Drucker, *Manual: SRA Youth Inventory, Form A.* Chicago: Science Research Associates, 1953.

Smith, L. M., and B. B. Hudgins, "The SRA Youth Inventory and mental health." *Personnel and Guidance Journal,* 1958, **37**, 303–304.

Name: SEARS SELF-CONCEPT INVENTORY

Author: Pauline S. Sears

Type of Measure: Rating scale

Availability: This instrument is available to qualified researchers and students from Pauline Sears, 1101 Golden Oak Drive, Portola Valley, California 94026.

Description: The Sears Self-Concept Inventory is a measure of self-esteem designed for bright third- through sixth-grade children. The original scale consisted of 100 items representing the following dimensions: Physical Ability; Attractive Appearance; Convergent Mental Ability; Social Relations with the Same Sex; Social Virtues; Divergent Mental Ability; Work Habits; Happy Qualities; and School Subjects. A revised form, developed in 1966, measures these factors using only 48 items.

It is suggested that parental consent be obtained prior to administering the scale since the items are of a very personal nature.

Sample Items: In response to each of the 48 items, the student rates himself or herself on a 5-point scale according to his or her standing, relative to other boys and girls, on the trait described. Items of the following type are included on the scale.

	Excellent	Very good	Better than most	OK	Not so good
Having self-confidence	⎯⎯	⎯⎯	⎯⎯	⎯⎯	⎯⎯
Having a good body size	⎯⎯	⎯⎯	⎯⎯	⎯⎯	⎯⎯
Being able to use what I've learned	⎯⎯	⎯⎯	⎯⎯	⎯⎯	⎯⎯
Having lots of friends	⎯⎯	⎯⎯	⎯⎯	⎯⎯	⎯⎯
Keeping up with my school work	⎯⎯	⎯⎯	⎯⎯	⎯⎯	⎯⎯

Reliability: The author computed the internal consistency of the 48-item Self-Concept Inventory on a sample of 32 third-graders. Kuder-Richardson reliability coefficients ranged from .56 (Happy Qualities) to .89 (Convergent Mental Ability). Internal consistency of the total scale was estimated at .90 (Sears, undated).

Spaulding (1963, 1964) and Sherman (1964), using an adaptation of the original form which included several new items relating to creativity, obtained reliabilities of .85 for Height of Self-Concept and .82 for Differentiation.

Validity: Gelfand (1962) related scores on the Sears Self-Concept Inventory to social suggestibility and obtained a negative correlation. The "height" of self-concept, as measured by this scale, was also found to vary according to sex and mental ability.

Norms: Normative data on the populations used in Sears' reliability studies are available from the author.

Administration and Scoring: The instrument may be administered to groups of children in approximately 40 minutes. Instructions are printed on the test form in language which third-graders can understand. The child is asked to rank himself on each item, compared to other children his age. It is emphasized that the responses will be confidential.

A score sheet is used to sum and average the values of selected responses within each of the 9 areas represented on the scale. A total self-concept is also computed.

Comments: The Sears Self-Concept Inventory is still in an experimental stage and, therefore, should be used only for research purposes. The reliability of the scale appears to be adequate, but more extensive validity and normative data are needed. Still, the instrument has potential value in counseling situations.

References: Gelfand, D. M., " The influence of self-esteem on rate of verbal conditioning and social matching behavior." *Journal of Abnormal and Social Psychology*, 1962, **64**, 259–265.

Johnson, O. G., and J. W. Bommarito, *Tests and measurements in child development*. San Francisco: Jossey-Bass, 1971.

Sears, P. S., *The effect of classroom conditions on the strength of achievement motive and work output of elementary school children*. Final Report to the U.S. Office of Education, Project No. 873. Palo Alto, California: Stanford University, 1963.

Sears, P. S., *Memorandum with respect to use of the Sears Self-Concept Inventory*. Unpublished mimeograph, undated.

Sherman, V., *Personality correlates of differential performance on intelligence and creativity tests*. Unpublished doctoral dissertation, Stanford University, 1964.

Spaulding, R., *Achievement, creativity and self-concept correlates of teacher-pupil transactions in elementary schools*. Urbana, Illinois: University of Illinois, 1963.

Spaulding, R., "Achievement, creativity and self-concept correlates of teacher-pupil transactions in elementary schools," in C. B. Stendler (ed.), *Readings in child behavior and development* (2nd ed). New York: Harcourt Brace, 1964.

Spaulding, R., "Affective dimensions of creative processes." *Gifted Child Quarterly*, 1963, **7**(4).

Name: SELF-CONCEPT SCALE

Authors: Mohindra P. Gill and Vincent R. D'Oyley

Type of Measure: Rating scale

Availability: Mohindra P. Gill and Vincent R. D'Oyley, c/o Request Instrument and Subscale Key, The Ontario Institute for Studies in Education, Ontario, Canada.

Description: The Self-Concept Scale was designed to measure self-concepts of high school students in an academic setting. Construction of the instrument was based on Rogers' (1951) self-concept theory, which stresses the multiplicity of self-preceptions and self-evaluations that are incorporated into one's self-concept. The scale measures 2 dimensions—the Real Self and the Ideal Self—represented by items selected through a review of pertinent literature. A factor-analysis identified 8 subscales constituting the Real Self dimension: Achievement-Related Characteristics; Acceptance by Peers and Teachers; Self-Confidence; Self-Perceived Originality; Feeling of Adequacy; Reaction to School Programs; Concentrating Ability; and Self-Satisfaction. Similarly, 6 factors emerged under the Ideal Self dimension: Self-Confidence and Achievement-Related Characteristics; Originality (Desired); General Characteristics; Acceptance by Peers and Teachers: Self-Satisfaction; and Reaction to School Program. The entire scale consists of 2 sets of 65 items.

Sample Items: The examinee rates himself on each statement according to a 4-point response scale ("this statement *never* describes me" to "this statement *always* describes me" on Part I; and "I would *never* wish to be like the student described" to "I would *always* like to be like the student described" on Part II). The instrument contains items of the following type.

	Never	Sometimes	Usually	Always

Part I (Real Self)

I make new friends easily.
I have difficulty making decisions.

Part II (Ideal Self)

A student who feels like people
  make fun of him.
A student who is willing to work hard.

Reliability: Two separate studies of reliability have been reported. The authors investigated test/retest reliability by administering the scale twice to 67 ninth-grade students over an 8-week interval. The Real Self coefficient for boys was .69 and for girls, .60. The Ideal Self coefficients were .60 for boys and .67 for girls.

An investigation of the instrument's internal consistency was also carried out, using Hoyt's (1941) analysis of variance approach. The obtained coefficients for Real Self were .89 for boys ($N = 227$) and .91 for girls ($N = 187$). Corresponding estimates for Ideal Self were .92 and .89 (Lake, Miles, and Earle, 1973).

Validity: Validity coefficients were determined for each dimension of the scale by correlating subscale scores with final grade point averages of 782 boys and 642 girls in the ninth grade in Toronto schools. Coefficients for total Real Self scores were .42 for boys and .35 for girls; while Ideal Self coefficients were .25 for boys and .19 for girls. The Achievement-Related Characteristics scale yielded the highest correlation for both sexes.

The validity coefficients for the Real Self scale (.42 and .35) were correlated with similar coefficients obtained for the Canadian Academic Aptitude Test (Verbal Reasoning), and with IQ as measured by the Henmon-Nelson Test of Mental Ability. Results suggested that self-concept is significantly correlated with academic achievement.

Norms: Normative data, based on the scores of 1,424 ninth-grade students (782 boys, 642 girls) from 5 high schools in Toronto, Canada, are provided in the form of means and standard deviations for each factor and for the two total scores.

Administration and Scoring: Directions for responding to the scale are printed on the test form. The scale requires about 30 minutes to complete. It can be easily administered to large groups and then scored by hand or machine. In scoring, items relating to each factor are identified and the student's responses to these items are summed. Factor scores under each of the two dimensions are averaged to provide two total scores (Gill and D'Oyley, 1970).

Comments: The Self-Concept Scale is in an experimental stage and thus requires further study to firmly establish its reliability and validity. Also, normative data on a wider range of ages, from a wider variety of settings, would be useful. However, the instrument does have potential as a predictor of academic achievement.

References: Gill, M. P., and V. R. D'Oyley, *The construction of an objective measure of self-concept.* Paper presented at the annual meeting of the American Educational Research Association, Chicago, 1968.

Hoyt, C., "Test reliability obtained by analysis of variance." *Psychometrika*, 1941, **6**, 153–160.

Lake, D. G., M. B. Miles, and R. B. Earle, Jr. (eds.), *Measuring human behavior.* New York: Columbia University Teachers College Press, 1973.

Rogers, C. R., *Client-centered therapy, its current practice, implications, and theory.* Boston: Houghton Mifflin, 1951.

Name: THE SELF-DIRECTED SEARCH

Author: John L. Holland

Type of Measure: Battery of checklists and rating scales.

Availability: Holland, J. L. *The self-directed search.* Palo Alto, California: Consulting Psychologists Press, 1970.

Description: The Self-Directed Search (SDS) is a self-administered vocational counseling instrument which allows high school and college students to identify a small group of occupations for further consideration. Based on Holland's (1966) theory of personality and vocational choice, the SDS includes 5 components each covering a separate domain (Occupational Daydreams, Activities, Competencies, Occupations, and Self-Estimates). Together these components permit the student to determine his resemblance to each of Holland's 6 proposed personality types: Realistic, Investigative, Artistic, Social, Enterprising, and Conventional. This resemblance is eventually expressed as a 3-digit summary code. Using this code and a booklet listing 456 vocations, the student can locate groups of occupations compatible with his pattern of interests and competencies.

Sample Items: The first part of the SDS, Occupational Daydreams, requires the subject to list jobs he has considered, or imagined doing. The 4 remaining components, however, ask the subject to rate or evaluate specified activities, competencies, occupations and aptitudes, all of which are scaled according to Holland's 6 personality types. These 4 components contain items similar to those below.

SDS Component	Scale	Item	Response Format
Activities	Realistic	Repair mechanical devices	Like ☐ Dislike ☐
Competencies	Conventional	I can do simple bookkeeping	Yes ☐ No ☐
Occupations	Artistic	Screenwriter	Like ☐ Dislike ☐
Selt-Estimates	Social	Teaching Ability	Low Average High 1 2 3 4 5 6 7

Reliability: The internal consistency of the individual SDS scales and the strong relationships between the scales and their corresponding profile totals are demonstrated in a correlational matrix presented by Holland (1971). This matrix, based on a population of college freshmen, shows high positive correlations between scales measuring the same personality type. Using a high school sample, Zener and Schnuelle (1972) essentially replicated this matrix, again finding the highest correlations among scales measuring the same personality type (for example, .68 between the Investigative scales on Occupations and Activities). A factor analysis of the responses of 718 college students also supports the internal organization of the SDS (Edwards and Whitney, 1972).

The stability of the SDS has also been investigated in several studies. Zener and Schnuelle (1972), retesting a high school sample after a 3- to 4-week interval, obtained scale reliabilities ranging over the 5 domains from .49 to .84 for males and from .41 to .80 for females. Coefficients for the summary scales ranged from .31 to .81 for males and from .44 to .78 for females. The reliability of the final summary code was estimated using a rank-order correlation of the 6 summary scales. The mean rank-order correlation for boys was .78, and for girls, .83. O'Connell and Sedlacek (1971) report a test/retest coefficient of .92 for SDS summary codes, obtained on a college population over a 7-month interval.

Validity: Though there is considerable evidence supporting the validity of Holland's formulations for the 6 personality types (Elton and Rose, 1970; Edwards and Whitney, 1972; Holland, 1968; Holland, 1971; Kristjanson, 1969; Morrow, 1970; Walsh and Lacey, 1969), research documenting the criterion-related validity of the SDS is more limited due to the instrument's relatively recent development. A study of the SDS conducted by Zener and Schnuelle (1972), however, offers a fairly comprehensive evaluation of the test. Using a sample of 1,092 students in the 10th, 11th, and 12th grades at 4 high schools, Zener and Schnuelle selected 2 treatment groups and a control group. To one treatment group they administered the published version of the SDS; to the other they administered a modified form of the SDS which removed the "self-directed" aspects of the test. The control group received no treatment. The effects of the SDS were evaluated according to a number of criteria, and the following results were obtained:

1. While both versions of the SDS were effective in increasing the number of occupations considered, the students who took the published version of the test were considering more appropriate occupations (based on their activities, competencies, interests and self-ratings) than those who took the modified version.

2. Both versions of the SDS were effective in increasing satisfaction and certainty about vocational plans. Students taking either version of the SDS reported more satisfaction with their current occupational choice than did control students, who expressed greater need for information about specific jobs and training programs. Those who took the published version of the SDS reported less need to see a counselor.

3. The published version of the SDS was more effective than the modified version in increasing students' understanding of the theory behind the SDS.

4. Students gave a positive evaluation to both forms of the SDS.

5. The SDS summary code corresponded well (better than the modified SDS

summary code) with the code of the vocation listed first under Occupational Daydreams.

Norms: Holland (1971) provides normative data based on the responses of 5,000 entering freshmen at the University of Maryland.

Administration and Scoring: The SDS is administered and scored by the respondent. After completing each part of the test, the student tallies his responses, obtaining six scale scores (corresponding to Holland's 6 personality types), which are charted to form a profile. The 3 highest points on the profile are used to determine a summary code, which represents the 3 areas (e.g., Realistic, Conventional, and Social) most compatible with the student's interests and abilities. This code may be used to locate appropriate occupations from a list of 456 which are similarly coded in a booklet accompanying the SDS.

Comments: The Self-Directed Search is a vocational guidance system which encourages the student to explore potential careers on his own. Because it is administered, scored, and interpreted by the respondent, it is more economical than most vocational interest inventories. Furthermore, there is some evidence indicating that this instrument offers a more effective way of presenting occupational information to students. In addition to teaching Holland's theory more successfully (and thus providing the student with a system to use in making future vocational decisions), the SDS expands the number of occupations the student is considering. Although several of the summary scales have demonstrated low reliabilities, these apparently have little effect on the reliability of the final summary code, which is satisfactory.

References: Edwards, K. J., and D. R. Whitney, " Structural analysis of Holland's personality types using factor and configural analysis." *Journal of Counseling Psychology*, 1972, **19**(2), 136–145.

Elton, C. F., and H. A. Rose, "Male occupational constancy and change: Its prediction according to Holland's theory." *Journal of Counseling Psychology*, 1970, **17**(6, Pt. 2), 1–19.

Holland, J. L., *The psychology of vocational choice: A theory of personality types and model environments*. Waltham, Mass.: Blaisdell, 1966.

Holland, J. L., "Explorations of a theory of vocational choice: VI. A longitudinal study using a sample of typical college students." *Journal of Applied Psychology*, 1968, **52**(1, Pt. 2).

Holland, J. L., *A counselor's guide for the Self-Directed Search*. Palo Alto, California: Consulting Psychologists Press, 1971.

Kristjanson, R. W., *Personality types and their hypothesized attributes: An application of Holland's vocational choice theory*. Unpublished master's thesis, University of North Dakota, 1969.

Morrow, J. M., Jr., *Satisfaction with choice of college major: A test of Holland's theory of vocational choice.* Unpublished doctoral dissertation, University of North Carolina, 1970.

O'Connell, T. J., and W. E. Sedlacek, *The reliability of Holland's Self-Directed Search for educational and vocational planning.* Counseling Center Research Report No. 6-71. College Park, Maryland: University of Maryland, 1971.

Walsh, W. B., and D. W. Lacey, "Perceived change and Holland's theory." *Journal of Counseling Psychology*, 1969, **16**, 348–352.

Zener, T. B., and L. Schnuelle, *An evaluation of the Self-Directed Search: A guide to educational and vocational planning.* (Report No. 124) Baltimore, Maryland: Johns Hopkins University, 1972.

Name: SELF-ESTEEM INVENTORY

Author: Stanley Coopersmith

Type of Measure: Self-report questionnaire

Availability: Coopersmith, S., *Self-esteem inventory*. Davis, California: Department of Psychology, University of California, 1967. Copies are also available in: Robinson, J. P., and P. R. Shaver, *Measures of social psychological attitudes*. Ann Arbor, Michigan: Institute for Social Research, University of Michigan, 1969; and Coopersmith, S., *The antecedents of self-esteem*. San Francisco: W. H. Freeman & Co., 1967.

Description: The Self-Esteem Inventory (SEI) measures self-attitudes in children aged 8 to 10 years. There are 2 forms of the scale: A and B. Most of the 58 items comprising Form A were selected from an earlier scale by Rogers and Dymond (1954). They were chosen on the basis of ratings by 5 psychologists and an item analysis performed on the responses of 121 children who were administered the experimental form. Items relate to 5 major dimensions determined by factor analysis: General Self, Social Self/Peers, Home/Parents, School/Academic, and a Lie Scale.

　　Form B of the SEI is composed of 25 items and has no subscales. It was developed on the basis of an item analysis of Form A, for use with individuals above age 8. Form B contains those items which demonstrated the highest item-total correlations. The 2 forms correlate .86.

Sample Items: Children are asked to respond to the SEI by checking either "like me" or "unlike me" according to how they usually feel about each statement. The following items are similar to those included on the inventory:

	Like me	*Unlike Me*
I am not making the kind of grades in school that I'd like to.	____	____
I am fun to be around.	____	____
I'd rather be alone than with other people.	____	____
My parents often push me.	____	____

Reliability: The author has investigated the reliability of Form A (Coopersmith, 1967). Using a group of 30 fifth-graders from Connecticut, he obtained a test/retest coefficient, after a 5-week interval, of .88. Test/retest reliability for a group of 56 public school children in Connecticut was .70 after a 3-year interval. No reliability information is reported for Form B of the SEI, which, due to its shorter length, is assumed to be somewhat less stable than Form A.

Validity: Many studies have been conducted to investigate the validity of the SEI. Form B was found to correlate .60 with the Rosenberg Scale for College Students on a sample of 300 students (Robinson and Shaver, 1969). Weinburg (in

Getsinger, Kunce, Miller and Weinburg, 1972) reports correlations of .63 between Form A and the Soares Scale and .60 between Form A and a derived picture test. Taylor and Reitz (1968) found that Form A correlates .45 with the Self-Acceptance scale of the California Psychological Inventory, and from .42 to .66 with the other CPI scales. They also found correlations of .75 with the Social Desirability scale of the Edwards Personal Preference Schedule and, .44 with that of the Marlowe-Crowne instrument.

Coopersmith (1967) found that parents of children scoring high on the SEI demonstrated greater acceptance of their children, setting clear rules, showing positive examples, and providing a high level of stimulation and interaction. Richmond and White (1971) found peer ratings positively related to the 5 areas of self-concept measured by the SEI, suggesting that children of low self-esteem are rated less favorably by their peers. Stein (1971) found no significant relationship between self-esteem, as measured by the SEI, and values, as measured by the Survey of Personal Values, except for Achievement, which was valued by high school seniors with high self-esteem. Using a sample of 111 14- and 15-year-old adolescents, Matteson (1974) found relationships between low SEI scores and dysfunctional family communication and between high SEI scores and facilitative family communication and marital adjustment.

Norms: Normative data are provided for a group of 70 females and 72 males, ages 9 through 15, and a group of 76 young adults, ages 16 through 23.

Administration and Scoring: Both forms of the SEI are self-administering. Form A requires about 20 minutes to complete and Form B, about 10 minutes.

Form A is usually scored by totaling the number of correct responses (those indicating high self-esteem) on all scales to produce one score. A separate Lie Reaction Score is computed by summing the total number of responses indicative of defensiveness. The first of these scores is multiplied by 2, making the maximum score 100. For the Lie Score the maximum value is 8. If subscales scores are desired, the correct responses are simply summed in each area.

Form B is scored by summing the number of correct responses and multiplying this number by 4.

Comments: The Self-Esteem Inventory measures overall self-concept, as well as discrete subareas of self-esteem. Though reliability and validity data are encouraging, high correlations with social desirability must be considered a drawback until they can be explained by systematic research findings. In general, however, this scale is useful as a measure of self-esteem for research, counseling and predictive purposes.

References: Coopersmith, S., *The antecedents of self-esteem.* San Francisco: W. H. Freeman & Co., 1967.

Getsinger, S., J. Kunce, D. Miller, and S. Weinburg, "Self-esteem measures and cultural disadvantagement." *Journal of Consulting and Clinical Psychology,* 1972, **38**, 149.

Matteson, R., "Adolescent self-esteem, family communication, and marital satisfaction." *Journal of Psychology*, 1974, **86**, 35–47.

Richmond, B. O. and W. F. White, "Socioeconomic predictors of the self concept among fifth and sixth grade children." *The Journal of Educational Research*, 1971, **64**, 425–429.

Robinson, J. P., and P. R. Shaver, *Measures of social psychological attitudes.* Ann Arbor, Michigan: Institute for Social Research, 1969.

Rogers, C., and R. Dymond, *Psychotherapy and personality change.* Chicago: University of Chicago Press, 1954.

Stein, S. L., "The interrelationships among self-esteem, personal values, and interpersonal values." *The Journal of Educational Research*, 1971, **64**, 448–450.

Taylor, J., and W. Reitz, *The three faces of self-esteem.* Research Bulletin No. 80. Ontario: Department of Psychology, University of Western Ontario, 1968.

Name: SELF-PERCEPTION INVENTORY

Authors: Anthony T. Soares and Louise M. Soares

Type of Measure: Rating scale

Availability: Soares, A. T., and L. M. Soares, *The self-perception inventory*. Princeton, New Jersey: Educational Testing Service, 1974.

Description: The Self-Perception Inventory (SPI) consists of a series of 4-step, bipolar scales, defined by pairs of matched traits derived from factor analyses reported in the literature. Each trait indicates some aspect of personal and social adjustment.

There are 3 versions of the SPI: a student form, an adult form, and a form for use with student teachers. The student form contains 20 scales, on each end of which bipolar traits are described in full sentences. Self-perception is divided into 6 components: Self Concept (how the individual sees himself at the moment); Ideal Concept (how he wishes he were or hopes to become); Reflected Self/Classmates (how he thinks his classmates see him); Reflected Self/Teachers (how he thinks his teachers view him); Reflected Self/Parents (how he thinks his parents perceive him); and Student Self (how he sees himself in the role of a student). The student form is appropriate for children in grades 3 through 9, for individuals who have a language difficulty, and for disadvantaged subjects.

The 36-scale adult form is very similar to the student form, except that scale endpoints are defined by adjectives rather than sentences. This form is appropriate for use with high school and college students. It includes 5 components: Self Concept; Ideal Concept; Reflected Self/Classmates; Reflected Self/Teachers; and Reflected Self/Parents.

The student teacher form of the SPI also consists of 36 bipolar scales, many of which are borrowed from the adult form. The student teacher form, however, includes only 4 components: Self Concept/Teacher (how the individual perceives himself as a teacher); Reflected Self/Cooperating Teacher (how he thinks the cooperating teacher sees him as a teacher); Reflected Self/Supervisor (how he thinks his college supervisor sees him); and Ideal Self/Teacher (what kind of teacher he would like to be).

Sample Items: The student form of the SPI contains items of the following type:

Self Concept:
1. I am usually happy. ____ ____ ____ ____ I am usually not happy.

Reflected
  Self/Classmates:
2. My friends think that ____ ____ ____ ____ My friends think that I
   I am always happy.   am always unhappy.

Reflected
  Self/Teachers:
3. My teachers think ____ ____ ____ ____ My teachers think my
   that I do good   school work is bad.
   school work.

Reflected Self/Parents:
4. My parents think ____ ____ ____ ____ My parents think that
   that I am calm.   I am very nervous.

Ideal Concept:
5. I wish I trusted ____ ____ ____ ____ I would not want to
   other people.   trust other people.

Student Self Concept:
6. I can be relied on ____ ____ ____ ____ I cannot be relied on
   in school.   in school.

Items on the adult and teacher forms are similar to the following:

Teacher Form:

Hard-working ____ ____ ____ ____ Lazy

Confident   ____ ____ ____ ____ Insecure

Adult Form:

Happy   ____ ____ ____ ____ Depressed

Sociable   ____ ____ ____ ____ Reserved

Reliability: Soares and Soares (1973) report that test/retest reliabilities, over unspecified intervals, are stable for all forms at around .88.

Validity: Soares, Soares, and Pumerantz (1973) report that SPI validity coefficients range from .44 to .68. The student form has been twice correlated with the Coopersmith Self-Esteem Inventory, producing coefficients of .68 and .63 (Soares and Soares, 1973). All components on the adult form of the SPI correlate .52 with the MMPI, except for Self Concept, which correlates .72 (Soares and Soares, 1973).

No validity information is provided for the student-teacher form of the SPI.

Norms: No normative data are currently available for the SPI.

Administration and Scoring: All forms of the SPI are easily administered, brief instructions being printed on the test sheets. Usually about 30 minutes are required to complete the inventory.

For scoring, values are assigned to each of the 4 response columns, depending on the positive or negative direction of the scales. Since scales are arranged with the positive poles on the left, check marks in the first column are added and multiplied by $+2$; those in the second column are added and multiplied by $+1$. The same procedure is followed for the third and fourth columns, using

-1 and -2, respectively. The masculine/feminine scale is the only exception to this procedure: males are scored $+2$, $+1$, -1, -2, while females are scored -2, -1, $+1$, $+2$.

An index score is obtained for each component by summing the column scores. Total discrepancy scores are calculated by determining the difference between any 2 index scores—e.g., between Reflected Self/Parents and Self Concept. A single-dimension discrepancy score is the difference between two individual scores on any one scale—e.g., "sociable" on Reflected Self/Parents and "sociable" on Self Concept.

Comments: The SPI is in a developmental stage, and, therefore, psychometric data are somewhat limited. This situation should soon be corrected, however, since Soares and Soares are undertaking continuing analysis of their instrument. Since preliminary data are encouraging, the SPI can be recommended for research use.

References: Soares, A. T., and L. M. Soares, *Description and validation of the Self-Perception Inventory.* Technical Report No. 5. Bridgeport, Connecticut: Also Corporation, 1973.

Soares, L. M., A. T. Soares, and P. Pumerantz, "Self-perceptions of middle-school pupils." *Elementary School Journal*, 1973, **73**, 381–389.

Name: SEMANTIC DISTANCE QUESTIONNAIRE

Author: Carl H. Weaver

Type of Measure: Rating scale

Availability: Weaver, C. H., "Semantic distance between students and teachers and its effect upon learning." *Speech Monographs*, 1959, **26**, 273–281. This instrument also appears in: Shaw, M. E. and J. M. Wright, *Scales for the measurement of attitudes.* New York: McGraw-Hill, 1967.

Description: The Semantic Distance Questionnaire (SDQ) was developed in a study (Weaver, 1959) of the semantic distance between 2 groups whose attitudes toward the educative process were expected to differ: high school students and their teachers. The SDQ measures attitudes toward teachers, high school, classrooms, study hall, studying, and school rules. These 6 attitude objects were selected by asking 147 twelfth-grade students to write statements describing attitudes held by their peer group toward various aspects of education. These statements were presented to 20 teachers who rated them on a 7-point continuum representing "good" to "bad" attitude. The 6 educative process variables mentioned above received the most consistent ratings and therefore were selected for inclusion on the final scale. Six items were chosen to measure each of these variables, creating a 36-item test. The items selected were those which showed the greatest scale distances between student responses and teacher ratings.

Sample Items: Items of the following type appear on the SDQ. The student responds on a 7-point scale, from "strongly disagree" to "strongly agree."

1. When I am in class, I think of what is going on after school.
2. Some teachers are stupid.
3. We should always follow the school rules.
4. I'm happy when school is closed.
5. I usually use the study hall period to relax.

Reliability: A split-half reliability of .92 was obtained during test development and used as a criterion for item selection (Weaver, 1959).

Validity: SDQ test items appear to have good content validity in relation to the 6 attitude dimensions toward which they are directed; the source and number of statements (2,100) from which the dimensions and items were drawn assures at least some content validity.

Since it was expected that the SDQ would have some value as a predictor of academic achievement, Weaver (1959) obtained intelligence quotients (Otis) and achievement scores for 269 students from one school. Achievement ratings were percentages representing grades received during the first $3\frac{1}{2}$ years of high school. Both of these criteria were significantly related to SDQ scores, with more positive attitudes toward education being associated with higher grades and IQ scores.

Norms: Profiles on the 6 attitudinal objects, obtained on 437 students and 16 teachers, are reported by Weaver (1959).

Administration and Scoring: The SDQ is easy to administer. Subjects can readily understand the simple instructions which precede the test.

In scoring the SDQ for research purposes, Weaver (1959) used the mean of the numbers selected by the subject from the response continuum, after reversing the weights for the negative items. Shaw and Wright (1967) suggest using a summated rating procedure, such as a standard Likert-type response continuum since there are no items possessing extreme scale values. In this way, items are weighted from 5 (strongly agree) to 1 (strongly disagree). Weights for negative items are reversed, and the sum of the weighted alternatives selected by the subject is his score.

Comments: The Semantic Distance Questionnaire appears to provide a reliable and valid assessment of general attitude toward the school situation and referents related to the school. Weaver (1959) feels that semantic distance between teacher and student on the six dimensions measured by the SDQ has some effect upon communicative behavior. If so, the SDQ could prove valuable in research efforts to further effective teacher/student communication and, in turn, student performance.

References: Shaw, M. E., and J. M. Wright, *Scales for the measurement of attitudes.* New York: McGraw-Hill, 1967.

Weaver, C. H., "Semantic distance between students and teachers and its effect upon learning." *Speech Monographs*, 1959, **26**, 273–281.

Name: SOUTHERN CALIFORNIA TESTS OF DIVERGENT PRODUC-
TION

Authors: J. P. Guilford, P. R. Christensen, and associates.

Type of Measure: Battery of creative ability tests

Availability: These tests are available to members of the American Psychological
Association (or psychologists sponsored by APA members), for research purposes, from: Sheridan Psychological Services, P.O. Box 6101, Orange, California 92667.

Description: This battery of creativity tests is a product of the factor analytic
research conducted over the past 2 decades by Guilford and his associates at the
University of Southern California. Following the lead of Thurstone (1938), who
theorized that the intellect was composed of several "primary factors," Guilford
and his various colleagues (1950; 1951; 1956; 1959; 1967) constructed a 3-
dimensional model (Structure of Intellect), subdividing the intellect into 120
structural and functional components. Though this model encompasses all
intellectual functions, the Southern California Tests of Divergent Production
represent only those measuring "divergent" thinking. Such thinking, according
to Guilford (1959, p. 381) is "the kind that goes off in different directions,"
leading to a diversity of solutions or products. Therefore, the Divergent Production tests present various tasks requiring creative and original problem solving.
They require the examinee to actually produce a quantity and variety of information. These tests are appropriate for students in grades 7 through 12 and for
adults.

The 11 tests described below are only a small sample of those in the Divergent Production series. As Guilford continues to identify the unlabelled cells in
his Structure of Intellect model, it is likely that even more tests will be
developed to measure these new factors.

Sample Items: Below are listed 11 of the Southern California Tests of Divergent
Production. Each is followed by: (1) the principal Structure of Intellect factor
measured; (2) an example of the kind of task required of the student; and (3) a
list of possible responses.

1. *Word Fluency*
   Measures divergent production of symbolic units.
   Requires examinee to list words containing a specified letter, such as "O":
   boat, lot, ocean, etc.

2. *Ideational Fluency*
   Measures divergent production of semantic units.
   Requires examinee to name things belonging to a given class, such as
   "things that ring": bells, telephones, alarm clocks, etc.

3. *Associational Fluency*
   Measures divergent production of semantic relations.

Requires subject to list words similar in meaning to a specified word, such as "short": small, low, lacking, insufficient, etc.

4. *Expressional Fluency*
   Measures divergent production of symbolic systems.

   Requires respondent to produce sentences containing 4 words, each beginning with a given letter, such as "p_____ u_____ y_____ n_____": Pick up your notes; Please use yellow needles; etc.

5. *Alternate Uses*
   Measures divergent production of semantic classes.

   Requires examinee to list possible uses, other than the intended use, for a specified object, such as "a book": paperweight, straight-edge, etc.

6. *Consequences*
   Measures divergent production of semantic units and transformations.

   Requires subject to list various consequences of a given hypothetical event: e.g., "What would happen if people no longer needed or wanted food?" Farmers would be out of work; Restaurants would go out of business; etc.

7. *Possible Jobs*
   Measures divergent production of semantic implications.

   Requires examinee to list jobs that might be represented by a given symbol, such as "a cat": tennis shoe manufacturer, detective agency, acrobat, etc.

8. *Making Objects*
   Measures divergent production of figural systems.

   Requires subject to draw specified objects, such as a face, using given geometric figures.

9. *Sketches*
   Measures divergent production of figural units.

   Requires respondent to make as many different sketches as possible by elaborating on a set of identical figures.

10. *Match Problems*
    Measures divergent production of figural transformations.

    Requires examinee to remove a specified number of matchsticks from a given configuration of matchsticks to form a certain number of squares or triangles.

11. *Decorations*
    Measures divergent production of figural implications.

    Requires subject to decorate outline drawings using as many different designs as possible.

Reliability: Split-half reliability coefficients reported in the manuals range from the .60s to the .80s. Although scorer reliability is not provided in the manuals, coefficients of approximately .90 have been obtained by independent investigators (Anastasi, 1968; Schaefer, 1967).

Validity: Guilford (1967) reports factorial validity data, based on extensive research, for all of the Southern California Tests of Divergent Production. His reliance on factorial, rather than predictive, validity has in the past been criticized. This criticism is becoming less appropriate, however, as evidence of criterion-related validity accumulates. In 2 independent studies (Cline, Richards, and Abe, 1962; Cline, Richards, and Needham, 1963), for example, a battery of Guilford's creativity tests (including Consequences, Alternate Uses, Associational Fluency, and Match Problems) successfully predicted several academic criteria and, to a substantial degree, accounted for criterion variance independent of that accounted for by IQ. The creativity battery correlated .65 with high school grade point average for male students ($N = 99$), and .63 for females ($N = 66$). When IQ (based on scores on the California Mental Maturity Inventory) was added to the creativity scores, these multiple correlations rose to .69 and .68, respectively (Cline, Richards, and Abe, 1962). The same battery also predicted 5 criteria of achievement in high school science, the correlations ranging from .32 to .68 for males and from .29 to .61 for females. Again, when IQ was added, these coefficients rose somewhat, ranging from .32 to .70 for males and from .36 to .74 for females (Cline, Richards, and Needham, 1963).

Guilford (1967) also reports evidence of criterion-related validity, citing relationships between the Divergent Production tests and several indices of creative potential. Verbal test composites, for example, correlated .46 and .58 with creative writing ability, while figural test composites correlated .50 and .54 with drawing ability. Yet the verbal tests correlated only .32 with the drawing criterion, and the figural tests only .40 with the writing criterion, thus demonstrating some differential validity. Three Divergent Production tests also correlated .30, .36, and .32 with staff ratings of originality among 100 Air Force captains. Similarly, the semantic divergent production tests successfully discriminated between criterion groups of public relations and advertising personnel rated by their supervisors as "more creative" or "less creative."

Comparing IQ and creativity, Guilford (1967) reports low correlations between tests of Divergent Production and IQ scores, noting that an above-average IQ is necessary, but insufficient, for high creativity scores.

Norms: Tentative norms, reported as *C*-scores and percentiles, are available for adult groups, ninth-grade students, or both.

Administration and Scoring: These tests can be administered to individuals or groups with minimal directions from the examiner. Subjects are instructed to produce answers as rapidly as possible within a specified time.

Scorers are required to use some judgment about the acceptability of responses, though each manual does present the test rationale and examples of correct answers. In many cases, 2 scores are computed—one indicating "obvious" responses, the other, "remote" responses.

Comments: The Southern California Tests of Divergent Production offer a battery of measures, based on sound factorial research, assessing specific aspects of creativity. Although evidence indicates that these tests measure something which is not covered by conventional IQ tests, further clarification of the relationship between creativity and IQ is needed. The provision of test/retest reliability data would also add to our understanding of these tests by addressing the question of variability in the examinee's capacity to "create" at a given point in time. Though it has been argued that scoring procedures are poorly standardized and norms too limited, these problems will probably be corrected with continued research and developmental work on the Southern California Tests of Divergent Production.

References: Anastasi, A., *Psychological testing* (3rd ed.). London: The Macmillan Company, 1968.

Cline, V. B., J. M. Richards, Jr., and C. Abe, "The validity of a battery of creativity tests in a high school sample." *Educational and Psychological Measurement*, 1962, **22**, 781–784.

Cline, V. B., J. M. Richards, Jr., and W. E. Needham, "Creativity tests and achievement in high school science." *Journal of Applied Psychology*, 1963, **47**(3), 184–189.

Guilford, J. P., "Creativity." *American Psychologist*, 1950, **5**, 444–454.

Guilford, J. P., "The relation of intellectual factors to creative thinking in science," in C. W. Taylor (ed.), *1955 Conference on the identification of creative scientific talent*. Salt Lake City: University of Utah Press, 1956.

Guildford, J. P., "Basic traits in intellectual performance," in C. W. Taylor (ed.), *1957 Conference on the identification of creative scientific talent*. Salt Lake City: University of Utah Press, 1958.

Guilford, J. P., "Intellectual resources and their value as seen by scientists," in C. W. Taylor (ed.), *1959 Conference on the identification of creative scientific talent*. Salt Lake City: University of Utah Press, 1959.

Guilford, J. P., *The nature of human intelligence*. New York: McGraw-Hill, 1967.

Guilford, J. P., R. C. Wilson, P. R. Christensen, and D. S. Lewis, *A factor analytic study of creative thinking: I. Hypotheses and description of tests*. Los Angeles: Psychological Laboratory, University of Southern California, 1951.

Schaefer, C. E., *Biographical inventory correlates of scientific and artistic creativity in adolescents*. Unpublished doctoral dissertation, Fordham University, 1967.

Thurstone, L. L., "Primary mental abilities." *Psychometric Monographs*, 1938, No. 1.

Name: TENNESSEE SELF CONCEPT SCALE

Author: William H. Fitts

Type of Measure: Rating scale

Availability: Fitts, W. H., *The Tennessee self concept scale.* Nashville, Tennessee: Counselor Recordings and Tests, 1970.

Description: The Tennessee Self Concept Scale (TSCS) is comprised of 100 self-descriptive statements, 90 of which assess self-concept and 10 of which assess self-criticism. The TSCS was designed for use with subjects aged 12 or older who have at least a sixth-grade reading level. The scale is appropriate for normal or mentally disturbed individuals.

In constructing the TSCS, a large pool of self-descriptive items were collected from other measures of self-concept and from individuals diagnosed as psychotic. These statements were then edited, classified, and used as a source from which qualified judges selected final TSCS items.

Although this scale was originally developed for research purposes, it can also be used in counseling, clinical diagnosis, or personnel selection. Because of its wide application, the TSCS is available in both a Clinical/Research form and a Counseling form. These forms differ only in regard to scoring and profiling, however. Both measure the same aspects of self: Identity; Self-Satisfaction; Behavior; Physical Self; Moral-Ethical Self; Personal Self; Family Self; and Social Self.

Sample Items: For each TSCS item, the subject must select 1 of 5 response options, from "Completely False" to "Completely True." The instrument contains items of the following type.

1. I am a good person.
2. I lie a lot.
3. Most people dislike me.
4. I succeed in anything I attempt.

Reliability: Fitts (1965) reports test/retest reliabilities, over a 2-week period, ranging from .60 to .92, on a sample of 60 college students. Congdon (1958), using a shortened version of the TSCS with psychiatric patients, obtained a reliability coefficient of .88 for total positive scores.

In addition, Fitts (1965) reports that profile patterns are remarkably stable for periods of a year or more. Although the profile details may change, the distinctive features remain the same.

Validity: High correlations have been reported between TSCS scores and other measures of personality functioning. McGee (1960) correlated TSCS scores with those from the MMPI and obtained coefficients in the .50s and .60s. Studies by Havener (1961) and Wayne (1963) yielded similar results. Fitts

(1965) reports a $-.70$ correlation between the TSCS total positive score and the Taylor Manifest Anxiety Scale. Correlations between the TSCS and the Edwards Personal Preference Schedule, the California F Scale, and the Cornell Medical Index are also in the expected direction.

The TSCS has also been shown to discriminate well between groups, on the basis of psychological status (Fitts, 1965). The scores of 369 psychiatric patients and 626 nonpatients were compared, and significant differences were found between the 2 groups at the .001 level.

Norms: The TSCS was standardized on 626 subjects of varying age, sex, race, and socioeconomic status. Norms are broken down according to these variables.

Administration and Scoring: The TSCS is self-administering and can be given to either individuals or groups. It can be completed in 10 to 20 minutes. Scoring may be done by hand or by a computer scoring service offered by the test publisher. Since scoring procedures are rather cumbersome (the Research/Clinical form produces 30 measures), machine scoring is recommended.

Comments: The content areas of the TSCS are well conceived and designed. Considering its relative brevity, the TSCS supplies an unusual variety of scores and a good deal of information. Its broad standardization sample makes this test widely applicable. The quality of the TSCS compensates for its tedious scoring procedure.

References: Congdon, C. S., *Self theory and chloropromazine treatment.* Unpublished doctoral dissertation, Vanderbilt University, 1958.

Fitts, W. H., *Manual, The Tennessee (Department of Mental Health) Self Concept Scale.* Nashville, Tennessee: Department of Mental Health, 1965.

Havener, P. H., *Distortions in the preception of self and others by persons using paranoid defenses.* Unpublished doctorial dissertation, Vanderbilt University, 1961.

McGee, R. K., Personal communication, 1960. Reported in W. H. Fitts, *Manual, The Tennessee (Department of Mental Health) Self Concept Scale.* Nashville, Tennessee: Department of Mental Health, 1965.

Wayne, S. R., *The relation of self-esteem to indices of perceived and behavioral hostility.* Unpublished doctoral dissertation, Vanderbilt University, 1963.

Name TEST ANXIETY SCALE FOR CHILDREN

Authors: S. B. Sarason, K. S. Davidson, F. F. Lighthall, R. R. Waite, and B. K. Ruebush

Type of Measure: Questionnaire

Availability: A copy of the instrument appears in: Sarason, S. B., K. S. Davidson, F. F. Lighthall, R. R. Waite, and B. K. Ruebush, *Anxiety in elementary school children.* New York: John Wiley, 1960.

Description: The Test Anxiety Scale for Children (TASC) is designed to measure anxiety in school children in grades 1 through 9. Maintaining that anxiety is a conscious experience which can be communicated, the authors constructed a test that measures anxiety by direct questioning. The TASC consists of 30 questions given orally to children by an examiner. These questions were designed to produce a test in which: (1) a "yes" answer reflects behavior experienced as unpleasant; (2) anticipation of dangerous or painful consequences is incorporated into each question; (3) bodily reactions to testing situations are included in a number of items; and (4) a variety of testing situations is represented. Both an original form and a revision of the TASC are available.

Sample Items: The child responds to all TASC questions by circling "yes" or "no" on his answer sheet. The first 18 items are of the following type:

1. When the teacher says she is going to ask you questions about your homework, do you get a funny feeling in your stomach?
2. Do you have a hard time sleeping some nights because you are worried about answering the teacher's questions the next day?

The last 12 items refer to "tests." Before administering them, the examiner explains that a test is any situation in which the teacher asks pupils to do something in order to find out how much they know. These questions are of this type:

1. When the teacher says that she is going to give the class a test, does your heart start beating faster?
2. Do you worry a lot about school tests?

Reliability: Dunn (1965) designed a study to test the stability of the TASC factor structure across 4 different sample groups. Groups 1 and 2 contained 223 boys and 191 girls, respectively, from the fourth and fifth grades of an upper-middle-class public school system. Group 3 was composed of 226 boys and Group 4 of 226 girls from the seventh and ninth grades. Using Hotteling's principal-axes method coupled with a normalized varimax rotation, Dunn factor analyzed the TASC scores of each sample. He then compared each factor with every other factor using Kaiser's coefficient of factor similarity (Kc). If a Kc of .71 or higher was obtained, the factor was judged to be replicated. The first two factors were Test Anxiety and Manifest Dream Anxiety. Test Anxiety accounted for 50% of the total common variance for preadolescent boys, but only 35% of the variance for other subjects. This factor was highly similar from group to group; the Kcs ranged from .94 to 1.00. Dream Anxiety accounted for 15 to 20% of the total common variance for all groups, with Kcs falling between .91 and .99

A Self-Doubt factor emerged and replicated most highly across the male groups ($Kc = .89$). This factor also appeared for adolescent females (Kcs = .61 to .89) but not for preadolescent females. The latter group seemed to utilize a Generalized School Anxiety dimension which was unrelated to the Self-Doubt factor.

Additional factors appeared in one group but not in others. For example, preadolescent boys produced a factor termed Awareness of Physiological Involvement, while adolescents and younger girls produced a more complex factor called Recitation Anxiety with Somatic Involvement.

Validity: The authors present extensive evidence of validity for the initial TASC and for subsequent revisions (Sarason et al., 1960). The original test correlated positively and highly with teachers' ratings of anxiety, and, as expected, negatively with intelligence and achievement. The size of these negative correlations increased with grade level. When TASC scores were compared to those on the General Anxiety Scale for Children (GASC), strong positive correlations were consistently obtained.

The revised TASC has been correlated with a number of other measures. Zweibelson (reported in Sarason, et al., 1960) compared the TASC to 3 group intelligence tests—the Davis-Eells Games, the Otis Beta, and the Otis Alpha—and obtained correlations of $-.14$, .28, and .24, respectively. These findings were in the expected direction, since the Davis-Eells games are far less "test-like" than the Otis measures.

The authors (Sarason, et al., 1960) report an overall correlation of .24 ($p < .001$) between the TASC and Thurstone's Tests of Primary Mental Abilities (PMA). The various tests composing the PMA related differentially to the TASC, depending on (1) their test-like vs. game-like nature; (2) their novelty, and (3) the degree of reading required.

Sarason and his associates (1960) also compared the TASC scores of English and American students. Since British primary schools create an intense concern with tests and evaluations among both parents and children, it was expected that the English students would score significantly higher than the Americans on the TASC. The correlations obtained confirmed this expectation. Though the 2 groups were similar in general anxiety, they differed in the level of *test* anxiety. Findings also showed that sex had a uniform effect on the TASC scores of both groups, with the girls revealing higher test anxiety levels.

Norms: Although the TASC has been administered to a variety of populations, Sarason et al. (1965) provide no systematic normative data.

Administration and Scoring: The TASC is easy to administer and takes only a short time to complete. The items are read to a group of children, who record their responses on a separate answer sheet. The children are told that there are no right or wrong answers, and assurance is given that only the examiner will see the answers. Detailed instructions for examiners are included in the test format. The subject's score is the total number of "yes" responses. It is suggested that a high score has more credence than a low score since there is probably less error in a self-report admitting "weakness" than in one denying it.

Comment: The TASC can be effectively used in studies of children's anxiety, especially in relation to school performance. Validity studies are diverse and impressive. However, the stability of the TASC across different sex and age groups is questionable, and further research is needed in this area.

References: Dunn, J. A., "Stability of the factor structure of the Test Anxiety Scale for Children across age and sex groups." *Journal of Consulting Psychology*, 1965, **29**, 187.

Sarason, S. B., K. S. Davidson, F. F. Lighthall, R. R. Waite, and B. K. Ruebush, *Anxiety in elementary school children*. New York: John Wiley, 1960.

Name: THINKING CREATIVELY WITH SOUNDS AND WORDS, RESEARCH EDITION

Authors: E. Paul Torrance, Joe Khatena, and Bert F. Cunnington

Type of Measure: Cognitive ability test

Availability: Torrance, E. P., J. Khatena, and B. F. Cunnington, *Thinking creatively with sounds and words.* Lexington, Massachusetts: Personnel Press, 1973.

Description: Thinking Creatively with Sounds and Words (TCSW) assesses creative thinking ability, using abstract sounds and spoken onomatopoeic words to stimulate originality of ideas. The TCSW consists of 2 independent tests, Sounds and Images (SI) and Onomatopoeia and Images (OI). The SI requires the subject to list ideas evoked by recorded abstract sounds. The OI requires him to react similarly to recorded spoken onomatopoeic words, which, according to the authors, have the potency to evoke the production of original responses. Thus, both tests provide sound or word stimuli under free associative conditions in order to encourage original thought. The originality of responses is determined largely by statistical infrequency.

    The TCSW tests are available at two levels: Level I is appropriate for children in grades 3 through 12, while Level II is designed for adults. Alternate forms (A and B) are available for both levels. All forms employ records to supply stimulus material and utilize certain built-in conditions, such as progressive warm-up, to free the subject's imagination and reduce the threat of evaluation.

Sample Items: The SI stimuli are recorded sound effects interspersed with narrated instructions which, in effect, force the listener to reject commonplace associations in favor of imaginative ideas. These sounds, which vary from the simple to complex, from the common to the unusual, are intended to evoke original responses.

    The OI stimuli are complete words, each of which is pronounced by a narrator and followed by a brief response interval. During this interval, the subject writes his reaction to the word he has just heard.

Reliability: The manual (Khatena and Torrance, 1973) reports a variety of reliability data for both tests. Interscorer reliability coefficients range from .88 to .97 for the SI and from .95 to .99 for the OI. An alternate form reliability coefficient of .77 is reported for Forms IIA and IIB of the SI, administered over a 7-day interval to 137 music majors at Westminster Choir College. Other alternate form studies have produced coefficients of .38 and .36 for adults and children, respectively, over a 3-month interval. Studies of the OI have yielded alternate form reliabilities of .76, .89, and .91 for college students, retested after varying intervals. Coefficients ranging from .77 to .92 have been obtained for elementary students, with no interval between OI administrations.

    Split-half reliabilities for the 2 tests are also presented in the manual. For the SI, coefficients obtained on Form IIA (corrected by the Spearman-Brown formula) were .88, .90, and .91, and on Form IIB, .82, .77 and .82. For the OI, odd/even coefficients ranged from .69 to .87, and administrative sequence coefficients ranged from .76 to .95.

Validity: The manual (Khatena and Torrance, 1973) presents extensive validity data for both the OI and the SI. Construct validity was approached by correlating both tests with the Runner Studies of Attitude Patterns (Runner and Runner, 1965). Results showed expected group differences between high and low scorers on the TCSW. For example, highly original repondents to Forms IIA and IIB of both the OI and the SI scored significantly higher than less original subjects on the Runner dimensions, Freedom Orientation ($p < .05$), Recognition Orientation ($p < .01$) and Achievement Orientation ($p < .05$).

A number of criterion-related studies, many correlating the TCSW to other measures of originality, are reported in the manual. For example, 2 tests of verbal originality, along with Forms IIA and IIB of the OI and SI, were administered to students from 3 universities. Correlations between the originality scores and Form IIA of both the OI and the SI ranged from .33 to .46. Those obtained for Forms IIB ranged from .31 to .43. Similarly, correlations between verbal originality scores on the Imaginative Story Test (Torrance, 1962) and the adult forms of the SI yielded coefficients of .44 and .39. Other studies of criterion-related validity, too numerous to describe here, are summarized in the manual.

Norms: Normative data for Sounds and Images are based on several groups of children and adults. The children's forms were administered to students in grades 3 through 12 in Minneapolis, Minnesota, and Huntington, West Virginia. The schools selected for testing, representing populations free from economic, academic, and ability extremes, were predominantly middle class and white. Students at the University of Minnesota, Marshall University, East Carolina University, the University of Georgia, and Westminster Choir College served as the standardization group for the adult forms. All of these college samples, except that at Westminster, were composed largely of education and psychology students.

Normative data for the OI are based on: (1) children in grades 3 through 12 from schools in South Point, Ohio, Commerce and Athens, Georgia, and Huntington, Westmoreland, and Guyandotte, West Virginia; and (2) students at the University of South Florida, the University of the South in Tennessee, Marshall University, East Carolina University, and Buffalo State College.

Means and standard deviations are presented for all the norm populations. Conversion tables are also available to obtain T-scores.

Administration and Scoring: The TCSW manual provides detailed instructions for test administration. Testing time is less than 30 minutes per test. All booklets are hand scored according to explicit instructions presented in the manual. Each response is credited with 0 to 4 points. A score of 0 on an item indicates that the response occurs with 5% or greater frequency. A score of 4 points indicates 1% frequency or less.

Comments: Thinking Creatively With Sounds and Words provides a new approach to creativity assessment. Because the normative data are preliminary, the TCSW is presently considered appropriate for research only. The authors suggest the use of local norms when data in the manual are inapplicable to subjects being tested. Further research efforts should clarify the apparently considerable potential of this measure.

References: Khatena, J., and E. P. Torrance, *Norms-technical manual. Thinking Creatively With Sounds and Words* (Research Edition). Lexington, Massachusetts: Personnel Press, 1973.

Runner, K., and H. Runner, *Manual of interpretation for the Interview Form III of the Runner Studies of Attitude Patterns.* Golden, Colorado: Runner Associates, 1965.

Torrance, E. P., *Guiding creative talent.* Englewood Cliffs, New Jersey: Prentice-Hall, 1962.

Name: TORRANCE TESTS OF CREATIVE THINKING, RESEARCH EDITION

Author: E. Paul Torrance

Type of Measure: Cognitive ability test

Availability: Torrance, E. P. *Torrance tests of creative thinking.* Lexington, Massachusetts: Personnel Press, 1966.

Description: The Torrance Tests of Creative Thinking (TTCT) are designed to measure creative thinking ability in children and adults. Developed as part of a research program investigating classroom experiences which stimulate divergent thinking, the TTCT assesses creativity on 4 cognitive dimensions: Fluency, Flexibility, Originality, and Elaboration. In designing the TTCT, Torrance devised situations intended to evoke the creative process in its natural complexity. Therefore, the individual Torrance tests are not factorially pure, but instead involve 2, 3, or all 4 of the above dimensions.

The TTCT is composed of 10 tests, grouped into 2 batteries, Thinking Creatively with Words and Thinking Creatively with Pictures. To reduce inhibition in respondents, these are called "activities" rather than "tests," and the emphasis is on "having fun." Thinking Creatively with Pictures includes 3 activities which require drawing responses, while Thinking Creatively with Words involves 7 parallel tasks requiring written responses. These activities sample various manifestations of creative thinking. Though each test relies on a somewhat different mental process, all require the subject to think in divergent directions.

Each battery is available in 2 equivalent forms, which can be used before and after special programs to determine changes in children's creativity. The entire verbal battery yields a total score in Fluency, Flexibility, and Originality, while the pictorial battery produces 4 scores: Fluency, Flexibility, Originality, and Elaboration.

The Torrance tests are suitable for group administration from kindergarten through graduate school, but the verbal battery must be administered individually and orally to subjects in kindergarten through grade 3. The author recommends that these tests be used in research evaluating cognitive functioning, individualized instruction, remedial programs, and innovative educational curricula. He also suggests that the TTCT can help teachers and clinicians recognize student potential which might otherwise be overlooked.

Sample Items: Thinking Creatively with Pictures consists of 3 activities, the first of which, Picture Construction, presents a brightly colored 2-dimensional form. The examinee pastes this form on a blank sheet and uses it as a starting point from which to draw an unusual picture "that tells an interesting and exciting story." The second test, Picture Completion, requires the subject to sketch "interesting objects or pictures" from a number of incomplete figures. The final activity, Repeated Figures, provides pairs of parallel lines or circles from which the subject produces as many different pictures as possible.

The verbal battery, Thinking Creatively with Words, contains 7 activities. The first 3 (Ask-and-Guess) present an intriguing picture to which the examinee responds by: (1) writing all the questions he or she would need to ask to understand what is happening in the picture; and (2) listing possible consequences of the action. The fourth activity requires the subject to think of methods to improve a toy so that children will have more fun playing with it. The fifth activity asks the respondent to list unusual uses for a common object, while the sixth requires him or her to reply to unusual questions which might be asked about this object. The last activity involves listing the consequences of an improbable happening.

Reliability: The author reports interscorer and test/retest reliabilities in the manual (Torrance, 1974). Coefficients computed between an experienced scorer and a scorer in training ranged from .86 to .99 and averaged .95. Untrained classroom teachers following prescribed rules, scored a sample of 25 TTCT booklets completed by children in the grade at which they were teaching. Mean reliability coefficients for the figural tests ranged from .88 for Originality to .96 for Fluency, and for the verbal tests, from .94 for Originality to .99 for Fluency.

Two test/retest studies, using alternate forms of the TTCT, are reported by Torrance (1974). One, involving 118 fourth-, fifth, and sixth-grade children in Wisconsin, produced coefficients ranging from .71 to .93 over an interval of 1 to 2 weeks. The other, using 28 experimental and 26 control subjects in the fifth grade in Minnesota, yielded reliability estimates ranging from .50 to .57 for experimental children and from .60 to .80 for controls, over varying intervals.

Other retest studies reported in the manual have involved incomplete forms of the TTCT batteries. Coefficients produced in these studies generally fell in the .60s, .70s or .80s.

Validity: The manual reports more than 50 validity studies, the majority of which deal with construct validation by focusing on the personalities of high and low scorers. For example, Weisberg and Springer (1961) compared the personality characteristics of highly creative children with those of less creative children (total $N = 32$). The highly creative children (determined by TTCT scores) were rated, according to a variety of personality indicators, significantly higher on: strength of self-image; ease of early recall; humor; availability of Oedipal anxiety; and uneven ego development. Results also indicated that creative preadolescents were more sensitive and more independent than less creative but equally intelligent children.

In regard to concurrent validity, the manual reports moderate correlations (mostly in the .20s and .30s) between TTCT scores and various indices of educational achievement. The author notes, however, that there are many reasons for *not* expecting strong relationships between creativity and educational achievement variables (Torrance, 1974). Peer and teacher nominations of creativity have yielded statistically significant but rather weak correlations (around .24) with TTCT scores (Yamamoto, 1960; 1964; Torrance, 1974).

The author reports studies of predictive validity in which the criterion was "real-life" creative accomplishment. One of these studies, involving a 12-year follow-up of the total enrollment of the University of Minnesota High School (1959), produced canonical correlations of .59 for males and .46 for females between the creativity predictor (a composite including the TTCT) and 3 criterion variables related to creative achievement.

Norms: The manual presents means and standard deviations, by grade level, for large samples of students, kindergarten through graduate school. These samples exclude students with special characteristics which might influence performance on the tests. For the figural tests, normative data are given for each of the 4 factors. For the verbal battery, factor norms are provided only for Fluency, Flexibility, and Originality.

The manual also presents 2 conversion tables, one based on the fifth-grade equivalency study sample and the other on a college population. The fifth-grade data are to be used in converting the raw scores of elementary school children and high school students to *T*-scores, and the college data are to be used with college students and adults.

Administration and Scoring: The TTCT manual provides clear and detailed instructions for administration and scoring. Both batteries can be administered individually or in groups, except the Verbal Form, which must be administered individually to subjects in kindergarten through third grade. The 3 figural tasks can be given in 30 minutes, while the 7 verbal tasks require 45 minutes. The tests must be scored by hand, though special training is not necessary to accomplish reliable scoring. It is recommended, however, that score interpretation be supervised by persons with psychometric training.

Comments: The Torrance Tests of Creative Thinking make a considerable contribution to the research on creative behavior. The tests and manual are well designed and provide a good basis for further research into the nature of creativity. Further normative and predictive validity statistics are needed before the tests' full potential for research and practice can be realized. However, considering the TTCT's relatively recent publication, the psychometric data available are impressive.

References: Torrance, E. P., "Examples and rationales of test tasks for assessing creative abilities." *Journal of Creative Behavior*, 1968, **2**(3), 165–178.

Torrance, E. P., *Norms-technical manual. Torrance Tests of Creative Thinking.* Lexington, Massachusetts: Personnel Press, 1974.

Weisberg, P. S., and K. J. Springer, "Environmental factors in creative function." *Archives of General Psychiatry*, 1961, **5**, 554–564.

Yamamoto, K., *Creativity and sociometric choice among adolescents.* Unpublished master's thesis, University of Minnesota, 1960.

Yamamoto, K., "Evaluation of some creativity measures in a high school with peer nominations as criteria." *Journal of Psychology,* 1964, **58**, 285–293.

Name: VINELAND SOCIAL MATURITY SCALE (1935–1965)

Author: Edgar A. Doll

Type of Measure: Interview/rating scale

Availability: Doll, E. A. *Vineland social maturity scale.* Circle Pines, Minnesota: American Guidance Service, 1965. An Australian edition is published by the Australian Council for Educational Research, Victoria, Australia.

Description: The Vineland Social Maturity Scale (VSMS) measures the social maturity, competence, and independence of individuals of any age, though it is most useful with younger or mentally retarded subjects. In administering the VSMS, an examiner interviews someone who is familiar with the individual being evaluated, interprets the information obtained, and scores the subject. The informant does not participate in scoring. Instead the examiner obtains as much detail as possible from which to judge the subject's performance in regard to a number of age-related behaviors. When older individuals are being evaluated, information may be obtained from the subjects themselves.

The VSMS includes 117 items scaled in order of difficulty and arranged according to 17 age levels, from 0–1 to 25+. These items cover 6 broad categories: Self-Help (general, eating, and dressing); Self-Direction; Occupation; Communication; Locomotion; and Socialization. The areas of Occupation, Locomotion, Communication, and Socialization include behaviors which allow the individual to interact with others, while those of Self-Help and Self-Direction involve the development of independence and freedom. A social age (SA) and a social quotient (SQ) are computed from the subject's ratings on the entire scale.

The VSMS has been used clinically in several ways: (1) to provide a measure of children's social development; (2) to reveal discrepancies among informants; (3) to distinguish between real and psuedo feeblemindedness; (4) to compare a child's level of functioning before and after a crisis; and (5) to appraise levels of social functioning among mentally or physically handicapped individuals. The scale has been particularly valuable in determining whether an individual who is intellectually deficient according to the Stanford-Binet will be able to adjust satisfactorily outside an institution. Though originally developed in 1936, the scale and manual have been revised as recently as 1965.

Sample Items: Items of the following type are included on the VSMS:

Category	Item	Age Level
Self-Help	Washes hands without assistance.	3 to 4
Locomotion	Walks around neighborhood unattended.	4 to 5
Occupation	Helps with minor household chores.	3 to 4
Self-Direction	Can be trusted with money.	5 to 6

Category	Item	Age Level
Communication	Uses the telephone to make calls.	10 to 11
Socialization	Plays cooperatively.	4 to 5

Reliability: Using 123 cases in the standardization sample, Doll obtained a test/retest reliability "across conditions" of .92. Retest intervals varied from 1 day to 9 months.

Validity: Although the validity of the VSMS has been established primarily through age differentiation and expected group differences between normal and retarded subjects, the scale has also been related to other measures of adjustment and maturity.

For example, Cassel (1964) correlated the VSMS social quotients of 800 children with teacher and parent ratings obtained on the Child Behavior Rating Scale, which assesses the personality adjustment of preschool and primary grade pupils. He found a high positive relationship ($r = .37$ to $.48$, $p < .01$) between the 2 ratings. Correlations between the Vineland Scale and the Stanford-Binet, though variable, are generally low enough to suggest that the 2 instruments are measuring different aspects of behavior (Anastasi, 1968).

According to Pedrini and Pedrini (1966), "item analysis and validation through internal-consistency procedures for the normative group are relatively well done through item 89" (p. 16). They suggest, however, that items 90 through 117 involve too much extrapolation, making the VSMS less valid above the level of 15 years. Pedrini and Pedrini also maintain that the VSMS contains some culturally biased items which perhaps favor individuals from a high socioeconomic or culturally advantaged background.

Norms: The VSMS was standardized on 620 subjects, including 10 males and 10 females at each age level, in Vineland, New Jersey, in 1936. Age norms of ratio social quotients are available for this sample.

Administration and Scoring: VSMS interviews and scoring should be conducted by a well trained examiner. An experienced interviewer can complete the scale in 20–30 minutes. The final score is computed from the total number of items which the subject can reportedly perform. In scoring the scale, lack of opportunity to perform certain behaviors and transitional stages of development are both considered. Raw scores are easily converted into social age figures or social quotients.

Comments: The Vineland Social Maturity Scale has been the subject of a great deal of research since its development in 1947. Its constant use has revealed certain weaknesses in the scale: (1) some items must be modified to accommodate children living in apartment houses or rural areas; (2) certain items seem to discriminate against girls; and (3) children in the standardization sample came chiefly from middle-class American homes, while many items have different meanings for children in different socioeconomic or ethnic groups. Yet, in spite of these limitations, the VSMS has proven valuable, particularly in interview and counseling situations. The scale has been used successfully by clinicians to gain insight into an individual's maturational interaction with his social environment.

References: Cassel, R. N., "A comparison of teacher and parent ratings on The Child Behavior Rating Scale for 800 primary pupils." *The Journal of Educational Research*, 1964, **57**, 437–439.

Doll, E. A., *Vineland Social Maturity Scale: Manual of instructions* (rev. ed.). Minneapolis, Minnesota: American Guidance Service, 1965.

Anastasi A., *Psychological testing* (3rd ed.). London: Macmillan Co., 1968.

Pedrini, D. T., and L. N. Pedrini, "The Vineland Social Maturity Scale: Recommendations for administration, scoring, and analysis." *Journal of School Psychology*, 1966, **5**, 14–20.

Name: THE VISUAL ANALYSIS TEST

Author: Jerome Rosner

Type of Measure: Perceptual performance test

Availability: Rosner, J. *The Visual Analysis Test: An initial report.* Pittsburgh: Learning Research and Development Center, The University of Pittsburgh, 1971.

Description: The Visual Analysis (VAT) quantitatively assesses the ability of 5- to 7-year-old children to analyze increasingly complex visual patterns. The VAT represents some of the objectives of the visual-motor component of the Perceptual Skills Curriculum (Rosner, 1969). Test items can thus be used as instructional objectives, with the expectation that competency in the behaviors they measure will be generalized to other, related tasks.

 The test consists of 27 items of varying complexity, each of which presents a pattern of lines drawn on a matrix of dots. The child is told to replicate the pattern on a matching dot matrix. According to Rosner (1971), the child's success in drawing geometric designs demonstrates the extent to which he or she has acquired certain basic skills, such as the ability (1) to discriminate individual graphic elements, (2) to plot spatial relationships between these elements, and (3) to apply mapping rules in reproducing these lines and spatial relationships on a blank space. Thus, the test's objective is to assess the child's visual analysis and synthesis skills, not his or her ability to draw specific geometric designs.

Sample Items: Each of the first 18 items on the VAT consists of a pattern of lines drawn on a matrix of dots. These are accompanied by corresponding dot matrices on which the child reproduces the line patterns. The last 9 items are accompanied by incomplete dot matrices. These item types are similar to the following:

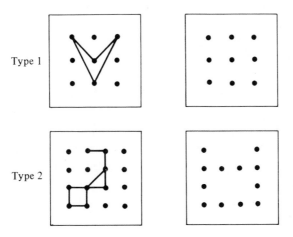

Reliability: A minimum interrater reliability of .98 was established between 3 project staff members scoring the VAT independently (Rosner, 1971).

Validity: The author (Rosner, 1971) presents several indices of the VAT's validity. Data from kindergarten through second-grade subjects in 3 schools shows that the lowest VAT scores were those of the youngest children and the highest, those of the oldest, thus confirming the developmental nature of the task.

Predictive validity was established by comparing VAT scores and performance on the norm-referenced Rutgers Drawing Test. Pearson product-moment correlation coefficients of .80 and .68 were obtained between VAT scores and Rutgers Form A and Form B, respectively.

Rosner, Levine and Simon (1970) report that design board training, using the VAT, was directly related to significant changes in the scores of kindergarten children on the Geometric Design Subtest of the Wechsler Preschool and Primary Scale of Intelligence, which entails design copying. Similarly, Rosner (1970) found that preschool children's copying skills, as measured by the Rutgers Drawing Test, were improved significantly after a period of design board training on the VAT.

Norms: The VAT was originally given to 667 children enrolled in 3 elementary schools in a suburban community in Western Pennsylvania.

Administration and Scoring: The VAT is easily administered and scored. The examiner gives the child a pencil with an eraser and explains that the task is to make the response matrix look like the stimulus matrix. Scoring transparencies are available for all items. If all the subject's lines fit within the correct paths, a score of 2 is given. One point is credited when the terminal points of the matrix are connected correctly, even though the lines may touch or extend beyond the borders of the path. No points are given if the child has connected the wrong terminal points or omitted a line.

Comments: Since visual/motor skills provide insight into one aspect of a child's maturation, the Visual Analysis Test may prove to be a valuable assessment device. Though the author speculates that the VAT is appropriate for children somewhat younger than 5 and older than 7, additional research is needed to support this hypothesis. Meanwhile, this instrument provides a reliable and valid measure of visual analysis skills for children in the age range for which it was designed.

References: Rosner, J., *The design of an individualized skills curriculum*. Pittsburgh: Learning Research and Development Center, The University of Pittsburgh, 1969.

Rosner, J., *Visual analysis training and the copying skills of 4-year-old children*. Pittsburgh: Learning Research and Development Center, The University of Pittsburgh, 1970.

Rosner, J., *The Visual Analysis Test: an initial report*. Pittsburgh: Learning Research and Development Center, The University of Pittsburgh, 1971.

Rosner, J., S. Levine, and D. Simon, *Effect of design board training on the performance scale and subtests of the WPPSI*. Pittsburgh: Learning Research and Development Center, The University of Pittsburgh, 1970.

Name: VOCATIONAL PREFERENCE INVENTORY

Author: John L. Holland

Type of Measure: Checklist

Availability: Holland, J. L., *Vocational preference inventory*. Palo Alto, California: Consulting Psychologists Press, 1965.

Description: The Vocational Preference Inventory (VPI) is a personality scale composed of 160 occupational titles to which the subject responds by indicating those that he likes and dislikes. According to Holland (1965), the inventory yields information about the subject's interpersonal relations, interests, values, self-concept, coping behavior and identifications, on 11 scales: Realistic, Intellectual, Social, Conventional, Enterprising, Artistic, Self-Control, Masculinity, Status, Infrequency, and Acquiescence. Most of these scales were developed through rational/empirical procedures rather than direct empirical methods using defined criterion groups. That is, variables were selected and scales constructed on the basis of a psychological rationale, which is summarized in the following assumptions, taken verbatim from the VPI manual (Holland, 1965).

1. The choice of an occupation is an expressive act which reflects the person's motivation, knowledge, personality, and ability.
2. People tend to see occupational titles and occupations in stereotyped ways.
3. The interaction of the person and his environment creates a number of favorite methods for dealing with interpersonal and environmental problems.
4. The development of adequate adjustive techniques requires accurate discrimination among potential environments.
4a. The total number of preferred occupations is a function of a number of personality variables.
4b. The inability to make discriminations among occupations is indicative of conflict and disorganized self-understanding.
5. Interest inventories are personality inventories.

Scales constructed in terms of this rationale were then tested empirically and modified accordingly. Six such revisions produced 11 relatively homogeneous and independent scales, each containing 14 items, with the exception of Acquiescence and Infrequency which contain 30 and 20 items, respectively.

Although the primary purpose of the VPI is personality assessment, it can also serve as an interest inventory since its content is occupational and its scales approximate those commonly represented on interest tests. Generally, subjects taking the VPI should be at least 14 years old, of normal intelligence, and free of brain damage. Holland (1965) cautions that the VPI should be used and interpreted only in combination with other psychological and sociological information.

Sample Items: The VPI contains 160 occupational titles, similar to those below, to which the subject responds by blackening "yes" or "no" on an answer sheet. If undecided about an occupation, the subject leaves the corresponding space on the answer sheet blank.

1. Airplane pilot
2. Opera singer
3. Palm reader
4. Mortician

Reliability: Coefficients of internal consistency (Kuder-Richardson formula 21) for the sixth revision of the VPI range from .28 (Masculinity) to .86 (Social) for employed adult males, from .57 (Masculinity) to .89 (Intellectual) for college males, and from .50 (Masculinity) to .89 (Intellectual) for college females. Test/retest coefficients for the sixth revision, computed on college student samples, range from .62 (Status) to .98 (Self-Control) over a 6-week interval, and from .61 (Conventional) to .93 (Acquiescence) over a 1-year interval. Coefficients based on data from 2 national mail surveys (rather than supervised test administrations), over a 4-year period, ranged from .41 to .61 for males, and from .27 to .56 for females (Holland, 1965).

Validity: The manual reports explicit evidence of construct and predictive validity which is too extensive to discuss in full. Briefly, the VPI has differentiated normals, psychiatric patients, and psychopaths as well as psychotic and nonpsychotic patients. Some VPI scales are significantly correlated with supervisory ratings of job satisfaction and with student self-ratings of personal traits and abilities, life goals and values, and coping behavior. Correlations between the VPI and a number of other personality inventories support the construct validity of the scales. Factor analysis (Forsyth and Fairweather, 1961) also lends some support to the VPI constructs.

In studies of vocational choice, the VPI has predicted choice of vocation and major field of study for high aptitude students (Holland, 1962). Selected VPI scales have also predicted academic and extracurricular achievement, though somewhat inefficiently (Holland, 1965).

Norms: The manual provides normative data (means and standard deviations) for 18 samples of normal adults and "abnormal" subjects (i.e., drug addicts, psychopaths, psychiatric patients, and tuberculosis patients). In addition, percentile ranks are presented for a sample of 12,433 college freshmen attending 31 colleges in 28 states. Holland (1965), however, recommends the use of local norms whenever possible.

Administration and Scoring: The VPI is self-administering and can be completed in 15 to 30 minutes. All scales, except Acquiescence, are scored by summing "correct" responses according to a scoring key. The Acquiescence score is the total number of "Like" responses to the first 30 items on the inventory.

Comments: The VPI is an extremely well designed instrument supported by a wealth of psychometric information and a clear, well organized manual. One of the instrument's chief assets is its nonthreatening item content, which *appears* unrelated to personal adjustment and therefore reduces the likelihood of "faked" responses. The VPI does have several limitations (e.g., somewhat restricted norms, questionable long-term reliability), but these are generally noted in the manual, which is remarkably straightforward. At this point, most of the research supporting the VPI has been in the area of vocational interest rather than personality measurement.

References: Forsyth, R. P., and G. W. Fairweather, "Psychotherapeutic and other hospital criteria: The dilemma." *Journal of Abnormal and Social Psychology*, 1961, **62**, 598–604.

Holland, J. L., "A theory of vocational choice." *Journal of Counseling Psychology*, 1959, **6**, 35–44.

Holland, J. L., "Some explorations of a theory of vocational choice: I. One- and two-year longitudinal studies." *Psychological Monographs*, 1962, **76**(26, Whole No. 545).

Holland, J. L., *Manual: Vocational Preference Inventory*. Palo Alto, California: Consulting Psychologists Press, 1965.

IIC

About the pupil from an observer

Name: BROPHY-GOOD SYSTEM (TEACHER-CHILD DYADIC INTER-ACTION)

Authors: Jere E. Brophy and Thomas L. Good

Type of Measure: Observation coding system

Availability: Brophy, J. E., and T. L. Good, *Teacher-Child Dyadic Interaction: A manual for coding classroom behavior.* Austin, Texas: Research and Development Center for Teacher Education, The University of Texas, 1969.

Description: The Brophy-Good System (Teacher-Child Dyadic Interaction) differs from most observation coding procedures by recording separately the teacher's interactions with each individual child. Maintaining that it is often inappropriate to treat the class as a unit without regard to intraclass differences in teacher/child contact (Good and Brophy, 1969), the authors have developed a system in which the student, rather than the class, is in the unit of analysis. Every interaction between the teacher and an individual child is coded. Situations in which the teacher addresses the class as a whole are not considered.

The following behavioral categories and coding distinctions are included in the system:

I. Response Opportunities
   A. Direct questions
   B. Open questions
   C. Call-outs
   D. Chorus questions
   E. Discipline questions
   F. Reading turns
   G. Recitation opportunities

II. Level of Question
   A. Process questions
   B. Product questions
   C. Choice questions
   D. Self-reference questions

III. Quality of Child's Response
   A. Correct response
   B. Partially correct response
   C. Incorrect response
   D. No response

IV. Teacher's Feedback Reactions
   A. Praise
   B. Criticism
   C. Product feedback
   D. Process feedback
   E. Repetition of the question
   F. Rephrasing the question
   G. Asking a new question
   H. Failure to provide feedback

V. Work-Related Contacts
   A. Teacher-afforded
   B. Child-created

VI. Behavior Evaluations
   A. Praise
   B. Warning
   C. Criticism

VII. Procedural Contacts
   A. Teacher-afforded
   B. Child-created (Good and Brophy, 1972)

Although the system has been used primarily in elementary classrooms, it is appropriate at all academic levels.

Sample Items: The manual describes behaviors typically recorded under each category. For example, a response opportunity is coded as a call-out only when: (a) the teacher asks a public question; (b) the child calls out an answer to the question before the teacher has a chance to call on anyone to respond; (c) the teacher then turns his or her attention to the child who called out the answer and says something in response.

Each behavioral dimension and the categories it subsumes are explicitly defined and illustrated.

Reliability: Reliability data were collected in normal classrooms by 4 different observers—2 doctoral students in educational psychology and 2 former classroom teachers. The coders reached 80% agreement or better on most categories within 1 or 2 weeks (Good and Brophy, 1972). Therefore, the authors suggest a 2-week training and practice period for observers and recommend specific procedures for insuring adequate intercoder reliability (Brophy and Good, 1969).

Validity: According to Brophy and Good (1969), since the system involves objective coding of observable behavior, content validity is automatically ensured if recommended procedures are applied.

Although no evidence of criterion-related validity is provided in the manual, the authors report in a more recent publication (Good and Brophy, 1972) that the instrument has uncovered some specific ways in which teachers differentially treat students for whom they have high or low performance expectations.

Norms: No normative data are presented in the manual.

Procedures for Use: The manual provides specific coding procedures for each behavioral category represented in the system, as well as general coding conventions which cut across all categories. This information is supplemented by very detailed instructions for using the 2 recording devices: the General Class Activities Coding Sheet and the Reading and Recitation Turns Coding Sheet.

The amount of time devoted to observation should be tailored to the purpose and context of data collection. Observations are coded continuously, usually on 2 occasions to ensure accuracy.

In order to score the data collected, frequency counts are made for each column on the coding sheets, producing a number of separate summary tabulations for each child. These frequency totals may be converted to percentage scores, which allow the user to compare teacher/child interaction among different individuals and groups. Frequencies and percentages may be used alone or in combination to draw inferences from the data collected.

Comments: The Brophy-Good system has many advantages and few apparent drawbacks. A single coder can record an entire classroom, following very explicit, but comprehensible, instructions provided in the manual. The observations recorded generally preserve the sequential nature of teacher/child interaction, so that the cycles of initiation and reaction are not lost in the coding process. Furthermore, the data collected may be treated individually or in combination. Thus, though the system focuses on teacher/child interaction, it can provide a class perspective when necessary. This instrument is easy to use, adaptable to a variety of research purposes, and capable of producing extensive data.

References: Brophy, J. E., and T. L. Good. *Teacher-Child Dyadic Interaction: A manual for coding classroom behavior*. Austin, Texas: Research and Development Center for Teacher Education, The University of Texas, 1969.

Brophy, J. E., and T. L. Good, *Teacher-student relationships: Causes and consequences*. New York: Holt, Rinehart & Winston, Inc., 1974.

Good, T. L., and J. E. Brophy, *Do boys and girls receive equal opportunity in first grade reading instruction?* Austin, Texas: Research and Development Center for Teacher Education, The University of Texas, 1969.

Good, T. L., and J. E. Brophy, *Teacher-child dyadic interactions: A new method of classroom observation*. Austin, Texas: Research and Development Center for Teacher Education, The University of Texas, 1972.

Good, T. L., and J. E. Brophy, *Looking in classrooms*. New York: Harper & Row, 1973.

Name: DISRUPTIVE BEHAVIOR SCHEDULE

Authors: Wesley C. Becker, Charles H. Madsen, Jr., Carole R. Arnold, and Don R. Thomas

Type of Measure: Observation coding system

Availability: Becker, W. C., C. H. Madsen, Jr., C. R. Arnold, and D. R. Thomas, "The contingent use of teacher attention and praise in reducing classroom behavior problems." *Journal of Special Education,* 1967, **1**(3), 287–307.

Description: The Disruptive Behavior Schedule was developed in a study of behavior modification in the elementary school classroom (Becker, Madsen, Arnold, and Thomas, 1967). After "problem" children had been selected for observation, preliminary coding categories were constructed to reflect pupil behaviors which: (1) interfered with classroom learning; (2) violated classroom rules; (3) were considered undesirable by the teacher (e.g., thumbsucking); (4) were similar within categories; (5) were different between categories; and (6) were observable rather than inferred. These categories were tested and revised over a 4-week period to insure that the pupil behaviors represented did in fact occur frequently enough to constitute a problem and be reliably rated. When interrater agreement of at least 80% could not be attained, the category in question was abandoned or redefined. These selection procedures produced the coding categories listed below, 7 of which were applied to each child observed and 4 of which were devised especially for particular children. The final category was included to record each child's "time on task."

A. General Categories of Disruptive Behavior
   1. Gross Motor Behaviors
   2. Disruptive Noise with Objects
   3. Aggression—Disturbing Others Directly
   4. Orienting Responses
   5. Blurting Out, Commenting, and Vocal Noise
   6. Talking
   7. Other
B. Special Categories of Disruptive Behavior
   1. Improper Position
   2. Sucking
   3. Bossing
   4. Ignoring
C. Relevant Behavior

Sample Items: Specific behaviors coded under each category are listed by the authors. For example, Orienting Responses includes "turning head or head and body to look at another person, showing objects to another child, attending to another child (Becker et al., 1967, p. 290)."

Reliability: Since the Disruptive Behavior Schedule has been employed in a number of studies, several estimates of interrater reliability are available. When the instrument was initially used, (Becker et al., 1967), reliabilities above 80% were obtained prior to baseline data collection. Checked periodically thereafter, these rarely fell below 80%. A similar level of interobserver agreement was obtained by O'Leary and Becker (1968), who ran 6 reliability checks, averaging 82%. O'Leary, Becker, Evans, and Saudargas (1969), studying the effects of a token reinforcement program in a public school, conducted numerous reliability checks throughout the various stages of their data collection and obtained interrater agreement figures ranging from 68 to 100%, and averaging well above 80%. Using a modified version of the Disruptive Behavior Schedule, O'Leary, Kaufman, Kass, and Drabman (1970) achieved comparable levels of interobserver reliability. In each of these cases, reliability was determined for each child observed by dividing the number of agreements between 2 observers by the total number of agreements plus disagreements. An agreement was scored if both raters recorded the same behavior within a given interval. A disagreement was scored if one observer recorded the behavior and the other did not.

Validity: Specific evidence of validity is not reported. However, the instrument has in several studies recorded a reduction in disruptive pupil behaviors following the introduction of behavior modification procedures into the classroom (Becker et al., 1967; O'Leary and Becker, 1968; O'Leary et al., 1969; O'Leary et al., 1970; Thomas, Nielsen, Kuypers, and Becker, 1967).

Norms: Normative data are not available.

Procedures for Use: In the initial study by Becker et al. (1967), coders underwent 4 weeks of training, during which time they learned to unobtrusively observe children in the classroom. Working in pairs, they observed target children for 20 minutes a day, 4 days a week. Using stop watches, which they synchronized every 5 minutes, the raters observed for 20 seconds and then took 10 seconds to record the observed behaviors according to a simple code. All data were reported as percentages of the time intervals in which deviant behavior occurred. Because classroom activities varied a great deal from day to day, weekly rather than daily averages were reported.

Comments: The Disruptive Behavior Schedule provides an economical and reliable method of assessing problem behavior in the classroom. With its restricted focus, this instrument offers a limited number of well defined categories and an uncomplicated coding system, which has consistently produced a high percentage of interobserver agreement.

References: Becker, W. C., C. H. Madsen, Jr., C. R. Arnold, and D. R. Thomas, "The contingent use of teacher attention and praise in reducing classroom behavior problems." *Journal of Special Education,* 1967, **1**(3), 287–307.

O'Leary, K. D., and W. C. Becker, "The effects of the intensity of a teacher's reprimands on children's behavior." *Journal of School Psychology,* 1968, **7**, 8–11.

O'Leary, K. D., W. C. Becker, M. B. Evans, and R. A. Saudargas, "A token reinforcement program in a public school: A replication and systematic analysis." *Journal of Applied Behavior Analysis*, 1962, **2**, 3–13.

O'Leary, K. D., K. F. Kaufman, R. E. Kass, and R. S. Drabman, "The effects of loud and soft reprimands on the behavior of disruptive students." *Exceptional Children*, 1970, **37**(2), 145–155.

Thomas, D. A., L. J. Nielsen, D. S. Kuypers, and W. C. Becker, "Social reinforcement and remedial instruction in the elimination of a classroom behavior problem." *Journal of Special Education*, 1967, **2**(3), 291–302.

Name: EMMERICH CLASSROOM OBSERVATION RATING SCALE

Author: Walter Emmerich

Type of Measure: Observer rating scale

Availability: This instrument may be obtained from Walter Emmerich, Educational Testing Service, Princeton, New Jersey 08540.

Description: This observation instrument assesses the personal/social behavior of preschool and kindergarten children. Two paraprofessionals observe a child independently in a play situation in which the subject is relatively free of adult control and formal teaching. Their observations are compared and combined to form a consensus rating for each child. The behaviors observed are arranged on 21 bipolar scales and 127 unipolar scales. The former assess broad personality dimensions, while the latter measure more specific behavior characteristics. This procedure links the more global dimensions of personality to precise behavioral cues. The observer rates the child first on the unipolar scales and then on the bipolar scales, deriving the more general judgments from the initial unipolar ratings.

The Emmerich Scale was developed in the Educational Testing Service/Head Start Longitudinal Study (Emmerich, 1971) to extend the general understanding of personal/social development, and to suggest ways in which Head Start and other compensatory educational programs might become more effective. The scale did in fact record global changes in the personal/social behavior of Head Start children over the school year. Most of these changes were consistent with accepted socialization goals for children of preschool and kindergarten age.

Sample Items: The 127 unipolar scales employ the following rating steps: (0) totally absent; (1) occasionally present; (2) frequently present; and, (3) continually present. Items similar to those below appear on the unipolar scales.

1. Seeks physical closeness to other children.
2. Often repeats verbal statements.
3. Exhibits poor physical coordination.

The 21 bipolar scales (the opposite ends of which are labelled X and Y) employ 7 rating steps: (1) extremely X, (2) considerably X, (3) slightly more X than Y, (4) X no more than Y, (5) slightly Y, (6) considerably Y, and (7) extremely Y. Behaviors of the following type appear on these scales.

        Reserved— — — — — —Outgoing
Socially Confident— — — — — —Shy, Timid

Reliability: Median scale scores of rater pairs who simultaneously observed at least 20 children were correlated yielding Pearson product-moment coefficients of .63 for the bipolar scales and .74 for the unipolar scales. These figures represent a composite of all raters, locations, and time periods. Median interrater reliabilities for individual observation sites and periods are reported by Emmerich (1971).

Validity: Evidence of validity for the Emmerich Scale is derived from the ETS/Head Start Longitudinal Study. Data from that study revealed expected group differences among the children observed. For example, younger children were rated more often than older children as submissive, withdrawn, and distrusting ($p < .05$). Similarly, cognitive activity was greater among the older subjects ($p < .05$). The scale also revealed significantly more masculine behavior among boys than girls ($p < .001$).

In addition to these group differences, the Emmerich ratings recorded changes in the children's behavior which signified a developmental trend toward more outgoing and independent behaviors. Autonomous achievement, for example, increased markedly ($p < .001$) over the year.

Norms: This test was standardized on children in the larger ETS/Head Start Longitudinal Study, all of whom were attending preschool in one of 3 sites (Portland, Oregon; St. Louis, Missouri; and Trenton, New Jersey) during the 1969–1970 academic year. Two fall ratings were obtained for 415 children, and a fall and spring rating for 596 children. Normative data for these groups are presented by Emmerich (1971). Included in these figures are mean scale differences by sex of child, age at entry into the program, and length of time in the program.

Procedures for Use: In using this scale, two trained raters simultaneously observe the target child continuously for 25 to 30 minutes during a "free play" period. The examiners independently rate the child on all scales and afterward discuss those scales on which their ratings differ, with the aim of arriving at a consensus rating for each scale. The bipolar scales call for a judgment regarding the relative strength of the attributes represented on each pole, while the unipolar scales require an estimate of the frequency of occurrence of 127 behaviors.

Comments: Although this instrument already appears to provide a fairly reliable measure of personal/social behavior among preschoolers, Emmerich (1971) suggests several ways to improve the unipolar and bipolar scales. If these improvements are made, the scale should effectively assess the success of preschool learning programs in developing appropriate personal/social behaviors in children.

References: Emmerich, W., "Personality development and concepts of structure." *Child Development*, 1968, **39**, 671–690.

Emmerich, W., *Disadvantaged children and their first school experiences. Structure and development of personal-social behaviors in preschool settings.* ETS/Head Start Longitudinal Study. Princeton, New Jersey: Educational Testing Service, 1971.

Name: FELS CHILD BEHAVIOR SCALES

Author: Fels Research Institute

Type of Measure: Observation rating scale

Availability: Fels Research Institute, Yellow Springs, Ohio. This instrument appears in: Richards, T. W., and M. P. Simons, "The Fels child behavior scales." *Genetic Psychology Monographs*, 1941, **24**, 259–309.

Description: The Fels Child Behavior Scales use observer ratings to measure personality traits in preschool children. Thirty scales assess 30 traits determined important in the longitudinal development of children, among them: Aggressiveness, Conformity, Cruelty, Friendliness, Leadership, Suggestibility, Social Apprehensiveness, and Vigor of Activity. After observing a child for a period of time, an examiner rates him or her on each trait, according to specified behavior cues and guidelines. The rater also indicates on a 5-point scale the consistency and saliency of each trait and his confidence in each scoring decision. While scores for individual traits may be correlated, no total "personality" score is computed. The authors suggest, however, that the scales measure certain general areas, including Desirability of Maturity of Behavior, Antagonism or Aggression, and Introversion/Extroversion (Richards and Simons, 1941).

Though designed for preschoolers, many of the Fels Scales may be used with older children, in settings other than the nursery school.

Sample Items: Each item presents a detailed definition or description of a particular trait, followed by 5 behavior cues. These cues represent varying amounts of the trait defined. The rater selects the cue which best describes the child's manifestation of the trait. Behavior cues of the following type are used:

Trait: Aggressiveness (an attempt to dominate social groups, to be the leader— regardless of success)

Cue 1: Child is bossy and continually tries to dominate others.

Cue 2: Child is usually bossy, but will take submissive role if older child or adult is directing a game.

Cue 3: When child feels that he is in a position of authority (taking care of a younger child or directing a game familiar only to him), he is aggressive.

Cue 4: Child shows very little aggressiveness.

Cue 5: Child shows no aggressiveness. He either follows or ignores others.

Reliability: Statistical evidence of interrater reliability is based on 2 groups of approximately 35 children, ages 22 to 72 months. Pearson correlations (corrected by the Spearman-Brown formula) were computed for all pairs of observers for each scale. The highest mean correlations between observers ranged from .77 for Curiosity to .98 for Quarrelsomeness. Mean interrater correlations for all scales combined ranged from .64 to .86.

The Fels Institute has conducted a number of reliability analyses and concluded that a scale will have satisfactory reliability if the following conditions are met: (1) a child's final score represents the average of 3 ratings; (2) the final rating is based on at least 1 month of observations; and (3) the raters are familiar with the child.

Validity: The validity of these scales has been determined in several different ways. The authors report Pearson intercorrelations for 29 of the scales, based on a sample of 40 children. Several of these were quite high, producing 3 prominent clusters of behavior: (1) Vigor, Frequency of Activity, and Fearlessness; (2) Aggressiveness, Gregariousness, Leadership, Competitiveness, and the reverse of Social Apprehensiveness; and (3) Suggestibility, Obedience, Conformity, Emotional Control, and the reverse of Resistance and of Cruelty (Richards and Simon, 1941).

The Fels Scales have also been correlated with external criteria, including; chronological age, Stanford-Binet IQ, Merrill-Palmer sigma score, and Vineland Social Maturity Quotients. Pearson coefficients indicated that Fels traits related to age were those associated with mature social or intellectual behavior. Except for jealousy, there appeared to be no relation between age and those traits the authors considered "emotional." Correlations with the Stanford-Binet and Merrill-Palmer scores showed little relationship between the 30 behavior scales and intelligence. The Fels scales showing the highest correlations with Vineland Social Maturity Quotients were Vigor of Activity (.35), Frequency of Activity (.33), and Resistance (.31).

Baldwin (1948) correlated the Fels ratings of 67 4-year-old children with the scores of their parents on the Fels Parent Behavior Rating Scales. He found that freedom and permissiveness in the home, combined with a high level of interaction between parent and child, were associated with active, outgoing and spontaneous behavior among children.

Norms: Mean scores and standard deviations for all 30 scales are reported for 2 groups, each composed of 35 children who attended the Fels Nursery School from 1938 to 1940 (Richards and Simons, 1941).

Administration and Scoring: The authors advise that these scales be used only after the child has been observed for at least 2 weeks in a preschool setting. Examiners are encouraged to rate each child in comparison to others in the group and to evaluate all the subjects on one trait before advancing to another trait. In using the scales, the rater indicates the degree to which the child exhibits a trait by checking the appropriate point on a rating line punctuated by 5 behavioral cues. Each rating line is 90 millimeters long, and the child's score for a given trait is the number of millimeters preceding the rater's check mark. Additional scores, determined on a 5-point scale, are included to indicate the consistency of the trait, its importance in relation to the child's total behavioral pattern, and the certainty with which it was rated.

Comments: Though developed over 3 decades ago, the Fels Child Behavior Scales still serve as a useful tool in measuring important personality traits in preschool children. The face validity of these scales has not been adversely affected by the passage of time. The authors thoroughly report the development and design of this test and present extensive evidence of validity and reliability (Richards and Simon, 1941). However, further research, using larger samples of children, would help to ascertain the test's true significance.

References: Baldwin, A. F., "Socialization and parent-child relationship." *Child Development*, 1948, **19**(3), 127–136.

Richards, T. W., and M. P. Simons, "The Fels child behavior scales." *Genetic Psychology Monographs*, 1941, **24**, 259–309.

Walker, D. K., *Socio-emotional measures for preschool and kindergarten children.* San Francisco: Jossey-Bass, 1973.

Name: OBSERVATION PROCEDURE FOR RECORDING THE PHYSI-
CAL CONTACTS OF NURSERY SCHOOL CHILDREN

Authors: Dorothy S. Thomas and associates

Type of Measure: Observation coding system

Availability: This instrument is fully described in: Thomas, D. S., et al., "Some
new techniques for studying social behavior." *Child Development Monographs*,
1929, **1**.

Description: This instrument is one of several developed by Dorothy Thomas
and her associates (1929) in an early attempt to study classroom interaction
through systematic observation. It requires an observer to record the physical
contacts made and received by each child in the class as well as the responses
to these contacts. These observations are coded according to the following
categories:

I. Contacts Made and Received
   A. Accident
   B. Support
   C. Assistance
   D. Caress
   E. Exploration
   F. Pointing
   G. Hitting
   H. Pushing
   I. Pulling

II. Responses to Contacts
   A. Cooperation
   B. Resistance
   C. Flight
   D. Passivity

Observations collected may be used individually as a measure of each child's
physical contacts or in combination as an index of classroom activity.

Sample Items: Behaviors to be coded under each category are listed by the
authors (Thomas et al., 1929). For example, included under "Hitting" are the
following actions: striking with the hand, foot, fist, or an object; biting; and
throwing sand at another child. These and other behaviors are coded on the
form appearing on the following page.

Reliability: To determine the consistency of the data collected (and the reliability
of the observers), the ratio of contacts made to those received was calculated
directly and indirectly for each of 13 children, and the 2 ratios were compared.
That is, the ratio computed from the child's own record was correlated with that
computed from data taken from the records of other children. The resulting
Pearson r was .50 $\pm$ .14.

    Data on each child, collected from the other children's records were also
analyzed separately. The contacts involving each child were numbered serially,
and subject/object ratios were calculated for odd and even numbered contacts.

PHYSICAL CONTACTS RECORD[1]

Children Present _____   Time _____   Date _____

Child Observed _____   Observer _____

Activity	As Subject											Type of Reaction								As Object											
	Accident		Aggression			Cooperation (R = requested) (G = game)						Cooper-ation		Resist-ance		Flight		Pass-ive		Accident		Aggression			Cooperation (R = requested) (G = game)						
	Accident	Support	Hits	Pulls	Push	Assistance	Caress	Explores	Points			S	O	S	O	S	O	S	O	Accident	Support	Pulls	Hits	Push	Assistance	Caress	Explores	Points			

[1]From Thomas, D. S., et al. Some new techniques for studying social behavior. *Child Development Monographs*, 1929, 1, p. 57.

These were correlated, and a coefficient of .79 ± .06 was obtained (Thomas et al., 1929).

Validity: No conclusive evidence of validity is provided (Thomas et al., 1929). Data collected did, however, differentiate individuals according to the ratio of contacts made to those received. While ratios for most children approximated 1, there were also clearly differentiated extremes: one group of children made twice as many contacts as they received and another received twice as many as they made. Other individual differences were found, but the authors considered the data from which they emerged too limited and unreliable to justify generalizations or conclusions.

Norms: Normative data are provided for 18 nursery school children, each of whom was observed for 30 to 60 minutes in 1928.

Procedures for Use: Thomas and her associates (1929) recorded the behavior of each child individually. Observers collected a number of brief, continuous accounts of behavior which were later interpreted and transferred onto the Physical Contacts Record. These brief accounts were similar to the one below made for a child named Diana.

/Acc. Agnes/0 Acc. Winifred/0 Push Arnold F/Asst. Connie Coop/

This means that: Diana accidentally touched Agnes, who responded passively; Winifred accidentally touched Diana, who responded passively; Arnold pushed Diana, who fled and then assisted Connie, who cooperated in response. Data such as these were grouped and transferred onto the final tally sheet.

Comments: Like the other instruments developed by Thomas and her associates, this behavior coding procedure is a pioneering attempt to measure classroom behavior through systematic observation. As such, it is less streamlined than its successors. It requires a separate record for each child, taken by a well trained, attentive observer. However, it focuses on a single, well defined aspect of behavior (physical contact) which, though relatively easy to observe, is not generally assessed by other observation coding systems.

References: Medley, D. M., and H. E. Mitzel, "Measuring classroom behavior by systematic observation," in N. L. Gage (ed.), *Handbook of research on teaching.* Chicago: Rand McNally, 1963.

Thomas, D. S., et al., "Some new techniques for studying social behavior." *Child Development Monographs*, 1929, **1.**

Name: OBSERVATION PROCEDURE FOR RECORDING THE SOCIAL-MATERIAL ACTIVITIES OF CHILDREN

Authors: Dorothy S. Thomas and associates

Type of Measure: Observation coding procedure

Availability: This instrument is fully described in: Thomas, D. S., et al., "Some new techniques for studying social behavior." *Child Development Monographs*, 1929, **1**.

Description: The Observation Procedure for Recording the Social-Material Activities of Children is the work of Dorothy Thomas and her associates (1929), who were among the first to assess classroom interaction through systematic observation. This instrument requires observers to record and time each child's activity as he interacts with materials and persons. The actual progress of the child as he moves from person to person and from thing to thing is mapped on a floor plan. Data obtained from these records yield several indices of social behavior: amount of time spent on each activity; number of contacts with things vs. contacts with people; and gross activity.

    After data are collected on the floor plans, they are classified according to the following revised categories:

I. Material   vs.   II. Nonmaterial

I. Material	II. Nonmaterial
A. Social	A. Social
1. Observation of material and persons using material	1. Observation of persons
2. Approach to material	2. Approach to persons
3. Contact with material	3. Contact with persons
a) Accidental	a) Accidental
b) Casual	b) Verbal
c) Manipulation of small objects (other persons involved)	c) Physical
d) Use of large objects (other persons involved)	d) Spatial
B. Nonsocial	B. Nonsocial
1. Observation of material	1. No overt reaction
2. Approach to material	2. Vocal reaction
3. Contact with material	3. Muscular reaction
a) Accidental	
b) Casual	
c) Manipulation of small objects	
d) Use of large objects	

Sample Items: A typical floor plan, on which an observer has recorded the child's activity for a 5-minute period, is represented below. Solid lines indicate spontaneous movement, while broken lines stand for directed activity. The letters and figures on the floor plan symbolize duration of activity, presence of other children, and so forth, according to a predetermined code.

Child Activity Record[1]

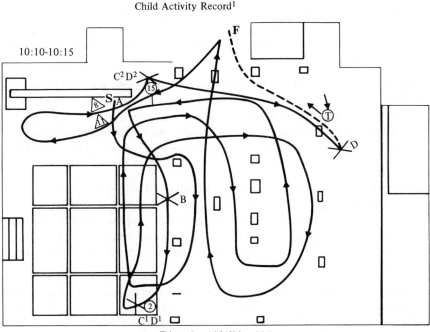

Edward — 12/6/28 — M.B.

AB — Trying to take cover from Alma to give to Ruth.	35″	C^1D^1 — Katherine says, "You knocked me down." He looks.	7″
CD — One foot on tricycle, pushing it with other. Then Henry comes up and sits on it and Henry pushes him. Falls off but doesn't cry. Gets on again.	243″	C^2D^2 — Looks at Ruth who is crying. Goes downstairs at end of five minute period.	10″

Reliability: To determine interobserver agreement, 16 children were observed for 20 5-minute intervals by 4 observers working in 6 different teams of 2. Reliability data, then, were derived from 324 records. The observations collected were correlated, and Pearson product-moment coefficients were computed to measure several dimensions of interobserver consistency. These ranged from .97 to .98 for space covered by the child; .92 to .98 for duration of activities; .63 to .89 for time of activities according to length of observation; and .47 to .80 for number of social contacts (Thomas et al., 1929).

[1] From Thomas, D. S., et al., "Some new techniques for studying social behavior." *Child Development Monographs*, 1929, **1**, p. 45.

Validity: Evidence of validity is limited. However, some validity may perhaps be inferred from correlations between mental age (measured on the Kuhlman-Binet test) and various indices of social and material activity obtained using this observation system. These data indicate that for 2- to 3-year-old children there is little relationship between mental age and number of activities, activities involving material objects, or space covered. There is, however, a small positive relationship between mental age and number of social contacts, and a strong positive relationship between space covered and number of activities per unit of time (Thomas et al., 1929).

Norms: The sample used by Thomas and her associates was composed of 16 children, aged 2 to 3 years, who were observed for 20 5-minute periods. For each of these children the following data are available: number of activities per unit of time; number of social contacts; space covered; proportion of time spent on material objects; and percentage of time spent on various activities (Thomas et al., 1929).

Procedures for Use: The space covered by each child within a 5-minute period is observed and mapped on a floor plan drawn to scale. Colored pencils and a simple activity code are used to indicate the child's progress from one person or object to another. Coded activities are then classified according to the nature of the social or material contact. These data may then be converted to frequencies or percentages.

Comments: Although developed in 1929, this observation procedure offers a unique method of studying children's behavior. It provides a comprehensive picture of each child's social/material activity, though it requires a good deal of effort on the observer's part. Since coding procedures are relatively complicated, observers must be carefully trained. Furthermore, because a record is made for each child, a relatively large number of observers may be needed.

References: Medley, D. M., and H. E. Mitzel, "Measuring classroom behavior by systematic observation," in N. L. Gage (ed.), *Handbook of research on teaching.* Chicago: Rand McNally, 1963.

Thomas, D. S., et al., "Some new techniques for studying social behavior." *Child Development Monographs,* 1929, **1**.

Name: PRESCHOOL OBSERVATION SCHEDULE

Authors: Thomas V. Busse, Malcolm Ree, and Marilyn Gutride.

Type of Measure: Observation coding system

Availability: Busse, T. V., M. Ree, and M. Gutride, "Environmentally enriched classrooms and the play behavior of Negro preschool children." *Urban Education*, 1970, **5**(2), 128–140.

Description: The Preschool Observation Schedule (POS) was developed to assess the social interaction of children in enriched and nonenriched environments (Busse, Ree, and Gutride, 1970). The POS measures 2 dimensions of the preschool child's activity: play and aggressive behavior. These dimensions are assessed according to the following categories:

I. Approaches to Play
  A. Solitary Play
  B. Parallel Play
  C. Cooperative Toy Play
     (equipment-centered)
  D. Cooperative Peer Play
     (peer-centered)
  E. Isolation
  F. Other

II. Aggressive Behavior
  A. Personal Physical Attack
  B. Taunting
  C. Threatening
  D. Destroying Property of
     Another's Labor
  E. Usurping Property
  F. No Aggressive Behavior

Sample Items: The authors (Busse et al., 1970) list specific behaviors recorded under each POS category. For example, Personal Physical Attack, includes hitting, biting, scratching, spitting, pushing, or shoving. Cooperative Peer Play refers to interaction with another child or other children in an activity in which no toys are involved.

Reliability: Interrater reliability figures are provided for both dimensions of the POS. Two observers' ratings of 30 half-minute intervals of play behavior agreed 74.8% of the time for 15 randomly selected boys and 79.7% of the time for 15 randomly selected girls. The corresponding figures for ratings of aggressive behavior were 97.3% and 97.7% (Busse et al., 1970).

Validity: Spearman rank-order intercorrelations of the play variables and the overall frequency of aggressive behavior provide some evidence of the validity of the POS. For boys, the frequency of Cooperative Toy Play correlated negatively with the frequency of both Solitary Play ($-.45$, $p < .01$) and Parallel Play ($-.62$, $p < .01$). The frequency of girls' Cooperative Toy Play was positively related to the frequency of Cooperative Peer Play ($.40$, $p < .05$) and negatively related to the frequency of Solitary Play ($-.37$, $p < .05$). Also, among girls the frequency of Cooperative Peer Play correlated $.56$ ($p < .01$) with the frequency of Aggressive Behavior (Busse et al., 1970).

Norms: Medians and semi-interquartile ranges for the play variables and overall aggressiveness are reported separately for each sex. (Because of low frequencies, aggressive behaviors were combined to form a single category.) These figures are based on a sample of 74 black children, including 37 males and 37 females with a median age of 4 years, 7 months. Approximately half of the children in each sex group were observed in an enriched preschool environment and half in a nonenriched atmosphere.

Procedures for Use: In the study by Busse et al. (1970), children were individually observed on the POS during free play for 3 15-minute periods separated by 1-month intervals. Each 15-minute observation was divided into 30 half-minute units. The type of play or aggressive behavior occurring during each 30-second period was recorded on a tally sheet as present or absent. Results were reported as frequency counts.

Comments: The Preschool Observation Schedule offers an uncomplicated method of observing and recording social interaction among children. Requiring little training and low inference on the observer's part, the POS is very easy to use and score. Furthermore, it demonstrates good interrater reliability, especially for the dimension of aggressive behavior. However, evidence of criterion-related validity is needed.

Reference: Busse, T. V., M. Ree, and M. Gutride, "Environmentally enriched classrooms and the play behavior of Negro preschool children." *Urban Education,* 1970, **5**(2), 128–140.

Section III

IIIA

About the classroom from the teacher

Name: BUREAUCRACY SCALE

Authors: Michael Aiken and Jerald Hage

Type of Measure: Rating scale

Availability: Aiken, M., and J. Hage, "Organizational alienation: A comparative analysis." *American Sociological Review*, 1966, **31**, 497–507.

Description: This instrument consists of four separate measures developed by Aiken and Hage (1966) which have been unified and labeled the Bureaucracy Scale (Grassie and Carss, 1972). These 4 components, or indices, were designed to assess organizational centralization and formalization. A companion instrument, the Satisfaction Scale (reviewed in this volume), was also developed to measure employee alienation. Two of the 4 components of the Bureaucracy Scale, a 4-item Index of Participation and 5-item Index of Hierarchy of Authority, assess centralization. The former reflects the degree of employee participation in making decisions which affect the entire organization, such as those involving the adoption of new programs or the hiring and promotion of new personnel, while the latter indicates the extent of reliance upon supervisors in performing individually assigned tasks. Items on the Index of Hierarchy of Authority were derived from a factor analysis of 21 items on a measure of organizational characteristics reported by Hall (1961). The factor analytic structure of these items also yielded several other discrete dimensions, 2 of which served as the basis for the remaining components of the Bureaucracy Scale—a 5-item Index of Job Codification and a 2-item Index of Rule Observation. Both of these scales measure formalization, i.e., the degree to which employees must consult rules in performing professional responsibilities and the extent to which they are observed for rule violations.

Although the Bureaucracy Scale was originally administered in social welfare agencies, it is applicable to a variety of formal organizations, including schools and school districts. It has been successfully used with teachers in a study of school structure, leadership quality, and teacher satisfaction (Grassie and Carss, 1972).

Sample Items: The following are items similar to those on each part of the Bureaucracy Scale:

Scale	Item	Response Format
I. Index of Participation in Decision-Making	How frequently are you involved in decisions to hire new staff members?	1 (never) to 5 (always)

II. Index of Hierarchy of Authority	I must consult my boss before taking action on almost any matter.	1 (definitely false) to 4 (definitely true)
III. Index of Job Codification	Each employee generally decides for himself how his work should be done.	1 (definitely true) to 4 (definitely false)
IV. Index of Rule Observation	Employees here are closely watched for rule violations.	1 (definitely false) to 4 (definitely true)

Reliability: The authors present no information on the reliability of the Bureaucracy Scale (Aiken Hage, 1966).

Validity: Validity information is also scarce, though some construct validity may be inferred from correlations among the Scale's 4 indices and between these indices and measures of alienation derived from the Satisfaction Scale. For example, there is a strong inverse relationship ($r = -.55$) between the Index of Participation in Decision-Making and the Index of Hierarchy of Authority. Other correlations which fall in the expected direction are: .49 between Hierarchy of Authority and Alienation from Work; $-.26$ between Participation in Decision-Making and Rule Observation; $-.59$ between Participation in Decision-Making and Alienation from Work; .51 between Job Codification and Alienation from Work; and .65 between Rule Observation and Alienation from Expressive Relations (Aiken and Hage, 1966).

Norms: The Scale was originally administered to professional and supervisory personnel in 16 social welfare agencies located in a large city in the midwestern United States (Aiken and Hage, 1966). It has since been administered to 441 teachers in 14 high schools in Brisbane, Australia (Grassie and Carss, 1972).

Administration and Scoring: The Bureaucracy Scale is brief and easy to administer. Scores range from 1 to 4 on all indices except Participation in Decision Making, which has a range of 1 to 5. Low score values indicate a relatively low degree of participation, reliance on supervisors, formalization, or rule observation. An organizational score for each variable is determined by averaging the scores of all respondents at a particular professional level and then computing the mean of these averages. Responses are standardized by occupational position and then combined to form an organizational score. This procedure is intended to avoid giving undue weight to the responses of employees lower in the organizational hierarchy.

Comments: Although its brevity, careful construction, and wide application are assets, the Bureaucracy Scale suffers from a scarcity of validity, reliability, and normative data.

References: Aiken, M., and J. Hage, "Organizational alienation: A comparative analysis." *American Sociological Review*, 1966, **31**, 497–507.

Grassie, M. C., and B. W. Carss, "School structure, leadership quality, and teacher satisfaction." *Educational Administration Quarterly*, 1972, **9**(1), 15–26.

Hall, R. H., *An empirical study of bureaucratic dimensions and their relation to other organizational characteristics*. Unpublished doctoral dissertation, Ohio State University, 1961.

Name: GROUP DIMENSIONS DESCRIPTION QUESTIONNAIRE

Author: John K. Hemphill

Type of Measure: Rating scale

Availability: This instrument may be obtained from the Educational Testing Service, Princeton, New Jersey   08540.

Description: The Group Dimensions Description Questionnaire measures 13 dimensions, which, according to Hemphill (1956), characterize groups. In developing the instrument, 1,100 items were classified into 13 categories. After extensive item analyses to insure internal consistency within categories and mutual independence between categories, 150 statements were retained for inclusion on the questionnaire. These items represent the following dimensions:

1. *Autonomy*—the extent to which the group functions independently;
2. *Control*—the degree to which a group regulates the behavior of its members;
3. *Flexibility*—informality of group procedures;
4. *Hedonic Tone*—the extent to which group membership is characterized by friendly or pleasant feelings;
5. *Homogeneity*—the degree of similarity among members;
6. *Intimacy*—the degree of mutual acquaintance among members;
7. *Participation*—the amount of effort and time which members apply to group activities;
8. *Permeability*—access to membership;
9. *Polarization*—the degree to which a group works toward a single goal;
10. *Potency*—the importance of the group to its members;
11. *Stability*—persistence of the group over time;
12. *Stratification*—the degree to which the group orders its members into status hierarchies; and
13. *Viscidity*—the extent to which group members act as a unit.

Sample Items: The Group Dimensions Description Questionnaire contains statements of the type below, to which subjects respond on a 1-to-5 scale, from "Definitely True" to "Definitely False":

1. Some members of the group express hostility toward other members.
2. The group has one primary purpose.
3. Members of the group do favors for one another.

Reliability: Estimates of internal consistency were obtained from several diverse populations. Split-half reliabilities ranged from .28 (Hedonic Tone) to .92

(Autonomy) across samples. Median coefficients were generally in the .70s (Hemphill, 1956).

Validity: One study of predictive validity is reported in the manual (Hemphill, 1956). Two confederates were assigned to two 4-man laboratory groups. In one group, the confederates were accepting and cooperative; in the other, they were rejecting and uncooperative. Group members were administered the Group Dimensions Description Questionnaire, and their responses revealed expected differences on the dimensions of Viscidity (4.5 stanines difference) and Hedonic Tone (4 stanines difference).

Norms: Normative data, collected in 1949, are provided on 950 subjects, in 5 subsamples. Sample 1 contained 100 college-age individuals who described military units, sororities, fraternities, and other groups. Sample 2 was composed of the faculty of a liberal arts college. Sample 3 consisted of 185 female office employees who described work groups, and Sample 4 contained 215 college students whose responses applied to religious groups affiliated with a large university. Sample 5, 320 elementary and secondary school teachers, described 45 school staffs.

Administration and Scoring: This questionnaire is self-administering. Answers are recorded on an IBM answer sheet which may be hand or machine scored. Response alternatives are assigned values ranging from 1 to 5, the direction of scoring depending on the positive or negative wording of the item. Thirteen scores are produced, one for each dimension. The manual (Hemphill, 1956) provides normalized scores, expressed as stanines, and a key for converting raw scores into stanines.

Comments: The Group Dimensions Description Questionnaire suffers from dated and somewhat limited norms (the author cautions that they should not be considered representative of the general population) and insufficient validity information. While the more reliable dimensions can probably be used with confidence, the instrument as a whole should be interpreted with caution.

References: Hemphill, J. K., *Group dimensions: A manual for their measurement.* Columbus, Ohio: Bureau of Business Research, Ohio State University, 1956.

Moran, G., and A. J. Klockhars, "Favorability of group atmosphere and group dimensionality." *Psychological Reports*, 1968, **22**, 3–6.

Name: ORGANIZATION DESCRIPTION QUESTIONNAIRE

Authors: Robert J. House and John R. Rizzo

Type of Measure: Rating scale

Availability: This instrument may be obtained from Dr. Robert J. House, Faculty of Management Studies, University of Toronto, 246 Bloor Street West, Toronto, Ontario, Canada   M5S 1V4.

Description: The Organization Description Questionnaire (ODQ) was designed to assess various internal organizational and managerial practices. Developed in a study of a heavy equipment manufacturing firm (House and Rizzo, 1972b), this measure was based on (1) interviews with selected managerial and professional employees, and (2) current literature and research concerning organic mechanistic organization structure (Burns and Stalker, 1961; Lawrence and Lorsch, 1967) and Theory X-Theory Y Leadership (McGregor, 1960).
   ODQ items are arranged on the following scales:

1. Conflict and Inconsistency
2. Decision Delay
3. Emphasis on Analytic Method
4. Emphasis on Personal Development
5. Formalization
6. Goal Consensus and Clarity
7. Communication Adequacy
8. Information Distortion and Suppression
9. Job Pressure
10. Adequacy of Planning
11. Provision for Horizontal Coordination
12. Selection on Ability and Performance
13. Tolerance of Error
14. Top Management Receptiveness
15. Upward Information Requirements
16. Adherence to Chain of Command
17. Work Flow Coordination
18. Adaptability
19. Adequacy of Authority

Although developed for use in business organizations, the ODQ could, with minor revision, be administered in school systems. In that setting, however, item content would be most applicable to school administrators and nonteaching personnel.

Sample Items: ODQ items describe various organizational characteristics or conditions. The respondent rates each statement twice, first according to its truth and then according to the desirability of the condition described. Ratings are made on a 7-point scale, from "Definitely Not True" to "Extremely True" or from "Extremely Undesirable" to "Extremely Desirable." Items of the following type are included on the questionnaire.

Scale	*Item*
Formalization	My work is guided by schedules, policy statements, or program descriptions.
Upward Information Requirements	My superiors require detailed reports of my job activities.
Job Pressure	There is not enough time, or help, to complete the work required of me.

Reliability: Kuder-Richardson reliabilities, corrected by the Spearman-Brown formula, were computed for each ODQ scale on 2 samples: (1) 199 office, plant, research and engineering employees; and (2) 91 research and engineering personnel. These ranged from .28 (Job Pressure) to .86 (Conflict and Inconsistency) for the first sample, and from .48 (Job Pressure) to .86 (Work Flow Coordination) for the second group (House and Rizzo, 1972b). More recent analyses indicate that all of the scales demonstrate internal reliability greater than .70 (House, 1975).

Intercorrelations among ODQ scales suggest moderate independence, with common variance (r^2) ranging from .00 to .48 (House and Rizzo, 1972b).

Validity: Eight of the 19 ODQ scales were validated against 8 criterion variables measuring role conflict and ambiguity, employee satisfaction, and leader behavior. It was assumed that this subset of ODQ scales should measure environmental characteristics also reflected by scores on the criterion scales. Using an adaptation of the Campbell and Fiske (1959) technique, the authors applied 4 tests of convergent and discriminant validity and found relationships between ODQ and criterion scales which indicated the construct validity of the ODQ. The Job Pressure and Tolerance of Error scales, however, were found to have relatively weak claims to validity (House and Rizzo, 1972b).

Norms: Means and standard deviations for the 2 samples used in the reliability studies are reported by House and Rizzo (1972b).

Administration and Scoring: The ODQ is easily administered and scored. The authors suggest that participation be voluntary and respondents be assured anonymity.

Comments: The 19 subscales of the Organization Description Questionnaire provide good coverage of organizational properties and managerial practices. Though this instrument is relatively new and has not yet been widely used, preliminary analyses indicate that it has some construct validity. The authors warn, however, that these analyses may have been affected by systematic, selective bias and suggest that other methods of validation be applied to the ODQ in order to substantiate its claim to validity. This instrument would require some minor modifications for use in schools or school systems.

References: Burns, T., and G. M. Stalker, *The management of innovation.* London: Tavistock, 1961.

Campbell, D. T. and D. W. Fiske, "Convergent and discriminatory validation by the multitrait-multimethod matrix." *Psychological Bulletin,* 1959, **56**, 81–105.

House, R. J., Personal communication, February 24, 1975.

House, R. J., and J. R. Rizzo, "Role conflict and ambiguity as critical variables in a model of organizational behavior." *Organizational Behavior and Human Performance,* 1972, **7**, 467–505. (a)

House, R. J., and J. R. Rizzo, "Toward the measurement of organizational practices: Scale development and validation." *Journal of Applied Psychology,* 1972, **56**, 388–396. (b)

Lawrence, P. R., and J. W. Lorsch, *Organization and environment.* Boston: Harvard University Press, 1967.

McGregor, D., *The human side of enterprise.* New York: McGraw-Hill, 1960.

Name: ORGANIZATIONAL CLIMATE DESCRIPTION QUESTIONNAIRE

Authors: Andrew W. Halpin and Don B. Croft

Type of Measure: Rating scale

Availability: Halpin, A. W., and D. B. Croft, *The organizational climate of schools.* Chicago: Midwest Administration Center, University of Chicago, 1963. This instrument is also available from Don B. Croft, Director, Claude C. Dove Learning Center, College of Education, New Mexico State University, Box 3 AC, Las Cruces, New Mexico, 88001.

Description: The Organizational Climate Description Questionnaire (OCDQ) was designed to assess the organizational climate of elementary schools, though its content appears appropriate for use in secondary schools as well. The OCDQ may be completed by teachers, principals, or other school personnel.

In developing this measure, Halpin and Croft (1963) determined that climate is to the school what personality is to the individual. Thus, the OCDQ bears some resemblance to a personality test. Focusing on perceived social interaction among teachers and between the principal and teachers, it yields scores on a continuum from openness/flexibility to closedness/rigidity.

The OCDQ was developed factor analytically. The authors initially assembled 1,000 items which demonstrated (1) task and socioemotional orientation, (2) social control and need satisfaction, and (3) leader behavior, group behavior, procedural regulation, and personality orientation. These items were screened to 600, pilot tested, and eventually reduced to 80, the first 12 of which request biographical information from the respondent. The remaining 68 items were organized into 8 moderately independent (median intercorrelation = .17) subscales. The first 4 of these subsclaes measure the following aspects of *teacher* behavior: Disengagement (alienation); Hindrance (the degree to which the teacher feels burdened by the principal with bureaucratic chores); Esprit (morale); and Intimacy (positive socioemotional relations among the teachers). The last 4 scales, on the other hand, reflect the *principal's* behavior: Aloofness (formal, impersonal behavior); Production Emphasis (directive, autocratic supervision); Thrust (active, task-oriented behavior); and Consideration. A factor analysis of subtest scores yielded 3 factors: Social Needs, Esprit, and Social Control.

Sample Items: The subject responds to the OCDQ by rating items of the following type on a 4-point scale, from "Rarely occurs" to "Very frequently occurs."

1. The principal sees the teachers every day.
2. The principal arrives at school before the teachers do.
3. A lot of time is wasted at faculty meetings.
4. The teachers socialize with each other outside of school.

Reliability: Split-half reliabilities for the OCDQ subtests range from .26 to .84, with a median of .64, while odd/even respondent subtest correlations fall between .49 and .76, averaging .63.

Though Halpin and Croft (1963) provide no test/retest data, Wilson (1966) reports that the OCDQ scores obtained for 88 Alberta schools changed very little over a 12-month period, suggesting that the instrument possesses some stability.

Validity: The OCDQ has been used in a great number of studies, and therefore a wealth of data bearing on its validity are available.

In regard to construct validity, Andrews (1965) has questioned the value of OCDQ "overall climate" scores, suggesting that they fail to predict anything "that is not better predicted by the subtests (p. 333)." He interprets the OCDQ as a measure of leadership, not climate, noting that the instrument deals primarily with teacher-principal interaction. This interpretation is supported by several studies which have indicated that the principal's own character and personality may largely determine OCDQ scores. Anderson (1965), for example, found a correspondence between principal personality and the openness of school climate, while Ford (1966) found a similar relationship between OCDQ scores and the principal's psychological health, as determined by Shostrom's Personal Orientation Inventory. Furthermore, Helsel, Aurbach, and Willower (1969) found only those subtests assessing perceptions of principal behavior (Aloofness, Thrust, Production Emphasis, and Consideration) or possible effects of his behavior (Hindrance) related to expectations of positive change.

The OCDQ, in addition to discriminating between different groups of principals, has also distinguished innovative from noninnovative schools (Hughes, 1968), middle-class from from lower-class schools (Tremko, 1969), and traditional schools from those with an emergent value orientation (Lupini, 1965).

Evidence of concurrent validity is provided by a great number of studies (reviewed by Brown and House, 1967). These have related the OCDQ to other measures of leader behavior or organizational climate, to academic achievement, to human relations training, and to several personality variables.

Norms: Original normative data are based on a 6-state sample of 1,151 teachers representing 71 schools. More recent norms are provided for a sample of 200,000 subjects.

Administration and Scoring: The OCDQ is self-administering, clear directions being provided on the test booklet. The 8 scale scores can be plotted to form one of 6 "climate profiles," which represent varying degrees of openness.

Comments: The Organizational Climate Description Questionnaire has been accepted and widely used by educational researchers, and thus there has accumulated a wealth of psychometric data concerning this measure. While these data are generally positive, there remains some question about the interpretation of climate scores. This instrument should probably be viewed as a measure of leadership or teacher/pupil interaction rather than climate.

References: Anderson, D. P., *Organizational climate of elementary schools.* Minneapolis: Educational Research and Development Council of the Twin Cities Metropolitan Area, University of Minnesota, 1964.

Andrews, J. H. M., "School organizational climate: Some validity studies." *Canadian Education and Research Digest,* 1965, **5,** 317–334.

Brown, A. F., and J. J. House, "The organizational component in education." *Review of Educational Research,* 1967, **37,** 399–416.

Ford, R. W., *The relationship of psychological health of elementary school principals to the organizational climate of schools.* Unpublished doctoral dissertation, Syracuse University, 1966.

Halpin, A. W., and D. B. Croft, *The organizational climate of schools.* Chicago: Midwest Administration Center, University of Chicago, 1963.

Helsel, A. R., H. A. Aurbach, and D. J. Willower, "Teacher's perceptions of organizational climate and expectations of successful change." *Journal of Experimental Education,* 1969, **38**(2), 39–44.

Hughes, L. W., "'Organizational climate'—another dimension to the process of innovation?" *Educational Administration Quarterly,* 1968, **4**(3), 16–28.

Lupini, D., "Values and social behavior in schools." *Canadian Administrator,* 1965, **5,** 5–8.

Tremko, M. S., *A study of school climate, socio-economic setting and inservice programs.* Unpublished doctoral dissertation, University of Illinois, 1969.

Wilson, W. G., *An analysis of changes in the organizational climates of schools.* Master's thesis, University of Alberta, 1966.

Name: ORGANIZATIONAL CLIMATE INDEX

Authors: George G. Stern and Carl R. Steinhoff

Type of Measure: True-false questionnaire

Availability: Stern, G. G., and C. R. Steinhoff, *Organizational climate index. Form 1163.* Syracuse, New York: Authors, 1963. A copy of this instrument also appears in: Stern, G. G., *People in context.* New York: John Wiley, 1970.

Description: The Organizational Climate Index (OCI) is one in a series of instruments developed by Stern and his associates (see Stern, 1970) to assess individual needs and environmental press. Though originally designed to determine the institutional press experienced by elementary and secondary school teachers, the OCI functions as a generalized measure of organizational climate, which may be applied in a variety of environments. References to students, teachers, and educational policy are avoided.

Derived from the more extensively researched College Characteristics Index (CCI), the OCI, like the other Stern instruments, is based on Murray's (1938) theory that environmental press can be inferred from the daily events occurring within an institution. Accordingly, the 300 OCI items describe procedures, activities, and expectations which characterize organizations. These items cover 30 scales, representing 6 first-order factors, which vary somewhat from sample to sample. Separate analyses, conducted on 3 different populations (school personnel, Peace Corps trainees, and industrial employees), produced 3 very similar 6-factor solutions. That derived from the school group included the following factors: Intellectual Climate; Achievement Standards; Practicalness; Supportiveness; Orderliness; and Impulse Control. In each of the 3 samples, 2 second-order factors, Development Press and Control Press, emerged.

Sample Items: The OCI contains items of the following type which the respondent marks "true" or "false":

1. Employees here are not informed of the standards by which they are rated.
2. If a committee were formed to control conduct and ethics, it would receive a great deal of support.
3. Knowing the right people here makes advancement easier.

Reliability: Scale reliabilities (KR_{20}) are reported for 3 samples: (1) 931 teachers in 43 schools; (2) 2,511 trainees in 63 Peace Corps training units; and (3) 223 industrial workers at 5 sites. These range from .23 to .87, .39 to .79, and .12 to .77, respectively. Factor score reliabilities are much higher, falling between .67 and .98 for the school district sample (Stern, 1970).

Validity: The similarity of the 3 OCI factor solutions to each other and to the factor structure of the parent CCI offers some evidence of construct validity.

Criterion-related validity is indicated by the instrument's ability to differentiate between groups. Elementary and high school climates, for example, were perceived differently on the OCI, the latter being described as colder, less solicitous, less formal, less achievement oriented, and less well organized. Similarly, OCI assessments of Peace Corps training centers were consistent with the centers' contrasting stated administrative policies. Furthermore, school climate, identified through combined analyses of scores on the OCI and the Stern Activities Index, was related to other measures, such as teacher turnover and pupil achievement (Stern, 1970).

Norms: Scale characteristics (including means and standard deviations) are provided for the 3 samples used in the reliability studies.

Administration and Scoring: Directions, printed on the test form, instruct the respondent to answer every item and to work as rapidly as possible. Answers are recorded on an optical scanning sheet, which permits hand or machine scoring. Thirty scale scores, 6 first-order factor scores, and 2 second-order factor scores are produced.

Comments: The Organizational Climate Index, pilot tested in 3 very disparate environments, provides a good, multipurpose measure of institutional press. Though this instrument has not been extensively developed, it is based on Stern's early and more comprehensive work with the CCI. The decision to use this instrument depends to some extent on one's acceptance of its conceptual foundation. Like the other Stern measures, the OCI assumes a relationship between environmental press and personal needs.

References: Murray, H. A., *Explorations in personality.* New York: Oxford University Press, 1938.

Steinhoff, C. R., *Organizational climate in a public school system.* Unpublished doctoral dissertation, Syracuse University, 1965. (a)

Steinhoff, C. R., *Organizational climate in a public school system. Final Report.* USOE Contract No. OE-4-10-225 (Project No. S-083), 1965. (b)

Stern, G. G., *People in context.* New York: John Wiley, 1970.

Name: SATISFACTION SCALE

Authors: Michael Aiken and Jerald Hage

Type of Measure: Rating scale

Availability: Aiken, M., and J. Hage, "Organizational alienation: A comparative analysis." *American Sociological Review*, 1966, **31**, 497–507.

Description: This instrument consists of 2 separate measures developed by Aiken and Hage (1966) which have been unified and labeled the Satisfaction Scale (Grassie and Carss, 1972). These 2 measures—the Index of Work Alienation and the Index of Alienation from Expressive Relations—were designed to assess, respectively, an employee's satisfaction with work and his satisfaction in social relations with supervisors and fellow workers. The items in these indices were derived from a factor analysis of a 13-item work satisfaction scale presented by Gross, Mason, and McEachern (1958).

Although the Satisfaction Scale was originally administered to supervisory and professional staff in social welfare agencies, it is appropriate for personnel in almost all formal organizations, including schools and school districts. It has been successfully used with teachers in a study of school structure, leadership quality, and teacher satisfaction (Grassie and Carss, 1972).

Sample Items: The Satisfaction Scale contains 8 items (6 on the Index of Alienation from Work and 2 on the Index of Alienation from Expressive Relations) of the following type:

Scale	*Item*
Alienation from Work	1. How satisfied are you with your job in relation to your career plans?
	2. How satisfied are you that your superiors accept you as a professional, with specialized knowledge and training?
Alienation from Expressive Relations	1. How satisfied are you with your colleagues?

Reliability: Though no test/retest data are provided, the authors report that a factor analysis was used to determine unidimensionality of the Satisfaction Scale (Aiken and Hage, 1966).

Validity: Evidence for the validity of the Scale is scarce, though some construct validity may be inferred from correlations between its two indices, and between these indices and those of a companion instrument, the Bureaucracy Scale (reviewed in this volume). For example, there is a strong relationship ($r = .75$) between the Index of Alienation from Work and the Index of Alienation from Expressive Relations. Correlations between Alienation from Work and all indices of the Bureaucracy Scale fall in the expected direction: .49 with Hierarchy of Authority; −.59 with Participation in Decision-Making; .51 with Job Codification (preponderance of rules); and .55 with Rule Observation (degree of supervision for rule violations). Alienation from Expressive Relations correlates similarly with these indices: .45 with Hierarchy of Authority; −.17 with Participation in Decision-Making; .23 with Job Codification; and .65 with Rule Observation.

Norms: The Scale was originally administered to professional and supervisory personnel in 16 social welfare agencies located in a large city in the midwestern United States (Aiken and Hage, 1966). It has since been administered to 441 teachers in 14 high schools in Brisbane, Australia (Grassie and Carss, 1972).

Administration and Scoring: The Satisfaction Scale is brief and easy to administer. For each item, the subject indicates the degree of his satisfaction on a 1 to 4 response continuum. Individual scores can be easily obtained through summation, or an aggregate score for a given organization can be determined by averaging the scores of all respondents at a particular professional level and then computing the mean of these averages.

Comments: Though the Satisfaction Scale can be easily administered and widely applied, its usefulness is limited by insufficient validity, reliability, and normative data.

References: Aiken, M., and J. Hage, " Organizational alienation: A comparative analysis." *American Sociological Review,* 1966, **31,** 497–507.

Grassie, M. C., and B. W. Carss, " School structure, leadership quality, and teacher satisfaction." *Educational Administration Quarterly,* 1972, **9**(1), 15–26.

Gross, N., W. Mason, and A. McEachern, *Explorations in role analysis.* New York: John Wiley, 1958.

Name: STRUCTURAL PROPERTIES QUESTIONNAIRE, FORM 4

Authors: Lloyd K. Bishop, Julius R. George, and Michael Murphy

Type of Measure: Rating scale

Availability: Murphy, M. J., L. K. Bishop, and J. R. George, *Defining organizational properties of schools: A focus on structure.* Paper presented at the meeting of the American Educational Research Association, Washington, D.C., April 1975.

Description: The Structural Properties Questionnaire (SPQ) is a Likert-type scale which measures the teacher's perception of the organizational characteristics within an elementary or secondary school. Based on Hage's (1965) axiomatic theory of organizations, the SPQ describes school structure in terms of four underlying organizational properties: Centralization, Formalization, Complexity, and Stratification.

    In developing the questionnaire, 350 items tapping each of the 4 structural properties were evaluated by 5 independent judges. Those items which were unanimously selected as best representing the constructs defined made up the first, 70-item version of the SPQ. This form and subsequent revisions were administered to various populations and results were factor analyzed. The 45 items which survived these tests were again subjected to factor analysis, which yielded 12 (unlabeled) factors.

Sample Items: The SPQ contains items of the following type. The respondent indicates on a 4-point scale ("Rarely" to "Very Frequently") the degree to which each statement characterizes his or her school.

1. Teachers must adhere to a prescribed curriculum.
2. Decisions about work methods are left up to the person doing the work.
3. Teachers must regularly submit lesson plans to the principal or to their department chairman.
4. Minor rules and regulations are generally ignored.

Reliability: Although no reliability data are provided for Form 4 of the SPQ, alpha coefficients are reported for the 38 items on the original form which had the most significant factor loadings (Bishop and George, 1973). Computed on the responses of 296 elementary school teachers, these coefficients ranged from .54 to .84 over 4 factors, with a total alpha of .87. Forty items on Form II, administered to 615 secondary school teachers, yielded similar estimates of internal consistency (.59 to .84, with a total alpha of .86).

Validity: Content validity of the SPQ was considered in the scale's development. Five students of organizational theory independently judged the adequacy of each item, and only those items on which they unanimously agreed were retained.

Some construct validity is suggested by the results of factor analyses. Although Form 4 yielded 12 factors, careful examination of item loadings indicates that each factor can be unambiguously assigned to one of the 4 structural properties originally hypothesized (Centralization, Formalization, Complexity, and Stratification). The factoring methods employed evidently revealed subscales of the major dimensions (Murphy, Bishop, and George, 1975).

Evidence of concurrent validity is provided by 3 major studies which have employed preliminary versions of the SPQ as a measure of organizational structure in elementary and secondary schools. In a study relating organizational structure and personality traits to organizational climate, George and Bishop (1971) confirmed the ability of the SPQ to distinguish traditional, highly bureaucratic schools from decentralized, nonbureaucratic schools. The discriminatory ability of the SPQ was supported at the .01 level of significance.

Barile (1971), investigating the relationship of organizational structure and teacher personality, found a significant positive correlation between Anxiety, measured on the 16PF (Cattell, 1967), and the structural properties of Formalization and Centralization. Kennedy (1973) found that elementary teachers with high professional orientations, working in schools with low organizational structure, were inclined to engage in innovative activities. A horizontal and diffuse distribution of power within the school was also associated with the teachers' proclivity toward innovation.

Norms: Means and standard deviations, derived from the responses of 1,170 teachers in rural, suburban, and urban schools, are reported for SPQ items (Murphy, Bishop, and George, 1975).

Administration and Scoring: The SPQ is self-administering and should take no more than 20 minutes to complete. Response alternatives are assigned values from 1 to 4 for purposes of scoring. Mean scores can be computed for each factor or each item. In their analyses, the authors generally used standardized factor scores (Mean = 0.00, standard deviation = 1.0) to facilitate comparison between groups.

Comments: The Structural Properties Questionnaire represents a dimensional, or structural (rather than process) approach to the measurement of organizational characteristics of schools. This instrument has been subjected to extensive empirical analyses involving a series of factor solutions, and, though still in a development stage, is a useful research tool.

References: Barile, P. A., Jr., *Relationship of organizational structure and teacher personality characteristics to teacher role behavior.* Unpublished doctoral dissertation, New York University, 1971.

Bishop, L. K., and J. R. George, "Organizational structure: A factor analysis of structural characteristics of public elementary and secondary schools." *Educational Administration Quarterly,* 1973, **9**(3), 66–80.

Cattell, R. B., *The sixteen personality factor questionnaire*. Champaign, Illinois: Institute for Personality and Ability Testing, 1967.

George, J. R., and L. K. Bishop, "Relationship of organizational structure and teacher personality characteristics to organizational climate." *Administrative Science Quarterly*, 1971, **16**, 467–475.

Hage, J., "An axiomatic theory of organizations." *Administrative Science Quarterly*, 1965, **10**, 289–320.

Kennedy, W. J., *Organizational structure and teachers' professional orientation to their involvement in innovative activities*. Unpublished doctoral dissertation, New York University, 1973.

Murphy, M. J., L. K. Bishop, and J. R. George, *Defining organizational properties of schools: A focus on structure*. Paper presented at the meeting of the American Educational Research Association, Washington, D.C., April 1975.

Name: TEACHER ATTITUDE AND CLASSROOM CLIMATE
QUESTIONNAIRE

Authors: Judith A. Agard and Martin Kaufman

Type of Measure: Rating scale

Availability: Agard, J. A., and M. Kaufman, *Teacher attitude and classroom climate questionnaire.* Austin, Texas: Project PRIME, undated.

Description: The Teacher Attitude and Classroom Climate Questionnaire is composed of 2 scales, one measuring the teacher's perception of classroom climate and the other measuring his or her attitude toward teaching and various educational practices. Part I contains 67 items about child and teacher behavior in the teacher's own classroom, while Part II presents 53 statements of opinion concerning educational practices. These 120 items represent 6 climate and 4 attitude factors. The climate factors are: Cooperation-Exploration; Unhappiness-Turmoil; Rigid Control; Individualization; Slow Students; and Competition. Attitude factors are: Traditional Authority; Personal Satisfaction; Teacher Cooperation; and Social-Emotional Development.

Although originally developed for Project PRIME (Programmed Re-Entry Into Mainstream Education) and intended for use with teachers whose classrooms include both handicapped and normal children, the questionnaire is suitable for all elementary and secondary teachers. Frequent references to "children," however, make the item content somewhat more appropriate for elementary teachers.

Sample Items: Items in Part I are followed by a 5-point response scale ("Always True" or "Never True"), while those in Part II are followed by a 4-point continuum ("Agree" to "Disagree"). The questionnaire contains statements of the following type.

Part	*Item*
I. Classroom Climate	1. The instructional resources used in this class include materials made or contributed by the children.
	2. I tailor classroom assignments to the needs of each child.
II. Teacher Attitude	1. To my knowledge, I am considered a good teacher by my colleagues.
	2. It is the responsibility of public schools to establish innovative educational practices.
	3. An academically oriented curriculum inhibits the development of critical thinking ability.

Reliability: Alpha coefficients were computed for each of the 6 climate and 4 attitude factors. Maximum alphas ranged from .66 for Social Emotional Development to .85 for Teacher Cooperation (Veldman, 1973).

Validity: Since this instrument is still in a developmental stage, little information is available concerning its validity. However, factor analysis gives some evidence of construct validity while a series of exploratory comparisons carried out with the Teacher Attitude and Classroom Climate Questionnaire suggests criterion-related validity. The scale was administered to regular and special education teachers (of both mentally retarded and learning disabled students), and responses revealed group differences in expected directions. For example, special education teachers scored higher than regular teachers on the Individualization and Slow Student dimensions, but lower on Competition and Traditional Authority. They also valued Social-Emotional Development more highly than did regular teachers (Veldman, 1973).

Correlations computed between the 4 teacher attitude factors and the 6 classroom climate dimensions also tend to suggest validity (Veldman, 1973).

Norms: Means and standard deviations derived from the responses of 555 teachers are reported by Veldman (1973) for all 10 factors.

Administration and Scoring: This instrument is self-administering. The 7-page test booklet provides the teacher with explicit instructions and a response column adjacent to the test items.

Likert scale scoring produces 10 factor scores, an overall attitude score, and an overall climate score.

Comments: The Teacher Attitude and Classroom Climate Questionnaire, though still in a developmental stage, appears to be a promising measure of teacher opinion and class environment. More extensive psychometric data should become available as Project PRIME analyses are completed and reported.

References: Agard, J. A., and M. Kaufman, *Teacher attitude and classroom climate questionnaire.* Austin, Texas: Project PRIME, undated.

Veldman, D. J., *Scale structure of the Teacher Attitude and Classroom Climate Questionnaire.* Austin, Texas: Project PRIME Data Analysis Center, The University of Texas, 1973.

Name: TEACHER QUESTIONNAIRE ON TEACHER GROUP BEHAVIOR

Authors: Douglas S. Finlayson, Olive Banks, and J. L. Loughran

Type of Measure: Rating scale

Availability: This instrument is available for research use from the National Foundation for Educational Research in England and Wales, The Mere, Slough, Bucks, England.

Description: The Teacher Questionnaire on Teacher Group Behavior is one component of a 4-part index measuring social climate in secondary schools. Although developed in England, the index is based on the work of two Americans, Halpin and Croft (1963).

This particular instrument assesses teachers' perceptions of their colleagues' behavior, while its 3 companion scales measure: (1) pupils' perceptions of the behavior of their peers and teachers; (2) teachers' perceptions of the department head's behavior; and (3) teacher's perceptions of the principal's behavior. One of these scales, the School Climate Index, is reviewed in this volume. Though any of the 4 components may be used in isolation, the climate of the school as a social system can be fully analyzed only when the entire index is administered (Finlayson, Banks, and Loughran, 1971).

The Teacher Questionnaire is composed of 7 scales which request teachers' opinions on the social behavior of their colleagues and the nature of communication within the school. The 4 scales relating to teacher group behavior are: Identification (work satisfaction); Familiarity (friendliness with colleagues); Social Disintegration (staff disunity); and Obstruction (lack of support from the school administration). The remaining scales, involving school communication, are: Teacher/Professional Communication; Teacher/Community Communication; and Teacher/Parent Communication. The entire questionnaire contains 54 items, many of which were modified from the Organizational Climate Description Questionnaire (Halpin and Croft, 1963).

Sample Items: The Teacher Questionnaire contains items of the following type, to which the subject responds by indicating the extent of his agreement on a 5-point scale ("Strongly Agree" to "Strongly Disagree").

Scale	*Item*
Familiarity	1. Teachers often see each other socially in their homes.
Teacher/Parent Communication	2. If a teacher wants to talk with a parent, he must do so either before or after school.

Reliability: Alpha coefficients were computed on a sample of 210 teachers from 10 comprehensive schools in England in order to determine the internal consistency of each scale on the Teacher Questionnaire. These ranged from .68 for Familiarity to .84 for Teacher/Community Communication (Finlayson, Banks, and Loughran, 1971).

Validity: Validity was investigated by the known-group method. Twelve schools known by reputation to have definite social climates were selected in an attempt to obtain a sample of distinct and diverse institutions. Teachers at these schools were administered the questionnaire, and their responses were subjected to a one-way analysis of variance. The F ratios, all significant at the .001 level, indicated that responses differed according to the school at which they were obtained (Finlayson, Banks, and Loughran, 1971).

Norms: Mean scores and standard deviations derived from the responses of 268 teachers in 12 English comprehensive schools are provided in the manual.

Administration and Scoring: The questionnaire may be administered to small groups of teachers in approximately one-half hour. This includes time to answer questions about the purpose of the test and the confidentiality of responses.

A scoring key is provided in the manual. A numerical score from 0 to 4 is assigned to each of the 5 response alternatives, the direction of scoring depending on the positive or negative wording of the item. One score is produced for each of the 7 scales on the questionnaire.

Comments: Use of the Teacher Questionnaire on Teacher Group Behavior may be limited in this country since its normative data and item content apply to British respondents. However, in combination with its companion scales, this instrument provides a comprehensive measure of social climate in secondary schools.

References: Finlayson, D. S., "How high and low achievers see teachers' and pupils' role behavior." *Research in Education,* 1970, **3**, 38–52.

Finlayson, D. S., "Measuring 'school climate.'" *Trends in Education,* 1973, **30**, 19–27.

Finlayson, D. S., O. Banks, and J. L. Loughran, *Administrative manual for Teacher Questionnaire on teachers' perceptions of teacher group behavior.* The Mere, Upton Park, Slough, England: NFER, 1971.

Halpin, A. W. and D. B. Croft, *The organizational climate of schools.* Chicago: Midwest Administration Center, University of Chicago, 1963.

IIIB

About the classroom from the pupil

Name: ATTITUDE TOWARD SCHOOL, GRADES K–12. REVISED EDITION

Author: Instructional Objectives Exchange

Type of Measure: Battery of affective tests, including self-report questionnaires and observation indicators.

Availability: Instructional Objectives Exchange. *Attitude toward school, grades K–12* (rev. ed). Los Angeles: Author, 1972. This battery may be obtained from the Instructional Objectives Exchange, Distribution Center, P.O. Box 24095, Los Angeles, California 90024.

Description: Attitude Toward School, Grades K–12 is one in a series of criterion-referenced test batteries published by the Instructional Objectives Exchange. This particular battery is referred to as a "collection of objectives and related measuring instruments ... devoted solely to *affective* goals (Instructional Objectives Exchange, 1972, p. 1)." The purpose of these objectives and measures is to evaluate instructional programs aimed at improving the learner's attitudes toward school.

The tests in this collection include direct and inferential self-report devices as well as observational indicators. The self-report scales are available in primary (grades K–3), intermediate (grades 4–6), or secondary (grades 7–12) forms. The direct self-report measures assess all of 6 dimensions of the learner's attitude toward school (Teachers; School Subjects; Learning; Social Structure and Climate; Peers; and General Orientation Toward Schooling), while the inferential self-reports each focus on one of these dimensions.

Commissioned in 1970 by representatives of Title III Programs, the Instructional Objectives Exchange developed and subsequently revised the Attitude Toward School battery based on a review of the literature, interviews with educators and students, pilot testing, and item analyses. The revised battery includes the following measures:

1. *School Sentiment Index* (Primary, Intermediate, and Secondary levels): This self-report inventory contains 37 items at the primary level, 81 at the intermediate level, and 82 at the secondary level, all of which involve student perceptions of, or attitudes toward, various aspects of school. Younger children respond by answering "Yes" or "No," intermediate pupils, by marking "True" or "False," and secondary students, by indicating agreement or disagreement on a 4-point scale.

2. *A Picture Choice* (Primary level), *Subject Area Preferences* (Intermediate and Secondary levels): These measures assess the student's relative interest in, or preference for, various school subjects. Children in the primary grades are presented (both orally and visually) 28 to 30 sets of 3 hypothetical activities and asked to choose which they would most like to do. Stu-

dents in the intermediate grades indicate which of 7 subjects they like and dislike and then evaluate each of these subjects according to its value, while secondary students rate 8 subjects on 6 bipolar (positive to negative) scales.

3. *Imagine That* (Intermediate and Secondary levels): This inventory presents 10 to 11 hypothetical situations describing teacher behavior in regard to Mode of Instruction, Authority and Control, or Interpersonal Relationships with Pupils. Each of these is followed by 4 response alternatives (2 negative, 2 positive), which at the intermediate level evaluate, and at the secondary level explain, the teacher behavior described.

4. *The Story* (Intermediate level): This instrument measures the student's perception of his peer group by asking him to select from a list of statements those which would make a realistic story about his school. The statements describe situations involving the student and his peer group.

5. *What Would Happen* (Secondary level): This scale presents students with 11 fictitious situations involving 2 new students at school. Respondents are required to select from 4 alternatives (2 positive and 2 negative), that which would be most likely to happen to the new students in each situation.

6. *Looking Back* (Intermediate level): This test asks the student to imagine that he is in junior high school and from that perspective to "look back" and remember his elementary school experience. He is instructed to select from a number of statements those which describe his feelings about his school.

7. *The School Play* (Intermediate level), *High School on TV* (Secondary level): These instruments assess school social structure and climate by asking students to select statements or alternative actions that could be used to write a play or a television script depicting life at their school.

8. *Take Your Pick* (Secondary level): This measure assesses the student's attitude toward learning by presenting him with 12 hypothetical situations, each followed by 4 response alternatives, indicating either a tendency to approach learning-related activities or to avoid them. The student must select the alternative which describes what he would be most likely to do in the situation depicted.

9. *Compliance with Assigned Tasks* (Primary and Intermediate levels): Based on the finding that compliance with assigned tasks is a correlate of liking for school, this instrument requires an observer to record both the frequency at which particular tasks are assigned and the frequency at which pupils comply with these assignments. A 20% sample of pupils is observed for 1 hour.

10. *School Conduct: Compliance with School Rules* (Primary-Intermediate and Secondary levels): This "observation" technique uses pupil discipline records as an indicator of school attitudes.

11. *School Tardiness* (Primary-Intermediate level): This observation indicator uses school records to compute a daily tardiness rate, from which to infer the student's attitude toward school.

12. *School Attendance* (Primary-Intermediate-Secondary level): Pupil attendance records are observed as an indicator of school attitude.

13. *Class Attendance* (Secondary level): Attendance records for individual classes are examined to provide information from which to infer the student's attitude toward a given class or subject area.

14. *Class Tardiness* (Secondary level): Tardiness records for particular classes are used as an indicator of the student's feelings about those classes.

15. *Grade Level Completion* (Secondary level, grades 11 and 12): On the assumption that students who leave school prior to graduation generally have negative attitudes toward school, the proportion of enrolled students completing a given semester of school is computed.

16. *Unwillingness to Transfer* (Secondary level): This observation indicator gives students the option to sign up for a new class section. Each student is asked whether or not he would be willing to transfer to the new section. Those who are willing to stay in their present situation are assumed to have positive feelings toward that class, and, conceivably, toward school in general.

Sample Items: Item format varies from test to test. The following items are similar to those on several of the measures included in this battery:

Test	*Item*	*Response Alternatives*
School Sentiment Index (Primary)	Do you get bored at school?	Yes No
Imagine That (Intermediate)	My teacher is returning school work which has just been graded.	a) I'm sure I'll get the grade I should have. b) I think my teacher grades too strictly. c) The grades probably won't be fair. d) My teacher's a pretty good grader.
Subject Area Preference (Secondary)	History	_ _ _ _ _ _ _ _ Valuable Worthless _ _ _ _ _ _ _ _ Difficult Easy

What Would Happen (Secondary)	This is Mary's first day at school. She enters her first class and sits near a group of students who are conversing with each other. The students will probably:	a) Ignore her. b) Say "hi" and continue their conversation c) Stop talking and look her over. d) Introduce themselves and include her in their conversation.
Looking Back (Intermediate)	I didn't enjoy having to go to school when I didn't feel like it.	Yes No
High School on TV (Secondary)	Two students need to see their history teacher about their homework. After school, they go to her classroom to see her.	a) She is talking with another teacher and tells them to go ask other students in the class. b) She is busy grading tests and tells them they should be able to figure out the assignment on their own. c) She is busy, but she arranges to see them in the morning, before class.
Take Your Pick (Secondary)	If you were to participate in only one extracurricular activity, it would be:	a) Athletics b) Community service work c) A social club d) A special interest group, such as the drama club, business club, or Spanish club.

Reliability: The Instructional Objectives Exchange (1972) presents internal consistency (KR_{20}) estimates and test/retest stability coefficients (computed over a 2-week interval) for the revised Attitude Toward School Measures. These are summarized below.

Tests	Internal Consistency	Test/Retest
Secondary		
School Sentiment Index—Total	.88	.49
Teacher: Instruction	.73	.68
Teacher: Authority	.71	.65
Teacher: Peers	.76	.81
Social structure and climate	.77	.64
Learning	.68	.62
Peer	.71	.71
General	.79	.68
Imagine That	.58	.51
High School on T.V.	.54	.61
What Would Happen?	.54	.54
Subject Area Preferences		
English	.74	.78
Math	.73	.80
Social studies	.62	.84
Foreign language	.62	.84
Art	.59	.76
Vocational education	.45	.80
Science	.67	.86
Physical education	.71	.84
Intermediate		
School Sentiment Index—Total	.80	.83
Teacher: Instruction	.76	.70
Teacher: Authority	.71	.77
Teacher: Peers	.65	.81
Peers	.54	.73
Learning	.71	.63
Social structure and climate	.47	.70
General	.73	.90
Looking Back	.67	.86
The Story	.68	.75
Imagine That	.62	.79
The School Play	.74	.69
Subject Area Preferences		
Spelling	.62	.53
Arithmetic	.46	.76
Social studies	.48	.76
Art	.51	.72
Music	.57	.82
Science	.56	.76
Physical education	.60	.75

Primary

School Sentiment Index—Total	.72	.87
Teacher	.62	.61
Peer	.42	.35
Subjects	.49	.68
Social structure and climate	.48	.55
General	.70	.85
A Picture Choice, K–1	No data	No data
A Picture Choice, 2–3	No data	No data

Validity: The thorough analyses undertaken during test development and revision assure at least some construct and content validity. While the direct self-report measures probably possess more content validity than the inferential self-reports, responses to the former are more easily faked. Furthermore, high intercorrelations among the subscales of the direct self-reports indicate that these measures are not assessing truly distinct characteristics.

Though the test developers provide no evidence of criterion-related validity, they report that validity analyses carried out by various educators throughout the nation have generally been positive (Instructional Objectives Exchange, 1972).

Norms: Because the tests in this battery are criterion-rather than norm-referenced, normative data are inapplicable.

Administration and Scoring: Although administration and scoring directions vary among the Attitude Toward School Measures, they are in each case well explained and easy to follow. In general, the tests require 10 to 30 minutes to complete. Since they are intended to yield information about the instructional program rather than the student, they should be answered anonymously. Questions on the primary level tests are read aloud to the children and are often color- or picture-keyed to the answer sheets.

All tests are distributed as preprinted spirit masters, each of which permits duplication of 200 to 300 copies. Alternate forms are available for every test in the battery.

Hand scoring is feasible when few respondents are involved. However, machine scoring is recommended for larger groups. Several scoring options, explained in the manual, are available.

Comments: Attitude Toward School, grades K–12, provides a battery of tests designed for use in evaluating programs aimed at improving learners' attitudes toward school. Carefully developed and periodically revised by the Instructional Objectives Exchange, this collection, when used in its entirety, gives broad coverage of student attitudes. Because the tests in this battery are criterion- rather than norm-referenced, they compare the student's attitudes to explicitly defined objectives rather than to the attitudes of other students. A typical objective might specify, for example, that the student will demonstrate favorable attitudes toward learning by expressing agreement with statements indicating interest in or involvement with learning-related activities. The use of such objectives makes this battery somewhat unusual, since criterion-referencing, while becoming more common among achievement measures, is still rare among attitude scales.

Considering their recent and continuing development, the Attitude Toward School tests show adequate psychometric properties. Still, evidence of criterion-related validity and efforts to raise the reliabilities of the primary level tests are needed. Stability coefficients in the .80s and .90s, however, should not be expected since these measures deal with attitude toward school, which may be expected to vacillate.

Reference: Instructional Objectives Exchange. *Attitude toward school, grades K-12* (rev. ed.). Los Angeles: Author, 1972.

Name: BARCLAY CLASSROOM CLIMATE INVENTORY

Author: James R. Barclay

Type of Measure: Questionnaire

Availability: Barclay, J. R., *Barclay classroom climate inventory.* Lexington, Kentucky: Educational Skills Development, 1971.

Description: The Barclay Classroom Climate Inventory (BCCI) is a multiple measurement device for assessing student needs and classroom characteristics. The BCCI is an assessment system which uses self-report judgments, peer nominations, and teacher expectations to measure the affective and social needs of third- through sixth-grade children within the context of the classroom. One of the unique aspects of this inventory is the fact that it is scored and interpreted by a computer, which integrates data from the 3 sources mentioned above to describe the forces that are creating and sustaining learning in the classroom.

The BCCI consists of 32 independent scales. Four of these ask the child about his skills, 6 involve peer judgment of skills, 10 concern the child's interest in and knowledge about the environment and vocations, 4 involve teacher ratings of children, and 8 assess the child's interest in, rewards from, and satisfaction with school. Data obtained on these scales describe the child in regard to: (1) realistic, outdoor, manual skills; (2) intellectual, scientific, and artistic skills; (3) social and interpersonal skills; (4) leadership, business and enterprising skills; (5) reinforcers; (6) basic temperament and methods of responding, such as extroversion versus introversion; and (7) support obtained from both peers and teachers.

Six major factors have been identified in the BCCI: Achievement-Motivation; Control-Stability; Introversion-Seclusiveness; Energy-Activity; Sociability-Affiliation; and Enterprising-Dominance. According to these factors, and the various scales and inputs, the computer analyzes the social interaction of each individual and describes his role in the classroom environment. The BCCI system provides: (1) summaries of each child in the classroom for teachers, counselors, and principals; (2) analyses of suspected problem areas that may be hampering learning; (3) a method for relating classroom problems to curriculum planning and interventions; (4) a comprehensive list of strategies that can be used by teachers to improve the quality of learning; (5) a special report designed for the child himself; and (6) summaries of children's reports that can be shared with parents.

BCCI development began in 1956. Since its completion in 1971, the test has been used in several teacher education projects and in a variety of educational programs at over 60 sites throughout the country. The BCCI is available in Spanish and Chinese, as well as English, and will soon be available in French, German, and Swedish.

Sample Items: Items of the following type appear on the various BCCI scales.

A. Vocational Awareness: 72 items, answered "yes" or "no."
   I would like to conduct a symphony orchestra.
B. Self-Competency: 25 items answered "yes" or "no."
   I enjoy playing softball.
C. Behavioral Interests or Reinforcers: 51 items, answered on a 3-point scale ("like very much," "sometimes," or "not at all").
   Going for a walk alone.
D. Sociometrics: 28 items answered with peer nominations.
   Who runs fastest?

Reliability: A number of reliability studies have been performed on this instrument. These have yielded internal consistency and test/retest estimates. The author points out that certain portions of the BCCI are more reliable than others since many short scales are used due to time constraints involved in dealing with children. Furthermore, the inventory assesses perceptions related to affective and social dimensions, which are subject to change.

The manual (Barclay, 1974) presents internal consistency coefficients for major BCCI scales. For teacher judgments, these ranged from .86 to .90. The Total Vocational Scale yielded a coefficient of .75, while Total Self Competency scores produced coefficients of .58 for boys and .50 for girls.

Test/retest coefficients for the major scales, over a 1-year interval, ranged from .34 to .71 for third-graders and from .34 to .77 for fourth- and sixth-graders. Test/retest correlations also indicate that the multisource factor scores are quite stable over a 1-year period.

Validity: Various approaches have been used in establishing the validity of the BCCI. First, face validity is based on the assumption that there is some correspondence between real attitudes of people and their responses on the test. The author maintains that responses are estimates of expectation. Even though the expectations may not be realistic, they do reflect the subject's feelings. Thus, the face validity of the inventory is related to the pooling of a set of expectations from self, peer and teacher sources.

In order to establish concurrent validity, the *Research Manual* (Barclay, 1972) cites correlations between the BCCI peer judgment scales and a global sociometric technique, the Kuder, and the Children's Personality Questionnaire. These have yielded generally appropriate positive and negative relationships.

Several BCCI scales have also been related to observed behaviors in the classroom. In one study, 5 substitute teachers observed 437 children in a number of classrooms over a period of 10 days. The children had been administered the BCCI several months earlier, but the observers were unaware of the test results. Their observations produced 43 correlations, 32 of which were significant at the .01 level and 10 at the .05 level. Though most of these correlations were rather low, they did reflect a relationship between empirically observed behaviors and the BCCI scales.

Other validity studies have related the BCCI scales to achievement measures. One of these studies, reported in the *User's Manual* (Barclay, 1974), involved 528 fourth- and sixth-graders and 302 third-graders. The BCCI scores obtained at the beginning of the school year served as predictors for achievement variables measured at the end of the year. Stepwise regressions were used to obtain multiple correlations. These data indicated that BCCI variables accounted for between 30 and 45% of the variance in achievement for third-graders and between 20 and 30% for fourth- and sixth-graders.

Norms: The preliminary standardization of the BCCI involved approximately 2,000 children assessed in 1967. These children were from 7 states in various regions of the nation. During the period from 1969 to 1973, over 5,000 additional children in the second through the seventh grades were tested. This sample included 1,400 black children, 600 Spanish-American children and 250 American Indians. They attended schools in urban, suburban, and rural areas. Scale scores and factor scores are provided for these groups.

Administration and Scoring: The BCCI can be administered by the classroom teacher in about 75 minutes. The answer sheets must be filled out accurately and checked by school personnel.

Because of its complexity, the BCCI cannot be scored by hand. After receipt of the data, processing requires about 2 weeks. The school district receives 2 bound copies of each classroom report.

Comments: The Barclay Classroom Climate Inventory is a social-affective assessment technique to be used in elementary classrooms. The BCCI manual and testing materials are well designed and effectively presented, and computer feedback, which is quite detailed and surprisingly personalized, yields a comprehensive analysis of the child and the classroom.

References: Barclay, J. R., *The Barclay Classroom Climate Inventory: A user's manual.* Lexington, Kentucky: Educational Skills Development, Inc., 1974.

Barclay, J. R., *A research manual for the Barclay Classroom Climate Inventory.* Lexington, Kentucky: Educational Skills Development, Inc., 1970.

Name: CLASS ACTIVITIES QUESTIONNAIRE

Author: Joe M. Steele

Type of Measure: Rating scale

Availability: This instrument can be ordered from Dr. Robert Rosemier, 520 College View Court, Northern Illinois University, DeKalb, Illinois 60115.

Description: The Class Activities Questionnaire (CAQ) is a measure of instructional climate administered to both the student (in grades 7 and above) and the teacher. CAQ results obtained from students suggest *actual* classroom emphases, while those from the teacher indicate *intended* emphases. These 2 sets of data can be compared for purposes of research or teacher self-assessment.

Developed in 1969 as part of a large-scale evaluation of gifted classes throughout the state of Illinois, the CAQ was designed to incorporate 2 theoretical domains of instructional climate: Cognitive and Affective. Results of field testing and factor analysis indicated that these domains are represented on the questionnaire by the 5 dimensions and 20 factors listed below:

Dimensions	*Factors*
1. Lower Thought Processes	1. Memory
	2. Translation
	3. Interpretation
2. Higher Thought Processes	4. Application
	5. Analysis
	6. Synthesis
	7. Evaluation
3. Classroom Focus	8. Discussion
	9. Test/Grade Stress
	10. Lecture
4. Classroom Climate	11. Enthusiasm
	12. Independence
	13. Divergence
	14. Humor
	15. Ideas Valued
	16. Ideas Enjoyed
	17. Teacher Talk
	18. Homework
5. Student Opinions	19. Qualities
	20. Deficiencies

These factors are in turn represented by items describing (1) cognitive demands made of students and (2) affective classroom conditions.

Sample Items: The CAQ contains 25 items of the following type to which the subject responds on a 4-point scale (from "Strongly Agree" to "Strongly Disagree"):

1. The student's main task is to remember or recognize factual material.
2. Students in this class are often required to decide whether things are good or bad, right or wrong, and to explain why.
3. Students are enthusiastic about and interested in class activities.
4. In this class there is very little laughing or kidding around.

Five additional CAQ items (3 of which are open-ended) request information about teacher activity, student preparation for class, and student preferences and opinions. The questionnaire also provides space for 20 optional, locally generated items.

Reliability: Though reliability figures are not reported for the most recent revision of the CAQ, estimates based on a preliminary version of the questionnaire are available (Steel, House, and Kerins, 1971). Using the Horst formula (1949), reliabilities were computed from within-class and between-class variances ($N = 131$ classes). These ranged from .76 to .88 for the CAQ dimensions and from .58 to .94 for the factors. Only 1 of 20 coefficients fell below .65.

Test/retest reliabilities, based on factor scores from 6 classes, were also computed for an early form of the CAQ. These figures, which ranged from .59 to .91, were viewed as tentative since the classes tested, being small and employing independent study modes, were considered atypical (Steele, House, and Kerins, 1971).

Validity: Studies conducted with preliminary versions of the CAQ offer some evidence of construct and concurrent validity. Factor analyses of CAQ results obtained from gifted classes substantially supported the logical construction of the instrument, though 2 factors, Divergence and Memory, proved to be weak. Generally, statistical components were closely related to the theoretical structure of the CAQ, with 8 of 10 logically paired items intact after empirical analysis (Steele, House, and Kerins, 1971). Using a normal rather than a gifted population, Wahlstrom (1971) analyzed the CAQ and confirmed its affective and cognitive dimensions, thus supplying further factorial validation of the scale.

Concurrent validity is suggested by differences (significant beyond the .001 level) between the CAQ subscores of average and gifted samples. Average classes as a group are seen as emphasizing 3 of the 7 cognitive processes represented on the scale, while gifted classes are seen as stressing 6. Only 8% of the average classes emphasized 4 or more cognitive levels, but 45% of the gifted classes emphasized from 4 to 6 levels.

On the affective dimensions of the CAQ, the contrast between average and gifted classes was also marked. Average classes were characterized by lack of enthusiasm, stress on grades and tests, and a greater proportion of time (75% to

90%) devoted to teacher talk. Gifted classes, on the other hand, stressed discussion and active student involvement. In almost one-third of these classes, teachers were seen as talking less than 40% of the time. Furthermore, gifted students reported less stress on tests and grades and a great deal more enthusiasm (Steele, House, and Kerins, 1971).

Norms: Extensive normative data are not reported (Steel, 1969; Steele, 1973). However, some comparative statistics (percentage of classes within a school or subject area which emphasize each factor, for example) are available from the Scoring Center at Northern Illinois University which services the CAQ.

Administration and Scoring: The CAQ can be administered by the classroom teacher in about 30 minutes. Printed on optical scanning forms for automated keypunching and computer scoring, test forms can be purchased and processed for $5.00 per class of 25. Completed questionnaires are sent to Dr. Robert Rosemier at Northern Illinois University, where they are scored, analyzed, and returned to individual teachers within 2 weeks. The CAQ's are usually treated by class, unless special analyses are requested. The user receives a 4-page computer printout containing: (1) frequency distributions and means of student responses to the open-ended items; (2) teacher intended and predicted responses for the same items; (3) results grouped by paired items with the proportion of individual students responding consistently calculated for each pair; (4) a summary of students' perceived emphases based on a scoring formula; and (5) a comparison of the students' perceptions with teacher intentions and predictions.

Comments: The Class Activities Questionnaire provides a measure of classroom climate by requiring students to make low-inference judgments about prevailing patterns of instruction. It is intended for use in large-scale evaluation of educational programs and in teacher self-assessment. CAQ authors have attempted to prevent its use as a tool for evaluating instructors, strongly discouraging administrators from using it " on " teachers. Considering its fairly recent development, this instrument is supported by substantial research, most of which confirms its validity.

References: Steele. J. M., *Class Activities Questionnaire (CAQ). General information.* Unpublished paper, 1969. (Available from the author, Evaluation Center, Mars Hill College, Mars Hill, North Carolina 28754).

Steele, J. M., *Availability and use of the Class Activities Questionnaire.* Unpublished paper, 1973. (Available from the author, Evaluation Center, Mars Hill College, Mars Hill, North Carolina 28754).

Steel, J. M., E. R. House, and T. Kerins, "An instrument for assessing instructional climate through low-inference student judgments." *American Educational Research Journal,* 1971, **8**, 447–466.

Wahlstrom, M. W., *Factorial validation of the Class Activities Questionnaire.* Paper presented at the meeting of the American Educational Research Association, New York, 1971.

Walberg, H. J., E. R. House, and J. M. Steele, "Grade level, cognition, and affect: A cross-section of classroom perceptions." *Journal of Educational Psychology,* 1973, **64**(2), 142–146.

Name: CLASSROOM CLIMATE QUESTIONNAIRE

Author: Herbert J. Walberg

Type of Measure: Rating scale

Availability: Walberg, H. J., *Classroom climate questionnaire*. Cambridge, Massachusetts: Harvard University, 1966. (multilithed)

Description: The Classroom Climate Questionnaire (CCQ) assesses the climate of a class as perceived by the students. Based on the framework developed by Getzels and Thelen (1960) for the analysis of the classroom as a unique social system, the CCQ was derived from the Group Dimensions Description Questionnaire (Hemphill and Westie, 1955), a measure of group characteristics. Walberg modified 80 items from 12 of the Hemphill and Westie scales, in order to make them descriptive of classroom climate. Factor analysis of these items revealed 18 structural and affective dimensions of classroom climate: Friction; Classroom Intimacy; Goal Direction; Social Heterogeneity; Interest Heterogeneity; Goal Diversity; Group Status; Democratic; Subserviant; Satisfaction; Strict Control; Disorganization; Alienation; Personal Intimacy; Stratification; Egalitarian; Formality; and Speech Constraint.

The 80 CCQ items describe characteristics of school classes. The subject responds to each by expressing agreement or disagreement on a 4-point scale. The questionnaire yields 18 subscores, 1 for each dimension.

Sample Items: Items of the following type appear on the CCQ:

1. Some members of the class have more influence than other members.
2. Personal dissatisfaction with the class is a big problem.
3. Success of the class is important to most members.
4. Certain members of the class enjoy special privileges.
5. Students in the class can work under no supervision.
6. Students are proud of their membership in the class.
7. Most ideas may be expressed freely within the class.

Reliability: Walberg and Anderson (1968) report individual split-half reliabilities for the 18 factor scores ranging from .41 to .86. Walberg (1968) obtained group reliabilities over .85 for all CCQ dimensions and over .94 for 9 of the 18 factors.

Validity: Since its development, the CCQ has been used in several research studies, which have yielded data pertaining to the test's validity. Walberg and Anderson (1968) tested the hypothesis that end-of-year individual student achievement and interest in a subject can be predicted from aspects of classroom climate measured at midyear by the CCQ. The predictor instruments (the Physics Achievement Test, the Test on Understanding Science, the Science Process Inventory, the Semantic Differential for Science Students, and the Pupil Activity Inventory) were administered to 2,100 high school juniors and seniors in 76 classes throughout the country participating in an experimental physics course. Correlations between these instruments and the CCQ produced over 4 times as many significant relationships ($p < .05$) as would be expected by chance. Simple and multiple correlations revealed significant and complex relations between classroom climate and learning. For example, Stratification and Friction both predicted science understanding, while the climate variables predicted physics achievement and attitudes toward laboratory work. The data indicated that students with various perceptions of classroom climate grow in different ways during a course.

Walberg and Anderson (1968) used the same sample and predictor instruments to measure the effect of classroom climate on the group, rather than the individual. Results showed that the class as a whole can vary along a dimension, and that its position on the scale is reflected in (or is predictive of) classroom climate. For example, the "achieving class" appeared to have a friendly, democratic, goal-directed character, while the "creative class" was typified by diverse interests, friction among its members, and high group status.

Another study by Walberg, using subjects in 72 of the classes from the physics sample, indicated that class structure is related to students' affective reactions. Class means on the 18 CCQ dimensions served as the units of analysis. Correlations between the structural and affective variables were calculated; each of the affective measures was regressed on all of the structural measures; and each of the structural measures was regressed on all the affective measures. Canonical correlations were computed between all the structural and all the affective aspects. Data revealed 23 correlations significant beyond the .05 level and 15 significant beyond the .01 level. All of the affective measures were predicted from the structural measures in the multiple regression analysis; and, with the exception of Strict Control and Speech Constraint, all of the structural measures were predicted from the affective measures ($p < .05$).

Norms: Statistical data are based on 2,106 high school juniors and seniors throughout the country, participating in the preliminary evaluation of the Harvard Project Physics, an experimental physics course.

Administration and Scoring: The CCQ is easily administered. The subject merely responds to each item on a 4-point scale. A score is obtained for each of the 18 dimensions by averaging the values of chosen response alternatives for items loading uniquely above .30 on each of the factors.

Comments: The Classroom Climate Questionnaire may prove valuable in predicting learning outcomes from assessments of class atmosphere. Walberg believes that the CCQ has implications for teacher education, behavior modification of inservice teachers, and the assessment of teaching effectiveness. Since the measurement of classroom climate is a relatively new area, more research is needed on the reliability and validity of the CCQ. At present this instrument is limited by its unique nonrandom standardization sample.

References: Hemphill, J. K., and C. M. Westie, "The measurement of group dimensions." *Journal of Psychology*, 1955, **29**, 325–342.

Walberg, H. J., "Structural and affective aspects of classroom climate." *Psychology in the Schools*, 1968, **5**(3), 247–253.

Walberg, H. J., and G. J. Anderson, "The achievement-creativity dimension and classroom climate." *Journal of Creative Behavior*, 1968, **2**(4), 281-291.

Walberg, H. J., and G. J. Anderson, "Classroom climate and individual learning." *Journal of Educational Psychology*, 1968, **59**(6), 414–419.

Name: HIGH SCHOOL CHARACTERISTICS INDEX

Author: George G. Stern

Type of Measure: True-false questionnaire

Availability: Stern G. G., *High school characteristics index. Form 960.* Syracuse, New York: Author, 1964. A copy of this instrument also appears in: Stern, G. G., *People on context.* New York: John Wiley, 1970.

Description: The High School Characteristics Index (HSCI) is one in a series of instruments designed by Stern and his associates (see Stern, 1970) to assess individual needs and environmental press. The HSCI specifically measures environmental forces operating in the high school to facilitate or impede expression of the students' needs. Derived from the more extensively researched College Characteristics Index (CCI), the HSCI, like the other Stern instruments, is based on the work of Murray (1938), who theorized that both needs and press can be inferred from activities and events (needs from things the individual commonly does and press from the things commonly done to him). Accordingly, the 300 HSCI items describe activities, attitudes, or conditions which commonly occur in high schools. These items cover 30 scales, each representing a different kind of press (i.e., an environmental characteristic which reinforces a particular behavior), and together representing the 7 first-order and 3 second-order factors listed below.

First-Order Factors	*Second-Order Factors*
1. Intellectual Climate	1. Development Press
2. Expressiveness	2. Orderliness
3. Group Life	3. Practicalness
4. Personal Dignity	
5. Achievement Standards	
6. Orderliness	
7. Practicalness	

Sample Items: The HSCI contains items of the following type which the student marks as "true" or "false":

1. When a student is called to the office, he is usually seen immediately by the counselor or administrator who called for him.

2. In class, students usually agree with the teacher.

3. Many teachers require students to recopy homework which isn't neat.

4. Dancing is popular among the students at this school.

5. Students feel free to voice their complaints around here.

Reliability: Stern (1970) reports Kuder-Richardson (formula 20) reliabilities, computed for the 30 scales on a sample of 947 students attending 12 high schools. These estimates ranged from .28 (Fantasized Achievement) to .77

(Objectivity-Projectivity). Herr (1965), using a sample of 725 secondary school students, also obtained scale reliabilities which were irregular and in some cases very low. KR_{20} coefficients reported by Stern (1970) for the HSCI first-order factors, however, were relatively high, falling between .74 (Practicalness) and .97 (Personal Dignity).

Validity: Factor analyses of the HSCI provide some evidence of construct validity, since the factors which emerged are similar to those of the parent scale, the CCI. Independent factorings (Kight and Herr, 1966; Mitchell, 1968), however, have yielded 6-, 5-, and 3-factor structures, though these results are possibly due to different extraction procedures.

Concurrent validity is indicated by the ability of the HSCI to differentiate various groups. Studies reported by Stern (1970) demonstrate that the scale has discriminated successfully and predictably between private, parochial, and public schools, and between schools with and without a guidance counselor. Furthermore, Herr (1962; 1963; 1965) found that the press suggested by the HSCI was congruent with that indicated by other sources. He also discovered that HSCI scores varied according to sex, grade level, IQ, occupation and education of parents, extracurricular participation, and grade-point average.

The close comparability of the HSCI and the CCI also gives the former some claim to validity, since numerous studies (Stern, 1970) suggest that the CCI reflects differences in institutional climate as perceived by students.

Norms: Stern (1970) provides scale means and standard deviations derived from the scores of 947 students attending 12 high schools located primarily in the Northeast. He also lists standard score means from each of these high schools as well as factor scores for private, parochial and public secondary schools.

Administration and Scoring: Printed on the HSCI test booklet are clear instructions to the student, directing him to answer every item and to work as rapidly as possible. Answers are recorded on an optical scanning sheet, which permits hand or machine scoring. Thirty scale scores and 7 factor scores are produced.

Comments: The High School Characteristics Index has been widely used to assess students' perceptions of the educational institutions they attend. Consequently, the user of the HSCI benefits from an accumulation of data concerning this scale. Yet, regardless of these data, the value of the test as a measure of school climate may depend on whether one wishes to view the school in terms of the conceptual structure offered by the HSCI—that is, in terms of forces facilitating or inhibiting certain personality needs. If, however, one is focusing on the student rather than the school, one need not accept the theoretical framework of the HSCI in order to successfully use the instrument. As Herr (1965) points out, HSCI results can be effectively used by counselors in an attempt to help maladjusted students.

References: Herr, E. L., *An examination of student achievement and activities as related to "perceptions" of environmental press: Implications.* Unpublished manuscript, Saddle Brook High School, Saddle Brook, N.J., 1962.

Herr, E. L., *An examination of differential perceptions of "environmental press" by high school students as related to their achievement and participation in activities.* Unpublished doctoral dissertation, Teachers College, Columbia University, 1963.

Herr, E. L., "Differential perceptions of 'environmental press' by high school students." *Personnel and Guidance Journal,* 1965, **43**, 678–686.

Kight, H. R., and E. L. Herr, "Identification of four environmental press factors in the Stern High School Characteristics Index." *Educational and Psychological Measurement,* 1966, **26**, 479–481.

Mitchell, J. V., Jr. "Dimensionality and differences in the environmental press of high schools." *American Educational Research Journal,* 1968, **5**, 513–530.

Murray, H. A., *Explorations in personality.* New York: Oxford University Press, 1938.

Stern, G. G., *People in context.* New York: John Wiley, 1970.

Name: LEARNING ENVIRONMENT INVENTORY

Author: Gary J. Anderson

Type of Measure: Rating scale

Availability: Anderson, G. J., *The assessment of learning environments: A manual for the Learning Environment Inventory and the My Class Inventory.* Halifax, Nova Scotia, Canada: Atlantic Institute of Education, 1973.

Description: The Learning Environment Inventory (LEI) measures classroom climate as perceived by secondary school pupils along 15 dimensions, reflecting both interpersonal relationships among students and organizational characteristics of the classroom.

The LEI was developed in an attempt to expand and improve Walberg's (1968) Classroom Climate Questionnaire. Seven items were included on each LEI scale to obtain internally consistent dimensions. Items were assigned to scales by 4 independent judges. Those which were misclassified by one or more of the judges were modified or replaced. After empirical testing, 6 items with poor scale correlations were revised. The final version of the LEI contains 105 statements describing typical school classes on the following scales: Cohesiveness, Diversity, Formality, Speed, Environment, Friction, Goal Direction, Favoritism, Cliqueness, Satisfaction, Disorganization, Difficulty, Apathy, Democratic, and Competitiveness.

This instrument can be used to assess an individual student's perception of his class or to measure the learning environment of the class as a whole. Anderson (1973) maintains that class means provide the best estimate of collective student perceptions and suggests their use when different treatments are being studied across classes.

Sample Items: The LEI contains items of the following type with which the respondent expresses his agreement or disagreement on a 4-point scale.

Scale	Item
Cohesiveness	1. Students in this class don't know each other well enough to like or dislike one another.
Formality	2. There are well established rules of behavior in this classroom.
Friction	3. There is an atmosphere of tension among groups of students in this class.
Satisfaction	4. Most students enjoy coming to class.

Reliability: Alpha coefficients, intraclass correlations, and test/retest reliabilities are reported in the LEI manual (Anderson, 1973). Alpha coefficients, based on the responses of 1,048 high school students range from .54 (Diversity) to .85 (Goal Direction), while intraclass correlations for the same sample fall between .31 (Diversity) and .92 (Formality and Disorganization). Test/retest estimates, computed on a sample of 139 11th- and 12th-graders, over a 4-week interval. range from .43 (Diversity) to .73 (Friction). Anderson, notes, however, that these results may be unrepresentative since unusual national political events, believed to have had a strong effect on high school students, occurred between test administrations.

Validity: The LEI manual summarizes validity studies on a scale-by-scale basis. Major relationships between each scale and selected other variables are reported. For example, the Cohesiveness scale has been related to class size, with smaller groups indicating greater cohesiveness. Large classes, on the other hand, were rated as more formal than small classes.

Science classes using the Harvard Project Physics Course, which promotes a variety of interests and activities and attempts to simplify physics, received higher scores on the Diversity scale and lower scores on the Difficulty scale than more traditional physics classes.

Other relationships, too numerous to mention here, were also in the expected directions.

Norms: Scale means and standard deviations are provided for 1,048 high school students in a variety of subject areas. Class means are also presented for 2 samples: (1) 47 Harvard Project Physics classes and 37 traditional physics classes, whose students were given an early (1967) version of the LEI; and (2) 62 diverse classes from 8 high schools in Montreal, where the 1969 version was administered.

Administration and Scoring: The test can be easily administered in 30 to 40 minutes. Students can respond on an optical scanning answer sheet, and their responses can then be punched onto regular IBM computer cards. Machine scoring is recommended due to the large number of subscales. Response alternatives are assigned values from 1 to 4. Scale scores are computed by totaling the item scores for each scale. Since all scales contain 7 items, scale scores range from 7 to 28.

Comments: The LEI is short, easy to administer, and supported by a wide variety of research. In general, its phychometric characteristics are satisfactory. The moderate internal consistency reliabilities are acceptable since the LEI attempts to measure many dimensions validly, rather than to measure a few dimensions very reliably.

References: Anderson, G. J., *The assessment of learning environments: A manual for the Learning Environment Inventory and the My Class Inventory.* Halifax, Nova Scotia, Canada: Atlantic Institute of Education, 1973.

Edwards, K. J., D. L. DeVries, and S. A. Livingston, *Changing the focus of response in assessing classroom learning environments.* Baltimore: Center for Social Organization of Schools, 1973.

Walberg, H. J., "Social environment as a mediator of classroom learning." *Journal of Educational Psychology*, 1969, **60**, 443–448.

Walberg, H. J., and G. J. Anderson, "Properties of the achieving urban classes." *Journal of Educational Psychology*, 1972, **63**, 381–385.

Name: MEASURES OF SELF CONCEPT, GRADES K–12. REVISED EDITION

Author: Instructional Objectives Exchange

Type of Measure: Battery of affective tests including self-report questionnaires and observation indicators.

Availability: Instructional Objectives Exchange. *Measures of self concept, grades K–12* (rev. ed.). Los Angeles: Author, 1972. This battery may be obtained from the Instructional Objectives Exchange, Distribution Center, P.O. Box 24095, Los Angeles, California 90024.

Description: This instrument is one in a series of criterion-referenced test batteries published by the Instructional Objectives Exchange. Like its companion battery, Attitude Toward School, Grades K–12 (reviewed in this volume), this group of tests is referred to as a "collection of objectives and related measuring instruments ... devoted solely to affective goals (Instructional Objectives Exchange, 1972, p. 1)." These objectives and measures are designed for use in evaluating instructional programs aimed at improving students' self-concepts.

The tests in this collection include direct and inferential self-report devices as well as observational indicators. The self-report scales are available in primary (grades K–3), intermediate (grades 4–6), or secondary (grades 7–12) forms. The direct self-report measures assess 4 dimensions of self-concept (Family; Peer; Scholastic; and General), thus providing subscale scores. The inferential self-reports, however, each focus on one of these 4 dimensions.

Commissioned in 1970 by representatives of Title III programs, the Instructional Objectives Exchange developed and subsequently revised the Measures of Self Concept battery based on a review of the literature, an examination of existing self-concept scales, interviews with educators and students, pilot testing, and item analyses. The revised battery includes the following measures.

1. *Self Appraisal Inventory* (Primary, Intermediate, and Secondary levels): This direct self-report scale contains 36 items at the primary level, 77 at the intermediate level, and 62 at the secondary level, all of which assess various aspects of self-concept. Younger students respond by marking "yes" or "no," intermediate students by answering "true" or "false," and secondary students by indicating extent of agreement on a 4-point scale.

2. *Television Actors* (Primary level): Based on the assumption that a child with a positive self-concept will be more willing than one with a negative self-concept to project himself into a wide variety of make-believe roles, this inventory measures general self-estimates by asking the pupil to select from a list of 18 television characters those which he would be willing to play.

3. *What Would You Do?* (Intermediate and Secondary levels): This instrument assesses general self-concept by presenting the respondent with 18 or 19 fictitious situations and asking him to select one of 4 actions or interpreta-

tions (2 positive, 2 negative) which best describes what he would think or do in the situation depicted. The problems presented were drawn from the self-concept literature, particularly the work of Coppersmith (1967) and Wylie (1961). They focus on the following dimensions: (1) accommodation to others; (2) expectations of acceptance; (3) courage to express opinions; (4) willingness to contribute; and (5) expectations of success.

4. *The Class Play* (Primary and Intermediate levels): This inventory measures self-esteem associated with peer relations by asking the student to select from a number of dramatic roles (both negative and positive) those which his peers would cast him to play.

5. *Word Choice* (Secondary level): This measure assesses self-concept in relation to peers, using 19 pairs of bipolar adjectives, each arranged on a 7-point scale. The student rates himself on each word pair, according to the way in which he feels his friends would describe him.

6. *How About You* (Intermediate level): Based on the assumption that the student with a positive self-concept will view himself as scholastically successful, or at least able, this test asks the respondent to imagine that he is writing an essay about himself and then to select from a number of descriptions those which he would include in the essay.

7. *For All I Know* (Secondary level): This inventory measures self-esteem by presenting the student with 10 hypothetical situations involving school achievement, academic integrity, confidence in school work, and scholastic initiative. The student must select one of 4 alternatives (2 positive, 2 negative) which best describes what he would do in the situation depicted.

8. *Parental Approval Index* (Primary and Intermediate levels): This instrument describes 10 activities, 7 of which would generally provoke parental disapproval. For each item, the child indicates: (1) how his mother would feel about the particular activity; and (2) how she would feel about *him* if he were to engage in the activity.

9. *Work Posting* (Primary and Intermediate levels): Based on the assumption that students with positive self-concepts will want to display their work, this instrument requires an observer to record the number of students who post their completed assignments on the bulletin board when given the opportunity to do so.

10. *Perceived Approval Situation* (Primary, Intermediate, and Secondary levels): This instrument measures self-concept through a contrived classroom situation, in which the teacher announces his approval of an unnamed group of students and then allows the individual student to decide whether or not he is included in this special group. If the student decides that he is included in the group, he indicates this by coming to see the teacher. This situation permits the pupil to display 3 aspects of self-esteem: (1) confidence in ability; (2) willingness to place himself in a vulnerable

social position; and (3) confidence in others' opinion of him. It is assumed that the student with a positive self-concept will be more likely to express these perceptions of self-worth.

Sample Items: Item format varies from test to test. The following items are similar to those on several of the measures included in this battery:

Test	*Item*	*Response Alternatives*
Self Appraisal Inventory (Primary)	Do most of the other children have more friends than you?	Yes No
Television Actors (Primary)	Will you play the part of a snail?	Yes No
What Would You Do? (Intermediate)	Both you and your friend are nominated to be captain of a class team. You know that your friend would like to be captain. You:	a) turn down the nomination. b) worry that your friend doesn't want you to run. c) accept the nomination. d) think that it's okay for both you and your friend to run for the position.
The Class Play (Intermediate)	Would your classmates choose you to play a coward?	Yes No
Word Choice (Secondary)	I think my friends would describe me as:	_ _ _ _ _ _ _ Relaxed Tense _ _ _ _ _ _ _ Thin Overweight
How About You (Intermediate)	Your class is putting on a skit. If you had one of the leading parts, you would be:	a) great b) okay c) not very good
For All I Know (Secondary)	If you had started a class test but discovered you did not understand the instructions for several questions, you would probably:	a) raise your hand and ask the teacher for help. b) just do the best you could. c) ask a classmate for help. d) complete all the questions except those which were unclear.

| Parental Approval Index (Intermediate) | If you had just stolen some comic books from the drugstore, what would your mother think about this? | Approve ____ Disapprove ____ Wouldn't Care ____ |

Reliability: The Instructional Objectives Exchange (1972) reports internal consistency (KR_{20}) estimates and test/retest stability coefficients (computed over a 2-week interval) for the revised Measures of Self Concept. These figures, summarized below, are based on samples ranging in size from 62 to 185.

Tests	Internal Consistency	Test/Retest Stability
Secondary		
Self Appraisal Inventory	.75	.87
General	.60	.67
Peer	.61	.62
Scholastic	.72	.53
Family	.74	.70
What Would You Do?	.78	.69
Word Choice	.54	.86
For All I Know	.74	.31
Intermediate		
Self Appraisal Inventory	.87	.88
General	.80	.75
Peer	.82	.85
Scholastic	.81	.78
Family	.70	.83
Class Play	.78	.80
Parental Approval	.73	.91
What Would You Do?	.58	.64
How About You?	.57	.68
Primary		
Self Appraisal Inventory	.37	.73
General	.50	.43
Peer	.60	.29
Scholastic	.62	.58
Family	.61	.50
Parental Approval	.55	.77
TV Actors	.60	.74
Class Play	.60	.75

Validity: The thorough analyses undertaken during test development and revision assure at least some content and construct validity. Items on the direct self-report measures, for example, were carefully screened according to 2 criteria. They were required to yield responses which showed both (1) appreciable variability among students, and (2) congruence with a predetermined objective reflecting an assumed aspect of self-concept. While the direct self-report measures probably possess more content validity than the inferential self-reports, responses to the former are more easily faked. Furthermore, high intercorrelations among the subscales of the direct self-reports indicate that these measures are not assessing truly distinct characteristics.

Though they provide no evidence of criterion-related validity, the test authors do report that validity analyses carried out by various educators throughout the nation have generally been positive (Instructional Objectives Exchange, 1972).

Norms: Because the tests in this battery are criterion- rather than norm-referenced, normative data are inapplicable to them.

Administration and Scoring: Although directions for administration and scoring vary among the Measures of Self Concept, they are in every case well explained and easy to follow. In general, the tests require 10 to 20 minutes to complete. Since they are designed to yield data about the instructional program rather than the student, they should be answered anonymously. Items on the primary level tests are read aloud to the pupils and are frequently keyed by pictures or colors to the answer sheets.

All of the Measures of Self Concept are distributed as preprinted spirit masters, from which 200 to 300 copies can be duplicated. Alternate forms are available for every test in the battery.

When a small group of children is tested, hand scoring is feasible. However, machine scoring is recommended for larger groups. Several scoring options, explained in the manual, are available.

Comments: Carefully constructed and periodically revised by the Instructional Objectives Exchange, Measures of Self-Concept, Grades K–12, when used as a complete battery, provides broad coverage of student self-concept. This collection of instruments is designed, however, for program rather than student evaluation. Because the measures in the battery are criterion-referenced, they compare the student's reported self-concept not to that of other students, but instead to explicitly difined objectives. Such an objective might specify, for example, that the student will demonstrate positive self-concept in relation to his peers by expressing agreement with questions reflecting positive perceptions of the self in social situations and disagreement with those reflecting negative perceptions. The use of these objectives makes this, and the other affective batteries published by the Instructional Objectives Exchange, somewhat unusual since criterion-referencing is uncommon among self-concept and attitude scales.

This collection shows adequate psychometric properties (and particularly good face validity), considering its recent development. However, it shares the weaknesses of its companion battery, Attitude Toward School. Evidence of criterion-related validity and efforts to raise the reliabilities of the primary level tests are needed.

References: Coopersmith, S., *The antecedents of self-esteem.* San Francisco: W. H. Freeman, 1967.

Instructional Objectives Exchange, *Measures of Self Concept, Grades K–12* (rev. ed.). Los Angeles: Author, 1972.

Wylie, R. C., *The self-concept, a critical study of pertinent literature.* Lincoln, Nebraska: University of Nebraska Press, 1961.

Name: QUESTIONNAIRE   FOR   STUDENTS,   TEACHERS,   AND ADMINISTRATORS

Authors: The Secondary School Research Program and the Educational Testing Service

Type of Measure: Questionnaire

Availability: This instrument may be obtained from Dr. Edward Dalton, Program Director, Secondary School Research Program, Box 2601, Educational Testing Service, Princeton, New Jersey 08540.

Description: The Questionnaire for Students, Teachers, and Administrators (QUESTA) was developed by the Secondary School Research Program (SSRP), an association of public, independent, and Catholic high schools, in collaboration with the Educational Testing Service (ETS) in order to obtain a systematic assessment of school environment from students, teachers, and administrators. A working committee of schoolmen and ETS professionals based the questionnaire on (1) a review of related research, (2) interviews with students, teachers, administrators, and counselors, and (3) findings from trial administrations of an experimental version.

QUESTA is a 2-part test containing a mixture of questions (some about the school and some about the respondent) covering the following content areas:

Leadership
Governance
Stress
Human relations
Counseling
Teachers, grades, and curriculum
The arts
Student status structure
Student and adult value systems
Use of drugs, alcohol, tobacco
Satisfaction with the school
   experience
Cheating
Relations of racial and ethnic
   groups

Career goals and life style
Athletics and physical education
Change in the school
Student's individual development
Leisure time
Sexual values
Purposes of the school
Tensions within the school
   community
Effect of the school on the
   student
Extracurricular activities
Rules and regulations
Ethical and spiritual values

These content areas are represented on both parts of the questionnaire. The first part, QUESTA I, is administered only to new students or entering freshmen in an attempt to gather baseline biographical, socioeconomic, demographic, and attitudinal data. The second part, QUESTA II, is administered to these same students either at the end of the senior year or the end of each school year. It yields information about the student's satisfaction with the school and with his own development, about the values of various subgroups within the school, and about sources of tension and discontent. By comparing Parts I and II, the administrator or researcher can estimate the impact of the school on the student's attitudes and values. To obtain a more comprehensive assessment of the school environment, QUESTA II may also be completed by teachers and administrators. In this way, areas of agreement and disagreement among students, teachers, and administrators can be pinpointed.

Because QUESTA is designed to assess the school, rather than the individual, it is completed anonymously and results are tabulated by ETS for groups only.

Sample Items: QUESTA I contains items and response alternatives of the following type:

1. Check the phrases below which you feel describe the relations between racial and ethnic groups at this school.

   ☐ They ignore each other.
   ☐ They are friendly with each other.
   ☐ They distrust each other.
   ☐ They make an effort to understand each other.
   ☐ They fight each other.
   ☐ They ridicule each other.
   ☐ They put up with each other.
   ☐ They treat each other as individuals rather than members of a group.

2. What would you do if you caught another student cheating?

   ☐ It would bother me, but I'd ignore it.
   ☐ It wouldn't bother me so I'd ignore it.
   ☐ It would depend on the circumstances and the identity of the cheater.
   ☐ I'd talk to the student about it.
   ☐ I'd mention it to a teacher without naming the student.
   ☐ I'd report the student to a teacher.

Items and responses similar to those below appear on QUESTA II.

1. Would you like your school to offer (or continue to offer) courses or counseling on the following?

	No	Yes	No opinion
Male/female relations	☐	☐	☐
Drugs	☐	☐	☐
Drinking	☐	☐	☐
Social relations	☐	☐	☐
Racial relations	☐	☐	☐
Vocational choice	☐	☐	☐
Differences between right and wrong	☐	☐	☐

2. To what degree do you feel each of the following groups determines school policy?

	Little influence	Some influence	Much influence	Don't know
Teachers	☐	☐	☐	☐
Students	☐	☐	☐	☐
The principal	☐	☐	☐	☐
The school board	☐	☐	☐	☐
Graduates	☐	☐	☐	☐
The public	☐	☐	☐	☐
Parents	☐	☐	☐	☐

Reliability: The *QUESTA Interpretive Manual* (Baird and Peterson, 1972) provides no information on reliability. Questions of internal consistency and stability over time, however, do not apply to this measure, since its content is intentionally varied, and responses are expected to change over a 1- or 4-year period.

Validity: No validity data are available at present.

Norms: Normative data on QUESTA I and II are compiled yearly for the following categories: (1) public schools; (2) Catholic boys' schools; (3) Catholic girls' schools; (4) Catholic coeducational schools; (5) independent boys' boarding schools; (6) independent girls' boarding schools; (7) independent coeducational boarding schools; (8) independent boys' day schools; (9) independent girls' day schools; and (10) independent coeducational day schools. These data are available from ETS.

Administration and Scoring: Because QUESTA I and QUESTA II are designed as longitudinal research instruments, they should both be used regularly and recurrently. Detailed guidelines for administering QUESTA, along with test forms, comment sheets, and preaddressed return envelopes for completed questionnaires are provided by ETS. Administration procedures usually require about 10 minutes, while QUESTA I takes approximately 40 minutes to complete and QUESTA II, 60 minutes.

ETS offers several scoring options. Standard Scoring Service provides a computer print-out of questions and responses arranged by subgroup (male students, female students, all students, teachers, administrators, and total staff). This print-out includes the number responding in each category and the percentages of responses to each choice in the questionnaire. Since QUESTA is designed primarily for internal use rather than external comparisons, scale scores are not provided.

If item-response percentages are desired for 1 to 4 additional subgroups (racial or age groups, for example), the Combined Scoring Service can be requested. Or, if the user wishes the data to be further subdivided, he may request "Batching," a method of obtaining information about subgroups specified by the school (i.e., experienced vs. new teachers).

Comment: Developed with the professional supervision and cooperation of ETS, the Questionnaire for Students, Teachers, and Administrators is a carefully constructed instrument covering a wide range of environmental variables. Although psychometric information on QUESTA is somewhat limited at present, ETS and SSRP, due to the longitudinal nature of the test, are accumulating data continuously. While QUESTA was designed primarily to help the school understand and evaluate its own environment, it can be used to compare schools in general ways or to satisfy a number of other research purposes.

References: Baird, L. L., and F. A. Peterson, "A new look at reality in the high schools, or why the Secondary School Research Program?" *Phi Delta Kappan,* 1971, **52**, 427–431.

Baird, L. L., and F. A. Peterson, *QUESTA interpretive manual.* Princeton, New Jersey: Educational Testing Service, 1972.

Educational Testing Service, *The Secondary School Research Program. A prospectus.* Princeton, New Jersey: Author, 1972.

Secondary School Research Program, and The Educational Testing Service. *SSRP Newsletter,* 1974, **2**(1).

Name: SCHOOL CLIMATE INDEX—NS1

Author: Douglas S. Finlayson

Type of Measure: Rating scale

Availability: This instrument is available for research use from the National Foundation for Educational Research in England and Wales, The Mere, Slough, Bucks, England.

Description: The School Climate Index—NS1 is one component of a 4-part instrument measuring social climate in secondary schools. Although developed in England, the index is based on the work of 2 Americans, Halpin and Croft (1963). This particular scale assesses pupils' perceptions of the behavior of their teachers and peers, while its 3 companion scales measure: (1) teachers' perceptions of their colleagues' behavior; (2) teachers' perceptions of the department head's behavior; and (3) teachers' perceptions of the principal's behavior. One of these scales, The Teacher Questionnaire on Teacher Group Behavior, is described in this volume. Taken together, these 4 tests provide a measure of the climate of the school as a social system.

In developing the School Climate Index, a large number of items, covering a wide range of pupil and teacher behaviors, was initially assembled, based on a review of the literature. After interviews with teachers and pupils, these items were modified and reduced in number. A final list of 170 items was administered to 314 15-year-old boys, whose responses were subjected to factor analyses. After further revision, the test was administered to a random sample of boys, and results were factor analyzed once more.

These analyses produced a final 34-item test, with 4 relatively independent scales, 2 of which concern peer behavior and 2, teacher behavior. The peer behavior scales are Task Orientation and Emotional Tone, while the teacher scales are Concern and Social Control.

Sample Items: The School Climate Index contains items of the following type, to which the subject responds on a 5-point scale, from "Strongly Agree" to "Strongly Disagree":

1. Pupils tear up or scribble in their textbooks.
2. Teachers here try to help pupils whenever they can.
3. Everybody tries to get into classes taught by the easy teachers.

Reliability: Alpha coefficients were computed as a measure of internal consistency. These ranged from .77 to .84 for the 4 scales (Finlayson, 1970a).

Validity: Validity was investigated by the known-group method. Fourteen schools were selected, representing differences in organization, geographic location, and administrative style. Pupils at these schools were administered the Index, and their responses were subjected to a one-way analysis of variance. The

F-ratios, all significant at the .01 level, indicated that responses differed according to the school at which they were obtained (Finlayson, 1970).

Norms: Mean scores and standard deviations for each of the scales, derived from the responses of 978 boys and girls attending 14 comprehensive schools in England, are provided in the manual.

Administration and Scoring: The Index is designed for administration to groups of approximately 30 secondary school pupils. After explaining the purpose of the test, guaranteeing confidentiality, and answering pupil questions, the administrator reads the instructions aloud to the examinees, who then complete the scale. Responses are recorded on a separate answer sheet. Usually, no more than 30 minutes are required for test administration and completion.

A scoring key is provided in the manual. Values ranging from 0 to 4 are assigned to each of the response alternatives, the direction of scoring depending on the negative or positive wording of the item.

Comments: Use of the School Climate Index may be limited in the United States since its normative data and item content apply to British respondents. However, with minor revision, it could easily acquire face validity for American students. In combination with its companion scales, this test could provide a comprehensive measure of social climate in secondary schools.

References: Finlayson, D. S., *Administrative manual for the School Climate Index (NS1)*. The Mere, Upton Park, Slough, England: NFER, 1970. (a)

Finlayson, D. S., "How high and low achievers see teachers' and pupils' role behavior." *Research in Education*, 1970, **3**, 38–52. (b)

Finlayson, D. S., "Measuring 'school climate'." *Trends in Education*, 1973, **30**, 19–27.

Halpin, A. W., and D. B. Croft, *The organizational climate of schools*. Chicago: Midwest Administration Center, University of Chicago, 1963.

Name: SCHOOL MORALE SCALE

Authors: Lawrence S. Wrightsman, Ronald H. Nelson, and Maria Taranto

Type of Measure: Questionnaire

Availability: Wrightsman, L. S., R. H. Nelson, and M. Taranto. *The construction and validation of a scale to measure children's school morale.* Nashville, Tennessee: George Peabody College for Teachers, 1968.

Description: The School Morale (SM) Scale is designed to assess the change in students' school-related attitudes and morale. The authors (Wrightsman, Nelson, and Taranto, 1968) believe that innovative programs in the schools will produce changes in student behavior. However, behavior changes must be preceded by changes in pupil morale. Improvement in student achievement and personal/social development cannot occur without attitudinal change. Thus, a device which accurately measures changes in students' attitudes and morale, according to the authors, is both necessary and important.

In selecting dimensions to be measured by the SM scale, the authors considered (1) the types of innovations proposed by various agents, including Title III Projects, Project Mid-Tenn and Project REACHIGH and (2) aspects of school life and relationships that affect the student's attitude about school. The 7 dimensions eventually chosen are represented by 12 items each, yielding a total of 84 items. Half of the items on each subscale are favorable toward school and half are unfavorable. The subject responds to the item by printing either A (agree) or D (disagree) in the appropriate space.

Sample Items: The 7 SM subscales are listed below, along with items similar to those appearing on the test.

Subscales	*Items*
1. Morale about the school plant	Compared with most school buildings I've seen, this building is not very good.
2. Morale about instruction and instructional materials	My teachers use very few audiovisual materials to help me learn.
3. Morale about administration, regulations, and staff	The principal of this school is unfair.
4. Morale about community support of schools and parental involvement in the schools	My parents are not very interested in the school.
5. Relationships with other students	I wish I had more friends at this school.

6. Morale about   Most teachers in this school have
   teacher/student relationships   "teacher's pets."
7. General feeling about   I wish I could attend another
   attending school   school.

Reliability: The authors (Wrightsman and Nelson, undated) report subscale homogeneity estimates for 3 samples (127 fifth-graders, 169 seventh-graders and 137 ninth-graders). Of the 21 coefficient-alphas obtained, 18 exceeded .50, and 15 exceeded .60. The authors concluded that each subscale showed adequate item homogeneity since alphas are conservative estimates of reliability. The least reliable subscale involved community support and parental interest in the school. This was expected since many students are not aware of teacher salaries and community support of schools. The highest coefficients were obtained for the teacher/student relationship subscale.

Correlations between SM subscales have also been computed, using four samples including a total of 477 subjects. All intercorrelations were significant and positive and did not increase with grade level. The subscale which correlated most highly with the others was that involving general feelings about the school. Parental involvement correlated the lowest. The authors concluded that the total SM score does reflect a basically unitary construct.

Validity: Validity of the SM scale is established in terms of: (1) school grade and sex differences; and (2) relationships between student scores and teacher ratings of students' attitudes. To test school differences, the author used four Tullahoma, Tennessee elementary schools which varied widely in regard to the socioeconomic status of their students. Mean scores on the subscales dealing with community support of the schools and general feeling about school were lower for lower SES schools. Children in older school buildings obtained lower scores on the school plant subscale. In a similar investigation, total SM scores of students attending New Providence Junior High, an innovative institution, were consistently higher than those of students attending a regular junior high in Chattanooga. The authors concluded that the morale of the average student at New Providence is much better than that of the average student at the Chattanooga school. Data collected in this study also revealed sex and grade differences. It was found that as grade level increased, average school morale decreased. This was true for both sexes at both schools. Girls, on the average, reported higher school morale than boys. Both of these findings were expected.

Teachers' nominations of students with good or poor school morale were also obtained and compared to SM scores. At each grade level, the "good morale" nominees had significantly higher total scores than "poor morale" students.

Further data, relating the SM Scale to other variables such as age, intelligence, grade point average, achievement, and authoritarianism, are presented by the authors (Wrightsman et al., 1968).

Norms: Median total and subscale scores are reported for grades 7, 8, and 9 of New Providence Junior High School and another junior high in Chattanooga, Tennessee. Grade means are presented for grades 4 and 5 in 4 Tullahoma, Tennessee, elementary schools. Research involving 2 upper-middle-class schools (grades 4, 5, and 6) also produced grade means and standard deviations for each of the subscales. In addition, total and subscale scores for experimental and control classes in 6 Tuscaloosa, Alabama elementary schools are reported (Wrightsman et al., 1968).

Administration and Scoring: This instrument is easily administered in a relatively short period of time. An SM Scale Score Sheet is used to record answers on appropriate subscales. For each subscale, the number of agreements with favorably worded statements and the number of disagreements with unfavorably worded statements are summed to determine the score on that subscale. A subscale score of 12 indicates very good morale, while 0 indicates extremely poor morale. The sum of the subscale scores produces a total score which can range from 0 to 84.

Comments: The authors point out that the School Morale Scale is still in a developmental stage. Although preliminary investigations indicate validity, additional control groups should be studied to more conclusively validate the instrument. Also, test/retest data should be obtained. Still, the SM Scale appears to be a useful research measure for gauging student morale and evaluating innovative programs.

References: Wrightsman, L. S., and R. H. Nelson, *The reliability of the School Morale Scale.* Nashville, Tennessee: George Peabody College for Teachers, undated.

Wrightsman, L. S., R. H. Nelson, and M. Taranto, *The construction and validation of a scale to measure children's school morale.* Nashville, Tennessee: George Peabody College for Teachers, 1968.

Name: SCHOOL ORGANIZATION INDEX—AS1

Authors: Douglas S. Finlayson, Olive Banks, and J. L. Loughran

Type of Measure: Rating scale

Availability: This instrument is available for research use from the National Foundation for Educational Research in England and Wales, The Mere, Slough, Bucks, England.

Description: The School Organization Index—AS1 was developed in England to measure the way in which high school students perceive the organizational structure of the classroom and the school as a whole. It is composed of 2 scales, one relating to pupil behavior and the other to teacher behavior. In Scale I, Pupil Participation and Integration, the student indicates the degree to which his peers can and do participate in school decision making and the extent to which they can and do interact with pupils of differing academic and social backgrounds. On Scale II, Promotion of Individual and Social Experience, he notes the degree to which teachers encourage organizational procedures compatible with individual interest and abilities, open social interaction, and a variety of social values.

Sample Items: The School Organization Index contains 36 items of the following type, to which the student responds on a 5-point scale, from "Strongly Agree" to "Strongly Disagree":

Scale	*Item*
I. Pupil Participation and Integration	1. Several groups of students here never attend school functions.
	2. There is no way for students to make their opinions known.
	3. There are a good number of clubs and extracurricular activities available to the students..
II. Promotion of Individual and Social Experience	1. Teachers don't trust us to do our own work unless they're watching.
	2. Teachers require all students to do the same kind of project in the same way.
	3. Teachers allow us to sit where we want in class.

Reliability: Estimates of internal consistency are provided in the manual for both scales. The alpha coefficient for Scale I is .85, for Scale II, .81 (Finlayson, Banks, and Loughran, 1970).

Validity: The manual presents no evidence of predictive or concurrent validity. Some content and construct validity may be inferred from analyses of the scales. In developing the test, 100 original items were administered to fourth-year classes in 14 comprehensive schools in England, and responses were factor analyzed. A principal components analysis was applied to both the pupil items and the teacher items. Though both first- and second-order rotated factors were examined, interpretation of the separate factors proved impossible. Each factor contained a number of items from each of the areas covered by the Index. The authors concluded that "in the perceptions of the pupils no distinction was made between the various dimensions of role behavior reported (Finlayson, Banks, and Loughran, 1970, p. 5)." Consequently, those pupil and teacher items with the highest loadings ($> .4$) on their respective principal components were included on the final scales.

The relationship between Scales I and II is also discussed in the manual. As would be expected, the scales are not independent of each other, though the degree to which they are related varies from school to school. Product-moment correlation coefficients, obtained from data collected at 14 English schools, ranged from .46 to .79. The authors suggest that further work is needed to clarify the relationship between Scale I and Scale II (Finlayson, Banks, and Loughran, 1970).

Norms: Means and standard deviations for 978 14-year-old students attending 14 diverse comprehensive schools in England are provided in the manual.

Administration and Scoring: The Index may be administered in a minimum of 25 minutes. This estimate allows time for the administrator to establish rapport with the subjects and assure them that their responses will be treated confidentially.

Responses are scored from 0 to 4, according to a key provided in the manual. The direction of scoring depends on the positive or negative wording of the item. A high score indicates that the respondent perceives the school organization as encouraging student participation and a variety of individual and social experiences.

Comments: Use of the School Organization Index may be limited in the United States since its normative data and item content apply to British students. Insufficient validity data may further restrict its use. However, if items were adapted for use with American students, the School Organization Index might prove valuable in research situations.

Reference: Finlayson, D. S., O. Banks, and J. L. Loughran, *Administrative manual for School Organization Index (ASI)*. The Mere, Upton Park, Slough, England: NFER, 1970.

Name: STUDENT OPINION POLL

Authors: Jacob W. Getzels and Philip W. Jackson

Type of Measure: Rating scale/adjective checklist/questionnaire

Availability: Getzels, J. W., and P. W. Jackson, *Creativity and intelligence.* New York: John Wiley, 1962.

Description: The Student Opinion Poll (SOP) is a 3-part instrument designed to assess the attitudes of secondary school students toward school. Part I is a 60-item opinionnaire concerning general satisfaction with various aspects of school, such as curriculum, teachers, instructional methods, and student body. Part II is a list of 24 adjectives (12 "negative" and 12 "positive") from which the student selects 6 that best describe his feelings in each of seven classes: English, mathematics, science, art or music, physical education, social studies, and foreign language. The third part of the SOP requires the student to write an essay describing the 1 hour of class during the past academic year which he feels was most worthwhile.

Sample Items: Part I of the SOP contains items and response alternatives of the following type:

1. In preparing students for college, the curriculum at this school is
   a) more difficult and demanding than it needs to be.
   b) just about right.
   c) easier than it should be.

2. In this school, students
   a) put too much emphasis on competition.
   b) put too much emphasis on cooperation.
   c) have achieved a good balance between cooperation and competition.

Part II contains adjectives similar to those below.

Positive	*Negative*
1. self-confident	1. misjudged
2. good	2. mad
3. enthusiastic	3. discontented
4. satisfied	4. uninterested

Reliability: No reliability data are reported by the test authors (Getzels and Jackson, 1962; Jackson and Getzels, 1959).

Validity: Most evidence supporting the validity of the SOP involves the instrument's ability to differentiate groups. In an exploratory study, Getzels and Jackson (1962) identified 2 samples of adolescents: a "highly moral" group selected according to their scores on tests requiring ethical or moral decisions; and a "highly adjusted" group, whose members scored in the top 20% on measures of adjustment. The mean SOP scores of these 2 samples differed significantly, those of the adjusted students suggesting greater satisfaction with their total school experience, particularly with other people in their environment. The free-response essays in Part III of the test also revealed differences between the 2 groups, with the adjusted students emphasizing the interpersonal and social aspects of their education and the moral students stressing intellectual stimulation.

In another study, Jackson and Getzels (1959) used the SOP to select 2 experimental groups, one composed of "satisfied" high school students, the other of "dissatisfied" students. Though these 2 groups did not differ in general intellectual ability or achievement, they did differ according to "psychological health," as determined by their scores on the California Test of Personality, the Indirect Sentence Completion Test, and (for girls) the Direct Sentence Completion and the Group Rorschach. On all of these measures the "satisfied" group obtained scores indicating more adequate psychological functioning. Furthermore, the "satisfied" and "dissatisfied" boys were perceived differently by their teachers. On 3 teacher ratings, "satisfied" boys received more favorable evaluations than did "dissatisfied" boys. The authors hypothesized that this finding did not appear among girls because girls are less likely than boys to express negative feelings publicly.

Further evidence of validity is provided by DuCette and Wolk (1972), who found that an abbreviated form of Part I of the SOP correlated .49 ($p < .01$) with scores on the Brown-Holtzman Survey of Study Habits and Attitudes.

Norms: Getzels and Jackson (1962) provide means and standard deviations derived from the SOP total scores and subscores (Curriculum, Pupils, Teachers and Classroom Procedures) of 58 secondary school students. These subjects were selected for high intelligence and/or creativity.

Administration and Scoring: The SOP is easily administered and scored. The student is provided with brief, printed instructions, a test booklet, and an answer sheet. The entire test requires approximately 60 minutes, 30 of which are allotted to the Part III essay.

The 60 multiple-choice questions in Part I are scored by giving 1 point for each "satisfied" response. Thus, the range of possible scores is from 0 to 60. Part II is scored by tallying the number of positive and negative adjectives marked by the respondent. There are no set of rules for scoring Part III; the procedure selected depends on the objectives of testing. For example, when comparing "moral" and "adjusted" students, the authors (Getzels and Jackson, 1962) scored the essays according to emphasis placed on "personal" versus "social" aspects of learning, "allegiance" versus "alliance" and "ideational" versus "existential" perspectives.

Comments: The Student Opinion Poll is an appealing instrument since it solicits the student's attitude toward school in 3 ways, providing both objective and free-response data. However, the SOP is weakened by the scarcity of published information describing it. Reliability data are reported in neither of the authors' studies (Getzels and Jackson, 1962; Jackson and Getzels, 1959), and the populations administered the SOP have generally been atypical (selected for intelligence or creativity), thus limiting the inferential statements which can be based on research using this test. It should be noted, however, that Spellman (1959) replicated the work of Jackson and Getzels (1959) on another atypical, but different, sample (seventh- and eighth-grade, lower-class blacks) and obtained very similar results. While this measure appears to be valid, the authors suggest caution in interpreting SOP scores since some degree of dissatisfaction seems to be the norm, even among "satisfied" students.

References: DuCette, J., and S. Wolk, "Ability and achievement as moderating variables of student satisfaction and teacher perception." *Journal of Experimental Education,* 1972, **41**, 12–18.

Getzels, J. W., and P. W. Jackson, *Creativity and intelligence.* New York: John Wiley, 1962.

Jackson, P. W., and J. W. Getzels, "Psychological health and classroom functioning: A study of dissatisfaction with school among adolescents." *Journal of Educational Psychology,* 1959, **50**(6), 295–300.

Spellman, R. J., *Psychological and scholastic correlates of dissatisfaction with school among adolescents.* Unpublished master's thesis, University of Chicago, 1959.

Name: YOUR SCHOOL DAYS

Authors: Judith A. Agard and Sandra M. Harrison

Type of Measure: Questionnaire

Availability: Agard, J. A., and S. M. Harrison, *Your school days (developmental stage). Administrator's handbook.* Austin, Texas: Project PRIME, undated.

Description: Your School Days is a measure of classroom climate from the student's point of view. It contains 65 questions representing 4 factors derived from an analysis of item means obtained from a sample of approximately 9,000 normal (as opposed to mentally retarded, emotionally distrubed, or learning disabled) elementary pupils. These factors are: Enjoyment, Positive Reinforcement (I); Unhappiness, Misbehavior (II); Cognitive Emphasis (III); and Variety, Individualization (IV). Factor I links happiness with the teacher's use of positive reinforcement, while Factor II associates unhappiness and misbehavior with the teacher's selective use of special assignments. The third factor stresses reasoning and task orientation, and the fourth, individualized activity and self-direction. According to Veldman (undated), the extent to which these factors represent major characteristics of all classes, rather than different *types* of classes, is at this point uncertain.

Though specifically developed for Project PRIME (Programmed Re-Entry Into Mainstream Education) in an attempt to assess the effect of climate on the behavior of handicapped pupils, Your School Days may be administered in any elementary classroom.

Sample Items: Your School Days requires the child to respond to 65 items of the following type by writing " yes " or " no " on an answer sheet.

Factor	*Item*
I. Enjoyment, Positive Reinforcement	1. When you behave well, does your teacher say nice things to you?
	2. Do the children in your class like their school work?
II. Unhappiness, Misbehavior	1. Are many of the children in your class punished for misbehaving?
	2. Do the children in your class fight with one another a lot?
III. Cognitive Emphasis	1. When you answer one of the teacher's questions, do you have to give reasons for your answer?
	2. When your teacher tells you not to do something, does she explain why you shouldn't do it?

IV. Variety, Individualization

1. Are you allowed to use games and materials without the teacher watching you?
2. Do several different activities happen at the same time in your class?

Reliability: Veldman (undated) assessed the reliability of scale scores using alpha coefficients and intraclass correlations. Alphas were computed for item-mean data from 602 classes and for individual protocols from 3 samples: 648 mentally retarded children; 305 learning disabled students; and 1,042 normal children. Those for item-mean data ranged from .57 to .86. Estimates for individual protocols ranged from .38 to .65 for the MR sample, from .30 to .72 for the LD group, and from .34 to .69 for the normal children. Generally, alphas were highest for Scale I (Enjoyment, Positive Reinforcement) and lowest for Scale IV (Variety, Individualization).

Intraclass correlations, computed on 41 classes of 27 pupils each, produced the following reliability estimates for the 4 scales: .94, .93, .74, and .87, respectively. The same procedure also yielded reliabilities of .37, .31, .10, and .21 for individual pupil scale scores.

Validity: Since this instrument is still in a developmental stage, little information is available concerning its validity. However, preliminary analyses of the deviations of pupil scores from their respective means indicated that Your School Days discriminates among MR, LD, and normal groups in integrated classrooms. As expected, the scores of normal pupils were much closer to their class means than were those of either of the handicapped groups. The MR and LD children perceived fewer cognitive demands than did normal pupils, and the LD group reported more variety and individual attention (Veldman, undated).

When class-mean scale scores from special education classrooms were compared with those from integrated classrooms, results indicated that handicapped students, even when segregated, experienced fewer cognitive demands than normal children. LD students in special LD classrooms, however, did not perceive greater individualization and variety (Veldman, undated).

Norms: Distribution statistics for scale scores from 602 classes are provided by Veldman (undated).

Administration and Scoring: In administering Your School Days an examiner reads each item aloud to the children, who respond by writing "yes" or "no" in an answer booklet. Item responses are later transferred from the answer sheets to machine-scoreable forms. Four scale scores are produced, and, except on Scale IV, low scores are consistent with scale names.

Comments: Class means obtained on Your School Days appear to be good measures of classroom climate. Reliability figures indicate, however, that individual pupil protocols may be too idiosyncratic to serve as accurate measures of classroom atmosphere—though the difference between a pupil's score and the class mean may yield valuable information about that pupil's perception of classroom reality. Like other Project PRIME measures, Your School Days is still in a developmental stage, and more extensive psychometric data should become available as studies using this measure are completed and reported.

Reference: Veldman, D. J., *Scale structure of Your School Days.* Austin, Texas: Project PRIME Data Analysis Center, University of Texas, undated.

IIIC

About the classroom from an observer

Name: CLASSROOM OBSERVATION CODE DIGEST

Authors: Francis G. Cornell, Carl M. Lindvall, and Joe L. Saupe

Type of Measure: Observation coding system

Availability: Cornell, F. G., C. M. Lindvall, and J. L. Saupe, *An exploratory measurement of individualities of schools and classrooms.* Urbana, Illinois: Bureau of Educational Research, College of Education, University of Illinois, 1952.

Description: The Classroom Observation Code Digest was developed to measure differences in classrooms as an index of differences in school systems. After an extensive review of the literature, an evaluation of related measurement attempts, and empirical testing, the following dimensions were selected for inclusion on the Digest:

1. Differentiation—the extent to which the teacher recognizes individual differences among students.
2. Social Organization—the group structure and the pattern of interaction characterizing the classroom.
3. Pupil Initiative—the extent to which pupils are allowed to determine the learning situation.
4. Content—what is taught in the classroom.
5. Variety—the degree to which a variety of activities or techniques are used.
6. Competency—the technical performance of the teacher.
7. Classroom Climate (Teacher)—the social/emotional atmosphere of the classroom as reflected in the teacher's behavior.
8. Classroom Climate (Pupils)—the social/emotional atmosphere of the classroom as reflected in the pupils' behavior.

Sample Items: Each of the 8 dimensions represented on the Digest is designed to measure 1 aspect of a classroom learning situation. The Digest contains brief definitions of behavioral codes which are recorded by the observer on an accompanying tally sheet, labeled the Classroom Observation Schedule. The specific behaviors listed below are similar to those included in several of the Digest categories:

Dimension	*Behavior*
Variety	1. Pupils involved in class discussion.
	2. Pupils performed a demonstration.
	3. Teacher read aloud from text.
	4. Teacher showed a film.

Competency   1. Teacher conducted a review lesson.

2. Teacher provided relevant examples.

3. Teacher allowed discussion to continue aimlessly.

4. Teacher's answers to pupil questions were vague and ambiguous.

Reliability: In order to determine the instrument's reliability, the Digest was tested in 32 classrooms, each visited 3 times by 6 observers in teams of 2. During each visit, observers independently recorded behaviors for 30 minutes. Coefficients reported by Cornell, Lindvall, and Saupe (1952) range from .42 to .89 for a single observer's measurement, and from .59 to .94 for a team's measurement. In each case, the Competency dimension was least reliable, while Social Organization was most reliable. The single observer coefficients are, according to the authors, "similar in meaning to the correlations of 2 forms of a test (Cornell, Lindvall, and Saupe, 1952, p. 36)." The team estimates, however, are best described as indices of observer agreement (Medley and Mitzel, 1963). As such, the latter assess the objectivity of the Digest, but do not indicate its power to discriminate among classrooms. In a later study, Medley and Mitzel (1958) produced reliability coefficients which do indicate the discriminating power of the dimensions, as well as indices of observer agreement. Their estimates, based on 25-minute observations of 33 New York City classrooms made by 6 observers in teams of 2, range from .00 (Climate—Pupil) to .66 (Social Organization) for interobserver agreement, and from .00 (Climate—Pupil) to .42 (Variety) for discriminating power. The lower reliabilities obtained by Medley and Mitzel are perhaps a reflection of the more homogeneous sample used in their study (Medley and Mitzel, 1963).

Validity: During the development of the Classroom Observation Code Digest, 118 teachers responded to a questionnaire asking them to name the dimensions they considered most likely to distinguish one classroom from another. Responses to this questionnaire served as a check on the validity of the dimensions included on the Digest. The results were analyzed, categorized, and found to support the authors' original selection of dimensions (Cornell, Lindvall, and Saupe, 1952).

Further evidence of validity was provided in a pilot study of the Digest, results of which indicated that the dimensions significantly discriminate among classrooms. Each dimension was found to differ significantly on at least 1 of 5 sources of variation (Cornell, Lindvall and Saupe, 1952).

Norms: Data used in the pilot studies were collected from 32 classrooms in 4 "rural/urban" school districts in a central Illinois county and 4 "suburban-metropolitan" districts in a high socioeconomic area near Chicago. For each school system, 1 class was observed at each of 4 grade levels: fourth, sixth, eighth, and tenth (Cornell, Lindvall, and Saupe, 1952).

Data have also been collected in 33 elementary classrooms in New York City (Medley and Mitzel, 1958).

Procedures for Use: The observer uses the Digest as a guide in recording behavior on the Observation Schedule, or tally sheet. For the first 4 dimensions, he or she enters a number, representing the appropriate description of the classroom situation, for each 5-minute interval in a 1-hour visit. For the fifth dimension, each kind of behavior observed during 5-minute intervals is checked. Behaviors observed on the remaining dimensions are recorded only once during each visit.

The scoring procedure yields a single value for each dimension except Variety, which is scored once for the number of different activities observed, and once for the duration of these activities.

Comments: The Classroom Observation Code Digest is an economical and relatively uncomplicated measure of classroom characteristics. Observers need only about 15 hours of training to code a wide variety of items, many of which require little inference.

References: Cornell, F. G., C. M. Lindvall, and J. L. Saupe, *An exploratory measurement of individualities of schools and classrooms.* Urbana, Illinois: Bureau of Educational Research, College of Education, University of Illinois, 1952.

Medley, D. M. and H. E. Mitzel, "Application of analysis of variance to the estimation of the reliability of observations of teachers' classroom behavior." *Journal of Experimental Education,* 1958, **27**, 23–25.

Medley, D. M. and H. E. Mitzel, "Measuring classroom behavior by systematic observation," in N. L. Gage (ed.), *Handbook of research on teaching.* Chicago: Rand McNally, 1963.

Name: CLASSROOM OBSERVATION RECORD

Author: Henry Morrison McGee

Type of Measure: Observation coding system

Availability: McGee, H. M., "Measurement of authoritarianism and its relation to teachers' classroom behavior." *Genetic Psychology Monographs*, 1955, **52**, 89–146.

Description: The Classroom Observation Record was developed by McGee (1955) to assess classroom behavior related to authoritarianism in teachers. The initial form of the Record contained 13 categories of teacher behavior and 4 categories of pupil behavior, all presumed on the basis of theoretical and empirical studies, notably those reported in *The Authoritarian Personality* (Adorno, Frenkel-Brunswick, Levinson, and Sanford, 1950), to be associated with authoritarianism. Each of these categories was accompanied by a set of specific behaviors defining it, and a hypothesis concerning its connection with authoritarianism. The behaviors composing all 13 categories in combination formed a Glossary of terms to be used by the observer in coding classroom activity.

   A preliminary study of 50 elementary and secondary school teachers revealed a number of deficiencies in both the Record and the Glossary. As a result, descriptive behaviors with low discriminating power were eliminated, and several categories were revised to accommodate the dichotomous nature of the authoritarian character structure.

   The dimensions of teacher behavior included on the revised form of the Record are: Aloof vs. Approachable; Unresponsive vs. Responsive; Dominative vs. Integrative; Irresponsible vs. Responsible; Harsh vs. Kindly; Immature vs. Mature; Inflexible vs. Adaptable; Insensitive vs. Sensitive; Narrow vs. Broad; Partial vs. Fair; Pessimistic vs. Optimistic; Stereotyped vs. Liberal; and Suspicious vs. Trusting. Pupil behavior categories are: Unresponsive vs. Responsive; Dependent vs. Initiating; Obstructive vs. Responsible; and Uncertain vs. Confident.

Sample Items: Each specific descriptive behavior included in the Record's 17 categories relates to 1 or more of the variables comprising the authoritarian syndrome. Furthermore, each is observable. The following behaviors are similar to those which are coded on the Classroom Observation Record.

Variable	*Behavior*
Harsh vs. Kindly	1. Teacher ridiculed child in front of class.
	2. Teacher pointed out positive aspects of pupil's performance.

Stereotyped vs. Liberal   1. Teacher treated pupils as a homogeneous group, rather than as individuals.
2. Teacher explored problems, leaving room for questions and exceptions.

Reliability: Reliability of the obtained behavior scores was computed on a sample of 150 teachers, classified according to volunteer/nonvolunteer status, sex, teaching level, and minority/majority group membership. Pearson rs, corrected by the Spearman-Brown formula, ranged from .85 to .97. Overall reliability was estimated at .90 (McGee, 1955).

Agreement between observations was computed by correlating the first and second observations of 2 coders, yielding a coefficient of .74. Also, one of these coders and a timed observer simultaneously but independently recorded the behavior of 10% of the sample ($N = 15$). A rank-difference correlation of .89 was obtained between the 2 sets of scores (McGee, 1955).

Validity: Evidence for validity is drawn from 3 sources: item analysis; relationship to similar constructs; and differences between groups.

Internal consistency of the behavioral dimensions, established through item analysis, suggests validity by demonstrating that even the least discriminating categories significantly differentiated between high and low scorers (McGee, 1950).

Empirical validity is indicated by a correlation of .58 between mean behavior scores obtained on the Record and a modified form of the F-Scale, a measure of authoritarianism devised by Adorno, Frenkel-Brunswik, Levinson, and Sanford (1955).

Further evidence of the validity of teacher scores is provided by a highly significant critical ratio of 3.3 between the mean pupil behavior score obtained in classrooms of less authoritarian teachers and that obtained in classrooms of more authoritarian teachers (McGee, 1955).

Norms: Normative data are available for the 184 regular classroom teachers whose behavior was originally coded on the Classroom Observation Record. This sample included men and women, 25 to 30 years of age, teaching at the elementary or secondary level in the public schools of Oakland, California. No one in the sample had taught more than 3 years (McGee, 1955).

Procedures for Use: Before employing the Classroom Observation Record, the user should carefully train prospective observers and then pilot-test the system for agreement among them. This procedure may take as long as 4 weeks.

When observers are ready to enter the classroom, they should do so unobtrusively, situating themselves at the side or rear of the room. Behaviors are recorded as they are observed, unless coding appears to be causing some anxiety on the subjects' part, in which case observed behaviors may be entered immediately after class. An observation period of 45 to 50 minutes is considered optimal length.

Numerical values are assigned to each category according to the number of specific behaviors recorded in that category during a single observation period. For the 13 categories of teacher behavior, total scores can range from 13 to 91 points, a high score indicating strong authoritarian behavior.

Comments: While this instrument does not claim to represent all features of the authoritarian personality, it does include a good sample of those which are commonly expressed in the classroom. Although it requires extensive observer training, the Classroom Observation Record can be a valuable research tool.

References: Adorno, T. W., E. Frenkel-Brunswik, D. S. Levinson, and R. N. Sanford, *The authoritarian personality.* New York: Harper, 1950.

McGee, H. M., "Measurement of authoritarianism and its relation to teachers' classroom behavior." *Genetic Psychology Monographs*, 1955, **52**, 89–146.

Name: CLASSROOM OBSERVATION SCALES

Author: Edmund T. Emmer

Type of Measure: Observation coding system

Availability: Emmer, E. T. *Classroom observation scales.* Austin, Texas: Research and Development Center for Teacher Education, University of Texas, 1971.

Description: The Classroom Observation Scales (COS) are intended to measure "classroom process variables for research on teaching and to provide an instructional tool in teacher education (Emmer, 1971, p. i)." They are designed for use in the classroom by trained observers. The 12 variables measured by this instrument are listed and briefly described below.

1. *Pupil Attention* refers to student orientation toward the teacher, the task at hand, or the predominant classroom activity.
2. *Teacher-Initiated Problem Solving* indicates a mode of teacher behavior characterized by frequent presentation of questions and problems to the entire class.
3. *Pupil-to-Pupil Interaction* includes substantive utterances of one student directed at another or at a group of students, as well as indirect or unsolicited responses to the teacher.
4. *Teacher Presentation* refers to the relative amount of class time devoted to teacher presentation of substantive information.
5. *Negative Affect* is used to record behaviors which reflect negative or hostile feelings on the part of either the teacher or the pupils.
6. *Positive Affect* encompasses teacher behaviors which support or show positive feeling for pupils and their behavior.
7. *Higher Level Cognitive Student Behavior* refers to pupil verbalizations which reflect more complex cognitive processes.
8. *Passive Pupil Behavior* measures the extent to which pupils demonstrate passive behaviors, such as visual wandering or withdrawal from engagement with surroundings.
9. *Convergent-Evaluative Interaction* is characterized by a focus upon obtaining the correct answer to a teacher question, with little or no attempt to continue contact once the answer has been obtained.
10. *Task Orientation* measures the degree to which the teacher works toward content-related, substantive goals.
11. *Clarity* refers to the degree to which the teacher's presentations and interactions are understood by the pupils.
12. *Enthusiasm* indicates the extent to which the teacher demonstrates interest, vitality, and involvement in his subject and his teaching.

Sample Items: The COS manual (Emmer, 1971) lists specific behaviors and interactions typical of those which are recorded on each of the 12 scales. For example, attention (Scale 1) may be inferred from the following pupil behaviors: maintaining eye contact with the teacher; working on an assigned activity; or raising hand to volunteer a response.

Reliability: Reliability of the COS was established using data collected by graduate and undergraduate students who received approximately 6 hours of training, including practice observations of both videotapes and live classrooms. For each of 2 data sets, the manual presents 2 indices of interobserver agreement (intraclass correlations and average difference scores) along with estimates of stability. Intraclass correlations for data set 1 yielded reliability estimates for single observer scores ranging from .07 (Task Orientation) to .71 (Teacher Presentation). Corresponding correlations for data set 2 ranged from .06 (Higher Level Cognitive Pupil Behavior) to .81 (Pupil Attention). Reliability estimates for the average of 2 observers' scores ranged from .13 (Task Orientation) to .83 (Teacher Orientation) for data set 1, and from .12 (Higher Level Cognitive Pupil Behavior) to .89 (Pupil Attention) for data set 2. Average difference scores ranged from .31 (Pupil Attention) to .90 (Pupil-to-Pupil Interaction) for data set 1, and from .59 (Pupil Attention, Teacher Presentation, and Enthusiasm) to .90 (Teacher-Initiated Problem Solving) for data set 2.

Stability estimates were computed for single observations and for the average of 5 observations of each class. The former ranged from .08 (Task Orientation) to .65 (Enthusiasm) for data set 1 and from .10 (Convergent-Evaluative Interaction) to .64 (Pupil Attention) for data set 2. Stability estimates for an average of 5 observations ranged from .27 (Task Orientation) to .89 (Enthusiasm) for data set 1, and from .30 (Convergent-Evaluative Interaction) to .87 (Pupil Attention) for data set 2.

Validity: All but 3 of the 12 Classroom Observation Scales are empirically based. In developing the scales, observations were collected on 5 occasions in 28 fifth- and eighth-grade classrooms, using 5 coding systems: CASES (Spaulding, 1970); CCS (Emmer and Albrecht, 1970); Dyadic Interaction System (Good and Brophy, 1970); FAIR (Fuller, 1970); and OScAR 5V (Medley et al., 1968). Categories in each of these systems were intercorrelated, and these intercorrelations were then factor analyzed. The factors which emerged were intercorrelated across systems to yield common factors. Scales were defined using the behavioral categories associated with each factor.

Three scales (Task Orientation, Clarity, and Enthusiasm) not derived through factor analysis were also included since they had been associated with positive pupil outcomes in several different studies (Emmer, 1971).

Norms: The Classroom Observation Scales have been used in several research studies. The samples which served as the source for reliability data were composed of 15 fifth-grade classrooms and 31 first- and second-grade classrooms, each videotaped on 4 or 5 occasions and coded independently by 2 observers.

Procedures for Use: In using the COS, the observer should be situated so that he can see both the teacher and the pupils. Ideally, he should be able to observe the faces of all students. Thus situated, he records, at 15-minute intervals, observed behaviors on a printed coding form.

Comments: The Classroom Observation Scales are easy to learn and use, and they are, for the most part, behaviorally based. They may be effectively used in research, evaluation, or teacher performance feedback. However, the user should note that several of the scales (Higher Level Cognitive Pupil Behavior, Task Orientation, and Passive Pupil Behavior) have produced marginal or inconsistent reliability data. Furthermore, in using the scales, at least 4 or 5 observations should be collected. Otherwise, the user may obtain data which are not sufficiently reliable.

References: Brophy, J. E., and T. L. Good, *Teacher-child dyadic interaction: A manual for coding classroom behavior.* Austin, Texas: Research and Development Center for Teacher Education, University of Texas, 1970.

Emmer, E. T., *Classroom observation scales.* Austin, Texas: Research and Development Center for Teacher Education, University of Texas, 1971.

Emmer, E. T. and I. D. Albrecht, *The Cognitive Component System* (*CCS*) *manual.* Austin, Texas: Research and Development Center for Teacher Education, University of Texas, 1970.

Fuller, F. F., *FAIR system manual.* Austin, Texas: Research and Development Center for Teacher Education, University of Texas, 1970.

Medley, D. M., C. G. Schluck, and N. P. Ames, *Assessing the learning environment in the classroom: A manual for users of OScAR 5V.* Princeton, New Jersey: Educational Testing Service, 1968.

Spaulding, R. L., *Classroom behavior analysis and treatment.* San Jose, California: San Jose State College, 1970.

Name: COGNITIVE COMPONENT SYSTEM

Authors: Edmund T. Emmer and I. Dorothy Albrecht

Type of Measure: Observation coding system

Availability: Emmer, E. T., and I. D. Albrecht, *The Cognitive Component System (CCS) manual.* Austin, Texas: Research and Development Center for Teacher Education, University of Texas, 1970.

Description: The Cognitive Component System (CCS) was designed to measure the cognitive functioning of students and teachers in the classroom. It is used by trained observers, who code cognitive behaviors according to 5 categories: Association, Description, Conceptualization, Generalization, and Inference. These categories are tallied in a manner which distinguishes teacher and student behaviors as well as presenting, responding, and soliciting behaviors. These distinctions produce 30 classifications of cognitive behavior, which are supplemented by 3 activity categories—Directing and Managing, Individual Seat Work, and Group Work—bringing the total number of CCS discriminations to 33.

Sample Items: The CCS manual explicitly defines the system's categories and lists behaviors which are typically coded under each heading. For example, Association is defined as "verbatim reproduction of verbal sequences, a stimulus/response chain without apparent mediators (Emmer and Albrecht, p. 5)." Teacher questions and student responses involving memorization, drill, and recall are coded in this category.

Reliability: Estimates of between-observer agreement, based on intraclass correlations, are presented in the manual for each CCS category. These range from .11 (Student Responds Inference) to .98 (Teacher Solicits Association), with most being in the .80s or .90s. Reliability coefficients are not reported for 7 categories in which insufficient behavior was observed.

Estimates of between-observer agreement for combined CCS categories range from .83 to .98.

Validity: The development of the CCS and the selection of its behavioral categories are not described in the manual. The system's theoretical rationale is not discussed, and no evidence from which to infer validity is provided.

Norms: Data in the manual are based on 15 $\frac{1}{2}$-hour videotapes made in fifth- and eighth-grade classrooms, with 2 observers coding each tape.

Procedures for Use: CCS codings can be made from audiotapes, videotapes, or live observations of classroom interaction. The observer indicates each cognitive statement on a tally sheet. Each entry on the sheet describes 1 unit of behavior—usually a sentence—which represents a single, complete thought. If a thought is repeated (if, for example, a teacher restates a student remark), it is coded only when it first occurs, unless it has been modified or expanded in some way.

Noncognitive behaviors, such as affective communications or routine response acknowledgements, are ignored. This rule, however, does not apply to the 3 classroom activity categories, which are included to provide an estimate of the amount of seat work, group work, and nonsubstantive activity (directing and managing). Behaviors falling in these 3 categories are coded in time, rather than thought, units. The observer records these behaviors at 3-second intervals— unless they are occurring over an extended period, in which case he or she merely "times" them with a stopwatch and enters the duration of occurrence directly onto the tally sheet.

After the observation is completed, entries on the tally sheet are totalled. These frequency counts can be used individually or in combination to yield a variety of information.

Comments: The Cognitive Component System is easy to learn and to use. Coders can be trained in a relatively brief period of time, and, since tallying is done using paper and pencil only, no elaborate or expensive equipment is required. Although CCS reliabilities are generally high, this system could be more confidently recommended if its manual provided some information from which to infer validity.

Reference: Emmer, E. T., and I. D. Albrecht, *The Cognitive Component System (CCS) manual.* Austin, Texas: Research and Development Center for Teacher Education, University of Texas, 1970.

Name: FLANDERS SYSTEM OF INTERACTION ANALYSIS

Author: Ned A. Flanders

Type of Measure: Observation coding system

Availability: Flanders, N. A. *Analyzing teaching behavior.* Reading, Mass.: Addison-Wesley, 1970.

Description: The Flanders System of Interaction Analysis is the observation instrument most frequently used to analyze the influence of teachers in the classroom. The instrument focuses primarily on teacher behaviors which restrict or increase student freedom of action. These behaviors are recorded, tallied, and arranged on a 10-by-10 matrix which provides a visual diagram of the classroom interaction pattern. The Flanders System is useful not only for research on teaching, but also for training teachers (Flanders, 1970).

Sample Items: The following 10 categories are used to classify teacher and student behaviors on the Flanders System (Flanders, 1970).

Teacher categories (indirect influence)
1. Accepts feeling
2. Praises or encourages
3. Accepts or uses ideas of students
4. Asks questions

Teacher categories (direct influence)
5. Lectures
6. Gives directions
7. Criticizes or justifies authority

Student categories
8. Student talk—response
9. Student talk—initiation

Other
10. Silence or confusion

Reliability: Procedures for establishing interjudge agreement are clearly defined by Flanders (1970), and decoding exercises are recommended to improve reliability. Using a formula suggested by Scott (1955), coefficients of observer agreement as high as .85 have been obtained (Medley and Mitzel, 1963).

Validity: Procedures for coding behavior are discussed in great detail by Flanders (1970) in order to insure accurate interpretation of data, which in turn enhances the instrument's validity. Though no formal studies of validity are available, Flanders (1970) has drawn several generalizations, which suggest validity, from a number of research projects examining the effects of Interaction Analysis. He has concluded that after studying Interaction Analysis: (1) individuals become more responsive to pupil ideas; (2) teaching behavior becomes more flexible; and (3) the attitudes of college students toward teaching and teacher education become more positive.

Norms: A formula for determining expected frequencies for each cell is provided in addition to a table containing normative expectations for matrix ratios (Flanders, 1970).

Procedures for Use: Only 1 trained observer is needed to collect and code behaviors. At the end of each 3-second period, the coder records the category number which best describes communications just observed. The time and a double line are recorded with each change in major class formations, communications, or subject area. Examples of classroom conversation and tally sheets with category ratings corresponding to classroom verbalizations are provided. The author also describes elementary tabulating and multiple coding procedures (Flanders, 1970).

Comments: The Flanders System of Interaction Analysis is a frequently used and easily adapted observation system for measuring teacher influence in the classroom. However, because the focus of this system is on teacher influence, information on students is limited to 2 of the 10 categories. Yet, the Flanders System is easy to learn and use, and its widespread popularity is an indication of its utility and flexibility. However, the system has also received its share of criticism (Mitchell, 1969), most of which has centered on the instrument's ground rules and its implied endorsement of certain teaching behaviors.

References: Dunkin, M. J., and B. J. Biddle, *The study of teaching.* New York: Holt, Rinehart and Winston, 1974.

Flanders, N. A., *Analyzing teaching behavior.* Reading, Mass.: Addison-Wesley, 1970.

Flanders, N. A., *Interaction analysis in the classroom: A manual for observers.* Ann Arbor, Mich.: University of Michigan, 1960.

Medley, D. M., and H. E. Mitzel, "Measuring classroom behavior by systematic observation," in N. L. Gage (ed.), *Handbook of research on teaching.* Chicago: Rand McNally, 1963.

Mitchell, J. V., "Education's challenge to psychology: The prediction of behavior from person-environment interactions." *Review of Educational Research,* 1969, **39**, 699–710.

Moskowitz, G., "Effects of training in interaction analysis on the behavior of secondary school teachers." *The High School Journal,* 1967, **51**, 17–25.

Simon, A., and E. G. Boyer, (eds.) *Mirrors for behavior. An anthology of observation instruments.* Philadelphia: Research for Better Schools, 1970.

Name: FLORIDA CLIMATE AND CONTROL SYSTEM

Authors: Robert Soar, Ruth Soar, and Marjorie Ragosta

Type of Measure: Observation coding system

Availability: Soar, R., R. Soar, and M. Ragosta, *Florida climate and control system*. Gainesville, Florida: Institute for the Development of Human Resources, College of Education, University of Florida, 1971.

Description: The Florida Climate and Control System (FLACCS) was developed for use in Project Follow Through (Soar, 1973), a study of the educational needs of disadvantaged children. Derived primarily from the South Carolina Observation Record (Soar, 1966), the Hostility-Affection Schedule (Fowler, 1962), and earlier versions of the Observation Schedule and Record (Medley and Mitzel, 1958), FLACCS was designed to record behavioral dimensions not covered by Interaction Analysis. Among these were classroom groupings, the degree of individual versus group work, the physical movement of teacher and pupils, and the nonverbal expression of affect in the classroom.

After several revisions, FLACCS emerged as a 2-part instrument, the first section of which focuses on the teacher's direction and control of the classroom and the pupils' response to such management. This section includes items describing Teacher Activity, Verbal Control, Nonverbal Control, Pupil Activity, Socialization, Materials, and Pupil Interest/Attention. The second portion of FLACCS assesses expression of negative and positive affect under the following categories: Teacher Verbal; Pupil Verbal; Teacher Nonverbal; and Pupil Nonverbal.

The control and affect sections of FLACCS were separately factored by Soar (1973). Items with the highest factor loadings were jointly analyzed, yielding the following 9 factors.

1. Strong Control
2. Pupil Free Choice vs. No Choice
3. Teacher/Pupil Supportive Behavior
4. Nonverbal Gentle Control
5. Gentle Control
6. Work Without the Teacher
7. Pupil Negative Affect
8. Teacher Attention in a Task Setting
9. Teacher Positive Affect

Sample Items: Most of the behavioral items included on FLACCS are specific, demanding little inference on the observer's part (e.g., "smiles, laughs, nods" under Positive Affect, Teacher Nonverbal). Other items, however, are more general, requiring some interpretation by the observer (e.g., "makes disparaging remark" under Negative Affect, Pupil Verbal).

Reliability: Soar (1973) reports correlations between observations taken at 3 points in time for all 9 FLACCS factors. The first and second observations correlated from −.16 to .77, the first and third from .09 to .89 and the second and third from −.05 to .72, indicating considerable variability in factor stability. Soar reports less variability among observers, presenting indices of interobserver agreement calculated by Hoyt's (1955) analysis of variance formula 5. These ranged from .77 to .99 and averaged .92.

Validity: Intercorrelations among the FLACCS factors, computed by Soar (1973), were generally low, indicating some construct validity. Only 2 were above .50—that between Strong Control and Pupil Negative Affect and that between Pupil Free Choice and Teacher Positive Affect. Further evidence of construct validity is provided by group differences which emerged on the FLACCS. Five of the 9 FLACCS factors showed F ratios which significantly discriminated grade levels. In general, kindergarten differed most often from the other grades, as might be expected. Kindergarten classrooms were characterized on the FLACCS by more Pupil Free Choice and Teacher Gentle Control and less Strong Control, Work Without Teacher, and Teacher Attention in a Task Setting.

Evidence of criterion-related validity is provided by correlations between FLACCS factors and other measures of classroom interaction. For example, the FLACCS factor, Pupil Free Choice, related negatively to Convergent Thinking, as measured on the Teacher Practices Observation Record (TPOR), but positively to the TPOR variables, Pupil Free Choice and Exploration of Ideas. This same FLACCS factor, Pupil Free Choice, also correlated positively with Varied Pupil-Initiated Interaction, measured on the Reciprocal Category System (RCS), and negatively with Drill, also on the RCS. Both of these correlations exceeded .50.

Relationships between FLACCS factors and measures of pupil behavior also have bearing on the system's validity. Pupil absences in the upper grade levels correlated positively with Strong Control and negatively with Teacher Positive Affect. In the lower grades, pupil skills gain related positively to Teacher Attention in a Task Setting and negatively to Pupil Free Choice. In general, the expected relationship between teacher expressions of affect and pupil gain did not appear. Instead, pupil gain was associated with the FLACCS dimensions reflecting structuring of classroom activity and pupil involvement with the teacher (Soar, 1973).

Norms: Soar (1973) presents factor means and standard deviations for several elementary grade levels.

Procedures for Use: FLACCS categories are presented on 2 pages, the first reflecting teacher control and pupil reaction, the second, teacher and pupil expression of positive and negative affect. Behaviors are recorded separately on each page. Certain items (such as "Praise") appear on both pages of the instrument. These may be coded once or twice, depending on the use and intent of the item. If a teacher praises a child's work in order to reinforce and encourage him, the item is coded in both the structural and affective areas. If, however, the teacher compliments a child's appearance, a check is placed only on the affective page.

In using the FLACCS, an observer views the classroom for a specified period of time, usually 2 to 5 minutes, and then tallies both pages of the code sheet. Behaviors are recorded only once, even if they recur several times within the brief observation period. This procedure is then repeated. The ratings thus reflect overall impression of the classroom.

Comments: The Florida Climate and Control System offers comprehensive assessment of classroom interaction, requiring little inference on the observer's part. The FLACCS has a strong affective component and is most appropriate for the elementary grades. The somewhat low reliabilities between observations reflect changes in pupil and teacher behaviors over the year and, therefore, should not necessarily be interpreted as a characteristic of the instrument.

References: Fowler, B. D., *Relation of teacher personality characteristics and attitudes to teacher-pupil rapport and emotional climate in the elementary classroom.* Unpublished doctoral dissertation, University of South Carolina, 1962.

Hoyt, C. J., "Relations of certain correlational to variance ratio estimates of test reliability." *Twelfth Yearbook of the National Council of Measurement Used in Education,* 1955, 50–55.

Medley, D. M., and H. E. Mitzel, "A technique for measuring classroom behavior." *Journal of Educational Psychology,* 1958, **49**, 86–92.

Soar, R. S., *An integrative approach to classroom learning.* NIMH project 5-R11 MH 01096. Columbia, South Carolina: University of South Carolina, 1966. (ERIC Document Reproduction Service No. ED 033 749).

Soar, R. S., Final report. *Follow Through classroom process measurement and pupil growth (1970–71).* Gainesville, Florida: Institute for Development of Human Resources, College of Education, University of Florida, 1973.

Name: FULLER AFFECTIVE INTERACTION RECORDS 33

Author: Frances F. Fuller

Type of Measure: Observation coding system

Availability: Fuller, F. F. *FAIR system manual. Fuller Affective Interaction Records.* Austin, Texas: Research and Development Center for Teacher Education, University of Texas, 1969.

Description: The FAIR observation system employs trained coders to assess interpersonal behaviors of preservice teachers and their students in self-contained (single classroom) settings. FAIR 33 is based on 5 interpersonal dimensions. The first of these, *Responsiveness,* includes behaviors which occur in response to another's actions (*R*) or serve to initiate a new action (*I*). The second dimension, *Self-Other,* describes actions directed toward the self (*S*) or toward others (*O*). The third dimension, *Approval,* includes behaviors ranging from approval (*A*), to noncommittal (*N*), to disapproval (*D*), and the fourth, *Inclusion,* describes behaviors ranging from an invitation to respond (*I*) to exclusion of another (*E*). The final dimension, *Control,* is comprised of behaviors which permit (*P*) or restrict (*R*) the responses of others. Combinations of the behaviors within these 5 dimensions produce 14 teacher categories, 14 student categories, and 5 noninteractive categories (Fuller, 1969; Manning, 1972).

Sample Items: The manual presents a series of dialogues illustrating the 33 categories generated from the behaviors included in the 5 dimensions. Sample categories produced from dimension combinations appear below (Fuller, 1969, p. 20):

Dimension Combination	*Teacher Category*	*Student Category*
ROAIP (*R*esponds, *O*ther, *A*pproval, *I*nvites, *P*ermits)	*Values.* Values feelings; identifies; shares. Listens attentively. Unqualified acceptance. Includes laughing or being sad *with* someone, "I feel that way too." (Person oriented)	*Zeal.* Student is responsive, participating. Listens attentively. Values or recognizes another's feelings. Waves hand, shows pleasure, appreciation, good mood, laughing *with* someone. "Oh, Boy!" (Affect)

ROAIR (*Responds, Other, Approval, Invites, Restricts*)

Nurtures. Teacher gives focused encouragement. Guides. Hints. "Come on, Johnny, you know this one." Gives praise, approval to previous behavior. Smiles. Includes recognition of student volunteer, and "Thank you for helping me." (Affect)

Encourages. Encourages teacher or another student to go on. Includes "Thank you for helping me." Gives approval; praises. "You got it right." Includes choosing in a game, election panel.

Reliability: The reliability of mean ratings of two coders is presented in the manual for each FAIR category. Coefficients range from .97 to .00, with an average of .56. Average reliability for teacher codes is .70; average reliability for student codes is .42. For 97% of the data collected, average intercoder agreement is .81 (Fuller, 1969).

Validity: No information on the validity of the FAIR 33 is reported in the manual. However, FAIR 33 categories were constructed from classroom behaviors recorded on sound films and videotapes. These included behaviors which were observed, as well as behaviors which were assumed to exist. For example, teachers were observed praising students, but students were not observed praising teachers. Yet the latter behavior probably occurs, and was therefore included on the FAIR 33. All behaviors observed in 360 films and videotapes have successfully been classified within this category system (Fuller, 1969).

Norms: No normative data are presented.

Procedures for Use: Each time behavior changes, a code is recorded on the FAIR 33. A single behavior may last for 1 second or several minutes. The length of the behavior is recorded according to procedures described in the manual. One coder records the behavior of both teacher and students. It is recommended that a coding desk or flexowriter be used in conjunction with the coding system. The flexowriter produces a punched paper tape which can be easily transferred to magnetic tape for computer processing, thereby permitting large quantities of data to be processed without tallying or keypunching.

Comments: The FAIR 33 categories allow the researcher to view behaviors in relation to one another. The FAIR system offers an efficient means of processing large quantities of observation data. However, because of heavy demands placed on the observers, some mechanical and electronic equipment is needed to eliminate tallying and key punching. FAIR reliabilities are generally high, and the instrument appears to be soundly constructed, although validity data are lacking.

References: Fuller, F. F., *FAIR system manual. Fuller Affective Interaction Records*. Austin, Texas: Research and Development Center for Teacher Education, University of Texas, 1969.

Manning, B. A., *Interpersonal interaction: A selective review*. Austin, Texas: Research and Development Center for Teacher Education, University of Texas, 1972.

Name: JACKSON AND LAHADERNE OBSERVATION SYSTEM

Authors: Phillip W. Jackson and Henriette M. Lahaderne

Type of Measure: Observation coding system

Availability: This instrument is described in: Jackson, P. W., and H. M. Lahaderne, "Inequalities of teacher-pupil contacts." *Psychology in the Schools*, 1967, 4(3), 204–211.

Description: This observation system was developed by Jackson and Lahaderne (1967) in a study of teacher/pupil interaction in elementary school classrooms. Designed to assess the communication between the teacher and individual students, this instrument requires an observer to sit in the classroom and record the following information for each verbal or nonverbal exchange: (1) the identity of the student involved; (2) the initiator of the message (i.e., teacher or student); and (3) the nature of the communication. Any given communication is classified as primarily Instructional, Managerial, or Prohibitory. Instructional messages refer in some way to curriculum content or educational objectives. Managerial messages, on the other hand, involve the interpretation of classroom rules and the definition of acceptable behavior, while Prohibitory remarks are intended to maintain order or punish misbehavior.

Sample Items: Jackson and Lahaderne (1967) illustrate the classification of several nonverbal behaviors, noting that "the ability to categorize messages that are only partially overheard or that do not entail words is particularly important in elementary classrooms where teachers and students are very mobile and where the occasion for certain messages recurs so frequently that their transmission becomes highly stylized and abbreviated (p. 205)." Thus, they explain that when a student approaches the teacher with an open workbook in his hand, the interaction, though inaudible to the observer, may safely be classified as Instructional. Or, when the teacher snaps his fingers and points to a student, it may be assumed that the message is Prohibitory even though no words are spoken.

The classification of verbal behavior is not similarly exemplified. The authors maintain that observers can usually differentiate the 3 types of communication, though Managerial and Prohibitory messages may sometimes be confused.

Reliability: Reliability data are not reported by Jackson and Lahaderne (1967).

Validity: Though no evidence of criterion-related validity is presented, many of the results which Jackson and Lahaderne obtained using this instrument reveal expected differences and similarities in classroom communication. Data from 4 sixth-grade classes in a relatively homogeneous community indicated a rapid rate of interaction and a preponderance of Instructional exchanges in all of the classrooms. The 4 groups were also quite similar in regard to the initiation of student/teacher interaction. In each room the teacher controlled the flow of communication, initiating about 80 individual exchanges per hour. Initiation rates for students, however, differed from class to class, and among those rooms with high student initiation rates, the focus of student queries differed.

Further differences emerged with regard to pupil sex, confirming the popular belief that boys are the source of most classroom misbehavior. Though only 44.8 to 58.8% of the children in each class were male, 69.6 to 90.1% of the Prohibitory exchanges involved boys rather than girls. Within each room and within each sex group, however, there remained wide individual differences in teacher/pupil interaction, with 1 or 2 students having fewer than 1 exchange per hour with the teacher and others being in contact with the teacher almost constantly.

Norms: The sample used by Jackson and Lahaderne (1967) was composed of 4 sixth-grade classrooms in 2 schools in a predominantly white, working-class community. Two of the classrooms contained 34 pupils each, and 2 others contained 29 each. Two of the 4 teachers were men and 2 were women.

Procedures for Use: In the Jackson and Lahaderne study (1967), observations were tallied in 20-minute units, 36 of which were recorded for each classroom. These observations, distributed throughout the school week, covered all of the activities of each room. The observation tally sheet required that an entry be made for each transmission of information between the teacher and individual students. Teacher remarks directed at more than 1 student were ignored.

Comments: The primary advantage of the Jackson and Lahaderne Observation System is its simplicity. It allows the observer to record both verbal and nonverbal classroom interaction using relatively few, fairly easily distinguished categories. However, it should be kept in mind that such simplicity may also produce a broad, general picture of classroom communication, which may suffer from lack of detail and depth. This possibility, along with the absence of reliability data, limits this instrument somewhat.

Reference: Jackson, P. W., and H. M. Lahaderne, "Inequalities of teacher-pupil contacts." *Psychology in the Schools*, 1967, **4**(3), 204–211.

Name: KOUNIN, FRIESEN, AND NORTON BEHAVIOR CODING PROCEDURE

Authors: Jacob S. Kounin, Wallace V. Friesen, and A. Evangeline Norton

Type of Measure: Observation coding system

Availability: Kounin, J. S., W. V. Friesen, and A. E. Norton, "Managing emotionally disturbed children in regular classrooms." *Journal of Educational Psychology*, 1966, **57**(1), 1–13.

Description: Developed in a study of the relationship between teaching style and the behavior of emotionally disturbed children in regular elementary classrooms (Kounin, Friesen, and Norton, 1966), this observation system focuses on the pupil's academic activity and the teacher's managerial techniques. In developing codes for teacher style, the authors were guided by several criteria. The categories were required to reflect: (1) concrete behaviors or managerial methods, rather than traits or characteristics; (2) dimensions on which teachers differed; and (3) behaviors which were relatively free of commitment to any philosophical orientation or value system. The teacher categories selected are listed below.

I. Desist Techniques
   A. Clarity
   B. Firmness
   C. Child treatment
      1. Negative
      2. Neutral
      3. Positive
   D. Intensity
   E. Focus
      1. Misbehavior
      2. Task
   F. Overlappingness
   G. With-it-ness
   H. Degree of success (coded on a 7-point scale)

II. Transition Incidents
   A. Behavior mode of children at time of transition
   B. Delineation
      1. Simple
      2. With clarity
      3. With group alerting
      4. With challenge/arousal
      5. With zest
   C. Attention property of the signal

    D. Presence of anti-resolution properties
    E. Appropriateness of timing
    F. Children's immediate reaction

The categories of pupil behavior selected for observation apply only to the child's academic activity. These categories, listed below, produce 2 indices of student behavior: Work Involvement rate and Deviancy rate.

    I. Definitely and completely involved in work
    II. Probably involved in work
    III. Definitely not involved in work
    IV. Restless
    V. Languishing
    VI. Languishing and restless
    VII. Engaged in task-related deviancy
    VIII. Engaged in non-task-related deviancy
        A. Mild
        B Serious
    IX. Contagion of deviancy

Sample Items: Kounin et al. (1966) define the categories included on this system and list behaviors typically coded under each. For example, "With-it-ness" refers to the extent to which the teacher communicates to the pupils that he knows what is happening in the classroom. A teacher indicates that he is not "with-it" when he acts upon a deviancy too late, or when he attends to a minor disturbance while a major deviancy is occurring behind his back.

Reliability: For the pupil behavior categories, interrater agreement between various pairs of 4 observers ranged from 82 to 96% and averaged 92%. The teacher behavior category, Degree of Success, produced an average of 74% agreement among observers, while the remaining teacher Desist categories yielded intercoder agreement averaging 90% (Kounin et al., 1966).

Validity: Evidence for validity is based on findings of Kounin et al. (1966), who used this system to observe emotionally disturbed and nondisturbed children in a variety of classroom subsettings. They obtained group differences and category intercorrelations which were almost all in expected directions. For example, in all classroom subsettings, nondisturbed children received higher work involvement and lower deviancy scores than disturbed children. The behavior of all children, however, varied with classroom subsetting, the highest degree of school-appropriate behavior occurring in subgroup recitation periods and the lowest occurring during seatwork situations. In all settings, the amount of school-appropriate behavior manifested by nondisturbed children was positively related to that exhibited by disturbed children.

    Correlations between observation categories were, for the most part predicted by the authors. Although Overlappingness (the extent to which the teacher attends to 2 aspects of the classroom at once) was not significantly associated with Deviancy or Work Involvement for either group of children, it was related to With-it-ness ($r = .50$, $p < .01$). The more with-it the teacher, the more work-involved and less deviant were the pupils. Teacher behavior during transition periods (in which the children were guided from one activity to another) also correlated with the Work Involvement and Deviancy rates of pupils: high antiresolution scores during these periods were associated with a decline in school-appropriate behavior.

Norms: The authors report mean Work Involvement and Deviancy scores for varying numbers of emotionally disturbed and nondisturbed children in regular elementary classrooms. Figures are provided for four classroom subsettings: (1) subgroup recitation; (2) class recitation; (3) seatwork in teacher's sphere; and (4) seatwork outside teacher's sphere. Normative data are not reported for the categories of teacher behavior (Kounin et al., 1966).

Procedures for Use: In the study by Kounin et al. (1966), classroom behavior was videotaped for entire mornings or afternoons. Observers categorized this behavior from tapes, treating each of the 4 subsettings separately and coding only academic activities. Observed behaviors were tallied in 10-second intervals. The mean percentage of intervals containing a tally for a particular behavior constituted the score for that behavior.

Comments: Although published information regarding this observation system is limited, the Kounin, Friesen, and Norton Behavior Coding Procedure appears to be a useful tool for those researchers who prefer to focus on concrete techniques of classroom management rather than on teacher personality characteristics. It has demonstrated adequate interobserver agreement and preliminary evidence of validity.

Reference: Kounin, J. S., W. V. Friesen, and A. E. Norton, "Managing emotionally disturbed children in regular classrooms." *Journal of Educational Psychology*, 1966, **57**(1), 1–13.

Name: A METHOD OF STUDYING SPONTANEOUS GROUP FORMATION

Authors: Dorothy S. Thomas and associates

Type of Measure: Observation coding system

Availability: This instrument is fully described in: Thomas, D. S., et al., "Some new techniques for studying social behavior." *Child Development Monographs,* 1929, **1.**

Description: Dorothy Thomas and her associates (1929) devised this Method of Studying Spontaneous Group Formation in an early attempt to quantify classroom interaction through live observation. This instrument was designed to record social situations as they occur in nursery schools. A social situation is "a group of two or more children playing together, either functionally or spatially (Thomas et al., 1929, p. 76)." The observations recorded yield several indices of a child's participation in social activities, including: total amount of time spent in social situations; daily variation in that time; number of social situations in which the child engages; number of children with whom he plays; and average size of groups in which he plays.

Sample Items: In using this system, the observer records social situations in terms of the activity of each child. For example, a social situation might be recorded as follows: "John was building a sand castle while Mary was offering a toy to him." Additional data (e.g., the initiator and the duration of the described activity) are also entered on the observation form.

Reliability: To determine the instrument's objectivity, simultaneous records were taken independently by 2 raters, who observed nursery school children ($N = 35$) playing both indoors and outdoors. The 2 records were correlated, and coefficients were computed for: (1) amount of time spent in social situations by each child; (2) number of social situations recorded for each child; and (3) number of children played with by each child. Rank-order correlations ranged from .69 to .77 for indoor observations, and from .86 to .88 for outdoor observations (Thomas et al., 1929).

Validity: Evidence for validity is scarce. However, some validity may be inferred from correlations between chronological age, mental age (measured on the Kuhlman-Binet test), and indices of social participation obtained using this observation system. These correlations indicated that the child with a higher chronological and mental age spent a larger percentage of time in social situations. Also, each child's mental age was positively related ($r = .41$) to the average mental age of the 3 children with whom he played the most. Similarly, the correlation between each child's mental age and the average mental age of the 3 children with whom he played the longest was .62. Furthermore, a consistently positive relationship was demonstrated between the amount of time a child spent in social situations and the number of children with whom he played and the size of groups in which he played (Thomas et al., 1929).

Norms: The sample used in the original Thomas study (1929) included 35 children, 18 of whom were observed at the Institute for Child Welfare Research and 17 at the Bethlehem Day Nursery. The Institute children averaged 30 months of age. Their mean mental age was 37 months, and their mean IQ, 122, as measured on the Kuhlman-Binet test. The Bethlehem children ranged in age from 18 to 50 months. However, figures describing their average chonological age, mental age, and IQ are not available (Thomas et al., 1929).

Procedures for Use: Observations are recorded on a blank divided into 7 vertical columns, labeled: Activity, Initiator, Children, Time, Function, Attraction, and Teacher. In the first column, the observed activity is described, and in the second, the initiator of that activity is named. Other children engaging in the activity are listed in the Children column. The time at which each child enters and leaves the group is recorded (in half-minute units) in the fourth column. In the Function column, each child's reaction to the social grouping is briefly described. The column headed Attraction is used to list each child's motive for entering the group, while the last column is intended to indicate the presence and function of a teacher in the group. An individual record is made for each child.

Comments: This observation system is one of the earliest attempts to measure "classroom" behavior through live observation. As such, it is a bit more cumbersome than its successors. It requires strict attention and quick notations on the observer's part. Also, since a record is made for each child, a number of observers may be needed.

References: Medley, D. M., and H. E. Mitzel, "Measuring classroom behavior by systematic observation," in N. L. Gage (ed.), *Handbook of research on teaching.* Chicago: Rand McNally, 1963.

Thomas, D. S., et al., "Some new techniques for studying social behavior." *Child Development Monographs,* 1929, **1**.

Name: NONVERBAL INTERACTION ANALYSIS

Author: Peggy Amidon

Type of Measure: Observation coding system

Availability: Amidon, P., *Nonverbal interaction analysis.* Minneapolis, Minnesota: Paul S. Amidon and Associates, 1971.

Description: Nonverbal Interaction Analysis (NVIA) provides a method of systematically observing and recording nonverbal behavior in the classroom. Designed to parallel the categories of verbal behavior in Flanders' Interaction Analysis (and capable of accomodating the 30 expanded IA categories), NVIA codes the following classroom dimensions, each of which affects teacher/pupil interaction.

   I. Room Arrangement
  II. Materials
 III. Nonverbal Behaviors
 IV. Activities

The first and second dimensions involve classroom setting—the physical arrangement of desks, chairs, bulletin boards, etc., and the presence or absence of certain materials, supplies, and equipment. The third dimension is concerned with the teacher's nonverbal behavior—gestures, facial expressions, posture, and so forth. The fourth dimension combines the previous 3 by focusing on the use of materials, by the teacher and the pupils, in conjunction with nonverbal behaviors.

Sample Items: Specific aspects of each NVIA dimension are coded pictorially. For example, under Dimension I (Room Arrangement) the chalkboard is symbolized by the following figure: ☐ . Or, under Dimension II (Materials and Supplies), printed items, such as textbooks, workbooks, and newspapers, are represented by the symbol, ⌂ . These symbols are further specified by the 10 numerical codes used in Interaction Analysis: (1) Accepts Feeling; (2) Praises or Encourages; (3) Accepts Student Ideas; (4) Asks Questions; (5) Lecturing; (6) Giving Directions; (7) Criticizing or Justifying Authority; (8) Student Talk—Response; (9) Student Talk—Initiation; (10) Silence or Confusion. By combining symbols from Dimensions I and II with Interaction Analysis category numbers, the *contents* of furniture or material may be described, as illustrated below.

   ☐ 4. symbolizes a chalkboard containing questions.

   ☐ 5 symbolizes a chalkboard containing lecture-type information.

   ⌂ 6 symbolizes printed material containing directions or instructions.

⌊8⌋ symbolizes printed material written by the student in response to an assignment or request made by the teacher (e.g., an essay or written answers to questions).

If a more precise description of content is desired, the Dimension I and Dimension II symbols can be combined with an *expanded* Interaction Analysis category number and code letter:

⌊4c⌋ symbolizes printed material containing convergent-type questions.

Items on the NVIA Dimensions III and IV are also coded using combinations of symbols and Interaction Analysis categories. For example, on Dimension III (Nonverbal Behaviors), use of the hands to give directions is indicated by the following figure: ⌒4⌒ . Recording items on Dimension IV (Activities) is a bit more complex, since this aspect incorporates symbols from all of the preceding dimensions and distinguishes verbal from nonverbal use of material. Thus,

5 ⌊⌋ represents the verbal use of a book during a lecture,
while

⌒⌋ represents the use of a gesture to hold a book.

Reliability, Validity, and Norms: The NVIA manual (Amidon, 1971) reports no reliability, validity, or normative data.

Procedures for Use: Data collected on Dimensions I and II of the NVIA are recorded *prior* to observing the actual teacher/pupil interaction. The physical arrangement of the classroom and the materials present can be coded before class starts. Items on Dimensions III and IV, however, are sequentially recorded *during* classroom interaction. Immediate (live), delayed (videotaped), or a combination of immediate and delayed observation may be used. It is generally recommended that behaviors be recorded in 3-second units over a 20-minute observation period, though these specifications may be modified to accomodate unusual circumstances related to class size, students' ability, and classroom setting. Such circumstances, along with the purposes of observation, also determine the number of coders employed per classroom or per videotape. All or as few as 1 of the NVIA dimensions can be recorded—with or without the Interaction Analysis and expanded Interaction Analysis categories—depending on the user's needs and objectives.

Amidon (1971) explains NVIA recording procedures in great detail, illustrating the coding symbols for each dimension and their modification by Interaction Analysis and expanded Interaction Analysis categories. Practice exercises are also provided for prospective coders.

Comments: Because it incorporates Flanders' Interaction Analysis categories, Nonverbal Interaction Analysis is capable of providing a complete picture of classroom activity (both verbal and nonverbal). Yet it may also be used to assess only one or a few dimensions of teacher/student interaction. The NVIA is adaptable to a number of situations and purposes and offers varying levels of specificity. The manual is very thorough in describing procedures for using the system. Although psychometric data are not reported, the NVIA, admittedly in an "infant stage," is based on an already researched and widely used observation instrument.

Reference: Amidon, P. *Nonverbal interaction analysis.* Minneapolis, Minnesota: Paul S. Amidon and Associates, 1971.

Name: OBSERVATION PROCEDURE FOR ASSESSING THE MICRO-ENVIRONMENTS OF INDIVIDUAL PRESCHOOL CHILDREN

Author: John Dopyera

Type of Measure: Observation coding system

Availability: Dopyera, J. *Assessing the micro-environments of individual preschool children.* Syracuse, New York: Head Start Evaluation Project, Syracuse University, 1969. This report may be obtained from William J. Meyer, Director, Syracuse University Early Childhood Education Center, 340 Huntington Hall, 150 Marshall Street, Syracuse, New York 13210.

Description: This observation procedure was developed in an evaluation of compensatory preschool programs to assess the micro-environments of children. The term "micro-environment" was used to describe (1) events in the child's immediate environment which were sensorily accessible to him or her and (2) other setting phenomena which served as a medium for the child's behavior. These events and phenomena were recorded in two 2-minute observations, the first of which concentrated on the following aspects of each child's behavior or environment:

1. Physical location and posture;
2. Focus and coordination;
3. Physical environments encountered (i.e., toys, people, equipment);
4. Affective verbal or vocal behavior;
5. Affective verbal or vocal behavior of other children in the immediate vicinity;
6. Interpersonal verbal and nonverbal encounters between the child and any adult or any other child;
7. Conditions which might affect the accuracy of observations;
8. Behavioral indicators of the child.

A second 2-minute observation provided the following information:

1. Context of the child's behavior;
2. The child's activity;
3. The group's activity;
4. Codes for child, peer, teacher, aide, or other adult activity;
5. Minimum distances between the child and others;
6. Sanctions given by adults to the target child or the other children.

Dopyera (1969) reduced data derived from the above categories to 33 variables representing 7 factors, 5 of which were interpretable. These 5 were labeled: Adult Directed and Highly Controlled Small Group Activities; Diffuse Activity

Structure; Undisrupted Independent Effort; Adult Tolerated Nonsettled Behavior; and Subject-Directed Striving.

Sample Items: Dopyera (1969) provides examples of the kinds of behaviors and environmental characteristics coded under each category on the system. "Behavioral indicators," for example, includes exaggerated gait, tics, and other physical idiosyncrasies of the child.

Reliability: Interrater reliabilities were computed for each of the observational items included in the factor analysis. These averaged .56, .59, .59, and .58 for 3 pairs of observers and for all 6 observers combined, respectively.

Validity: Dopyera (1969) related factor scores to a number of criteria. He found that Adult Directed and Highly Controlled Small Group Activities correlated negatively with posttest Stanford-Binet mental age scores. Factor III, Undisrupted Independent Effort, was negatively related to the amount of time the child required to complete the Caldwell Preschool Inventory and the Animal House subtest of the Wechsler Preschool and Primary Scale of Intelligence. Similarly, Factor IV, Adult-Tolerated Nonsettled Behavior, was negatively associated with mental age change. A positive relationship emerged between Factor IV, Subject-Directed Striving, and posttest mental age and Animal House scores.

Norms: The sample used by Dopyera (1969) was drawn from Head Start classes in upstate New York during 1969–70. It included 68 children (males and females, blacks and whites) from 10 different classes.

Procedures for Use: In the study reported by Dopyera, raters observed the children for two 2-minute periods and recorded their observations immediately afterward. Their task was simply to indicate the occurrence or absence of specified events. Generally, 25 to 30 observations were recorded for each half-day session.

These records were date-time coded and transferred to tally sheets for data reduction. This involved converting the data to proportions to adjust for variations in the number of observations made. Proportion of item occurrence, or base rate, then, was the unit of analysis used.

Comments: Although reliabilities are somewhat low and two factors are uninterpretable, this observation procedure has several theoretical and practical advantages. Because it allows the researcher to record the child's actual encounters, this system is free from the assumption that the classroom environment is the same for all children. Information about the environmental factors confining or supporting each child's behavior is particularly valuable for purposes of program evaluation. Furthermore, the system can be used in almost any setting by minimally trained and relatively inexperienced observers.

Reference: Dopyera, J., *Assessing the micro-environments of individual preschool children.* Syracuse, New York: Head Start Evaluation Project, Syracuse University, 1969.

Name: OBSERVATION PROCEDURE FOR MEASURING THE "SOCIAL CLIMATE" OF CHILDREN'S GROUPS

Authors: Ronald Lippitt, Kurt Lewin and Ralph K. White

Type of Measure: Observation coding system

Availability: This instrument is fully described in: Lippitt, R., and R. K. White, "The 'social climate' of children's groups," in R. G. Barker, J. S. Kounin, and H. F. Wright (eds.), *Child behavior and development.* New York: McGraw-Hill, 1943.

Description: This observation system was developed in an attempt to describe the social climate of children's groups and to quantitatively record the effects of different atmospheres on group life and individual behavior. Although the authors of this measure focused on the effects of "democratic," "authoritarian," and "laissez-faire" social climates, the observation procedure they used provides a complete and integrated record of group behavior which can be adapted to measure other variables. This record is composed of 8 kinds of observational data, the 4 most important of which are listed below.

I. Social Interactions—a quantitative running account of the social interactions among the children in the group, coded in symbols representing directive, compliant, and objective behaviors, including a category of intentional refusal to respond to a social approach.

II. Group Structure—a minute-by-minute record of subgroup formation, goal identification, goal initiation, and subgroup unity.

III. Interpretation—an interpretive, continuing account of significant actions of group members and definite changes in group atmosphere.

IV. Stenographic Records—continuous records of all conversation.

Sample Items: Lippitt and White (1943) provide excerpts from the stenographic records of 4 different groups, along with interpretive comments. These groups represent 4 climates: authoritarian, with a submissive reaction; authoritarian with an aggressive reaction; democratic; and laissez faire. The example below is similar to an excerpt from the record of a democratic group.

Excerpt	*Interpretation*
John and Bob enter together. John notices a pad of paper and says, "Look, here's the paper for the drawings we decided on."	"We" decided, rather than "I" decided or "our leader" decided.
Jim and Freddie come in, and Jim says excitedly, "That's the best kind of drawing paper!"	High interest in the proposed tasks—even in the absence of the leader.

Reliability: Lippitt and White (1943) present 2 different kinds of reliability data: the degree of agreement between the records of 2 observers making simultaneous observations of the same group; and the degree of agreement between 2 investigators independently categorizing the same behavioral record.

Simultaneous observations recorded by 2 group-structure analysts achieved an agreement of 85%. In preliminary training, stenographic recorders produced indices of agreement ranging from .78 to .95, with a mean of .84.

Two investigators independently coding conversation units from stenographic records achieved 86% agreement. Categorizing the data into units of social climate, they produced indices of agreement ranging from .90 to .98 for the number of units per meeting, the exact length of each unit, and the classification of each unit.

Validity: Some evidence of validity is provided by analyses conducted by the authors (Lippitt and White, 1943). Four groups, each composed of five 10-year-old boys and an adult leader, were observed over several 6-week periods. During each of these periods, the group leaders exercised a different form of control: authoritarian, democratic, or laissez-faire. Recorded observations indicated that about 60% of the authoritarian and only 5% of the democratic and laissez-faire leadership behavior limited the scope and spontaneity of child activity. Similarly, the number of " guiding suggestions " was significantly lower under authoritarian and laissez-faire than democratic conditions. Also, democratic leaders exhibited eight times as much "jovial, confident" behavior as authoritarian and laissez-faire leaders.

Similar differences emerged in relation to group discussion and group morale. For 30 observations, 234 minutes of group discussion were recorded under democratic leadership, as compared to a total of 3 minutes under authoritarian control. The morale of the democratic groups, determined by (1) the ratio of the members' "we" statements to "I" statements and (2) the number of friendly remarks made by the average member to other members, was higher than that of the authoritarian and laissez-faire groups.

Norms: No true normative information is provided, though limited frequency data are reported (Lippitt and White, 1943).

Procedures for Use: In the studies reported by Lippitt and White (1943), 5 coders were used to observe each group of 5 children. Each observer focused his or her attention not on a particular child but on a particular facet of group functioning. The data collected were synchronized at 1-minute intervals. When placed side by side, the observers' reports provided a complete and integrated picture of the continuing activities of the group.

Comments: This instrument provides a comprehensive measure of group behavior. Though more complex than recently developed observation procedures, it yields a variety of data and can be applied to a number of different research purposes. This system is unusually flexible since the behavioral record it produces can be used to assess almost any variable of interest to the individual researcher.

References: Lewin, K., R. Lippitt, and R. K. White, "Patterns of aggressive behavior in experimentally created 'social climates'." *Journal of Social Psychology*, 1939, **10**, 271–299.

Lippitt, R., *An analysis of group reaction to three types of experimentally created social climate*. Unpublished doctoral dissertation, University of Iowa, 1940.

Lippitt, R., and R. K. White, "The 'social climate' of children's groups," in R. G. Barker, J. S. Kounin, and H. F. Wright (eds.), *Child behavior and development*. New York: McGraw-Hill, 1943.

Name: PUPIL-TEACHER RAPPORT SCALE

Author: J. Wayne Wrightstone

Type of Measure: Observation rating scale

Availability: Wrightstone, J. W., "Measuring the social climate of a classroom." *Journal of Educational Research*, 1951, **44**, 341–351.

Description: Wrightstone (1951) developed the Pupil-Teacher Rapport Scale in an attempt to measure the social climate of classrooms. Assuming that he could economically obtain an estimate of classroom atmosphere by observing and rating important components of pupil-teacher rapport, Wrightstone constructed a scale incorporating the following categories: Pupil-Teacher Interaction Pattern; Degree of Social Interaction; Quality of Social Interaction; Interest; Enjoyment; Role Structure; Emotion of Teacher; Teacher Orders or Suggestions; Physical Tension of Group; and Emotional Tone of Pupil Group.

The scale appears to be appropriate for use in either elementary or secondary classrooms.

Sample Items: An observer rates the classroom according to each of the categories listed above, using a 3-, 4-, or 5-point scale similar to the following:

Category	*Rating Scale*
Enjoyment	1. No pleasure—signs of displeasure or aversion.
	2. Little pleasure—minimal enjoyment.
	3. Some pleasure—a few signs of enjoyment.
	4. Moderate pleasure—generally restrained, occasionally active enjoyment.
	5. Extreme pleasure—enthusiasm.
Teacher Orders or Suggestions	1. Teacher demands compliance.
	2. Teacher expects compliance.
	3. Teacher generally suggests rather than coerces.
	4. Teacher allows options, commanding only in emergencies.

Reliability: Two estimates of interrater agreement are provided by Wrightstone (1951). Trained observers who had used the scale for 5 to 10 observations made independent ratings of the same classroom and achieved 90% agreement on item ratings. In addition, total scores given to 25 teachers by 2 independent observers correlated .92.

Validity: In order to test the validity of the scale, supervisors were asked to make detailed, anecdotal notes, over a period of months, describing the rapport between the teacher and the children in 25 classrooms. These supervisory reports covered the same general categories as those on the observation scale. Both quantitative and qualitative analyses were made, comparing the data provided by supervisors to that obtained on the rating scale. These comparisons convinced Wrightstone (1951) that the scale had a "high degree of correspondence (p. 435)" with the anecdotal records.

Norms: No normative data are provided by Wrightstone (1951).

Procedures for Use: In using the scale, the observer visits the classroom on several occasions. The rating form provides space for 3 different ratings to be completed on 3 separate occasions. Identification data (name of teacher, school, class or grade, number of pupils, date, name of observer, length of observation, topic of class activity, and group structure) are recorded prior to observation. The rater then checks the items on the scale which best describe the social climate of the classroom.

Comments: The assumption underlying the Pupil-Teacher Rapport Scale—that the degree of compatibility between the teacher and his pupils is an indicator of social climate in the classroom—appears to be sound. Evidence of reliability and validity is positive, though limited, and the observational categories represented on the scale cover the major aspects of classroom interaction. This instrument does, however, require a high degree of inference on the rater's part and therefore requires extensive training of observers to insure that they are interpreting behavioral categories and observed behaviors similarly.

References: Wrightstone, J. W., "Measuring the social climate of a classroom." *Journal of Educational Research*, 1951, **44**, 341–351.

Wrightstone, J. W., J. Justman, and I. Robbins, *Evaluation in modern education.* New York: American Book Co., 1956.

Name: SEQUENTIAL ANALYSIS OF VERBAL INTERACTION

Authors: Yvonne Agazarian and Anita Simon

Type of Measure: Observation coding system

Availability: Agazarian, Y., and A. Simon, *Sequential analysis of verbal interaction*. Philadelphia, Pennsylvania: SAVI Associates, 1974.

Description: Sequential Analysis of Verbal Interaction (SAVI), originally developed in 1960 and revised in 1974, is a system for analyzing verbal communication among people. SAVI is based on the assumption that the way in which something is said influences what is heard. This instrument provides a "mental snapshot" of what happens when people talk and predicts what is likely to happen next.

The SAVI categorizes verbal behavior as either approaching or avoiding problems to be solved. Approach Behaviors facilitate the transfer of information, while Avoidance Behaviors tend to distort or confuse information. In addition to these 2 types of behavior, the SAVI also describes Contingent Behaviors, the direction and effect of which are not always obvious. The impact of Contingent Behaviors on problem solving is, as the name implies, contingent upon the interactional context.

The SAVI also classifies messages as either Person, Factual, or Orienting. Person Messages address the person rather than what is said. Factual Messages contain the kinds of information that are basic to data input and data processing, and Orienting Messages determine the level of abstraction and sequence of context characterizing communication. Each of these types of messages is associated with 1 of the 3 categories of behavior, producing 9 classes of communication: (1) Person Avoidance Messages; (2) Person Approach Messages; (3) Person Contingent Messages; (4) Factual Avoidance Messages; (5) Factual Approach Messages; (6) Factual Contingent Messages; (7) Avoidance Orienting Messages; (8) Approach Orienting Messages; and (9) Contingent Orienting Messages. When communication is categorized by this procedure, patterns of verbal behavior emerge. For example, if the frequency of Avoidance Messages is high, the overall pattern indicates defensive communication. In such a situation it is unlikely that information relevant to some objective goal or target will be transferred in ways that lead to effective problem solving.

The authors believe that identifying patterns of communication is the first step toward influencing them. They designed SAVI to allow individuals to gain practical and theoretical knowledge of *how* to say *what* in order to resolve the problems inherent in communicating. Such an instrument has obvious implications for teacher training and analysis of classroom interaction.

Sample Items: The 9 classes of communication are characterized by behaviors of the following type.

Person Avoidance Message: self-defensive behavior

Person Contingent Message: personal history

Person Approach Message: personal support

Factual Avoidance Message: small talk

Factual Contingent Message: factual question

Factual Approach Message: factual answer

Orienting Avoidance Message: being obscure

Orienting Contingent Message: opinion

Orienting Approach Message: building on ideas

Reliability: Reliability estimates are reported by Agazarian (1968), who observed a group of people and taped their voices, later categorizing the recorded verbal behaviors on the SAVI. Intercoder agreement, calculated for 10-minute periods, ranged from 87 to 96%. During a later phase of this study, reliability was checked by obtaining judgments from two separate raters on a systematic sampling of SAVI classifications. Agreement between judges and agreement with the initial coding was 100%.

Validity: Agazarian (1968) selected 2 external criteria against which to validate the SAVI: targetness (the goal orientation of the group) and convergence (continuity of topic). Communication was viewed as convergent when the topic of a message was the same as that of the preceding message, and as divergent when a new topic was introduced. Subjects observed were a group of people attending a conference to solve a specific problem. Their communication was categorized on the SAVI. Incidents of verbal behavior were also independently judged according to the selected criteria, i.e., as either on or off target, and convergent or divergent. Fisher's discriminate function yielded data which confirmed the ability of the SAVI categories to discriminate targetness and convergence at less than the .01 level of probability. A *chi* square statistic showed that 9 specific categories were significantly related to targetness, 3 in an off-target direction and 6 in an on-target direction. Three categories related significantly to convergence and seven to divergence. These findings, along with the overall distribution of the categories, revealed a pattern of cross-purpose talk. Since the group observed had a cross-purpose goal, it was expected that both interpersonal maintenance and interpersonal conflict behaviors would be avoided, as they were.

Norms: No normative data are reported (Agazarian, 1968; Agazarian and Simon, 1974).

Procedures for Use: In using the SAVI, verbal behavior is recorded on tape (usually in 10-minute samples) and later transcribed. Listening to the tape, a coder classifies the verbal interaction by labeling the transcribed statements according to the appropriate SAVI category. The coded transcript is scored in terms of frequency of occurrence of various kinds of behavior.

Comments: The SAVI system provides a unique perception of communication using 9 classes of behavior which are well defined and illustrated. These 9 classes can accommodate all verbal behavior to provide an objective basis on which to analyze the effectiveness of communication. Additional research data, including further evidence of reliability and validity, should be obtained and reported. Since this instrument appears to have value for teacher training or classroom interaction assessments, data collected in educational settings would be of interest.

References: Agazarian, Y., *A theory of verbal behavior and information transfer.* Unpublished doctoral dissertation, Temple University, 1968.

Agazarian, Y., and A. Simon, *Sequential analysis of verbal interaction.* Philadelphia, Pennsylvania: SAVI Associates, 1974.

Name: SOCIAL INTERACTION AND CREATIVITY IN COMMUNICA-
TION SYSTEM

Author: David L. Johnson

Type of Measure: Observation coding system

Availability: Johnson, D. L., *Social Interaction and Creativity in Communication
System. Coding manual.* Streator, Illinois: Institute of Human Resources, 1975.

Description: The Social Interaction and Creativity in Communication System
(SICCS) was designed to assess the social and environmental conditions facilitating, hindering, or otherwise affecting creative performance. The product of
extensive and continuing developmental work, SICCS is based on a well
defined, social/psychological conceptualization of creativity. This conceptual
model focuses on verbal acts in the context of social interaction. According to
Johnson (1975), "verbal acts may be creative, and creative *processes* may be
examined sequentially in relation to antecedent and subsequent speaker acts
(p. 6)." Creativity is viewed as an unexpected, original verbal act emitted spontaneously by a speaker in social interaction and affected by the verbal acts of
antecedent speakers. The verbal act (a phrase, clause or simple sentence) and
the interact (a verbal act followed by at least 1 verbal act emitted by another
speaker) serve as the units of analysis employed by the SICCS. They are observed and coded according to the following categories:

I. Antecedent Modes of Verbal Activity
   A. Appraisal
      1. Positive Judgment
      2. Negative Judgment
   B. Prescriptive
      1. Direction
      2. Standard
   C. Informational
      1. Certain
      2. Uncertain
   D. Questioning
      1. Narrow
      2. Broad

II. Subsequent Student Performance
   A. Self-Reference
      1. Positive
      2. Negative
   B. Self-Initiated
      1. Volunteering
      2. Redirecting
      3. Interrupting

C. Productivity
  1. Productive
  2. Elaboration
  3. Construction
  4. Reinterpretation
D. Quantity
  1. Length
  2. Number

Sample Items: Johnson (1975) defines the categories listed above and provides numerous examples of verbal acts typically recorded under each one. For instance, a self-referenced verbal act is " one in which the speaker makes explicit reference to his own characteristics (p. 21)." It is coded positively if the speaker asserts responsibility for the content (e.g., "I think people usually do what is expected of them."). However, when the speaker repudiates or denies responsibility for the content of a verbal act (e.g., "I didn't say that."), it is coded negatively.

Reliability: Using a Kappa (K) coefficient of agreement, Johnson (1971) calculated mean interrater reliabilities for all SICCS categories based on sixth- and eleventh-grade lesson transcripts. These ranged from .85 to .93 for the antecedent mode categories and from .87 to 1.00 for the student performance categories. Mean percentages of intercoder agreement computed on 10 bilingual transcripts from kindergarten and first- through third-grade classes ranged from 95.6 to 97.6% for the mode categories, and from 91.5 to 100.0% for the performance categories (Johnson, 1974).

Validity: Although the SICCS is a relatively new instrument, various forms have been employed in a number of studies, and evidence of validity is accumulating. For example, Smith (1972), using the SICCS to observe 6 small group sessions in a drug-abuse treatment center, found that uncertain rather than certain informational acts and broad rather than narrow questions were positively related to a greater number of subsequent verbal acts. Childers (1974), studying open and closed school systems, observed fourth- through sixth-grade classrooms and reported a higher incidence of self-initiated, positive self-referenced, and longer interactions in the open rather than the closed environments.

Studies by Johnson have also produced results in the expected directions. Observing 4 classrooms in a small, coeducational community college, he found the teachers' use of broad questioning, more than any other mode category, to be significantly and consistently associated with student creativity recorded on the SICCS performance categories. Also, the teachers' uncertain informational acts were more consistently related to student talents than were the prescriptive or appraisal modes (Johnson, 1972). Similarly, in an analysis of 24 taped social studies lessons from sixth- and eleventh-grade classrooms, Johnson (1973) found that both broad questioning and uncertainty in teacher informational acts were associated with a higher quantity and quality of student verbal performance. Teacher appraisals, on the other hand, appeared to terminate or inhibit student participation.

Norms: No comprehensive normative data are provided in the SICCS *Coding Manual* (Johnson, 1975). However, classroom interaction outcomes for various groups are reported (as frequencies and percentages) in his individual studies (Johnson, 1972; 1973; 1974).

Procedures for Use: Student/teacher interaction can be studied on the SICCS using: (1) direct observation; (2) direct observation and audio tape recording; or (3) direct observation and audio/video tape recording. When either of the last 2 procedures is employed, the tape, rather than the live interaction, is coded. Johnson (1975) provides detailed instructions, including an explanation of codes, the sequence of coding steps, and examples of tape transcripts and completed coding sheets, for all 3 procedural alternatives.

Comments: The Social Interaction and Creativity in Communication System is based on the idea that student creativity is affected by the social/psychological conditions present in the classroom. Though carefully developed and revised according to an explicit theoretical model, this instrument is more complex than many of the observation coding systems available, and its manual is less clear than it might be. However, the SICCS demonstrates good reliability and validity and, when used by trained observers, is a useful research tool.

References: Childers, V., *Open-closed school system expectations and observed pupil behavior*. Unpublished master of arts thesis, Baylor University, 1974.

Johnson, D. L., *Classroom interaction and student creativity*. Unpublished doctoral dissertation. University of Missouri, 1971.

Johnson, D. L., *Teacher and student classroom interaction and student verbal creativity*. Paper presented at the annual meeting of the Southwestern Social Science Association, San Antonio, Texas, March 1972.

Johnson, D. L., "A conceptual model of teacher and student classroom interaction and observed student verbal creativity." *Psychology in the Schools*, 1973, **10**, 475–481.

Johnson, D. L., *Teacher-pupil interaction in bilingual elementary school classrooms*. Paper presented at the annual meeting of the Southwestern Social Science Association, Dallas, Texas, March 1974.

Johnson, D. L., *Social Interaction and Creativity in Communication System. Coding manual*. Streator, Illinois: Institute of Human Resources, 1975.

Smith, R., *The effects of various verbal modalities on the quantity of subsequent verbal acts*. Senior research paper, Missouri Southern State College, 1972.

Name: THE SOCIAL WEATHER RATING SCALES

Author: James E. Simpson

Type of Measure: Observer rating scale

Availability: Simpson, J. E., "A method of measuring the social weather of children," in R. G. Barker (ed.), *The stream of behavior*. New York: Appleton-Century-Crofts, 1963.

Description: The Social Weather Rating Scales were designed to measure "social weather," that is, "the over-all social treatment given a particular individual in a behavior setting (Simpson, 1963, p. 219)." Based in part on the Fels Parent Behavior Rating Scales, this instrument assesses 9 specific factors which may be grouped to form 3 general dimensions of social weather. Each dimension and its component scales are listed below:

Dimension	*Scales*
1. Warmth (emotional tone of social weather)	1. Acceptance 2. Affectionateness 3. Approval
2. Tendance (direct efforts made for the child)	1. Attention 2. Assistance 3. Communication
3. Indulgence (the freedom allowed the child)	1. Adaptation 2. Privilege 3. Choice

The scales may be used to assess an individual child's treatment by the group, the teacher's behavior toward children, or, combining the ratings of individual children, to obtain an aggregate picture of group atmosphere.

Sample Items: Each bipolar scale is arranged vertically and punctuated by 5 objectives, which become progressively negative. The child's rating is indicated by checking the appropriate spot on the scale. Following each adjective is a brief definition, clarifying for the rater the conditions which warrant a check mark at that particular point on the scale. The Choice scale, for example, is similar to that below.

CHOICE: the freedom of choice or option allowed the child.

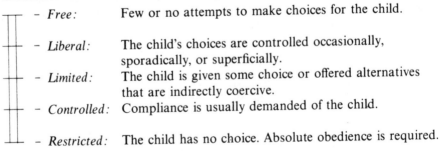

- *Free:*   Few or no attempts to make choices for the child.

- *Liberal:*   The child's choices are controlled occasionally, sporadically, or superficially.

- *Limited:*   The child is given some choice or offered alternatives that are indirectly coercive.

- *Controlled:* Compliance is usually demanded of the child.

- *Restricted:* The child has no choice. Absolute obedience is required.

Reliability: Interobserver and test/retest reliabilities are reported by Simpson (1963) for 2 observational situations. In Situation A, raters observed a child and his parents at dinner; in Situation B they observed the same child on the school playground at recess. Situation A was judged moderately difficult to rate, while Situation B was considered socially chaotic and thus very difficult to rate. The ratings of 4 observers correlated .83 for Situation A and .38 for Situation B, using Kendall's coefficient of concordance.

Test/retest estimates, over a 6-week interval, were computed on: (1) the investigator's ratings; (2) the investigator's ratings and median ratings of 3 untrained observers; and (3) the investigator's ratings and the average ratings of 3 untrained observers. Kendall's coefficients of concordance were, respectively: .98 for Situation A and .85 for Situation B; .87 (A) and .71 (B); and .91 (A) and .69 (B). Coefficients obtained for Situation A were significant at the .001 level, for Situation B at the .01 or .02 level.

Validity: Data describing the validity of the Social Weather Rating Scales are scarce. Findings reported by Simpson (1963), however, indicate that: the social weather of preschool children (measured on these scales) differs from that of elementary school children in shared behavior settings; social weather varies for each child from setting to setting; and variance for preschool children is smaller within the home and greater outside the home than that for school children.

Norms: Normative data are not reported (Simpson, 1963).

Procedures for Use: The Social Weather Rating Scales are used in conjunction with very explicit behavior setting records described by Simpson (1963). The rater does not observe the child directly but instead rates his social weather using an episodic account of his interactions, recorded previously. He rates the child's treatment by marking an X at that point on the scale which best describes the variable in question. Procedures are outlined for recording variations or exceptions in the behavior of significant individuals interacting with the child.

The rater must attempt to make "objective" judgments, relying on his own perception of the overall behavior toward the child—and not on the child's (or anyone else's) apparent perception of it. That is, if the teacher treats the child in a neutral way, this behavior should be rated "neutral," even though the child may feel that it is cold and rejecting.

Comments: The Social Weather Rating Scales offer a technique for assessing the atmosphere of a setting or the overall treatment received by an individual. Though validity and normative data are inadequate, these scales can be recommended for research use. They are particularly appropriate for research assessing the effect of environment on behavior.

Reference: Simpson, J. E., "A method of measuring the social weather of children," in R. G. Barker (ed.), *The stream of behavior*. New York: Appleton-Century-Crofts, 1963.

Name: A SYSTEM FOR OBSERVING BEHAVIORAL CONTAGION IN GROUPS

Authors: Norman Polansky, Ronald Lippitt, and Fritz Redl

Type of Measure: Observation coding system

Availability: Polansky, N., R. Lippitt, and F. Redl, "An investigation of behavioral contagion in groups." *Human Relations*, 1950, **3**, 319–348.

Description: This instrument was designed by Polansky, Lippitt, and Redl (1950) to assess behavioral contagion in groups of children. The authors define behavioral contagion as a form of social influence in which a change in the behavior of one individual (the "initiator") appears to unintentionally produce a change in the behavior of others (the "recipients"). Though the focus of their efforts was on *unintentional* influence, the observation system they developed codes status indicators and direct attempts at influence, as well as incidents of behavioral contagion—that is, events in which the recipients' behavior alters to resemble that of the initiator, who has not communicated intent to evoke such a change. These incidents are recorded by an observer, or observers, on precategorized data sheets.

Sample Items: Observers code a wide variety of behavior. In recording contagion, for example, they typically note the initiator, the recipient(s), and the contagious content, which may include behaviors such as singing a song, throwing food, or playing a game.

Reliability: Reliabilities were calculated for all observational categories (except status categories for which insufficient information was collected) from data gathered by 3 pairs of observers on children attending boys' or girls' summer camp. These were reported as average Spearman rank-order coefficients (*rhos*), broken down according to 2 categories, initiation and reception of behavior. Coefficients ranged from .56 to .87 for initiation and from .34 to .84 for reception. The behavioral contagion categories yielded *rhos* ranging from .62 to .87 for initiation and from .56 to .76 for first reception and .68 to .76 for subsequent reception.

The percentage of agreement (PA) between each pair of observers was also calculated for several categories. PAs ranged from 79 to 100.

Validity: Validity is suggested by correlations between influence, as observed on the behavioral contagion system, and a prestige index based on attributes such as athletic ability, sex sophistication, independence of adults, and good looks. Average *rhos* for 16 groups of children showed prestige positively correlated with Contagion Initiation (.61), Frequency of Successful Direct Influence Attempts (.55), and Frequency of Direct Influence Attempts (.49). Furthermore, high-prestige children were observed to be less susceptible to direct influence than were low-prestige children (Polansky, Lippitt, and Redl, 1950).

Norms: In the study which originally employed this instrument (Polansky, Lippitt, and Redl, 1950), data were collected at the University of Michigan's Fresh Air Camp for boys and the Community Service Society of New York Camp Greybarn for girls. Eight groups of children, 11 to 15 years old, were studied at each camp for 4-week periods. Four to 9 boys or girls were in each group.

Procedures for Use: This system uses mobile observers who record behavior on precategorized data sheets. In the Polansky, Lippitt, and Redl study, one observer was assigned to each group (except during reliability checks), usually for the entire day. The observer followed the children through all activities in which they remained a group. Coding at 15-minute intervals, he assigned an identifying number to each child and then indicated the source and object of each interaction. Three observers were rotated among groups to equalize the interaction between observer and group.

Comments: This unique instrument provides a variety of data related to social interaction among children. It is relatively easy to use, and although it demands an alert observer, it does not require him to make many inferences. More extensive psychometric data would make this coding system a more valuable research tool.

Reference: Polansky, N., R. Lippitt, and F. Redl, "An investigation of behavioral contagion in groups." *Human Relations*, 1950, **3**, 319–348.

Name: WISPÉ OBSERVATION SYSTEM

Author: Lauren G. Wispé

Type of Measure: Observation coding system

Availability: Wispé, L. G., "Evaluating section teaching methods in the introductory course." *Journal of Educational Research*, 1951, **45**(3), 161–186.

Description: This observation coding system was developed by Wispé (1951) in a study of the general effects of directive and permissive teaching. After observing 8 graduate student instructors, all teaching an introductory college course in social relations, Wispé identified 4 whose styles were "permissive" (i.e., student-centered, informal, and characterized by less instructor talk) and 4 whose styles were "directive" (subject-centered, formal, and characterized by more instructor talk). He then asked each instructor to "sharpen" his natural teaching style for the remainder of the semester, during which time all 8 sections of the class were observed according to the following categories:

1. Instructor defines problem area for discussion.
2. Instructor asks open-ended questions, requiring student reflection.
3. Instructor provides factual information about the course or class procedures.
4. The ratio of the instructor's student-commending behavior to his or her total commending plus rejecting behavior.
5. Instructor asks for information, values, or personal experiences from students.
6. The amount of general instructor activity (composed of 2, 3, and 4 above).
7. Students ask the instructor for information, administrative help, or personal experiences.
8. Students volunteer information, administrative help, or personal experiences.
9. Students tell humorous stories, laugh, smile, etc.
10. The amount of general student activity (composed of 7, 8, and 9 above).
11. Students give information in response to open-ended questions.
12. The total amount of student participation disregarding the nature of the participation.

Sample Items: Wispé (1951) does not provide examples of specific behaviors coded under the above categories.

Reliability: Interobserver reliability coefficients are reported to average .91 (Wispé, 1951).

Validity: The final form of this observation system was pilot tested over a 3-week period to insure that selected categories included behaviors relevant to the proposed study. Only those categories which were successful in distinguishing the directive from the permissive sections (beyond the .05 level of significance) were used in the final study. The categories, themselves, then, provide operational definitions of "directive" and "permissive" teaching (Wispé, 1951).

Norms: No true normative data are provided by Wispé. The sample he observed, however, was composed of 8 instructors, each of whom taught a section of approximately 20 students.

Procedures for Use: In Wispé's study (1951), a total of 14 class meetings were observed via a one-way screen by 2 observers using a categorized scoring instrument.

Comments: Very little information is available on this observation system, and, according to Medley and Mitzel (1963), that which is available suffers from a number of technical faults. However, Wispé's system may be of interest to researchers developing methods of observing teacher style. Although designed for use in a college setting, it is also suitable for high school classrooms.

References: Medley, D. M., and H. E. Mitzel, "Measuring classroom behavior by systematic observation," in N. L. Gage (ed.), *Handbook of research on teaching.* Chicago: Rand McNally, 1963.

Wispé, L. G., "Evaluating section teaching methods in the introductory course." *Journal of Educational Research,* 1951, **45**(3), 161–186.

Indexes

Index of Instrument Authors

Index of Instruments